T

Se...

John Stott (NT)
Derek Tidball (Bible Themes)

The Message of
Spiritual Warfare

The Lord is a warrior;
the Lord is his name

The Bible Speaks Today: Bible Themes series

The Message of Spiritual Warfare

The Lord is a warrior;
the Lord is his name

Keith Ferdinando

Associate Pastor at Woodford Evangelical Church
Formerly lecturer at Shalom University,
Bunia, Democratic Republic of Congo
and London School of Theology

InterVarsity Press

InterVarsity Press
P.O. Box 1400
Downers Grove, IL 60515-1426
ivpress.com
email@ivpress.com

©2016 by Keith Ferdinando

Published in the United States of America by InterVarsity Press, Downers Grove, Illinois, with
permission from Inter-Varsity Press, England.

All rights reserved. No part of this book may be reproduced in any form without written permission
from InterVarsity Press.

InterVarsity Press® is the book-publishing division of InterVarsity Christian Fellowship/USA®,
a movement of students and faculty active on campus at hundreds of universities, colleges and
schools of nursing in the United States of America, and a member movement of the International
Fellowship of Evangelical Students. For information about local and regional activities, visit
intervarsity.org.

Unless otherwise stated, Scripture quotations are taken from the Holy Bible, New International
Version. Copyright © 1973, 1978, 1984 by International Bible Society. Used by permission of
Hodder & Stoughton, a division of Hodder Headline Ltd. All rights reserved. "NIV" is a trademark
of International Bible Society.

Quotations marked ESV are from The Holy Bible, English Standard Version® (ESV®),
copyright © 2001 by Crossway, a publishing ministry of Good News Publishers. Used by permission.
All rights reserved.

Scripture quotations marked NIV 2011 are taken from the Holy Bible, New International Version
(Anglicized edition). Copyright © 1979, 1984, 2011 by Biblica (formerly International Bible
Society). Used by permission of Hodder & Stoughton Publishers, an Hachette UK company. All
rights reserved. "NIV" is a registered trademark of Biblica (formerly International Bible Society).

One Scripture quotation is taken from the New King James Version. Copyright © 1982 by Thomas
Nelson, Inc. Used by permission. All rights reserved.

One Scripture quotation is taken from the New Revised Standard Version of the Bible, Anglicized
Edition, copyright © 1989, 1995 by the Division of Christian Education of the National Council of
the Churches of Christ in the USA. Used by permission. All rights reserved.

ISBN 978-0-8308-2418-2 (print)
ISBN 978-0-8308-9211-2 (digital)

Printed in the United States of America ∞

 As a member of the Green Press Initiative, InterVarsity Press is committed to
protecting the environment and to the responsible use of natural resources. To learn
more, visit greenpressinitiative.org.

Library of Congress Cataloging-in-Publication Data
A catalog record for this book is available from the Library of Congress.

P	20	19	18	17	16	15	14	13	12	11	10	9	8	7	6	5	4	3	2	1
Y	32	31	30	29	28	27	26	25	24	23	22	21	20	19	18	17	16			

To my African students, colleagues and friends
with deep gratitude for our fellowship in Christ

Contents

BST The Bible Speaks Today

GENERAL PREFACE

THE BIBLE SPEAKS TODAY describes three series of expositions, based on the books of the Old and New Testaments, and on Bible themes that run through the whole of Scripture. Each series is characterized by a threefold ideal:

- to expound the biblical text with accuracy
- to relate it to contemporary life, and
- to be readable.

These books are, therefore, not 'commentaries', for the commentary seeks rather to elucidate the text than to apply it, and tends to be a work rather of reference than of literature. Nor, on the other hand, do they contain the kinds of 'sermons' that attempt to be contemporary and readable without taking Scripture seriously enough. The contributors to The Bible Speaks Today series are all united in their convictions that God still speaks through what he has spoken, and that nothing is more necessary for the life, health and growth of Christians than that they should hear what the Spirit is saying to them through his ancient – yet ever modern – Word.

ALEC MOTYER
JOHN STOTT
DEREK TIDBALL
Series editors

Author's preface

In the 'Song at the Sea' Moses and the people of Israel boldly sang, 'The LORD is a warrior; the LORD is his name' (Exod. 15:3). There on the seashore they celebrated his transcendent victory over the enemy who had so long oppressed them, and rejoiced in the deliverance the Lord had brought. Spiritual warfare is first of all God's own warfare against those who rise up against him – 'the dragon, that ancient serpent, who is the devil, or Satan' (Rev. 20:2) and all the supernatural forces of evil, as well as rebellious and unrepentant humanity. God himself is the great 'man of war', but his warfare becomes also that of his redeemed people, and to enable them to carry it out he equips them with his own armour. The greatest wonder and profoundest mystery of all, however, is that the divine warrior wins his decisive victory at the cross. There his own beloved and eternal Son, 'his form marred beyond human likeness' (Isa. 52:14), bore the sins of his people and, in so doing, freed them from the dominion of darkness. And then, as they follow the one who died in their place, their warfare also takes the shape of a cross.

I am very grateful to Derek Tidball, BST Themes series editor, and Philip Duce, Senior Commissioning Editor at IVP, for the privilege of working on this book and having the opportunity to explore such immense and awesome themes, and for their encouragement and the many helpful suggestions they have made. I also thank Garry Williams, Director of the John Owen Centre, for reading the manuscript and commenting on it. And I thank my wife, Margaret, for patiently bearing my prolonged periods of seclusion with my computer.

Various friends and colleagues have encouraged me as I have slowly progressed through the chapters, and I am very grateful to them. I would, however, particularly like to thank my students, colleagues and friends in Africa with whom at different times and in varied situations I have shared parts of what is now reproduced here. I am grateful for their questions, challenges and contributions, all of which have helped me grow in my own understanding, but much more for the hospitality, warmth and fellowship I have experienced as a stranger but a brother in Christ among them over many years.

Abbreviations

BS	*Bibliotheca Sacra*
BZ	*Biblische Zeitschrift*
ESV	English Standard Version
EvQ	*Evangelical Quarterly*
ExpT	*Expository Times*
JETS	*Journal of the Evangelical Theological Society*
NIV	New International Version
NT	New Testament
OT	Old Testament

Select bibliography

Allen, J. L., 'The War on Christians', *The Spectator* (5 October 2013), at <http://www.spectator.co.uk/2013/10/the-war-on-christians/>, accessed 29 February 2016.

Andersen, F. I., *Job*, Tyndale OT Commentaries (Leicester: Inter-Varsity Press, 1976).

Arnold, C. E., *Ephesians: Power and Magic* (Cambridge: Cambridge University Press, 1989).

———, *Powers of Darkness* (Leicester: Inter-Varsity Press, 1992).

———, *3 Crucial Questions about Spiritual Warfare* (Grand Rapids: Baker, 1997).

———, 'Early Christian Catechesis and New Christians' Classes in Contemporary Evangelicalism', *JETS* 47.1 (2004), pp. 39–54.

———, *Ephesians*, Zondervan Exegetical Commentary on the NT (Grand Rapids: Zondervan, 2010).

Bandy, A. 'The Hermeneutics of Symbolism: How to Interpret the Symbols of John's Apocalypse', *Southern Baptist Journal of Theology* 14.1 (2010), pp. 46–58.

Barrett, C. K., *From First Adam to Last: A Study in Pauline Theology* (London: A & C Black, 1962).

Beale, G. K., *The Book of Revelation*, New International Greek Testament Commentary (Grand Rapids: Eerdmans and Carlisle: Paternoster, 1999).

———, *The Temple and the Church's Mission: A Biblical Theology of the Dwelling Place of God* (Leicester: Apollos and Downers Grove: InterVarsity Press, 2004).

Beasley-Murray, G. R., *Revelation*, 2nd edn (London: Marshall, Morgan and Scott and Grand Rapids: Eerdmans, 1981).

Beattie, J. H. M., 'Sorcery in Bunyoro', in J. Middleton and E. H. Winter (eds.), *Witchcraft and Sorcery in East Africa* (London: Routledge and Kegan Paul, 1963), pp. 27–55.

Begg, A. and S. B. Ferguson, *Name above All Names* (Wheaton: Crossway, 2013).

Beilby, J. K. and P. R. Eddy (eds.), *Understanding Spiritual Warfare: Four Views* (Grand Rapids: Baker Academic, 2012).

Beker, J. C., *Paul the Apostle: The Triumph of God in Life and Thought* (Edinburgh: T&T Clark, 1980).

Berger, P., *A Rumour of Angels* (Harmondsworth: Penguin, 1970).

Berglund, A.-I., *Zulu Thought-Patterns and Symbolism* (London: C. Hurst, 1976).

Birkett, K. R., *Spells, Sorcerers and Spirits: Magic and the Occult in the Bible* (London: Latimer Trust, 2015).

Blocher, H., '*Agnus Victor*: The Atonement as Victory and Vicarious Punishment', in J. G. Stackhouse, Jr (ed.), *What Does It Mean to Be Saved? Broadening Evangelical Horizons of Salvation* (Grand Rapids: Baker, 2002), pp. 67–91.

Block, D. I., *Judges, Ruth*, New American Commentary (Nashville: B&H Publishing Group, 1999).

Boice, J. M., *Foundations of the Christian Faith: A Comprehensive and Readable Theology* (Downers Grove: InterVarsity Press and Leicester: Inter-Varsity Press, 1986).

Bolt, P. G., 'Towards a Biblical Theology of the Defeat of the Evil Powers', in P. G. Bolt (ed.), *Christ's Victory over Evil: Biblical Theology and Pastoral Ministry* (Nottingham: Apollos, 2009), pp. 35–81.

Bonhoeffer, D., *The Cost of Discipleship* (London: SCM Press, 2001).

Bosch, D., *Transforming Mission: Paradigm Shifts in Theology of Mission* (Maryknoll: Orbis Books, 1991).

Boyd, G., 'The Ground-Level Deliverance Model', in J. K. Beilby and P. R. Eddy (eds.), *Understanding Spiritual Warfare: Four Views* (Grand Rapids: Baker Academic, 2012).

Brown, M. L., *Israel's Divine Healer* (Carlisle: Paternoster, 1995).

Bruce, F. F., *Romans*, Tyndale NT Commentaries (Leicester: Inter-Varsity Press and Grand Rapids: Eerdmans, 1963).

———, *The Acts of the Apostles: The Greek Text with Introduction and Commentary*, 3rd edn (Grand Rapids: Eerdmans and Leicester: Apollos, 1990).

Budd, P. J., *Numbers*, Word Biblical Commentary 5 (Waco: Word, 1984).

Caird, G. B., *Principalities and Powers* (Oxford: Clarendon Press, 1956).

———, 'On Deciphering the Book of Revelation', *ExpT* 74 (1962–3), pp. 13–15, 51–53, 82–84, 103–105.

Calvin, J., *Institutes of the Christian Religion*, ed. J. T. McNeill (Philadelphia: The Westminster Press, 1960).

———, *Genesis* (Edinburgh: The Banner of Truth Trust, 1965).

Carson, D. A., 'Matthew', in *The Expositor's Bible Commentary*, vol. VIII, 1st edn (Grand Rapids: Zondervan, 1984), pp. 1–599.

———, *How Long, O Lord?: Reflections on Suffering and Evil* (Leicester: Inter-Varsity Press, 1990).

———, *The Gospel According to John*, Pillar NT Commentary (Leicester: Inter-Varsity Press and Grand Rapids: Eerdmans, 1991).

———, *The Gagging of God: Christianity Confronts Pluralism* (Leicester: Apollos, 1996).

———, *The God Who Is There: Finding Your Place in God's Story* (Grand Rapids: Baker, 2010).

Ciampa, R. E. and B. S. Rosner, *The First Letter to the Corinthians*, Pillar NT Commentary (Grand Rapids: Eerdmans and Nottingham: Apollos, 2010).

Collins, J., 'A Syntactical Note (Genesis 3:15): Is the Woman's Seed Singular or Plural?', *Tyndale Bulletin* 48.1 (1997), pp. 139–148.

Cranfield, C. E. B., *Mark* (Cambridge: Cambridge University Press, 1959).

———, *The Epistle to the Romans, Volume II* (Edinburgh: T&T Clark, 1979).

Davids, P., *The Epistle of James* (Exeter: Paternoster, 1982).

Davis, R. D., *2 Samuel: Out of Every Adversity* (Fearn: Christian Focus Publications, 1999).

Day, P. L., *An Adversary in Heaven: śāṭān in the Hebrew Bible* (Atlanta: Scholars Press, 1988).

Dimock, N., *The Doctrine of the Death of Christ in Relation to the Sin of Man, the Condemnation of the Law, and the Dominion of Satan*, 2nd edn (London: Elliot Stock, 1903).

Dowden, R., *Africa: Altered States, Ordinary Miracles* (London: Portobello Books, 2008).

Edersheim, A., *The Life and Times of Jesus the Messiah*, vol. I, 7th edn (London: Longmans, Green and Co., 1892).

Ellis, E. E., *The Gospel of Luke* (London: Nelson, 1966).

Erickson, M. J., *Christian Theology* (Grand Rapids: Baker, 1985).

Evans, C. A., 'Typology', in J. B. Green and S. McKnight (eds.), *Dictionary of Jesus and the Gospels* (Downers Grove: InterVarsity Press, 1992), pp. 862–866.

Everts, W. W., 'Jesus Christ, No Exorcist', *BS* 81 (1924), pp. 355–362.

Fee, G. D., *The First Epistle to the Corinthians*, New International Commentary on the NT (Grand Rapids: Eerdmans, 1987).

Ferdinando, K., *The Triumph of Christ in African Perspective* (Carlisle: Paternoster, 1999).

———, *The Battle Is God's: Reflecting on Spiritual Warfare for African Believers* (Bukuru: African Christian Textbooks, 2012).

————, 'Evil and AIDS – an African Perspective', *Africa Journal of Evangelical Theology* 31.1 (2012), pp. 67–84.

Ferguson, S. B., 'Christus Victor et Propitiator: The Death of Christ, Substitute and Conqueror', in S. Storms and J. Taylor (eds.), *For the Fame of God's Name: Essays in Honor of John Piper* (Wheaton: Crossway, 2010), pp. 171–189.

Fernando, A. 'Is Western Christian Training Neglecting the Cross?', *Trinity World Forum* (Fall, 1998), pp. 1–5.

Foulkes, F., *Ephesians: An Introduction and Commentary*, Tyndale NT Commentaries (Leicester: Inter-Varsity Press, 1989).

Frame, J., *Systematic Theology: An Introduction to Christian Belief* (Phillipsburg: P&R Publishing, 2013).

France, R. T., *Jesus and the Old Testament* (London: The Tyndale Press, 1971).

————, 'Exegesis in Practice: Two Examples', in I. H. Marshall (ed.), *New Testament Interpretation* (Exeter: Paternoster, 1977), pp. 252–281.

————, *Matthew*, New International Commentary on the NT (Leicester: Inter-Varsity Press, 1985).

Garland, D. E., *2 Corinthians*, New American Commentary (Nashville: B&H Publishing Group, 1999).

————, *1 Corinthians* (Grand Rapids: Baker, 2003).

————, *Luke*, Zondervan Exegetical Commentary on the NT (Grand Rapids: Zondervan, 2012).

Garrett, S. R., 'Light on a Dark Subject and Vice Versa: Magic and Magicians in the New Testament', in J. Neusner, E. S. Frerichs and P. V. M. Flesher (eds.), *Religion, Science and Magic: In Concert and in Conflict* (New York and Oxford: Oxford University Press, 1989), pp. 142–165.

Goldsworthy, G., *According to Plan* (Leicester: Inter-Varsity Press, 1991).

Grbich, N., *Repentance: Cleansing Your Generational Bloodline* (Helderkruin, SA: Ariel Gate International Kingdom Communications, 2009).

Guelich, R. A., *Mark 1–8:26*, Word Biblical Commentary 34A (Dallas: Word, 1998).

Hagner, D. A., *Matthew 1–13*, Word Biblical Commentary 33A (Dallas: Word, 1998).

Hamilton, J., 'The Skull Crushing Seed of the Woman: Inner-Biblical Interpretation of Genesis 3:15', *Southern Baptist Journal of Theology* 10.2 (2006), pp. 30–54.

Harrison, G., 'Witchcraft in Salem', in *Fulfilling the Great Commission* (London: The Westminster Conference, 1992), pp. 108–129.

Hartley, J. E., *The Book of Job*, New International Commentary on the OT (Grand Rapids: Eerdmans, 1988).

Hay, D. M., *Glory at the Right Hand: Psalm 110 in Early Christianity* (Nashville and New York: Abingdon Press, 1973).

Hemer, C. J., 'Medicine in the New Testament World', in B. Palmer (ed.), *Medicine and the Bible* (Carlisle: Paternoster, 1986), pp. 43–83.

Hendriksen, W., *More Than Conquerors: An Interpretation of the Book of Revelation*, 2nd edn (Grand Rapids: Baker, 1962).

Hiebert, P. G., 'The Flaw of the Excluded Middle', *Missiology* 10.1 (1982), pp. 35–47.

Hughes, P. E., *The Second Epistle to the Corinthians* (Grand Rapids: Eerdmans, 1962).

———, *The Book of Revelation*, Pillar NT Commentary (Leicester: Inter-Varsity Press and Grand Rapids: Eerdmans, 1990).

Imasogie, O., *Guidelines for Christian Theology in Africa* (Achimota, Ghana: Africa Christian Press, 1993).

Johnson, A. F., 'Revelation', in *The Expositor's Bible Commentary*, vol. XII (Grand Rapids: Zondervan, 1981), pp. 397–603.

Kaiser, W. C., *Toward an Old Testament Theology* (Grand Rapids: Zondervan, 1978).

Kampling, R., 'Jesus von Nazaret – Lehrer und Exorzist', *BZ* 30 (1986), pp. 237–248.

Kee, H. C., *Medicine, Miracle and Magic in New Testament Times* (Cambridge: Cambridge University Press, 1986).

Keller, T., *Prayer: Experiencing Awe and Intimacy with God* (London: Hodder and Stoughton, 2014).

Kidner, D., *Genesis*, Tyndale OT Commentaries (Leicester: Inter-Varsity Press, 1967).

Klein, W. W., C. L. Blomberg and R. L. Hubbard, *Introduction to Biblical Interpretation* (Dallas: Word, 1993).

Köstenberger, A. J. and P. T. O'Brien, *Salvation to the Ends of the Earth: A Biblical Theology of Mission* (Leicester: Apollos and Downers Grove: InterVarsity Press, 2001).

Kruse, C. G., *2 Corinthians: An Introduction and Commentary*, Tyndale NT Commentaries (Leicester: Inter-Varsity Press, 1987).

———, *Letters of John*, Pillar NT Commentary (Grand Rapids: Eerdmans and Leicester: Apollos, 2000).

———, *John: An Introduction and Commentary*, Tyndale NT Commentaries (Leicester: Inter-Varsity Press, 2003).

———, *Paul's Letter to the Romans*, Pillar NT Commentary (Grand Rapids: Eerdmans and Nottingham: Apollos, 2012).

Lane, W. L., *The Gospel of Mark*, New International Commentary on the NT (Grand Rapids: Eerdmans, 1974).

Langton, E., *Essentials of Demonology* (London: Epworth Press, 1949).

Leahy, F., *Satan Cast Out: A Study in Biblical Demonology* (Edinburgh: The Banner of Truth Trust, 1975).

Lewis, C. S., *The Screwtape Letters* (London: Geoffrey Bles/The Centenary Press, 1942).

Lewis, I. M., *Social Anthropology in Perspective* (Cambridge: Cambridge University Press, 1985).

Lincoln, A. T., *Ephesians*, Word Bible Commentary 42 (Dallas: Word, 1990).

Ling, T., *The Significance of Satan: New Testament Demonology and Its Contemporary Relevance* (London: SPCK, 1961).

Lloyd-Jones, D. M., *Healing and Medicine* (Eastbourne: Kingsway Publications, 1987).

Lohse, E., *Colossians and Philemon*, Hermeneia (Minneapolis: Fortress Press, 1971).

Longman III, T. and D. G. Reid, *God Is a Warrior* (Grand Rapids: Zondervan, 1995).

Lowe, C., *Territorial Spirits and World Evangelisation* (Fearn: Mentor/OMF, 1998).

McConville, J. G., *Chronicles* (Edinburgh: The Saint Andrew Press and Philadelphia: The Westminster Press, 1984).

Macleod, D., *Christ Crucified: Understanding the Atonement* (Nottingham: Inter-Varsity Press, 2014).

Marshall, I. H., *The Epistles of John*, New International Commentary on the NT (Grand Rapids: Eerdmans, 1978).

———, *Acts: An Introduction and Commentary*, Tyndale NT Commentaries (Leicester: Inter-Varsity Press, 1980).

Marshall, P., L. Gilbert and N. Shea, *Persecuted: The Global Assault on Christians* (Nashville: Thomas Nelson, 2013).

Martin, R. P., 'A Footnote to Pliny's Account of Christian Worship', *Vox Evangelica* 3 (1964), pp. 51–57.

———, *2 Corinthians*, Word Biblical Commentary 40 (Dallas: Word, 1998).

———, *James*, Word Biblical Commentary 48 (Dallas: Word, 1998).

Miller, D. L., *Discipling Nations: The Power of Truth to Transform Cultures* (Seattle: YWAM Publishers, 1998).

Moo, D. J., *James: An Introduction and Commentary*, Tyndale NT Commentaries (Leicester: Inter-Varsity Press, 1985).

———, 'The Problem of *Sensus Plenior*', in D. A. Carson and J. D. Woodbridge (eds.), *Hermeneutics, Authority and Canon* (Leicester: Inter-Varsity Press, 1986).

———, *The Letter of James*, Pillar NT Commentary (Grand Rapids: Eerdmans and Leicester: Apollos, 2000).

————, *Romans*, NIV Application Commentary (Grand Rapids: Zondervan, 2000).

————, *The Letters to the Colossians and to Philemon*, Pillar NT Commentary (Grand Rapids: Eerdmans and Nottingham: Apollos, 2008).

Moon, R., 'Warning on Witches: Missionaries May Be Encouraging Witchcraft Accusations', *Christianity Today* 55.3 (2011), at <http://www.christianitytoday.com/ct/2011/march/warningonwitches.html>, accessed 10 January 2015.

Moreau, A. S., 'Gaining Perspective on Territorial Spirits', at <https://www.lausanne.org/content/territorial-spirits>, accessed 29 January 2016.

Moreau, A. S., G. R. Corwin and G. B. McGee, *Introducing World Missions: A Biblical, Historical and Practical Survey* (Grand Rapids: Baker, 2004).

Morris, L., *1 Corinthians: An Introduction and Commentary*, Tyndale NT Commentaries (Leicester: Inter-Varsity Press, 1985).

————, *New Testament Theology* (Grand Rapids: Academie Books, 1986).

————, *Revelation: An Introduction and Commentary*, Tyndale NT Commentaries (Leicester: Inter-Varsity Press, 1987).

Motyer, J. A., *The Message of James: The Tests of Faith*, Bible Speaks Today (Leicester: Inter-Varsity Press and Downers Grove: InterVarsity Press, 1985).

Moule, C. F. D., *The Epistles to the Colossians and to Philemon* (Cambridge: Cambridge University Press, 1957).

Murray, J., *The Epistle to the Romans* (London: Marshall, Morgan and Scott, 1974).

Murray, J. J., *Behind a Frowning Providence* (Carlisle, Pennsylvania: The Banner of Truth Trust, 1990).

Nevius, J. L., *Demon Possession and Allied Themes: Being an Inductive Study of Phenomena of Our Own Times* (Chicago: F. H. Revell, 1894).

————, *The Planting and Development of Missionary Churches* (New York: Foreign Mission Library, 1899).

Nicole, J. M., *Précis de Doctrine Chrétienne* (Nogent-sur-Marne: Éditions de l'Institut Biblique, 1983).

O'Brien, P. T., *Colossians, Philemon*, Word Biblical Commentary 44 (Waco: Word, 1982).

————, 'Principalities and Powers: Opponents of the Church', in D. A. Carson (ed.), *Biblical Interpretation and the Church: The Problem of Contextualization* (Nashville, Camden and New York: Thomas Nelson, 1985), pp. 110–150.

————, *The Letter to the Ephesians*, Pillar NT Commentary (Grand Rapids: Eerdmans and Leicester: Apollos, 1999).

Oesterreich, T. K., *Possession Demoniacal and Other among the Primitive Races, in Antiquity, the Middle Ages and Modern Times* (London: Kegan Paul, Trench, Trubner & Co. Ltd, 1930).

Osborne, L., 'Entertaining Angels: Their Place in Contemporary Theology', *Tyndale Bulletin* 45.2 (1994), pp. 273–296.

Oswalt, J. N., 'Is Balaam's Donkey the Real Prophet (Numbers 24:1–4)?', in D. G. Firth and P. D. Wegner, *Presence, Power and Promise: The Role of the Spirit of God in the Old Testament* (Nottingham: Apollos, 2011), pp. 208–219.

Ott, C., S. J. Strauss and T. C. Tennent, *Encountering Theology of Mission: Biblical Foundations, Historical Developments, and Contemporary Issues* (Grand Rapids: Baker, 2010).

Page, S. H. T., *Powers of Evil: A Biblical Study of Satan and Demons* (Grand Rapids: Baker and Leicester: Apollos, 1995).

Peterson, D. G., *The Acts of the Apostles*, Pillar NT Commentary (Grand Rapids: Eerdmans and Nottingham: Apollos, 2009).

Powlison, D., *Power Encounters: Reclaiming Spiritual Warfare* (Grand Rapids: Baker, 1995).

————, 'The Classical Model', in J. K. Beilby and P. R. Eddy (eds.), *Understanding Spiritual Warfare: Four Views* (Grand Rapids: Baker Academic, 2012), pp. 89–127.

————, 'Response to C. Peter Wagner and Rebecca Greenwood', in J. K. Beilby and P. R. Eddy (eds.), *Understanding Spiritual Warfare: Four Views* (Grand Rapids: Baker Academic, 2012), pp. 204–209.

Priest, R. J., T. Campbell and B. A. Mullen, 'Missiological Syncretism: The New Animistic Paradigm', in E. Rommen (ed.), *Spiritual Power and Missions: Raising the Issues* (Pasadena: William Carey Library, 1995), pp. 9–87.

Rowland, C., *The Open Heaven* (London: SPCK, 1982).

Salier, W. H., 'Deliverance without Exorcism? Jesus and Satan in John's Gospel', in P. G. Bolt (ed.), *Christ's Victory over Evil: Biblical Theology and Pastoral Ministry* (Nottingham: Apollos, 2009), pp. 81–103.

Schaeffer, F. A., *How Should We Then Live?: The Rise and Decline of Western Thought and Culture* (Grand Rapids: Revell, 1976).

Schnabel, E., *Early Christian Mission*, vol. I, *Jesus and the Twelve* (Leicester: Apollos and Downers Grove: InterVarsity Press, 2004).

————, *Early Christian Mission*, vol. II, *Paul and the Early Church* (Leicester: Apollos and Downers Grove: InterVarsity Press, 2004).

Schnackenburg, R., *The Epistle to the Ephesians* (Edinburgh: T&T Clark, 1991).

Schreiner, T., *Paul, Apostle of God's Glory in Christ: A Pauline Theology* (Downers Grove: InterVarsity Press and Leicester: Apollos, 2001).

Sire, J. W., *Naming the Elephant: Worldview as a Concept* (Downers Grove: InterVarsity Press, 2004).

Smalley, S. S., *1, 2, 3 John*, Word Biblical Commentary 51 (Waco: Word, 1984).

Stark, R., *The Rise of Christianity* (New York: HarperOne, 1996).

Stott, J. R. W., *The Message of Ephesians: God's New Society*, Bible Speaks Today (Downers Grove: InterVarsity Press, 1979).

———, *The Letters of John: An Introduction and Commentary*, Tyndale NT Commentaries (Leicester: Inter-Varsity Press, 1988).

———, *The Message of Romans: God's Good News for the World*, Bible Speaks Today (Leicester: Inter-Varsity Press, 2001).

Strange, D., *'For Their Rock Is Not as Our Rock': An Evangelical Theology of Religions* (Nottingham: Apollos, 2014).

Talbert, C. H., *Ephesians and Colossians*, Paideia Commentaries on the New Testament (Grand Rapids: Baker, 2007).

Thomas, J. C., *The Devil, Disease and Deliverance: Origins of Illness in New Testament Thought* (Sheffield: Sheffield Academic Press, 1998).

Thomas, K., *Religion and the Decline of Magic* (Harmondsworth: Penguin, 1978).

Treat, J. R., *The Crucified King: Atonement and Kingdom in Biblical and Systematic Theology* (Grand Rapids: Zondervan, 2014).

Twelftree, G., *Christ Triumphant: Exorcism Then and Now* (London: Hodder and Stoughton, 1985).

Unger, M. F., *What Demons Can Do to Saints* (Chicago: Moody Press, 1977).

Wagner, C. P. and R. Greenwood, 'The Strategic-Level Deliverance Model', in J. K. Beilby and P. R. Eddy (eds.), *Understanding Spiritual Warfare: Four Views* (Grand Rapids: Baker Academic, 2012), pp. 173–198.

Ware, B. A., *The Man Christ Jesus: Theological Reflections on the Humanity of Christ* (Wheaton: Crossway, 2012).

Weinandy, T., *Does God Suffer?* (Edinburgh: T&T Clark, 2000).

Wenham, G. J., *Numbers*, Tyndale OT Commentaries (Leicester: Inter-Varsity Press and Downers Grove: InterVarsity Press, 1981).

———, 'Christ's Healing Ministry and His Attitude to the Law', in H. H. Rowdon (ed.), *Christ the Lord: Studies in Christology Presented to Donald Guthrie* (Leicester: Inter-Varsity Press, 1982), pp. 115–126.

———, *Genesis 1–15*, Word Biblical Commentary 1 (Waco: Word, 1987).

Wilkinson, J., 'The Case of the Epileptic Boy', *ExpT* 79.2 (1967–8), pp. 39–42.

——, 'The Case of the Bent Woman in Luke 13v10–17', *EvQ* 49 (1977), pp. 195–205.

——, *Health and Healing: Studies in New Testament Principles and Practice* (Edinburgh: The Handsel Press, 1980).

Williamson, H. G. M., *1 and 2 Chronicles* (Grand Rapids: Eerdmans and London: Marshall, Morgan and Scott, 1982).

Wright, N. T., *Colossians and Philemon: An Introduction and Commentary*, Tyndale NT Commentaries (Leicester: Inter-Varsity Press, 1986).

Yamauchi, E. M., 'Magic in the Biblical World', *Tyndale Bulletin* 34 (1983), pp. 169–200.

——, 'Magic or Miracle? Disease, Demons and Exorcisms', in D. Wenham and C. Blomberg (eds.), *Gospel Perspectives*, vol. VI (Sheffield: JSOT, 1986), pp. 89–184.

Introduction

In 1692 in Salem Village in Massachusetts, then a British colony in North America, there was an outbreak of witch hysteria as a result of which nineteen people were executed by hanging and one other crushed to death. At one stage over 150 people were in prison awaiting trial for witchcraft, and nobody was safe from accusation. Evidence was assembled, including the testimony of those allegedly bewitched, that 'spectres' came out of the bodies of the accused and tormented their victims.[1] Almost 300 years later, and at the other extreme, an American television channel transmitted a brief interview with a woman who claimed that the devil was haunting her toaster. She was, nevertheless, still using it because, 'when all is said and done, it makes good toast'! Few would be inclined to accept her evaluation of the sounds she heard coming from the toaster, but many more might attribute their own anger or adultery to the influence of demons. The notion that our sins can be blamed on invisible spirits may find no support in the Bible but it does offer an easy absolution from guilt. 'Satan made me do it.' 'Spiritual warfare' is understood in many ways, ranging from hysterical paranoia to total farce.

These days there are those who insist on the necessity of deliverance for people who suffer from curses transmitted to them down through the generations. Others proclaim the necessity of 'identificational repentance' to deal with corporate sins of the past as well as the present, and so to break the stranglehold of whatever demonic powers may exploit those sins.[2] One such describes 'a prayer journey to West Africa, where he along with others "confessed and remitted" some of the corporate sin rooted in the slave trade'.[3] Meanwhile the novels of Frank Peretti, which 'vividly portray angels and demons

---

[1] G. Harrison, 'Witchcraft in Salem', in *Fulfilling the Great Commission* (London: The Westminster Conference, 1992), pp. 108–129.

[2] See C. E. Arnold, *3 Crucial Questions about Spiritual Warfare* (Grand Rapids: Baker, 1997), pp. 177–185.

[3] K. Sjöberg, quoted in Arnold, *3 Crucial Questions*, p. 179.

in fierce battles over schools, towns, and whole territories',[4] have had significant influence, to the point that 'in some quarters' they have been 'used as manuals for training in spiritual warfare'.[5]

1. Spiritual warfare

There is in fact no explicit use of the expression 'spiritual warfare' anywhere in the Bible, but there are numerous references to the conflict of God and of his people with what Paul calls the 'dominion of darkness'.[6] For many the classic 'spiritual warfare' text would doubtless be Paul's description of the struggle believers must face with spiritual powers of darkness (Eph. 6:10–20), in which he reminds his readers that as they seek 'to live a life worthy of the calling' they have received[7] they must face the hostility of fallen, rebellious spirits. As other texts of Scripture inform us, however, the conflict of God's people is not only with Satan and the 'powers of darkness' but also with the fallen world which surrounds them and with the continuing pull of the old sinful nature. Christian life is in fact a life of spiritual warfare as believers battle temptation and the pressure to conform to the world, while seeking by their words and their lives to be light in a dark place. Following Jesus means conflict.

Before it is the warfare of God's people, however, spiritual warfare is the warfare of God himself. 'The LORD is a warrior; the LORD is his name.'[8] Satan, sin and the world are all expressions of cosmic rebellion against the Creator and his will and purposes, and God himself addresses that opposition and brings it to nothing. The climactic act of his warfare is the extraordinary, utterly paradoxical victory of the cross, where through the death of his Son God redeemed his people from sin and its penalty, and by that same act also liberated them from bondage to the world and the devil. Their redemption transfers them from the 'dominion of darkness' to the kingdom of Christ (Col. 1:13), and as a result God's warfare becomes theirs too. It is, however, a warfare in which he has already prevailed, and his triumph also becomes theirs. Their conflict may often be hard and painful, but they know for sure that the ultimate victory has already been won. They are, indeed, 'more than conquerors'.[9]

---

[4] A. S. Moreau, 'Gaining Perspective on Territorial Spirits', at <https://www.lausanne.org/content/territorial-spirits>, accessed 29 January 2016.

[5] L. Osborne, 'Entertaining Angels: Their Place in Contemporary Theology', *Tyndale Bulletin* 45.2 (1994), p. 274, n. 3.

[6] Col. 1:13.

[7] Eph. 4:1.

[8] Exod. 15:3.

[9] Rom. 8:37.

2. Differing views

Like much else in theology the notion of spiritual warfare is a contested one. There are no doubt honest differences of interpretation over the meaning of the biblical text, but differences also arise when cultural assumptions are read into the text, resulting in syncretism.

a. Deficient views of spiritual warfare

Too often spiritual warfare has turned into warfare of a much more physical nature as the church has taken up worldly weapons of various sorts against its human 'enemies' in order to crush them, coerce them, exclude them, annihilate them, manipulate them or whatever else. The brutal imposition of baptism on unwilling 'converts', the persecution of 'heretics', the emotional and psychological manipulation that may take place in some forms of evangelism, and the power plays that too often characterize church politics are all illustrations of the point. In the words of Paul, however, 'the weapons we fight with are not the weapons of the world' but rather weapons with 'divine power to demolish strongholds'.[10] At the heart of *spiritual* warfare there is the work and leading of the Spirit of God, and his weapons are such things as truth, righteousness, the gospel itself, prayer and faith. Moreover, far from trying to eliminate human 'opponents', those who engage in truly *spiritual* warfare fight as their Saviour did, by not loving 'their lives so much as to shrink from death'.[11]

A different misunderstanding arises when animistic concepts of the nature and activities of spirits distort the interpretation of biblical references to Satan, demons, magic and so on. For quite some time it has been an issue for churches in traditionally animistic contexts, but it has also had an impact in Western situations through the thinking, writing and teaching of some Western missiologists and missionaries, themselves powerfully impacted by experiences of traditional folk religions. The issue is debated from both sides in a book entitled *Spiritual Power and Missions*, in which critics of the new approach identify it as a missiological syncretism, arguing that 'some missiologists are promoting a pre-scientific and magical worldview rather than a biblical one'.[12] While recognizing that there are indeed

[10] 2 Cor. 10:4.
[11] Rev. 12:11.
[12] R. J. Priest, T. Campbell and B. A. Mullen, 'Missiological Syncretism: The New Animistic Paradigm', in E. Rommen (ed.), *Spiritual Power and Missions: Raising the Issues* (Pasadena: William Carey Library, 1995), p. 12.

3

similarities between biblical and animistic concepts of spirits, they claim that the new approach fails to recognize the very substantial differences that also exist between the two. 'Many of these authors are overly impressed with the extent of continuity they find between the biblical view of spirits and the views of spirits found in folk religions around the world, and are insufficiently attuned to the degree of discontinuity between the two.'[13]

At the other end of the spectrum there is a rationalistic syncretism which demythologizes biblical references to Satan and spirits. On this view, Satan, demons, principalities and powers and the rest should be understood not as independent spirit beings, but rather as metaphors for 'structures of thought (tradition, convention, law, authority, even religion), especially as embodied in the state and its institutions'.[14] J. C. Beker, for example, argues that Paul uses 'mythical' terminology to speak about the human condition, such that the principalities and powers are personifications of sin, the flesh, law and death.[15] However, while it is true that in various texts the Bible identifies a demonic or satanic presence behind, for example, pagan worship (1 Cor. 10:20–21) or political power (Rev. 13:1), this is far from *equating* demons and Satan with those things as if they were simply identical. The demythologizing approach is in fact a secularizing process in which 'the traditional language is transferred from other worldly to this worldly referents',[16] thereby eliminating a dynamic, supernatural element of the biblical narrative and replacing it with a meaning more congenial to the interpreter's own context and assumptions. However, both the authors and readers of the Bible understood the language of Satan, demons, principalities and powers to refer to spiritual beings of wickedness 'in heavenly places', which existed independently of human beings, their thoughts, institutions and common life. Interpretations which see them as human 'structures' vitiate a very significant element of the biblical testimony.

b. Four approaches to spiritual warfare

Recently four distinct concepts of spiritual warfare have been identi-fied, explained and critiqued in a volume which aims to facilitate a conversation between their respective advocates. The editors classify

[13] Priest et al., 'Missiological Syncretism', p. 11.

[14] J. R. W. Stott, *God's New Society: The Message of Ephesians*, Bible Speaks Today (Downers Grove: Inter-Varsity Press, 1979), p. 267.

[15] J. C. Beker, *Paul the Apostle: The Triumph of God in Life and Thought* (Edinburgh: T&T Clark, 1980), pp. 188ff.

[16] P. Berger, *A Rumour of Angels* (Harmondsworth: Penguin, 1970), p. 35.

them as the 'world systems' model, the 'deliverance' model, the 'strategic-level' model and the 'classic' model.[17] The 'world systems' model, elaborated in several books by Walter Wink, is an expression of the rationalistic approach discussed briefly above. Wink rejects the idea that Satan and the powers are to be seen as independent supernatural beings and argues that they symbolize the 'inner aspect' of human structures and systems, and as such epitomize institutional attitudes, values and so on. In his view, although they may be evil, they can nevertheless be redeemed and transformed.

Greg Boyd presents the case for a 'ground-level deliverance model' and puts his emphasis on the presence of a cosmic conflict that he sees running through the Bible. He regards it as central to Jesus' own ministry as he revolts 'against cosmic powers that fuel sociopolitical systems that privilege the few by oppressing the masses'.[18] From this perspective the centre of Christian faith lies in the imitation of Jesus' ministry in terms of fighting poverty, racism, dehumanizing religion, violence and the demonization of territories and individuals. Boyd's approach fails to recognize, however, the centrality of human sin as the enemy that Jesus came to battle, and as a result he accords little place to his death which atones for sin and, in consequence, also brings about Satan's defeat.

The 'strategic-level deliverance model', associated with missiologists such as Peter Wagner and Charles Kraft, distinguishes ground, occult and strategic levels of spiritual warfare. Its focus is on the last of these, which involves liberating whole territories from control by evil spirits through various means such as 'spiritual mapping' and 'prayer walking'. The approach is based on anecdotal evidence rather than biblical exegesis and critics of 'missiological syncretism' would tend to see it in those terms.[19]

Finally, the 'classical' model identifies spiritual warfare as the moral conflict of the Christian life. From this perspective, 'to win spiritual warfare is simply to live as light in a dark world', while to lose it is 'to live the darkness, to revert to what comes naturally to every fallen heart'.[20] It is rightly termed 'classical' for two reasons. First, it is the most securely rooted in the Bible itself and, second, it is the dominant way in which spiritual warfare has been understood

[17] J. K. Beilby and P. R. Eddy (eds.), *Understanding Spiritual Warfare: Four Views* (Grand Rapids: Baker Academic, 2012).

[18] G. Boyd, 'The Ground-Level Deliverance Model', in Beilby and Eddy (eds.), *Understanding Spiritual Warfare*, p. 139.

[19] See Priest et al., 'Missiological Syncretism', pp. 19–21, 68–76. There is fuller discussion on pp. 165–166.

[20] D. Powlison, 'The Classical Model', in Beilby and Eddy (eds.), *Understanding Spiritual Warfare*, p. 98. Much of the discussion in this section comes from my review of *Understanding Spiritual Warfare* in *Trinity Journal* 35.2 (2014), pp. 379–380.

through the centuries. Its best-known expression is John Bunyan's 1678 allegory of the Christian life, *Pilgrim's Progress*. It is this view that the present work leans towards, while not ignoring Jesus' ministry of expelling demons from possessed people and its implications for his people, nor the Bible's response to magic and sorcery.

3. Foundational truths

a. Biblical reticence

In the light of the brief discussion above, the essential criterion of a true understanding of spirits, of the relationship they have with human beings, and of the nature of spiritual warfare is their conformity with the biblical testimony. The point is especially important in that the Bible itself is reticent in what it says about Satan and demons, and indeed quite remarkably so when compared with the complex and exotic notions found in the cultures neighbouring those in which it was written. As Peter Bolt points out:

> The Old Testament (OT) is practically silent about demons, then an explosion of references as Jesus appears in the biblical story – at least according to Matthew, Mark and Luke; then there is a tiny demonic dribble into the period of history recorded by the Acts, and only an occasional drip elsewhere in the New Testament (NT).[21]

This can easily give rise to the temptation to read between the lines of the Bible in order to fill in 'the gaps' with unfounded and sometimes extravagant speculation about Satan and his activities, a temptation to which theologians, missiologists and others have not always been immune. For some 'it has for a long time been common practice . . . to turn to the demonology of surrounding cultures to supplement the paucity of biblical evidence'.[22] Others, as we have noticed, turn to ideas gleaned from their experience of animistic contexts. And there are even those who claim they have gained an enhanced comprehension of the powers of darkness by interrogating demons in the course of 'deliverance ministry', an approach both 'idolatrous and foolish – they are liars and cannot be trusted – and will be judged by God'.[23] The result in all cases, however, is a

---

[21] P. G. Bolt, 'Towards a Biblical Theology of the Defeat of the Evil Powers', in P. G. Bolt (ed.), *Christ's Victory over Evil: Biblical Theology and Pastoral Ministry* (Nottingham: Apollos, 2009), p. 39.

[22] Bolt, 'Towards a Biblical Theology of the Defeat of the Evil Powers', p. 40.

[23] K. R. Birkett, *Spells, Sorcerers and Spirits: Magic and the Occult in the Bible* (London: Latimer Trust, 2015), p. 86.

distorted perception with inevitably negative consequences in terms of understanding and living the Christian life.

It is important to respect what the Bible does not say as well as what it does. Much that we might like to know about the spiritual powers of evil is not disclosed in its pages. 'God seems to think we don't need to know all the details' and tells us only what we do need to know.[24] Indeed, when he speaks, whether about Satan and the forces of darkness or about anything else, it is not to satisfy our human curiosity but to fulfil his own purposes. He speaks to accomplish things: creation, judgment, salvation. And so, as far as the devil is concerned, 'Scripture points out the person and work of Satan only as he stands in relationship to God's purposes with us, as we live for either good or ill.'[25] His purpose is redemptive and pastoral; from that perspective there are things we do not need to know and God does not tell us them.

b. Basic issues

There are a relatively few central truths of biblical theology that must particularly define our thinking about Satan, spirits and spiritual warfare.

First of these is the fact that God is sovereign over all. He alone made everything that exists, it is all his, and he rules over it all. Satan and the powers of darkness do not constitute a realm or sphere independent of him, for he created them, he reigns over them, and even through them he efficaciously accomplishes his purpose. So immense is the disparity between God and the devil that there can never be any doubt about the final outcome of the cosmic conflict between them. In consequence an invincible optimism pervades the Bible, however desperate the spiritual conflict on earth may sometimes seem. And insofar as Satan exercises power over fallen humanity, he does so only because their own sin brings them into servitude to him; he possesses no legitimate authority over them.

Second, then, Satan is a creature of God, possessed of intelligence, will, moral responsibility and an ability to communicate and persuade. He cannot be seen as a mere force, nor as 'the spirit of a society, a society alienated from God'[26] or whatever. Similarly his 'angels', the principalities and powers, are not 'structures' of human existence but 'personal, supernatural intelligences, emissaries of the god of this world, which seek to influence the world and mankind

---

[24] Powlison, 'The Classical Model', p. 90.
[25] Ibid.
[26] T. Ling, *The Significance of Satan: New Testament Demonology and Its Contemporary Relevance* (London: SPCK, 1961), p. 84.

for ill at every level'.[27] As a creature Satan was made good, but he has of his own volition rebelled against God and corrupted himself, becoming utterly evil. There is profound mystery in this which is considered below, albeit very briefly. Nevertheless, Jesus' concise description of Satan identifies the two most critical things we need to know about him: 'He was a murderer from the beginning, not holding to the truth, for there is no truth in him. When he lies, he speaks his native language, for he is a liar and the father of lies.'[28] He is the enemy of God, of his purposes and his people, and he seeks to destroy.

Third, human beings are created in God's own image. They are persons, morally responsible, as Satan is also, and so guilty for their sin. When they sin, therefore, they are not mere victims of Satan, nor are their sins due to demonization, but they knowingly and willingly yield to temptation. Their great problem, therefore, is not Satan and the powers of darkness, but the corruption of their own hearts and the guilt that belongs to their own sin. The gospel of Jesus Christ is first of all good news to men and women of freedom from the penalty and power of sin through his cross and, in consequence, good news too of freedom from Satan who is parasitic on their sin.

Finally, then, Christ has decisively defeated Satan at the cross by atoning for the sin which brings men and women under his power. His people know freedom from Satan through his blood shed for them, and God equips them with his own armour so that they may prevail in their struggle against him. By God's grace they may therefore be confident, but never complacent: they must fight.

4. The big question

The big question is why Satan should exist at all. God of course did not and could not create him evil, but he created him nevertheless, knowing what he would become, indeed even ordaining it in the purpose of his will by which he works out all things (Eph. 1:11). So *why*? And, indeed, *how* could a creature made good become evil? By what process of spontaneous generation did that initial impulse to rebel arise? The same questions apply also, of course, to the fall of Adam and Eve.

Two false turnings must be dismissed from the outset. First, the existence of Satan cannot be the result of some inadequacy or incompetence on God's part. The Bible declares him to be omnipotent and

[27] P. T. O'Brien, 'Principalities and Powers: Opponents of the Church', in D. A. Carson (ed.), *Biblical Interpretation and the Church: The Problem of Contextualization* (Nashville, Camden, New York: Thomas Nelson, 1985), p. 146.
[28] John 8:44. See discussion below, ch. 2.

utterly sovereign over all that he has made, and there is never a hint that Satan is some sort of rogue elephant out of control and causing devastation simply as he wills. On the contrary, in Job for example, he 'is on a short leash, acting only within limits prescribed by God'.[29] Second, God is just. Whatever may finally prove to be the answer to the question of Satan's emergence as an incarnation of evil, the biblical testimony to God's nature is clear: he 'is the Rock, his works are perfect, and all his ways are just. A faithful God, who does no wrong, upright and just is he'.[30] His relationship to sin and Satan is certainly perplexing beyond human comprehension, but his perfect holiness is unquestionable.

Beyond that, an initial and limited answer is that all that exists and all that happens has its own place in God's own story planned by him. In the end everything is all about him – the whole drama of creation and redemption. And through it all, why does he do anything but to manifest his glory, to display his own being – his eternal power and divine nature (Rom. 1:20), his wondrous grace and truth (Exod. 34:6; John 1:14, 17)? It is for that reason that 'the heavens declare the glory of God',[31] because they were created to do so. And so too does the story of salvation from its inception in eternity to its consummation in the new heaven and new earth. Somehow, Satan's role in that story is necessary if the story as a whole is to declare, as God intends it to declare, his own glory. Somehow, without Satan, the story would be diminished and something of the grace, majesty, holiness and utter transcendence and glory of the Creator would not be displayed. Speculation beyond that point seems risky and futile.

And ultimately, of course, the only answer is one of humble and awed silence as we are faced with realities far beyond our experience and the possibility of our knowing. When Job demands explanation for his trials, God does not give it but instead questions Job and draws attention to his frailty and inability to understand even the finite, created things that surround him. How then will he be able to grasp the unsearchable ways of God himself? At so many points there is an inscrutability about the purposes and the actions of a God beyond all space and time; and our minds, wonderfully made but finite and limited, are by their very nature unable to trace out his paths. 'How unsearchable his judgments, and his paths beyond tracing out.'[32] Thomas Weinandy reminds us that since God is who

---

[29] J. Frame, *Systematic Theology: An Introduction to Christian Belief* (Phillipsburg: P&R Publishing, 2013), p. 297.

[30] Deut. 32:4.

[31] Ps. 19:1.

[32] Rom. 11:33.

he is, we will never comprehend the mystery of his being and acts, not even in eternity, although we may indeed hope to contemplate it with increasing clarity.

> The reason for the open-ended nature of true theological and doctrinal development is that we are ultimately engaged with the mystery of God in himself and with his actions in time and history. God, in himself, is incomprehensible, and thus his relationship to the created order and his actions within that order throughout history and in the lives of human beings can never be fully comprehended. We can come to know who the mystery of God is, and we can come to know the mysteries embodied in his dealings with human persons, but we will never be able to fully comprehend him or his actions – not even in heaven.[33]

5. Surveying the issues

There are four sections in this work. The first, entitled 'The sovereign Creator and a fallen world', is concerned with the nature of Satan and his activity in the world God has made. It focuses initially on the fact that he is a created being, and then moves on to his temptation of the first human couple which, although bringing about their fall into sin, did not thereby divest them of moral responsibility for what they did. Two further chapters look at his role in human suffering and at magic and sorcery, both underlining the biblical emphasis on God's sovereignty over both.

The second section, 'The warfare of the Son of God', looks at the different dimensions of Christ's victory over Satan. The first two chapters consider respectively the temptations he underwent in the desert and his expulsion of unclean spirits from possessed people. Two further chapters discuss passages in Colossians and Revelation which enable us to see the impact of his death on Satan and the powers of darkness. These chapters are the real centre of the book as they deal with the crucial and decisive moment of God's warfare. A final chapter looks at the accounts in Revelation of the final defeat of Satan and his minions at the end of this age.

The third section, under the title 'Liberated and liberating', considers ways in which Christ's victory over Satan impacts his people. Taking texts from Colossians and Ephesians respectively, the first two chapters in this section discuss their deliverance from 'the dominion of darkness' and their security in Christ, with whom they are seated already 'in the heavenly places' far above the

---

[33] T. Weinandy, *Does God Suffer?* (Edinburgh: T&T Clark, 2000), pp. 36–37.

principalities and powers. Two further chapters then focus on the spread of the gospel to men and women of all peoples as the Lord Jesus Christ sends out his messengers with a summons to faith and repentance. All authority 'in heaven and on earth' has been given to him and Satan cannot prevail against him and his church, and nor can he deceive the nations any longer. A final chapter examines the way in which even Paul's experience of suffering at the hands of a 'messenger of Satan' was a demonstration of Christ's victory over all the works of darkness.

The fourth and last section, 'Fighting in hope', looks first at various areas in which believers must fight sin and Satan. These include the battle for the renewal and integrity of their own minds, the pursuit of unity in their churches, the temptation to share in the desires of the fallen world which surrounds them, and the danger of complacency and carelessness. Two concluding chapters then look at the weapons with which God endows his people for their spiritual warfare, so that Christians and churches may fight the good fight, and overcome, and finish their course with joy.

Part 1
The sovereign Creator
and a fallen world

Colossians 1:15–17
1. The sovereign Creator of all

It is doubtless unusual to begin a book with a confession of ignorance. Nevertheless, as has already been said,[1] much that we might like to know about the spiritual powers of evil is not disclosed to us. All that we can know of them with any confidence is what God reveals, and one thing he discloses that *is* vital to know is that Satan and his fallen angels are created beings. They are not eternal, as God is, but have a beginning; they do not have life in themselves, as God has (John 5:26), but owe their existence and continued being to him; and they do not possess the divine attributes of omnipotence, omnipresence and omniscience. In the beginning, when 'God created the heavens and the earth',[2] Satan was included in that creative act along with everything else. That assumption is implicit when John speaks of the role in creation of the divine and eternal Word of God. 'Through him all things were made; without him nothing was made that has been made.'[3] More explicit and deliberate are Paul's words in Colossians 1:15–17.

1. A problem

Paul wrote to the church at Colosse during his imprisonment, probably at Rome in about AD 60. Colosse was in the Roman province of Asia (now part of western Turkey) and situated on an important trade route. It was a cosmopolitan place with a significant Jewish population, and it had once been quite important, but when Paul wrote to the Colossian church the town had experienced significant economic and political decline. Paul had not personally

---

[1] See Introduction, above.
[2] Gen. 1:1.
[3] John 1:3.

encountered the recipients of his letter but he had heard of their positive and enthusiastic response to the gospel from Epaphras who first brought it to Colossae (1:7–8), quite likely as part of the overflow from Paul's own ministry at Ephesus which was not too far away (Acts 19:10).[4]

He was motivated to write by the news Epaphras brought him of false teaching which had penetrated the young church and was beginning to cause serious damage. The exact nature of the doctrinal deviation is unclear; as with all Paul's letters we hear only one side of the conversation, and must infer the nature of the 'Colossian heresy' on the basis of Paul's response to it. Nevertheless, like many other towns and cities Colossae was characterized by religious diversity, and it is probable that the problem stemmed from syncretism of some sort. At heart it involved an unhealthy preoccupation with angels as objects of devotion. This included attributing to them a role in the work of creation and especially seeing them as mediators of admittance into God's presence. To enjoy their favour, and so to gain access to God himself, the false teachers were insisting on the observance of certain holy days ('a religious festival, a New Moon celebration or a Sabbath day'),[5] on the implementation of certain ascetic practices concerning both food ('"Do not handle! Do not taste! Do not touch!"')[6] and physical discipline ('harsh treatment of the body'),[7] and on mysticism, possibly including participation in angelic worship (Col. 2:18). 'All of this was presented as advanced teaching for a spiritual elite',[8] and it is clear that in their desire for spiritual progress some of the Colossian believers were going along with it (Col. 2:16–23). However, the fatal flaw of the teaching was that it undermined the absolutely central place of the Lord Jesus Christ as the unique and all-sufficient mediator between God and human beings (1 Tim. 2:5), and substituted something else. Such additions to the apostolic gospel of the New Testament, offering a super-spirituality of one sort or another through some new experience or revelation or ritual, have occurred over and over again through the centuries and are familiar today. The answer for us as for the Colossian church, and the focus of Paul's response in this letter, is to insist on the absolute sufficiency of the Lord Jesus, who by virtue of his divine person and atoning work reconciles his people to the Father once

[4] P. T. O'Brien, *Colossians, Philemon*, Word Biblical Commentary 44 (Waco: Word, 1982), p. xxvii.
[5] Col. 2:16.
[6] Col. 2:21.
[7] Col. 2:23.
[8] O'Brien, *Colossians, Philemon*, p. xxxiii.

and for all, assuring their ongoing and unfettered access into his holy presence (Heb. 10:19–23).

2. A hymn

In one of the very earliest references to Christian worship outside the Bible, written about AD 111–12, Pliny, Roman governor of Pontus and Bithynia, reported to the emperor Trajan that when Christians met they sang 'a hymn to Christ as to a god'.[9] His letter reflects New Testament testimony to the singing of hymns and psalms in early Christian worship (Eph. 5:19–20; Col. 3:16). Not only that, but on a few occasions New Testament writers seem actually to have included extracts of such hymns of worship to the Lord Jesus Christ in their writings. Most likely they composed these themselves, although in some cases they may have quoted from Christian songs already known to their readers which they used to underscore or illustrate the point they were developing.[10] One such passage is Colossians 1:15–20, a text, as one commentator says, 'almost intolerably weighty, *of Christ and of his position in relation to the universe and the Church*'.[11]

The text has a number of poetic features, including the repeated use of parallelism and other rhetorical devices, and division into two complementary stanzas in which Christ Jesus is exalted as Lord in the spheres of both creation and redemption – God's two great works. Paul highlights the parallel between Christ's creative and redemptive works when he describes him as 'the firstborn over all creation' in the opening stanza, and then 'the firstborn from among the dead' in the second. It is in and through him that God realizes his great purposes. 'The Lord through whom you are redeemed (Paul is telling the Colossians) is none other than the one through whom you (and all the world) were created.'[12]

It is the first stanza with its focus on creation which is of particular interest here.

---

[9] *Carmenque Christo quasi deo dicere*. Quoted in R. P. Martin, 'A Footnote to Pliny's Account of Christian Worship', *Vox Evangelica* 3 (1964), p. 51.

[10] See in general R. P. Martin, 'Hymns, Hymn Fragments, Songs, Spiritual Songs', in G. F. Hawthorne, R. P. Martin and D. G. Reid (eds.), *Dictionary of Paul and His Letters* (Downers Grove: InterVarsity Press, 1993), pp. 419–423.

[11] C. F. D. Moule, *The Epistles to the Colossians and to Philemon* (Cambridge: Cambridge University Press, 1957), p. 3. The italics are Moule's.

[12] N. T. Wright, *Colossians and Philemon: An Introduction and Commentary*, Tyndale NT Commentaries (Leicester: Inter-Varsity Press, 1986), p. 70.

3. Christ the Lord (1:15)

a. The image of the invisible God

First, in two phrases Paul exalts Christ as *the image of the invisible God* and *the firstborn over all creation*. The former phrase recalls the Jewish tradition which personified wisdom as the image of God, present with him and one with him before all things, and the one by whom God brought about his work of creation. Like other New Testament writers, Paul uses that tradition to speak of Christ: it is in Christ that the Jewish concept of wisdom finds its true fulfilment, with all that that implies in terms of his divinity, his pre-existence and his role in creation. The same theme is taken up in the opening of the prologue to John's Gospel, where the wisdom tradition is again implicit. John calls Christ the 'word' rather than the image or wisdom of God, but the meaning is largely identical in terms of the ascription to him both of divinity and of a crucial role in creation: 'In the beginning was the Word, and the Word was with God, and the Word was God . . . Through him all things were made . . .'[13]

More than this, as image (or Word) of God Christ is the climax and focus of revelation. Through the one who is his image, the invisible God acts to make himself truly known to human beings. Elsewhere Paul makes the same point using similar terminology when he tells the Corinthians that 'the light of the knowledge of the glory of God' is made known in Christ 'who is the image of God'.[14] And again, the same idea is present at the end of John's prologue: 'No one has ever seen God, but God the One and Only, who is at the Father's side, has made him known.'[15]

Further, the reference also links Christ's identity to God's purpose in the creation of humanity, when he said, 'Let us make man in our image, in our likeness'.[16] As a result of Adam's rebellion and fall the image of God in human beings has been grievously marred, but through the obedience of Christ, the second Adam and bearer of the true image of the Father, that image can be restored in redeemed men and women. As a phrase, *the image of the invisible God* points, therefore, not only to the divine identity of Christ who in his own person is a true revelation of the Deity, but also to his redemptive mission as Saviour and 'image-restorer' of a fallen humanity.

[13] John 1:1, 3.
[14] 2 Cor. 4:6, 4.
[15] John 1:18; see also Heb. 1:3.
[16] Gen. 1:26.

b. The firstborn over all creation

The second phrase, *firstborn over all creation*, has been much discussed and indeed, from the time of the heretical Arius, much misunderstood. However, in a context in which Paul describes Christ as creator and sustainer of all things (16–17), it is scarcely possible to suppose that he is also identifying him as part of the created order which he himself brought about. The point is rather to refer to his temporal priority, that is his pre-existence, and also to his supremacy over all that has been created.[17] He it is who has all the rights of the firstborn Son in his Father's house. The parallel description in verse 18, describing Christ as 'the firstborn from among the dead', confirms this when Paul concludes 'so that in everything he might have the supremacy'. In other words, as *firstborn over all creation* he is supreme over the first creation, and as 'the firstborn from among the dead' he is supreme over the new, redeemed creation. In everything therefore, Christ Jesus, the image of God, is Lord.

4. Christ the creator (1:16)

Paul goes on to explain that the reason for which Christ is to be identified as *firstborn over all creation* is that in him *all things were created*. As the argument then progresses Paul steadily responds to the Colossians' preoccupation with spirits, and their fears of provoking their displeasure.

At this point the argument moves through four stages.

a. In him

First, there is a general introductory declaration that everything was created '*in* Christ'. The NIV translation *by him all things were created* is potentially misleading as it may imply that Christ was the unique agent of creation to the exclusion of the Father. However, the way in which Paul phrases his sentence, using the passive voice – *all things were created* – implies as so often elsewhere that while God the Father is the unstated subject of the act of creation, he created them all *in* Christ. But what does that mean? One possible meaning is that Christ was the instrument or executive of creation, the one through whom God created. It is certainly true that this is expressed elsewhere in the New Testament, including the end of this very verse as well as in 1 Corinthians 8:6 and John 1:3. However, Paul seems to be

---

[17] O'Brien, *Colossians, Philemon*, p. 44, points out that the word 'firstborn' is used 130 times in the Septuagint 'to indicate temporal priority and sovereignty of rank'.

saying more than this: he is describing Christ not only as the executive of creation but also as the *sphere* in which it took place, just as in Ephesians 1:4 he declares that election also takes place 'in him'. In other words, none of the works of the Godhead, whether creation or redemption, take place independently of him: nothing escapes him, nothing is apart from him or autonomous of him. Father and Son are never apart in what they do – there is never a division between them but always total unity and harmony. All, whether creation or redemption, is 'in him'.

b. All things

Second, Paul clarifies what he means by *all things*. This is an absolutely central point in the argument. The issue he is addressing is so critically important for believers troubled by concerns about placating potentially hostile spirits, that Paul enumerates the *things* which were created in Christ in order to demonstrate that those very spirits are among them. He does so by means of synonymous parallelism in which each line contains two contrasting pairs:

> *things in heaven and on earth*
> *[things] visible and invisible*

There is clear repetition: the *things in heaven* in the first line are the *invisible* things of the second, and equally the *[things] on earth* are the *visible* things. Further, Paul presents the contrast between the heavenly (invisible) and earthly (visible) things in a different order the second time round, an example of chiasm – a repetition of ideas in reverse order – which avoids the monotony of simple repetition. In brief, he wants the Colossians to get hold of the fact that absolutely all things were made in Christ, and to grasp the implications of that for their own situation. There is absolutely no sphere of creation independent of him, including the spiritual, invisible, heavenly sphere. The spirits that some Colossian Christians were apparently trying to appease do not belong to some autonomous realm of the cosmos outside the 'sphere' of Christ: they are simply another part of a creation which in its entirety came to being 'in him'.

c. Whether thrones or powers or rulers or authorities

But Paul is still concerned to make sure that his readers get hold of the point he is making. Like any serious preacher he hammers the nail again and again to drive it home. So, third, he defines yet more exactly what he means by the *things in heaven*/the *invisible things*. In doing so he seriously unbalances the symmetry of his writing, and thereby focuses particular attention on his main concern. Thus, while he specifies what he means by heavenly and invisible things, he does not trouble himself or his readers with a clarification of the identity of the earthly and visible things. It was not the latter which troubled them, but the heavenly and invisible things, and so he names them: *whether thrones or powers or rulers or authorities.*

The terminology he uses here was well known at the time, and present in both Jewish and Greek literature. In the New Testament it is found uniquely in Paul's writings, apart from one reference in 1 Peter 3:22. It is, however, imprecise and fluid language. While the different terms – *thrones, powers, rulers* and so on – certainly refer to spiritual powers, they do so without exact definition: on the basis of the literary sources in which the terms are found, it is impossible to distinguish between thrones, powers and so on, or to establish any sort of hierarchy among them, and in his own writings Paul similarly uses the nouns in an unsystematic and fluid way. His intention is not to give definition to the spirit world, far less to engage in some sort of 'spiritual mapping' exercise, but simply to suggest its reality, its multiplicity and diversity, perhaps even its power, but ultimately its submission to Christ. 'It does not matter whether the list is complete or whether the angelic powers are arranged in the order of their particular classes. The emphasis is rather that all things that exist in the cosmos were created in Christ. Thus he is lord of the powers and principalities.'[18]

Furthermore, in the New Testament the terminology usually refers to spiritual beings hostile to God and his people. There are indeed some texts in which there is ambiguity such that the thrones or powers might in principle be angelic beings faithful and obedient to God. However, wherever the context makes their spiritual orientation quite clear, as in Ephesians 6:12 or Colossians 2:15 for example, they are evidently hostile to him, and it is therefore reasonable to interpret the ambiguous instances from that perspective too. Paul's point here, however, does not depend on the orientation of the spirits towards God, whether hostile or obedient; his purpose is simply to assure the Colossian believers that this element of the cosmos is also and entirely part of God's creation. It is not eternal as God is, it does not have life in itself, but it is among the *all things* which God made in Christ.

---

[18] E. Lohse, *Colossians and Philemon*, Hermeneia (Minneapolis: Fortress Press, 1971), p. 51.

d. By him and for him

Nor is that all. In his conclusion to this section Paul states, fourth, that not only were the powers and authorities made *in him* but also *by him* and *for him*, and that he is *before* them all. He is indeed the one by whom God carried out his work of creation. More than that, he is also the goal and purpose of creation, and so of the whole course of history too.[19] And that being so, even the spirits ultimately serve the fulfilment of his purpose, however much some of them may resist and oppose his will. Further still, he is *before all things* (17). As *firstborn over all creation* (15) Christ existed before the whole of creation, including the thrones, powers, rulers and authorities.

5. Christ the sustainer (1:17)

Paul adds one final point: *in him all things hold together*. Christ is the one in whom and by whom creation finds its origin, and he is the goal for which it exists. He is also the one in whom it continues to hold together. Paul, along with all the rest of biblical revelation, resists any deistic notion that God created a cosmos that would function independently of himself. On the contrary, it owes its existence at every moment to his sovereign and almighty sustaining power, and this too is exercised in Christ, as the writer of Hebrews also affirms: 'The Son is the radiance of God's glory and the exact representation of his being, sustaining all things by his powerful word.'[20] It could not, therefore, be argued that while God may have created the cosmos in Christ, he had subsequently left it under the rule of powerful spirits whom the Colossians needed somehow to appease in order to have access to him. On the contrary, just as the spirits owed their origin to Christ, so also at every moment they owed their ongoing existence to him, even those in a state of rebellion.

6. Drawing conclusions

Paul's major purpose throughout this first brief stanza of his hymn of praise to Christ was to put firmly in its place the spirit world which some of the Colossian Christians were seeking to appease. He denies the spirits any autonomous role or place in the universe. Like everything else they are mere creatures, called into existence by and in Christ and constantly dependent upon him for their very existence. The terminology Paul uses to describe them – *thrones,*

---

[19] O'Brien, *Colossians, Philemon*, p. 47.
[20] Heb. 1:3.

authorities and so on – may suggest their power, but as created beings they are infinitely inferior to Christ and can have no right to any cult of worship or veneration. It is Christ, in whom, by whom and for whom all things were made, including the powers and authorities themselves, who deserves worship. For the Colossian Christians, therefore, who had been both created and redeemed through the work of Christ, there could be no reason to fear mere creatures so totally subject to him; nor to suppose that they needed the mediation of beings so inferior to him who by his sacrifice had already opened up full access into the presence of the Father for his redeemed people.

It is easy to suppose that at the level of ontology – of being – there is a fundamental divide between the visible, 'natural' world on the one hand and the invisible, 'supernatural' world on the other. According to such a view, on the one side there are the spirits including God himself and the holy angels, along with Satan and the powers and demons that are subject to him, while on the other side there is the vast physical universe including the world of men and women, animals, plants and all the rest. This text – and the witness of the whole Bible – indicates that such an approach is fatally flawed in that it suggests a metaphysical dualism in which Satan would somehow be on a level of equality with God. On such a view all notion of God's sovereignty is compromised and history is the scene of a titanic struggle between more or less evenly matched foes, with the result inevitably uncertain. Assurance of God's ultimate triumph over the rebellious forces of darkness and of the final redemption of his people becomes impossible. Similarly, confidence in the unfailing operation of his benevolent providence in the often adverse circumstances of the daily lives of his children is unfounded.

However, this text, and indeed the whole of Scripture, loudly, constantly and vehemently refute such an approach. The great divide lies not between the visible and the invisible, but between the sovereign Creator God and all that he has created. Angels, demons and Satan may be invisible and supernatural spirits but they are nevertheless part of the created order: they are creatures. They are indeed immensely powerful, possessed of vast intelligence, capable of rapid displacement and undoubtedly in many respects far superior to human beings, but they fall infinitely short of the transcendent and almighty God who made them. They are not eternal; they cannot create from nothing; they cannot bring life to inanimate matter; they are not omnipotent, omniscient, omnipresent. God alone can create, for he alone has 'life in himself';[21] he alone could breathe the breath

---

[21] John 5:26.

of life into the first man such that he 'became a living soul'.[22] Compared with the Lord God Almighty all created spirits – *powers*, *thrones* and even Satan himself – are of small significance indeed.

In terms of history this means that God's purposes cannot for a moment be thwarted by the *thrones* and *authorities*, for he made them, and he both sustains them in existence and overrules the courses that they trace throughout their little histories. They may rebel and seek to frustrate God's purposes, but he uses even that rebellion to advance his own righteous design. The truth is that their resistance to him is characterized by utter futility, like the rebellion of an insignificant city state against a global superpower. It faces the certainty of defeat, not just at the moment of final downfall but in every single individual act of defiance. Indeed, Satan himself 'knows that his time is short'.[23]

Finally, the text cautions against all merely speculative interest in invisible beings, such as seems to have been at the root of the Colossian 'heresy'. There is no biblical foundation for the notion that lesser spirits are gatekeepers to the presence of God. On the contrary, the gospel tells us that the veil of the temple has been torn from top to bottom as a result of the work of Christ, and that his people may come freely before their Father through him. The speculations that propelled the Colossian 'heresy' were rooted in error, engendered a flawed religious practice, and deprived Christ of the worship that was due to him alone. Efforts to know more of the invisible world than God has revealed, for example by interrogating occult practitioners or even the demons themselves, are both foolish and sinful. God himself has spoken: why would anyone consult members of the kingdom of darkness to learn what he has not seen fit to reveal, especially in the light of Jesus' own description of Satan as 'a liar and the father of lies'?

Paul teaches the Colossians to see the spirit world in the light of Christ. Viewed in isolation from him it may indeed seem powerful and threatening, but it does not exist in some autonomous realm independent of him. Christ himself *made* all the *thrones* and *authorities*, and he is sovereign ruler over them all and over their history. Paul wanted the Colossians to *know* Christ, and to know him as the almighty sovereign Creator and Lord that he is. Their vision of him was too small and their grasp too feeble, and that led almost inevitably to an obsession with fears and preoccupations almost identical to those that afflicted their pagan neighbours. It is always so, whatever the time and place and culture, and whether the fears

---

[22] Gen. 2:7.
[23] Rev. 12:12; cf. Rom. 16:20.

concerned are those of witches and spirits or of social exclusion and financial hardship. Paul's response is the only one that can effectively answer every human fear. All the time he preaches Christ – Christ in all his glory and in all the wonder of his being – *the image of the invisible God, the firstborn over all creation, [the one by whom] all things were created [and in whom] all things hold together.*

Genesis 3:1–5; John 8:44
2. A liar and a murderer

Very early in the biblical narrative a talking serpent appears without explanation and immediately corrupts the human inhabitants of Eden. Much later, in the New Testament, the serpent is unmasked as Satan, but the Bible is largely silent about his origins, reflecting indeed a habitual reticence about the supernatural powers of darkness. He is undeniably a creature made by God like everything else, but the issue is that of his wickedness: how did it come about that a creature of evil was present in Eden, given that the creation narrative in Genesis 1 repeatedly affirms that God created all things good?

Quite often answers are sought by seeing Satan as the real object of the laments of Isaiah 14:12–20 and Ezekiel 28:12–19, and so attributing his fall and wickedness to the vaunting pride and ambition of which they speak. Isaiah speaks of the fall 'from heaven' of a 'morning star, son of the dawn', and Ezekiel of the expulsion from Eden of one 'anointed as a guardian cherub'. Both texts are explicitly addressed, however, not to Satan but respectively to the kings of Babylon and Tyre. It is the apparent extravagance of the language used by the prophets that has caused some interpreters to identify an implicit reference to Satan behind the laments. Nevertheless, such a view goes far beyond the stated intention of the two authors and fails to take account of the often hyperbolic nature of poetic language.

A more secure reference to Satan's fall may perhaps be found in John 8:44. The words translated in the NIV as *not holding to the truth* are more literally rendered with a perfect tense, 'he did not hold to the truth'. So, as John Stott argues, 'this seems to indicate a fall from the truth in which he once "stood" (RV), in which case the following clause, "for there is no truth in him", indicates not why he fell, but how we know that he fell'.[1] 'Indeed, when Christ states that Satan

---

[1] J. R. W. Stott, *The Letters of John: An Introduction and Commentary*, Tyndale NT Commentaries (Leicester: Inter-Varsity Press, 1988), p. 141.

"abode not in the truth," he hints that he was once in it, and when he makes him "the father of lies," he deprives him of imputing to God the fault which he brought up himself.'[2] It is certainly true that the only satisfactory theological explanation of the existence of a malign supernatural being is that a once perfect creature somehow corrupted itself of its own free volition. The other options, either that God created it evil or that it is eternally evil, are incompatible with the biblical understanding that God alone is eternal, and that in his utter holiness he is incapable of creating that which is evil.

1. A serpent

In Genesis 3 it is indeed a serpent which tempts the human couple. The text does not explicitly identify it with supernatural evil and it is only exposed as Satan in the literature of postbiblical Judaism, notably the Wisdom of Solomon 2:24, and in the New Testament where the identification made in Revelation is especially clear: 'the great dragon . . . that ancient serpent called the devil, or Satan'.[3] However, even in the Old Testament there are hints as to the real identity of the serpent that tempted Eve. 'According to the classification of animals found in Lev 11 and Deut 14, the snake must count as an archetypal unclean animal . . . at the farthest point from those pure animals that can be offered in sacrifice.'[4] Moreover, the serpent of Isaiah 27:1 – 'Leviathan the gliding serpent, Leviathan the coiling serpent' – was undoubtedly understood as symbolic of a supernatural being in rebellion against God, but described in terminology drawn from Ancient Near Eastern mythology. Israel's neighbours certainly believed demons might take the form of a snake,[5] and, as Wenham observes, 'for any Israelite familiar with the symbolic values of different animals, a creature more likely than a serpent to lead man away from his creator could not be imagined'.[6]

Nevertheless, the narrative suggests that an actual reptile, *more crafty than any of the wild animals the LORD God had made*, was really involved, and not just a bodiless supernatural being metaphorically described as a serpent. It is, however, a peculiar serpent, one that has intelligence and guile, that converses, and that is clearly ill-disposed towards God and his human creation. Interpreters have

---

[2] J. Calvin, *Institutes of the Christian Religion*, ed. J. T. McNeill (Philadelphia: The Westminster Press, 1960), 1.14.15, p. 174.

[3] Rev. 12:9; cf. John 8:44; Rom. 16:20; 2 Cor. 11:3, 13–15; Rev. 20:2.

[4] G. J. Wenham, *Genesis 1–15*, Word Biblical Commentary 1 (Waco: Word, 1987), p. 73.

[5] E. Langton, *Essentials of Demonology* (London: Epworth Press, 1949), p. 37.

[6] Wenham, *Genesis 1–15*, p. 73.

made various, often very speculative, suggestions to explain what is going on, of which the simplest and most ancient is that a real snake is employed by Satan as his instrument, which allowed him to approach Eve in an apparently quite harmless, albeit a distinctly unsettling, form.[7] At the same time, the agency of a serpent meant that she was not under duress; in her eyes it was only an animal that addressed her, part of the physical creation and inferior to her. It tempted her, but could not coerce.[8]

2. A murderer

The words with which the serpent addressed the woman refer back to God's command to Adam in the preceding chapter: 'You are free to eat from any tree in the garden; but you must not eat from the tree of the knowledge of good and evil, for when you eat of it you will surely die.'[9] There is a depth of meaning in the divine prohibition. Clearly God was not simply concerned about the fruit of a particular tree, but his words indicated that somehow the eating of that fruit embodied for Adam the possibility of asserting his independence of his creator, while warning him that such a move would mean the judgment of death. At the same time, rather like the serpent, the narrative suggests that the fruit was not purely symbolic, for Eve later saw 'that the fruit of the tree was good for food and pleasing to the eye',[10] and both she and Adam ate it.

In truth, of course, anything like total independence from God is mere illusion, for the universe he created continues at every moment to be sustained by him. Adam was dependent on God for the air he breathed, the food he ate, the functioning of his own body and the regular operation of the world around him – night and day, seedtime and harvest and so on. In that sense truly to rebel against God would be to opt for non-being. In practice, however, what eating the fruit of the 'tree of the knowledge of good and evil' represented was refusal of submission to the Creator's will, a repudiation of that trusting and obedient relationship with him which God had intended, a determination to have for oneself 'the ability to pronounce what is good and pronounce what is evil'.[11] It meant

[7] See the discussion in S. H. T. Page, *Powers of Evil: A Biblical Study of Satan and Demons* (Grand Rapids: Baker and Leicester: Apollos, 1995), pp. 12–16.

[8] D. Kidner, *Genesis*, Tyndale OT Commentaries (Leicester: Inter-Varsity Press, 1967), p. 67.

[9] Gen. 2:16–17.

[10] Gen. 3:6.

[11] D. A. Carson, *The God Who Is There: Finding Your Place in God's Story* (Grand Rapids: Baker, 2010), p. 32.

living 'without reference to revelation' and in repudiation of 'the fear of the LORD' which 'is the beginning of knowledge (Prov 1:7)'.[12] So when they did in fact eat, Adam and Eve apparently expected to continue to enjoy the life and all the accompanying blessings that the Creator had given, while living in defiance of his gracious purpose and wisdom and substituting goals and wisdom of their own. It was an act of the most stunning and arrogant folly and death was the inevitable consequence, not only because death is the logically necessary result of repudiating the giver of life, but also because such an act of rebellion would bring divine justice down upon them as God had warned Adam.

All this the serpent knew. As he tempted the couple, therefore, he did so with the conscious, deliberate intent of bringing about their destruction. In the words of the Lord Jesus, he revealed himself as *a murderer from the beginning* (John 8:44): at his very first appearance in Scripture Satan came to kill, for at the very deepest level murderer is what he is. He was the hunter, baiting the trap and enticing his prey towards its own death. However, his goal was far more ambitious than the destruction of just one human couple. While not explicit in the Genesis narrative, Adam stood in a unique relationship of headship to all of humanity, such that his sin, condemnation and death would be the sin, condemnation and death of all his posterity. Paul makes this clear when he compares Adam and Christ as representatives respectively of fallen and redeemed humanity: 'by the trespass of the one man, death reigned through that one man . . . through the disobedience of the one man the many were made sinners'.[13] In tempting Adam to sin, Satan sought the destruction of all those whom he represented as head.

More even than that, however, the fall of the human race also entailed that of the physical creation of which they were a part. This is first indicated by the curse that God pronounced on the ground as a judgment on Adam (Gen. 3:17–19), the primary effect of which was that in order to draw food from the soil human beings would have to engage in a far more toilsome labour than would otherwise have been the case. However, Paul's words in Romans 8:19–23 suggest that the implications of the divine curse are more far-reaching than a diminution of the productive capacity of the soil alone. He refers to the 'frustration' and 'bondage to decay' to which the non-human creation has been subjected, and compares its situation with the pains of childbirth: 'We know that the whole creation has

[12] Wenham, *Genesis 1–15*, p. 63.
[13] Rom. 5:17, 19.

29

been groaning as in the pains of childbirth right up to the present time.'[14] In Fitzmyer's words,

> The world, created for humanity and the service of it, was drawn into Adam's ruin; the blessing given to him (fertility of the soil, fecundity of trees, brilliance of stars, friendliness of animals, limitation of insects) were [sic] all lost ... [Paul] realizes that through Adam came not only sin and death (5:12–14), but 'bondage to decay' and the 'slavery of corruption', which affect all material creation.[15]

Therefore, as Satan tempted Eve what he envisaged was nothing less than the destruction of God's created order as a whole. This would be accomplished by the corruption of Adam, representative of the whole human race and vice-regent of God within his creation. Evidence of the same murderous ambition is found throughout the Bible. On each of the three occasions that he is explicitly named in the Old Testament he is in the process of causing or seeking the death of his victims: the denunciation of Job followed by the murderous assault on him and his entire household, intended to goad him to curse God (Job 1 – 2); the incitement of David to number Israel, which exposed him and his people to divine judgment (1 Chr. 21:1–14); and the accusation of Joshua, high priest and representative of Israel, thereby implicitly demanding his and their punishment (Zech. 3:1–2). In the New Testament Satan torments men and women by means of demonic possession, which invariably produced physical afflictions and sometimes self-harm (Mark 5:5; 9:22). On at least one occasion purely physical illness is attributed to demonic aggression (Luke 13:11, 16). And Satan inspired Judas' betrayal of Jesus (John 13:2, 27, 30), and then the war of the beast from the sea against all the saints of God (Rev. 13:7). The target of his murderous venom is, therefore, not only God's original creation, but also the new one that has been redeemed through Christ.

3. A liar

There is a unique and unrepeatable particularity in the serpent's temptation of Adam and Eve. It was the one defining moment which brought condemnation and death to all their race. However, there is also a universality about the event, a paradigmatic quality which

---

[14] Rom. 8:22.
[15] J. A. Fitzmyer, quoted in C. G. Kruse, *Paul's Letter to the Romans*, Pillar NT Commentary (Grand Rapids: Eerdmans and Leicester: Apollos, 2012), pp. 347–348.

demands the attention of every succeeding generation as each comes face to face with the serpent's malignant guile.

It is significant, first, that throughout the Genesis account of the temptation Satan addresses the woman alone: at no point is Adam a participant in the conversation. According to the narrative flow in Genesis 2 Eve was not present to hear the voice of God himself prohibiting consumption of the fruit of the tree of the knowledge of good and evil, for when the command was given she had not yet been made. The text therefore implies rather that her knowledge of the command came to her through Adam. One might suppose, therefore, that the words of interdiction were perhaps not so profoundly embedded in her consciousness as they would have been for Adam. Further, the fact that she was made from the rib of the man and twice named by him (2:23; 3:20) suggests that, while equal to him in nature and bearer of God's image just as he was (Gen. 1:27), her relationship to him was nevertheless characterized by a certain functional subordination. The serpent's shrewdness is first seen, therefore, by the fact that he focuses his attention on the more vulnerable of the two humans in the garden.

He begins his attack with apparent mildness. Wenham points out how his conversation seems 'smooth and urbane' throughout, while the 'snake's opening question appears to be innocent curiosity'.[16] In his approach he avoids awakening Eve's suspicions and disturbing her sense of security, a security which up to this point in her life she had never had reason to question. Subtly and with gentle words he gradually draws her into a discussion of the commandment of the Lord God. His opening question, therefore, introduces just a hint of doubt: 'In the very first words אַף כִּי "really," there is possibly a touch of scepticism or at least surprise, which carries through into "you must not eat from *any* of the trees," a total travesty of God's original generous permission (2:16).'[17] His reference to God, also, suggests a tone of distance and impersonality. Instead of referring to him as 'the LORD God', the name used throughout the narrative of Genesis 2 – 3, he speaks simply of *God*: 'God is just the remote creator, not Yahweh.'[18]

Eve responds in terms that suggest she may already be influenced by the serpent's perspective,[19] for she exaggerates the extent of the divine prohibition – *and you must not touch it* – and so unnecessarily magnifies God's strictness. Perhaps spotting the subtle inaccuracy of her reply, the serpent closes in for the kill and begins a direct

---

[16] Wenham, *Genesis 1–15*, p. 88.
[17] Ibid., p. 73.
[18] Ibid.
[19] Kidner, *Genesis*, pp. 67–68; Wenham, *Genesis 1–15*, p. 73.

assault on her obedience. It moves beyond the mere implantation of doubt and directly contradicts the divine command. The content of its temptation is briefly communicated, but comprehensive in its attempt to undermine Eve's confidence in the truth of what God had spoken to Adam.

First and most crucial of all, the serpent denies the truth of God's speech – of his word. The moral and spiritual universe in which Adam and Eve existed was one shaped by God's own words. The Creator himself had established the fundamental markers which were to mould their world view. He had, for example, told them to multiply; to fill the earth and subdue it; to rule over the animals; to eat the produce of the soil including the fruit of the trees; but not to eat the fruit of the tree of the knowledge of good and evil. He had put the man in the garden 'to work it and take care of it',[20] and had then created the woman as his helper and 'brought her to the man', giving her to him in marriage (2:22). Up to the moment when the serpent intervened, Adam and Eve had structured their lives on this foundation of God's words and acts, in all of which they had displayed implicit trust. Now, however, the serpent confronted them with a rival word, an opposing truth, and urged them to believe that rather than the word God had given them. Indeed, it encouraged the woman to regard the word of God as a subject for debate and discussion among other possible words, rather than as the very definition of truth, the absolute and final arbiter in terms of which all human debate must be evaluated and resolved. Implicitly, therefore, it proposes that finite human reason become the criterion of truth, and that the word of the one who is truth in his own very being be evaluated by those he had created. The absurdity of the proposition evidently escaped Eve, and Adam too.

Second, the serpent contradicts God's warning, that eating the fruit of the tree of the knowledge of good and evil would result in death: *you will not surely die* (4). The categorical denial means, of course, that God's word could not be trusted and that he had simply lied to Adam. By its contradiction, the serpent seeks to remove an otherwise insuperable disincentive to eating the fruit, and to clear the way for speculative experimentation on the part of the human couple in defiance of God's expressed will. Most fundamental of all, however, it subverts the moral structure which Eve had known from her first conscious moments: the belief that God's word was good just as God himself was good, and that obedience to it would bring about good; that disobedience to God would correspondingly issue in profoundly negative consequences, and so was foolish as well as

---

[20] Gen. 2:15.

wrong; that notwithstanding the serpent's words there was, therefore, such a thing as judgment for disobedience to the Creator; that human beings consequently inhabit a moral universe in which their acts have positive or negative value, which is objectively defined in terms of the conformity or otherwise of those acts with the Creator's nature and will; and that as human beings they are, therefore, moral actors, responsible for their choices and for the consequences of those choices. In place of all that, the serpent suggests that morality, like truth itself, is essentially subjective, something to be negotiated by the human couple themselves rather than determined by their creator, an approach strikingly in tune with contemporary and very secular Western culture. Accordingly it urges Eve and Adam too to decide their own course, and not to be deterred by needless fear of the warnings of God. It subverts the foundational moral structure of reality and, in so doing, it lures the human couple onto the path that leads to death. The serpent lies with knowingly murderous intent.

Third, the serpent impugns the goodness of God. Implicit in its words is the suggestion that, far from bringing judgment, eating the fruit was necessary for human fulfilment and would bring positive benefits. By forbidding Adam and Eve from eating the fruit of the tree God was therefore holding them back, stunting their growth and denying them the possibility of achieving the intellectual and moral maturity of which they were capable. There is again profound absurdity in the notion that the Creator had made them with capacities the fulfilment of which he himself was intent on frustrating. Nevertheless, the serpent suggests that there is a selfishness, a destructive confinement of human freedom and potential, in the divine interdiction. Adam and Eve could indeed be like God himself, *knowing good and evil* – making their own choices and shaping their own course, but God had forbidden them from eating the fruit and lied to them about the consequences of doing so in order to prevent that happening and stifle them.

Finally, then, having lied about God, the serpent lies about what constitutes human identity and the true locus of human fulfilment and joy. It claims that Adam and Eve would find freedom and fulfilment only by breaking away from their relationship with their creator. Like the prodigal son in Jesus' parable (Luke 15:11–32) they must leave home to gain their liberty, which consists in a self-determination that is independent of God. The Genesis narrative itself, however, indicates rather that Eden was a place of fulfilment and bliss for the couple precisely because of the presence of God with whom they lived in intimate fellowship as he walked in the garden (Gen. 3:8). In the same way the Lord Jesus Christ declared to his Father, 'Now this is eternal life: that they may know you, the only true God, and Jesus Christ, whom you have sent.'[21] Men and women are made not only by God but also for him, and it is in him alone that they are complete. The serpent offered a false prospectus which left them lost and alone in a futile and hopeless emptiness. In the words of Augustine, 'You made us for yourself and our hearts find no peace until they rest in you.'[22]

4. A character

Jesus' testimony in John 8:44 summarizes Satan's character in just two words – *murderer* and *liar*: [The devil] *was a murderer from the beginning, not holding to the truth, for there is no truth in him. When he lies, he speaks his native language, for he is a liar and the father of lies.* Not only is the characterization concise but also immensely significant, highlighting as it does the two essential and defining elements which constitute the biblical understanding of Satan's nature. Jesus almost certainly draws it from the narrative of the fall of Adam and Eve.

Identifying the serpent quite simply as Satan, Jesus underlines the deceitful and murderous nature of his temptation. However, he goes further than this, for in Jesus' definition the devil does not simply tell lies, but he *is* a liar. He does not deploy lies as a merely occasional strategic manoeuvre, but when he lies 'he speaks from his own self'.[23] *There is no truth in him*, and the act of lying therefore reveals his fundamental nature as liar, just as the manifestation of 'grace and truth' in Jesus revealed his true being as 'the One and Only, who came from the Father'.[24] Similarly, the word *murderer* defines the essence of Satan's being as one who destroys: he is Abaddon or Apollyon – the destroyer.[25] *Liar* and *murderer* are what he *is* in the depths of his self-corrupted being, and his lies accomplish his murders as they did in Eden.

In both respects he is therefore exposed as the adversary – the unwavering *śāṭān*[26] – of God. In Jesus Christ God reveals himself as

---

[21] John 17:3.

[22] Augustine, *Confessions*, tr. R. S. Pine-Coffin (Harmondsworth: Penguin, 1961), p. 21.

[23] The literal rendering of 'he speaks his native language'. See C. G. Kruse, *John: An Introduction and Commentary*, Tyndale NT Commentaries (Leicester: Inter-Varsity Press, 2003), p. 212.

[24] John 1:14.

[25] Rev. 9:11. As king of the demonic locusts (Rev. 9:1–11) with a name that means 'destroyer', Abaddon or Apollyon can be identified as Satan. See Page, *Powers of Evil*, p. 213.

[26] In Hebrew the noun *śāṭān* means adversary. In the Old Testament it is frequently used of human adversaries, but it gradually emerges in the Scriptures as the proper name of the great adversary of God.

both truth and life (John 14:6). This is what he *is*. And as such he is the one who speaks the truth that Satan denies, and who gives the life that Satan seeks to destroy. While the outcome of this cosmic conflict between God and Satan is never in doubt, the Bible nowhere understates the malevolent ambition of Satan to destroy the works of God, but consistently warns God's people of Satan's purpose and of the means he employs to accomplish it.

Jesus' words have other implications too. First, they suggest that lies are always there at the heart of every temptation. Whenever Satan speaks there is a lie, echoing the lies he told the woman in Eden. This may be more obvious in his inspiration of theological or religious error, but it is no less true with respect to temptation of a moral kind. There is the lie that God's word is no more true than other words, and can be picked over, debated and discarded, giving human beings freedom to construct their own 'truth' and morality. There is the lie that sin, rebellion against God, will go unpunished, and that the sinner need not fear hell and eternal separation from God's presence and blessing. There is the lie that God's will and words are unnecessarily restrictive and inhibit human fulfilment and happiness, and that liberation from God rather than relationship with him is the route to self-realization.

Nor is this true only at the personal level. Whole societies embrace lies that become rooted in their cultures and are lived out by their members: the lies of consumerism perhaps, or of ethnic and racial superiority, of hedonism, of human self-sufficiency. All of them are ultimately delusory and fatal, for individuals as well as for the cultures they have shaped – and by which they are shaped in their turn. They all find their origin in the great lie: *you will not surely die . . . you will be like God, knowing good and evil* (Gen. 3:4). And so men and women shape their own lives and determine their own morality – but they die, all of them, estranged from the Creator they have defied and subject to his righteous judgment.

Second, therefore, Jesus' words mean that these same men and women take on something of the character of Satan himself, as Jesus suggests to his interlocutors: *you belong to your father, the devil* (John 8:44). The lies they believe come apparently from themselves – from their own philosophies and ideologies, their fallen cultures, their self-justification. They share them with one another and propagate them – indeed, more and more effectively with every technological advance. But all the time, behind human beings and their lies there lurks the figure of Satan, not felt perhaps nor recognized but present and shrewdly manipulating lost men and women in whom he is 'at work'.[27]

---

[27] Eph. 2:2.

This is why Paul warns the Ephesian believers, 'our struggle is not against flesh and blood, but against the rulers, against the authorities, against the powers of this dark world and against the spiritual forces of evil in the heavenly realms'.[28] Christians face a spiritual battle with the liar who seeks to deceive in order to destroy.

The answer to lies is truth. It is truth that liberates victims of the lie and delivers them from the death which it brings. And that truth is Christ: 'If you hold to my teaching, you are really my disciples. Then you will know the truth, and the truth will set you free.'[29] Jesus Christ came to destroy the devil's work of lies and murder (1 John 3:8), and so to liberate his captives. The proclamation of the good news that he has done so is at the very heart of his redeemed people's spiritual warfare: exposing the lies of Satan, bringing good news of life to those deceived by him, and offering reconciliation with the Father to those who will believe in the Son.

[28] Eph. 6:12.
[29] John 8:31–32.

Genesis 3:6–24
3. Sinners, not victims

In the summer of 2014 New Zealand international cricketer Lou Vincent very publicly admitted taking money to fix cricket matches. In a video recording he began his statement with a stark confession: 'My name is Lou Vincent and I am a cheat.'[1] In what followed he made no excuse for his conduct: 'The decisions I made were wrong . . . It is entirely my fault . . . I accept my punishment . . .' It is a remarkable and, indeed, a very rare confession.

David's brief and simple confession when the prophet Nathan confronted him over his adultery with Bathsheba and subsequent murder of Uriah, her husband, is similarly one of the most remarkable statements in Scripture. 'Then David said to Nathan, "I have sinned against the LORD."'[2] At first glance, of course, his words might not seem so striking. The facts of the case are made transparently clear in the preceding narrative, and in the light of them David's words are nothing but plain truth. What else, indeed, could he have said? The reality is, however, that men and women invariably do all they can to evade such forthright confessions of personal responsibility and guilt. Elsewhere in the Old Testament prophets bearing messages similar to Nathan's could easily become the objects of the rage and violence of the kings they rebuked (2 Chr. 16:7–10; 24:20–21). David himself might have tried to transfer some of the guilt to Bathsheba and her indiscreet bathing habits, even perhaps have presented himself as a victim of feminine guile. Certainly, when Moses censured his brother Aaron for making the golden calf, Aaron initially responded by blaming the people and then implied that the calf had made itself (Exod. 32:22–24)! He tried to present himself not as a sinner but as a victim.

[1] 'Lou Vincent: Full Text of Shamed Cricketer's Apology', at <http://www.bbc.co.uk/sport/0/cricket/28105561>, accessed 5 July 2014.
[2] 2 Sam. 12:13.

And Adam and Eve did the same. They were indeed the first to use that line of defence, pioneers of the tactical denial of personal responsibility in favour of victimhood. So, Adam testified that he was the victim of his wife, and Eve that she was the victim of the serpent. Untold multitudes of guilty descendants have followed in their steps, protesting themselves to be victims of parents and elders, of poverty and ignorance, of culture and society – and, indeed, of the devil himself. Eve's claim, 'Satan made me do it', may perhaps be the commonest defence of them all. The Judge of all the earth, however, would not have it. Although he certainly did not find the serpent innocent, in God's eyes its treachery did nothing to mitigate the disobedience of Adam and his wife. They were sinners and guilty; they were not mere helpless, hapless victims.

1. Choice (3:6)

The narrative which recounts Eve and Adam's eating of the fruit takes particular care to draw attention to their personal responsibility for the act. When the tempter stops talking and the moment of decision arrives, he simply drops out of the story. His part has been played and he leaves the stage, not to reappear until God summons him to give account. He sowed his perfidious seed in the minds of the human couple, but he did not have the power to constrain them to act in accordance with his wishes. And so at this, the crucial and defining moment of human history, the narrator's spotlight falls on the couple alone, for all that matters is the choice that they will make. A cliché sometimes used in describing moments of critical decision is to say that 'time stood still'. The moment described in Genesis 3:6 truly merits such a description, for no other human decision has ever been so critical as this one. It is as if the entire created cosmos stood spellbound at the tipping point of history, waiting to see how Adam and Eve would use the liberty God had given them. For with wills free and uncoerced they alone would determine how they would respond to the temptation to disbelief, ambition and rebellion, and whether they would set God's word aside in favour of that of the serpent.

So the focus moves to Eve, and the narrator recounts her three decisive, and apparently quite rapid, acts: *she saw . . . she took . . . she gave*. At the beginning, in three brief clauses a particular emphasis is laid on Eve's observation, giving the reader privileged access to the working of her mind: *the woman saw that the fruit of the tree was good for food and pleasing to the eye, and also desirable for gaining wisdom.* The first two of these three assessments had formed no part of the serpent's temptation: however, it was not only the wisdom that the serpent had offered that she was now coveting, but also the aesthetic quality and nutritional value of the fruit. Taken together they indicate a movement in her thinking towards a total reassessment of the fruit, and one based on her own autonomous judgment altogether detached from the word of the God who had made both her and the fruit, and had assigned to each of them their place and meaning. Significantly then, the woman was already taking upon herself the role of God which the serpent had held out, for in Genesis 1 it is the Creator who repeatedly 'saw that it was good' – whether 'it' was the light, or the separation between dry ground and seas, or the vegetation that grew from the soil, or whatever else he had made. Now the woman usurped his role as she *saw that the fruit . . . was good*.[3] Her own evaluation – her independent and inherently rebellious 'seeing' – reversed that which God had communicated to Adam, and at once she acted on it. It was at that point in the story that Eve took the fruit and ate it: the decisive act of rebellion followed immediately on her own reflection and not on the serpent's words. She was no victim.

Nor indeed was Adam, *who was with her*. He was apparently the silent spectator throughout the interchange between his wife and the serpent, and a significant dimension of the story is his passive acquiescence in Eve's decision. That passivity, however, and the fact that he allowed Eve to entice him do not make him any less a responsible actor in what occurred – far, far, indeed, to the contrary. Adam's responsibility and the consequent significance of his disobedience were immeasurably greater than Eve's, for it was his sin rather than Eve's that would be imputed to the whole race which they would engender: 'through the disobedience of the one man the many were made sinners'.[4] He was the head of that race, his sin would be the sin of them all and so it is 'in Adam' that 'all die'.[5] Sin, condemnation and death all flow from the act of the one person, the man, Adam. This is reflected in the text of Genesis where it was Adam alone who had heard the very voice of God, forbidding him to eat from the tree of the knowledge of good and evil (Gen. 2:16–17), while Eve's knowledge of the interdiction was indirect and presumably mediated through his instruction. Yet, far from reminding her of the word they had received from God, restraining her rashness and assuming the role of headship God had conferred on him, he implicitly abdicated responsibility. As the serpent spoke he held back while

[3] G. J. Wenham, *Genesis 1–15*, Word Biblical Commentary 1 (Waco: Word, 1987), p. 75.

[4] Rom. 5:19.

[5] 1 Cor. 15:22.

Eve responded, tacitly approving her disobedience as she plucked the fruit and gave him some to eat too.

At the crucial moment of decision the man and the woman stood poised between two contradictory words, and their choice was determined by their own wills alone. On the one hand there was the word of the one who had made them, who sustained them, who had endowed them with all the riches of his creation, who had indeed given them each other. Moreover, and greatest of all those gifts that they enjoyed, he had blessed them with an infinitely satisfying relationship with himself. On the other hand there was the word of a serpent with which they had no relationship, from which they had derived not a single one of their many blessings, in which they had no reason to trust. Everything they knew and had experienced should have disposed them to choose the word of God in preference to that of a snake ominously exercising an abnormal power of speech. Surely, as Carson suggests, the woman should have cried out to the snake, 'Are you out of your skull? Look around! This is Eden; this is paradise! . . . God made everything; he even made me . . .'[6] But in full possession of minds perfectly balanced and knowing all that they did, Adam and Eve deliberately chose to take the fruit and eat it. It was an act of flagrant rebellion and sin.

2. Guilt (3:7–13)

The consumption of the fruit is followed by an apparent anticlimax. Has anything really changed? They are still alive, apparently unaltered and unharmed; the sun shines on; the garden is as it was before they ate, with its rich vegetation and animal life. But in fact everything had changed. It was signalled first of all by a subtle and highly significant shift deep in the consciousness of both Adam and Eve; for they are perturbed about the nakedness which had previously caused them no shame. It is indeed a deeply ironic let-down, 'a grotesque anticlimax to the dream of enlightenment':[7] the serpent had promised that their eyes would be opened and they would be like God, but far from that their eyes are *opened* and they know that they are *naked*. It is no doubt the first time they had experienced distress, anxiety and pain, and it is more than the mere state of being physically unclothed that concerns them. The shame they feel in their nakedness is an indicator, pointing beyond itself to the fact that the innocence and transparency which had previously characterized

---

[6] D. A. Carson, *The God Who Is There: Finding Your Place in God's Story* (Grand Rapids: Baker, 2010), p. 31.

[7] D. Kidner, *Genesis*, Tyndale OT Commentaries (Leicester: Inter-Varsity Press, 1967), p. 74.

their relationship with each other (Gen. 2:25), and also with God, have been replaced by a powerful psychological need to hide from one another and, in due course, from God too. What they experience is not the sense of violation felt by a victim but the guilt of the wilful transgressor, and they try to hide this profound sense of lost innocence from one another. Their feeble and inadequate attempts to cover themselves with fig leaves point towards their own intense awareness that what they had done was wrong, and that they were personally responsible for their act. Calvin says it plainly: 'This opening of the eyes in our first parents to discern their baseness, clearly shows them to have been condemned by their own judgment.'[8]

When God then appears *in the garden*, walking to and fro and pursuing the fellowship with them which they were accustomed to, their flight from his presence has the same meaning. The physical avoidance is quickly followed by verbal prevarication as Adam tries pathetically to throw responsibility onto the woman, and Eve onto the serpent, all in a forlorn effort to claim the innocence of victimhood and cover up their own guilt. And all in vain. Their attempts at self-justification are as derisory as the fig leaves with which they cover their naked bodies, and their mute submission as God pronounces judgment shows that in the depths of their consciousness they know themselves to be guilty and his verdict to be just.

3. Judgment (3:14–19, 22–24)

God indeed holds them accountable. The terse statement, *the LORD God called to the man* (9), informs the reader that 'the Judge of the whole earth is calling man in order to demand an account of his conduct'.[9] A judicial enquiry takes place and after the man and the woman have each presented their case God proceeds to pronounce judgment on all three actors: he finds each of them responsible for their acts and consequently guilty. In the eyes of the divine Judge neither Adam nor Eve can be exonerated: both Adam's claim that he was enticed by his wife, and Eve's that she was seduced by the serpent, meet with a divine silence that communicates rejection of their pleas.[10] God finds them guilty of grievous sin, committed freely and intentionally, as the preceding narrative has already made clear.

Nevertheless, distinctions are made. Alone of the three the serpent is not invited to offer an explanation of its act. So obviously did its temptation spring unprovoked from the wanton, murderous malice

[8] J. Calvin, *Genesis* (Edinburgh: The Banner of Truth Trust, 1965), p. 157.
[9] Wenham, *Genesis 1–15*, p. 76, alluding to U. Cassuto.
[10] Ibid., p. 77.

of its own heart, that no mitigation of its offence was even conceivable and cross-examination would be superfluous. It had lied and seduced, and its purpose could be nothing other than the destruction of the human couple and, indeed, of the whole divine purpose in their creation. Accordingly, the serpent alone suffered the explicit curse of God: *Because you have done this, cursed are you above all the livestock and all the wild animals!* (14). It would experience the very opposite of his blessing – the withdrawal of all that is good. More precisely it was condemned both to slither on the earth and to experience an enduring and violent state of mutual hostility between itself and its *offspring* on the one hand, and the woman and her 'offspring' on the other, through the long generations to come, culminating finally in its own total overthrow.[11]

Nevertheless, while the serpent was utterly guilty in what it had done, it had not forced the man and the woman to sin: indeed, it was not able to do such a thing. They disobeyed freely and God punishes them for their disobedience, but he does not do so with a curse. His judgment reflects the qualitative distinction between their sin and that of the serpent, and they will continue to experience something of his blessing. Nevertheless, the consequences of their rebellion are most grievous, as for the first time humanity experiences God's just anger against sin.

First, they suffer individual judgments which focus on the primary spheres God had assigned to each of them. Accordingly, the woman will experience anguish in the two human relationships most fundamental to her, those of mother and wife: childbirth will be painful to her, and her relationship with her husband will become problematic. The exact meaning of God's word to Eve concerning her relationship to her husband is not entirely clear: *Your desire will be for your husband, and he will rule over you* (16). It may mean that she will continue to be irresistibly drawn to her husband, while endlessly and helplessly finding the relationship oppressive as his headship tends constantly towards tyranny. Alternatively, it may refer to persistent conjugal strife as she seeks to control him while he is able to impose his will on her by brute force. The latter interpretation is somewhat supported by the closely parallel Genesis 4:7 where the desire of sin is for Cain, clearly not in the sense of having a personal relationship with him but rather of taking control of him. Moreover, Eve's implicit assumption of headship over the man earlier, when she took the initiative and led him to eat the forbidden fruit, may suggest that God's judgment is precisely that she will continue to act in the same way, seeking to direct her husband but

---

[11] We return to this later in the chapter, pp. 45–47.

repeatedly suffering harsh suppression in response. Whatever the exact meaning of God's word of judgment, it is clear that the marital relationship will cease to be a source of unmitigated delight and comfort for the woman, but instead and all too frequently become one of conflict, oppression and grief.

Adam's sentence is the longest and fullest of the three, for 'he bore the greatest responsibility in following his wife's advice instead of heeding God's instructions personally given to him'.[12] God's initial words to him stress the wilfulness of the rebellion of which he was guilty: *because you listened to your wife and ate from the tree about which I commanded you, 'You must not eat of it . . .'* (17). Not only had he failed to assume the role of headship which was his, but he had listened to the word of his wife instead of the word of God. Therefore, the work of tending the earth which God had committed to him (Gen. 2:15) would be toilsome and *painful* as God cursed the ground such that it became resistant to his labour, too readily producing *thorns and thistles* (18) while yielding food reluctantly and only after arduous labour on his part. The punishment 'strikes at the innermost nerve of his life: his work, his activity, and provision for sustenance'.[13] And finally, after a lifetime of struggling with the soil, he will return to it and die.

Finally, as a couple Adam and Eve are banished from the garden. Eden was the blessed location in which they had experienced God's presence as he walked to and fro there (3:8). It had, indeed, the character of a temple, the very dwelling place of God. The two verbs which define Adam's work in the garden resonate with deeper meaning than may be obvious on the surface: 'The LORD God took the man and put him in the Garden of Eden to work it and take care of it.'[14] For when they are used together elsewhere the verbs translated 'to work' and 'to take care of' refer 'either to Israelites "serving" God and "guarding [keeping]" God's word (approximately 10 times) or to priests who "keep" the "service" (or "charge") of the tabernacle (see Num. 3:7–8; 8:25–26; 18:5–6; 1 Chron. 23:32; Ezek. 44:14)'.[15]

Thus, in Genesis 2 Adam is identified as the original priest who was appointed to serve in and take care of God's first temple. The banishment of the couple from Eden therefore signifies their expulsion from the temple and so from the very presence of God, and not simply from a particularly fertile tract of land. The intimacy

---

[12] Wenham, *Genesis 1–15*, p. 82.

[13] G. Von Rad, quoted by Wenham, *Genesis 1–15*, p. 82.

[14] Gen. 2:15.

[15] G. K. Beale, *The Temple and the Church's Mission: A Biblical Theology of the Dwelling Place of God* (Leicester: Apollos and Downers Grove: InterVarsity Press, 2004), p. 67; for a fuller discussion see pp. 66–80.

of fellowship with him, for which they were made and which they had begun richly to enjoy, is abruptly ended. Furthermore, it was in Eden, in the presence of God, that *the tree of life* flourished. Expulsion from his presence inevitably entailed removal also from the source of life represented by the tree. In other words, it meant immediate spiritual death and, in due course, physical death too.

The divine judge of all the earth held the man and the woman responsible for their defiance of his explicit word of command. He did not see them as innocent dupes and victims of the serpent's undoubted guile and wickedness. They were accountable, and he found them guilty, and he punished them.

4. Grace (3:15, 20–21)

Paradoxically the very fact of their guilt and the dire consequences that flowed from their rebellion reveal the unique glory possessed by Adam and Eve – and all their descendants – as God's human creation. The reality of their guilt powerfully affirms that these are not mere dumb beasts acting on the basis of instinct for which they are not responsible; nor are they machines or automata controlled by some external operator, including perhaps a serpent. On the contrary, they are reflective, moral beings possessed of an inalienable freedom, and therefore responsible for their acts. Made in the image of their creator, they have a dignity and nobility which sets them apart from all the rest of the physical creation, and part of that dignity consists precisely in a moral nature rooted in moral freedom. Human beings were made such creatures as *can* be guilty: this is central to the glory they possess. Therefore, to deny the guilt arising from transgression, and so to deny personal responsibility for sin, was lethally to diminish the grandeur of their own humanity – the glory that God conferred upon the human race he had made.

Accordingly, when God confronts Adam and Eve with direct questions – *Have you eaten from the tree from which I commanded you not to eat?* (11) and *What is this you have done?* (13) – he is compelling them to face up to the implications of their humanity, and so to confess that they themselves of their own free volition had acted in defiance of his command. He confronts them in order that they should recognize themselves as fully human, and so as capable of guilt – and indeed guilty. He will not allow them to degrade the glory which he has bestowed on them by an infantile appeal to victimhood. Adam is not the victim of his wife, nor is she the victim of the serpent. And so, even as he prosecutes them, God acts not only in justice but also in grace. He acts to save Adam and his wife from a false and delusional self-justification which evades confession and thereby makes forgiveness impossible; for if there is no recognition of sin to confess, then there can be no confession, and so no forgiveness or redemption either. God interrogates Adam and Eve not simply to make them grovel in the dust, but out of grace and to make a way for grace. He takes the role that his Spirit will assume, convicting of sin, righteousness and judgment (John 16:8–11).

The character of that grace, both present and future, becomes clearer as the chapter progresses. Most important of all there is 'the first glimmer of the gospel'[16] as future judgment is pronounced on the serpent: *I will put enmity between you and the woman, and between your offspring and hers; he will crush your head, and you will strike his heel* (15). The brief declaration, exhaustively discussed over the centuries, speaks first of an *enmity* that God himself would put between the serpent and the woman, and then between their respective offspring or 'seeds'. The serpent was, of course, already enemy to the woman, bent on her destruction and that also of her husband. The issue was rather that of the woman's easy but suicidal complicity with a murderous foe, signalled by her earlier acquiescent response to its words of seduction. Accordingly, God himself would disrupt the burgeoning relationship and put enmity in its place, thereby drawing the woman – and her offspring – back towards himself and so to a participation in his own warfare with the enemy. It is here that we find the beginning of the 'spiritual warfare' of his people.

There is then the question, however, of the identity of the respective offspring or seeds. Is the woman's offspring to be understood as the whole human race? And who are the offspring of the serpent? There have been various responses to those questions, but in the context of the whole biblical narrative the two sets of offspring must surely be identified as divergent branches of humanity. On the one hand are those who would continue to go the way of the serpent, seduced by its lies, unwittingly enslaved to its murderous tyranny, and partners in its rebellion against God; on the other hand there are those who are offspring of the woman, not so much by biological descent but rather in that they share in her enmity against the serpent. Soon after God's declaration, the enmity he spoke of is evident in the fratricidal conflict between Eve's two sons when 'one who pleased God, Abel, was slain by one who did not please God and then rejected a divine warning, Cain (Gen. 4:1–16)'.[17] In the much later words of the apostle John, Cain 'belonged to the evil one' – he

---

[16] Kidner, *Genesis*, p. 74.

[17] J. Hamilton, 'The Skull Crushing Seed of the Woman: Inner-Biblical Interpretation of Genesis 3:15', *Southern Baptist Journal of Theology* 10.2 (2006), p. 33.

was indeed offspring of the serpent – and he murdered Abel 'because his own actions were evil and his brother's were righteous'. [18] And the Lord Jesus Christ told those who opposed him that they too were offspring of the serpent: 'You belong to your father, the devil.'[19]

There is, however, a fluidity in the concept of *offspring*, which may be understood not only in a collective sense but also later in verse 15 as a reference to one individual (*he* in the NIV) who might represent the whole group.[20] God's words in Genesis 3:15 not only speak, therefore, of an ongoing conflict running down through the generations, but also look forward to the one who will come as a second Adam, himself offspring of a woman, to wage war on the serpent on behalf of all her offspring and to *crush his head*. Human rebellion would not be the end of the story, for Eve *would become the mother of all the living* (20) and from her descendants would come a deliverer (15). There is amazing grace in God's use of woman, deceived though she was by the serpent (1 Tim. 2:14), to be mother of the coming Saviour. He would be sent into a desert by the Spirit to confront Satan; where the first Adam had failed he would stand firm in the face of Satan's attack (Matt. 4:1–11; Mark 1:12–13; Luke 4:1–13); and finally, in dying on a cross he would break the serpent's tyranny by delivering his captives from the guilt and condemnation of their sin (Col. 2:13–15). He would indeed crush the serpent's skull, as God had promised, but in so doing would himself be smitten as Satan struck his heel.

Indeed, God's word to the serpent underlines the fact that, beginning with Abel and climaxing in the incarnate Son of God, suffering would be integral to the renewal of his creation – would lie, indeed, at the heart of his divine warfare against sin and Satan. The theology of the cross begins here. 'Victory is gained only through injury; it is in being crushed that Christ crushes Satan.'[21] And to this day the dragon, 'that ancient serpent',[22] still makes war against the woman and 'against *the rest of her offspring* – those who obey God's commandments and hold to the testimony of Jesus'.[23] 'From this point on, the road for the human race will pass through suffering to glory, through struggle to victory, through the cross to a crown,

---

[18] 1 John 3:12.

[19] John 8:44.

[20] W. C. Kaiser, *Toward an Old Testament Theology* (Grand Rapids: Zondervan, 1978), pp. 36–37. See also J. Collins, 'A Syntactical Note (Genesis 3:15): Is the Woman's Seed Singular or Plural?', *Tyndale Bulletin* 48.1 (1997), pp. 139–148.

[21] S. Ferguson, 'Christus Victor et Propitiator: The Death of Christ, Substitute and Conqueror', in S. Storms and J. Taylor (eds.), *For the Fame of God's Name: Essays in Honor of John Piper* (Wheaton: Crossway, 2010), p. 181.

[22] Rev. 12:9.

[23] Rev. 12:17.

through the state of humiliation to that of exaltation. This is the fundamental law that God here proclaims before the entrance into the kingdom of heaven.'[24]

Finally, as well as the promise of future redemption God also acts in Eden to cover the present nakedness of the couple (21). His intervention indicates the irreversibility of what has taken place; clothing is now necessary and God provides it far more adequately than the couple had been able to do. In this way the text suggests the incapacity of sinful human beings to respond other than superficially to their own guilt and shame, and points them once again to their absolute need of God's grace. Moreover, the means by which God clothed them, with *garments of skin*, implies the death of the creatures from which the skins were taken, and so perhaps points towards the necessity of blood sacrifice if human sin and its consequences are to be dealt with effectively. The text, therefore, anticipates and evokes the sacrificial system established in the law by which human guilt could be covered, and beyond that it looks forward to Christ's climactic sacrifice of himself 'once to take away the sins of many people'.[25] So, Boice says, God 'killed animals, clothed the man and the woman with skins, covering their shame, and began his teaching of the way of salvation through sacrifice'.[26]

Some interpreters have commented on the terseness of David's confession of his sin regarding Bathsheba and Uriah – 'I have sinned against the LORD'[27] – as if he should have multiplied words in order to demonstrate his sincerity. However, the brevity of his statement indicates rather its simple honesty. 'There is no excuse, no cloaking, no palliation of the sin. There is no searching for a loophole . . . no pretext put forward, no human weakness pleaded. He acknowledges his guilt openly, candidly, and without prevarication.'[28] Through his prophet God brought David to recognition and confession of his guilt, as he sought also to do directly with Adam and Eve. When we sin, we are guilty; Satan does not make us sin; we are not mere victims of his guile; nor are we victims of whatever circumstance or condition

[24] H. Bavinck, quoted in J. R. Treat, *The Crucified King: Atonement and Kingdom in Biblical and Systematic Theology* (Grand Rapids: Zondervan, 2014), p. 58.

[25] Heb. 9:28.

[26] J. M. Boice, *Foundations of the Christian Faith: A Comprehensive and Readable Theology* (Downers Grove: InterVarsity Press and Leicester: Inter-Varsity Press, 1986), p. 54. It may be worth noting that Kidner (*Genesis*, p. 72) and some others regard this approach to the clothing of Adam and Eve as 'unduly subtle', and see it rather as a forerunner of measures of 'welfare' that human sin will make necessary.

[27] 2 Sam. 12:13.

[28] The Berleburg Bible (1726–9), quoted by R. D. Davis, *2 Samuel: Out of Every Adversity* (Fearn: Christian Focus Publications, 1999), p. 127.

we might like to hide behind. The appeal to victimhood diminishes us as human beings, and it cuts us off from the possibility of forgiveness. 'Unfortunately, victimization convinces men and women who should be looking for a Savior to search for a scapegoat. After all, if I am not to blame for what I do, the Cross is much ado about nothing.'[29] In his grace God acts to prevent us taking refuge in victim status. He confronts and convicts, demolishing our evasions in order to lead us to confession, and so to redemption. There may be intense pain in the sinner's encounter with the grace of a holy God, but with it there comes everlasting healing. Each of us has to say it: 'I have sinned against the LORD.'

[29] H. W. Robinson, quoted in D. A. Carson, *The Gagging of God: Christianity Confronts Pluralism* (Leicester: Apollos, 1996), p. 208.

Job 1 – 2
4. Satan and suffering

Human beings constantly ask the question, 'why?', and never more so than when they suffer. 'Why', Job asked, 'is light given to those in misery, and life to the bitter of soul . . . ?',[1] and the question recurs incessantly in one form or another through most of the book. At its heart lies the assumption that life ought to make sense, and that there should be some meaning to what happens, especially when things go 'wrong'. It is striking that in the functionally atheistic West people continue to ask the same question, although in a universe from which the notion of God has been largely expunged one might have supposed that any expectation of meaning and significance beyond the vagaries of chance would have disappeared. But in fact, when faced by some bleak medical prognosis or a serious misfortune in family or social life, for many people the questions, 'why me?', 'why this?', 'why now?' spring quickly to mind.

A foundational assumption in most traditional African cultures is that 'there is always somebody'.[2] In the face of misfortune the afflicted quickly consult a diviner to find out whether a jealous neighbour has resorted to sorcery, a neglected ancestor is demanding his due, or a capricious spirit is looking for some sort of relationship with its victim. Occult explanations of misfortune of various sorts – a witch, an ancestor, the evil eye, a spirit – have in fact been accepted by the vast majority of humanity and for most of its history. So, while such 'weird, mystical "fantasies"' may seem strange to many of us, in reality 'it is not the presence of such beliefs that is odd or unusual but their absence'.[3] They stubbornly persist in so-called

[1] Job 3:20.
[2] This is specifically a proverb of the Zulu. See A.-I. Berglund, *Zulu Thought-Patterns and Symbolism* (London: C. Hurst, 1976), p. 270.
[3] I. M. Lewis, *Social Anthropology in Perspective* (Cambridge: Cambridge University Press, 1985), p. 33.

animistic cultures as well as in the 'folk' forms of the great religious traditions, including Islam and Christianity, despite the disapproving incomprehension of Western rationalists. And they persist precisely because they respond to the question, 'why?', and enable the members of such societies to make sense of the adversities they face, and then to respond to them. To what extent then, might the Bible also sanction the view that evil powers, and specifically Satan, are at the root of human suffering?

1. Satan and Job's afflictions

Job suffered terribly. He lost his very substantial wealth along with the herdsmen who were guarding it, and then his ten adult sons and daughters, in a series of devastating blows through the course of just one day. Shortly afterwards his own health collapsed and he was afflicted *with painful sores from the soles of his feet to the top of his head* (2:7). The destruction of his herds and his family was occasioned by assorted political and climatic factors: Sabeans carried off his oxen and donkeys, Chaldeans took his camels, a *fire of God* falling from the sky destroyed his sheep and a *mighty wind* sweeping in from the desert brought the house in which his children were feasting crashing down on top of them (1:13–19). No diagnosis of Job's illness is possible at this distance but it was clearly chronic and very severe, and the text indicates that he suffered a wide range of unpleasant symptoms.[4]

Unknown to Job, however, and indeed to all the human participants in the story, a being identified as 'the satan (*śāṭān*)' stood behind these events. Both his identity and his unexpected appearance in the narrative are unexplained. The word by which he is labelled, *satan*, is Hebrew for adversary and it is preceded in the text by an article, probably specifying the title or the role of the being concerned rather than his name. The same is true of the one identified as '*the* satan' who accused the high priest, Joshua, in Zechariah 3:1, and it is only when Satan tempted David to number Israel (1 Chr. 21:1) that it is clear the word has become a proper name. Elsewhere in the Old Testament 'satan' is also used quite frequently of human adversaries,[5] while in Numbers 22:22 the angel of the Lord who resists Balaam is identified as a 'satan', in this case the adversary of Balaam. Here in Job, however, it is clear that a being of a rather different order is in view, and certainly not the angel of the Lord. The episodes

---

[4] J. E. Hartley, *The Book of Job*, New International Commentary on the OT (Grand Rapids: Eerdmans, 1988), p. 82.
[5] 1 Sam. 29:4; 2 Sam. 19:22; 1 Kgs 5:4; 11:14, 23, 25; Ps. 109:6.

in which he appears take place in the divine assembly, where the Lord is surrounded by the *sons of God,*[6] celestial beings or angels who serve the Creator (1:6–7; 2:1) and which we also encounter elsewhere in the Old Testament (1 Kgs 22:19–22; Dan. 7:9–10). The flow of the narrative suggests, however, that Satan's appearance in such a body was somehow incongruous. The words, *and Satan also came with them* (2:1), imply that his attendance was unusual, even inappropriate. While clearly a supernatural being, he is apparently not to be numbered among the sons of God and his true character quickly becomes evident. His brusque and contemptuous dismissal of God's testimony to Job's righteousness, his cynicism regarding the integrity of Job's faith, and his enthusiastic assumption of the role of torturer all indicate that this satan is a malignant being, in fact an adversary of God himself as also of one who fears and serves him. 'His insolence shows a mind already twisted away from God.'[7] Indeed, his denial of God's words and relentless determination to bring about the destruction of a God-fearing human being are suggestively reminiscent of the serpent's disposition in Genesis 3. Further, his apparently restless wandering across the earth (1:7; 2:2) will echo in Peter's much later warning, 'Your enemy the devil prowls around like a roaring lion looking for someone to devour.'[8] Here he has his sights set on Job.

While the narrator does not explicitly assert that Satan brings about the disasters which subsequently befall Job's wealth and children, the sequence of events shows that such is certainly his intended meaning. In Job 1:12 he tells how God allowed Satan to test Job: '. . . *everything he has is in your hands, but on the man himself do not lay a finger.' Then Satan went out from the presence of the LORD.* The text then immediately recounts the series of disasters that ensued, leaving little doubt that Satan is to be seen as the one who brought them about. A little later, in Job 2, the physical sufferings of Job himself are explicitly attributed to Satan: *So Satan went out from the presence of the LORD and afflicted Job with painful sores from the soles of his feet to the top of his head* (2:7).

Job 1 – 2 affirms, therefore, that this satan was able to manipulate the climate, to exploit the human greed and violence of Sabeans and Chaldeans, and to inflict physical disease in order to press his attack on Job. Nevertheless, his purpose was not simply the elimination of Job's wealth and offspring, nor the infection of his body – he was far more ambitious than that. By afflicting Job Satan's goal was that

---

[6] See NIV footnote.

[7] F. I. Andersen, *Job,* Tyndale OT Commentaries (Leicester: Inter-Varsity Press, 1976), p. 83.

[8] 1 Pet. 5:8.

he would curse God *to his face* (1:11; 2:5). His claim was that Job's apparent righteousness and fear of God were insincere. The only possible object of any truly personal relationship is communion with the person himself or herself, rather than whatever incidental benefit might accrue from knowledge of the person: in other words, in a relationship persons are ends in themselves and not means towards other ends.[9] Satan was suggesting, however, that Job saw God precisely as a means to his own prosperity rather than an object of personal knowledge and worship for his own sake. So Job's fear of God was hypocritical, motivated by the blessings which God could give; God himself was not the true end of Job's righteousness and worship. Accordingly, if God withdrew the blessing, the shallowness of Job's piety would be disclosed and he would curse God because of the loss of the good things he had once enjoyed. In afflicting Job Satan was aiming to elicit that curse, and so to bring about Job's spiritual destruction: the vicious and pitiless testing to which he subjected Job contained at its heart the potentially lethal temptation to apostasy.

2. Satan and God's sovereignty

The narrative is unambiguous, however, in its repudiation of any suggestion of metaphysical dualism. Each of Satan's two attacks on Job, initially on what he has and then on Job's own body, is only carried out following God's explicit verbal authorization. The implication is that Satan is totally unable to carry out any attack on Job except with divine permission. Further, in each case God sets a limit to Satan's action beyond which he cannot go. So, in Job 1 God authorizes Satan to *strike everything* [Job] *has* but adds, *on the man himself do not lay a finger* (1:12). When, after the series of attacks on Job's property and children, God then permits Satan to attack Job's own person, he again sets a boundary, *but you must spare his life* (2:6). In each case Satan does not transgress the boundary, suggesting indeed that he *cannot* transgress it. And finally, of course, he drops out of the story entirely.

A fundamental assumption of the book of Job is, therefore, that God is sovereign and that Satan, although undoubtedly antagonistic and malevolent, is emphatically subject to the divine will. Accordingly, the confrontation between God and Satan is in no way a dualistic clash between supernatural beings of an essentially similar nature or ontology. Here in Job as everywhere else the Bible is unequivocally monotheistic, and for all his guile and power Satan

---

[9] M. J. Erickson, *Christian Theology* (Grand Rapids: Baker, 1985), p. 270.

remains a mere creature who 'can only do what God permits him to do'.[10]

In his second letter to the Corinthians Paul spoke in similar terms when he described the 'thorn in the flesh' with which he was tormented at the hands of a 'messenger [angel] of Satan'.[11] The messenger was almost certainly a demon, and the affliction probably a physical ailment.[12] If that is so, then Satan is once again identified as a source of physical illness; but Paul saw his suffering in the much greater context of God's sovereignty. It is God who is the ultimate cause of his affliction, whose purpose was 'to keep me from becoming conceited' and so to ensure Paul's ongoing usefulness as an apostle of Christ.

Other passages too affirm Satan's subservience to the purposes of God. The writer of 2 Samuel 24 tells us that God's anger burned against Israel and he incited David to take a census, an act which then led to judgment. According to the Chronicler, however, it was Satan 'who rose up against Israel and incited David' to number the fighting men.[13] The contrast between these two parallel texts suggests, 'as indeed does the prologue of Job, that behind and above the spiritual agent of evil God reigns'.[14] And, indeed, in the Chronicler's narrative the outcome of the incident was 'the divine choice of the Temple site'. The writer 'looked on Satan as one who, as in Job, was strictly limited by God's overriding sovereignty, and . . . could be an instrument of the ultimate divine will'.[15] Similarly, in Luke 22:31 Jesus told Peter, 'Satan has asked to sift you as wheat', indicating again that his temptations take place only by divine permission. And ultimately, of course, Satan's role in the crucifixion of the Lord Jesus Christ, especially his inspiration of Judas' act of betrayal (Luke 22:3–4; John 13:2, 27), served only to advance God's 'set purpose'[16] which included Satan's own defeat.

Satan is certainly able to inflict pain, even on those who fear God, but, whatever malign plans he may have, they can only be put into effect subject to God's will and in accordance with his overriding purpose. Despite his rebellion, Satan is subject to the rule of the Creator. Not only that, but his very malignancy is turned to good by God. Satan gets away with nothing. Calvin says it like this:

[10] Andersen, *Job*, p. 83.

[11] 2 Cor. 12:7.

[12] See pp. 184–186.

[13] 1 Chr. 21:1.

[14] J. G. McConville, *Chronicles* (Edinburgh: The Saint Andrew Press and Philadelphia: The Westminster Press, 1984), p. 70.

[15] H. G. M. Williamson, *1 and 2 Chronicles* (Grand Rapids: Eerdmans and London: Marshall, Morgan and Scott, 1982), pp. 143–144.

[16] Acts 2:23.

But because with the bridle of his power God holds him bound and restrained, he carries out only those things which have been divinely permitted to him; and so he obeys his Creator, whether he will or not, because he is compelled to yield him service wherever God impels him.[17]

3. Satan and Job's response

An extraordinary feature of the story of Job is his ignorance throughout of the source of his affliction; he is never made aware of the events that had taken place in the divine assembly, nor of Satan's role. Reflecting a powerful Old Testament theme, his counsellors, Zophar, Bildad, Eliphaz and, later, Elihu, all interpret it in terms of retribution for Job's supposed sin, but none of them suggests the possibility of demonic or satanic intervention, and neither does Job.

This feature of the story is the more surprising in that the Ancient Near Eastern world that Job inhabited was one in which demonic explanation of suffering was widespread. This was especially the case for Assyria and Babylon, where gods and demons were often identified as causes of affliction. In Egypt there is evidence for more empirico-rational approaches to illness but it was nevertheless 'frequently believed to be the work of malevolent demons from which even the gods were not immune'.[18] In addition to empirical medicine, therefore, treatment for illness tended to involve appeasing gods and expelling demons, while protection was sought through the use of charms.[19]

The Old Testament, however, is characterized in general by an almost complete absence of such thinking. This is not to deny that it may have been present in popular conception and practice, the more so perhaps at times of spiritual decline. Nevertheless, that it should be absent from the debate between Job and his friends, focused as it was precisely on the reason for Job's awful suffering, is particularly striking. It is even more striking given that unlike Job readers of the book *do* know that there was satanic involvement in his trial. At no point in the narrative, however, does Job suggest that he may be the victim of demonic attack, nor do his counsellors ever advise him to consult a diviner or priest to ascertain whether demonic powers might be involved and, if so, to advise

---

[17] J. Calvin, *Institutes of the Christian Religion*, ed. J. T. McNeill (Philadelphia: The Westminster Press, 1960), 1.14.17, p. 176.

[18] M. L. Brown, *Israel's Divine Healer* (Carlisle: Paternoster, 1995), p. 42.

[19] E. M. Yamauchi, 'Magic or Miracle? Disease, Demons and Exorcisms', in D. Wenham and C. Blomberg (eds.), *Gospel Perspectives*, vol. VI (Sheffield: JSOT, 1986), p. 100.

on appropriate responses. In the context of the time, the silence is remarkable.

It is testimony again to the all-transcending impact of the revelation of God which permeates and saturates the Old Testament throughout its length, including the book of Job. While demons or evil spirits play an occasional role in the Old Testament, the presence of the living God, sovereign over all that he has made, totally overshadows them and reduces them to relative insignificance. Indeed, on more than one occasion they explicitly serve his purpose.[20] Job's verbal response to his suffering reflects that view, for he recognizes that whatever secondary factors may have been involved in causing his suffering, ultimately it is God who has permitted it to happen and it is, therefore, he who can bring relief. Accordingly, throughout the book, and often in the most blunt language, his discourse focuses uniquely on God himself as he questions him and demands that God give him an audience.

> I will say to God: Do not condemn me,
>   but tell me what charges you have against me.
> Does it please you to oppress me,
>   to spurn the work of your hands,
>   while you smile on the schemes of the wicked?[21]

> Only grant me these two things, O God,
>   and then I will not hide from you:
> Withdraw your hand far from me,
>   and stop frightening me with your terrors.
> Then summon me and I will answer,
>   or let me speak, and you reply.
> How many wrongs and sins have I committed?
>   Show me my offence and my sin.
> Why do you hide your face
>   and consider me your enemy?[22]

Despite the audacity of his complaining, which indeed comes close at times to insolence, Job demonstrates throughout a profound faith in God, and one far from the insipid, conventional piety of his friends and counsellors. His insistence, even his provocative language, display an invincible belief in the constantly forbearing grace and mercy of a God who will not be affronted by the anguished pleading

[20] Judg. 9:23; 1 Sam. 16:14; 18:10; 19:9.
[21] Job 10:2–3.
[22] Job 13:20–24.

of a desperately wounded human being. His vision of God is not of one who will respond to complaint like some petty despot, insecure, prickly and vengeful. Rather he believes in the breadth of God's loving heart and the depth of his understanding and compassion, and despite the apparently lengthy silence on God's part, Job's trust at times shines out luminously. It is there immediately after he loses his wealth and children:

> *Naked I came from my mother's womb,*
> *and naked I shall depart.*
> *The* LORD *gave and the* LORD *has taken away;*
> *may the name of the* LORD *be praised* (1:21).

And it is there again during his frequently impassioned exchanges with his counsellors:

> Though he slay me, yet will I hope in him;
> I will surely defend my ways to his face.
> Indeed, this will turn out for my deliverance,
> for no godless man would dare come before him![23]

In the extremity of his pain Job demonstrates the absolute importance of the conception we have of the God in whom we believe. 'The single most important thing in our mind is our idea of God and the associated images.'[24] Job knew God in all his sovereignty, grace and faithfulness even before he encountered him at the end of the narrative.

Unlike Job, in 2 Corinthians Paul was able explicitly to identify the immediate source of his affliction as a demon sent by Satan. Nevertheless, his reaction was in key respects the same as Job's. There is no suggestion in the text that he attempted any direct dealing with the demon responsible, either to bind it or to drive it out. In his pain he addresses himself neither to Satan nor to the 'messenger of Satan' but takes his affliction directly into the presence of God: 'Three times I pleaded with the Lord to take it away from me.'[25] When after such repeated appeals his prayer was not answered positively, he accepted the Lord's response. Like Job he understood that ultimately it was God who had permitted the disease to invade his body, and it was God who must bring him relief or refrain from doing so.

---

[23] Job 13:15–16.
[24] D. Willard, quoted in J. W. Sire, *Naming the Elephant: Worldview as a Concept* (Downers Grove: InterVarsity Press, 2004), p. 128.
[25] 2 Cor. 12:8.

4. God and Job

God did not allow Job to know the origin of his sufferings; Job was not made privy to what had taken place in the divine assembly, indeed to what every reader of the book knows. God's decision to keep him in ignorance is surely significant. Nevertheless, somewhat in response to Job's demand, God finally met with him and responded to his complaint. He did so with an unrelenting series of questions which drew out the immeasurable distance between his own wisdom and knowledge and Job's infinitely more limited understanding. In the course of the encounter Job responds twice, confessing his unworthiness and incomprehension, recognizing indeed the absurdity of his challenge to the Almighty.

> I am unworthy – how can I reply to you?
> I put my hand over my mouth.
> I spoke once, but I have no answer –
> twice, but I will say no more.[26]

> I know that you can do all things;
> no plan of yours can be thwarted.
> You asked, 'Who is this that obscures my counsel
> without knowledge?'
> Surely I spoke of things I did not understand,
> things too wonderful for me to know.[27]

The encounter focuses on the vastness and complexity of the universe God has made, such that no human being could truly grasp the particular meaning of his or her own small life and experience apart from divine revelation, which in Job's case God does not give. What he does, however, is enable Job to comprehend his own human finitude, and give him a glimpse of God's immeasurable glory and the inscrutability of his purposes. By revealing himself but not explaining himself, God summons Job to trust where he cannot see, and so to quieten his heart. In short, Job's questions evaporate as he contemplates the wonder and glory of the sovereign Creator, just as shadows disappear in the overwhelming light of the sun. And although they remain, therefore, unanswered, what he gains is a glimpse of God far more profound than he had ever conceived and far richer than any explanation of his own trials: 'My ears had heard

[26] Job 40:4–5.
[27] Job 42:2–3.

of you, but now my eyes see you.'[28] His experience anticipates that of Martin Luther and countless others: 'Affliction is the Christian's theologian. I never knew the meaning of God's Word until I came into affliction. My trials have been my masters in divinity.'[29]

Nevertheless, our own question remains: does Satan cause all suffering? Is that the explanation? The book of Job does not give an answer. Insofar as Satan seduced Adam and Eve, then in a general way he certainly bears massive responsibility for the presence of all suffering in the world. It may be in that sense that Peter describes Jesus as 'healing all who were under the power of the devil'.[30] Moreover, apart from Job the Bible does attribute some other particular cases of suffering to Satan. Paul's 'thorn in the flesh' has already been mentioned. The Gospels refer to people who suffered demon 'possession' which Jesus himself attributed directly to Satan,[31] and Jesus healed a woman suffering from curvature of the spine which Luke attributes to a spirit and Jesus himself to Satan – 'a daughter of Abraham, whom Satan has kept bound for eighteen long years'.[32] Paul, too, explained the disciplining of a notoriously immoral member of the Corinthian church as handing him 'over to Satan' for the destruction of his 'flesh', which may well mean that his expulsion from the church and return to the world would expose him to the physical aggression of Satan (1 Cor. 5:4–5). Nevertheless, in the vast majority of cases of illness and healing Satan and demons are not explicitly identified as the specific cause of the problem. 'For the New Testament writers there was no simple equation between infirmity and the demonic.'[33]

Perhaps, then, the question must remain open although, as Carson says, the Bible's big answer is that suffering is 'the effluent of the fall, the result of a fallen world'.[34] The very disordered nature of the natural world of itself engenders pain. Further, it may be that part of the message of Job is that faced with our own trials the specific question of Satan's role in suffering really does not matter. After all, God did not judge it necessary to let Job know where his trials came

[28] Job 42:5.

[29] Quoted in J. J. Murray, *Behind a Frowning Providence* (Carlisle, Pennsylvania: The Banner of Truth Trust, 1990), p. 18.

[30] Acts 10:38.

[31] Matt. 12:24–29; Mark 3:22–30; Luke 11:17–22.

[32] Luke 13:10–17. According to J. Wilkinson, the woman's condition was spondylitis ankylopoeitica ('The Case of the Bent Woman in Luke 13v10–17', *EvQ* 49 [1977], pp. 196–200).

[33] J. C. Thomas, *The Devil, Disease and Deliverance: Origins of Illness in New Testament Thought* (Sheffield: Sheffield Academic Press, 1998), p. 302.

[34] D. A. Carson, *How Long, O Lord?: Reflections on Suffering and Evil* (Leicester: Inter-Varsity Press, 1990), p. 48.

from, and even before his encounter with God Job himself understood that whatever the cause of his suffering, God alone, unique
Creator and almighty King, was necessarily sovereign over it. Health,
illness, accident and so on all occur in a universe over which God
rules. They are ordained by him.

> I am the LORD, and there is no other.
> I form the light and create darkness,
> I bring prosperity and create disaster;
> I, the LORD, do all these things.[35]

The significance of Satan, then, is not so much that he may or may
not be involved in the genesis of this or that illness or of whatever
other trials arise, but rather the deadly use that he wants to make of
them. From this perspective the importance of Job's story does not
lie in the discovery of answers to questions, for his questions were
not answered. It lies rather in the fact that in the face of terrible
suffering he remained faithful to God and did not curse him, contrary
to Satan's prediction. He truly knew God, and sincerely feared him
even in the darkness. In all his anguish he kept trusting in the one
who had allowed him to pass through such pain. Wherever it comes
from, suffering tests the reality of a believer's faith, and Job knew this:
'when he has tested me, I shall come forth as gold'.[36] His suffering
proved that his faith was real. But much more than that, his experience
led to inexpressible blessing in a fresh vision and knowledge of God,
who used Satan's very malignancy to bring that about.

And there is a final point. Job's experience dimly foreshadows that
of another righteous sufferer, and a far greater one. The Lord Jesus
Christ also endured suffering inspired by the hostility of Satan and
the powers of darkness; through all his sufferings, far worse than
those Job experienced, he too remained faithful to the God who had
ordained them; and, like Job's, his sufferings also led to blessing.
Indeed, they led to blessing *infinitely* greater than any Job could even
have conceived of, for the reward Jesus received was the justification
of the many – 'his offspring' – whose iniquities he bore.

> After the suffering of his soul,
> he will see the light of life and be satisfied;
> by his knowledge my righteous servant will justify many,
> and he will bear their iniquities.[37]

[35] Isa. 45:6–7.
[36] Job 23:10.
[37] Isa. 53:11.

Numbers 22 – 25
5. A curse transformed

It is striking how prevalent malevolent sorcery and use of the curse have been through most of human history and among widely different peoples right across the world.[1] In 1493 in the City of London, 'Elena Dalok of St Mary Abchurch had appeared before the Commissary of London's court after bragging that everybody she cursed had subsequently died.'[2] Among the African Nyoro people, at least up to the twentieth century, 'medicine' was used along with words to inflict harm on a victim: 'There is *kuhuha* ("to puff") . . . which consists in blowing from the palms of the hands a powder made from the dried leaves of a plant called *bihoire* (literally "it is finished"). The powder is blown, at sunset, in the supposed direction of the victim, and the practitioner orders it to find and kill his enemy.'[3]

In the Bible such practices almost never take centre stage. However, they are present in the background, for in the pagan societies surrounding Israel throughout the periods of both Old and New Testaments sorcery was widely practised and feared. 'There can be no doubt that both the Old Testament and the New Testament were born in environments permeated with magical beliefs and practices.'[4]

---

[1] The word 'sorcery' is a slippery one and is used in a number of different senses. In the present context it denotes the use of occult or mystical means to do harm to other human beings. The 'curse' is one such means, although it may also be used as a religious sanction, as when God cursed the serpent in Gen. 3:14, or when curses were proclaimed on Mount Ebal against those who break God's law in Deut. 27:9–26. The word 'witchcraft' is used here in a similar sense. Many societies distinguish between different occult or mystical means of inflicting suffering on others.

[2] K. Thomas, *Religion and the Decline of Magic* (Harmondsworth: Penguin, 1978), p. 610.

[3] J. H. M. Beattie, 'Sorcery in Bunyoro', in J. Middleton and E. H. Winter (eds.), *Witchcraft and Sorcery in East Africa* (London: Routledge and Kegan Paul, 1963), p. 29.

[4] E. M. Yamauchi, 'Magic in the Biblical World', *Tyndale Bulletin* 34 (1983), p. 169.

Accordingly, Old Testament law condemns occult practices on a number of occasions,[5] and Malachi is still declaring God's judgment on sorcerers in the fifth century BC at the other end of Old Testament history.[6] In his letter to the Galatians Paul identified witchcraft or sorcery as one of the acts of the sinful nature with which the Galatian believers would doubtless have been familiar (5:19–21). The Greek word he uses, *pharmakeia*, is related to *pharmakon* which initially denoted a drug used in erotic magic. 'For the most part, however, the cognates of φάρμακον [*pharmakon*] refer more often to magical material used for purposes of hate rather than love.'[7] Meanwhile, Ephesus was a city renowned for its magic, the purpose of which was to manipulate spiritual powers either for personal advantage or to harm enemies.[8] The famed 'Ephesian Letters', which were written magical spells, are first mentioned 'as early as the fourth century B.C. in a Cretan tablet'.[9]

1. Balaam and Balak

In the episode involving Balak and Balaam the issue of malevolent sorcery briefly comes to the fore. The incident took place close to the end of Israel's wanderings in the desert, not long before Moses' death and Israel's subsequent entry into the Promised Land. Balak, king of Moab, had noted *all that Israel had done to the Amorites* (22:2), including their defeat and conquest of the realms of Sihon king of the Amorites and Og king of Bashan somewhat to the north of Moab. As a result he and his people were terrified: *Moab was filled with dread because of the Israelites* (22:3). He concluded that Moab would be powerless to resist them by military force alone: *this horde is going to lick up everything around us* (22:4). Alerting the leadership of the neighbouring Midianites to the danger he saw, Balak therefore decided to seek supernatural help, and both Moabite and Midianite elders were sent to summon Balaam to curse Israel so that he could then defeat them and drive them away (22:4–7). It was a critical moment. But who was Balaam?

The biblical text tells us that he came to Moab from *Pethor, near the River* (22:5), probably Pithru on the Euphrates in northern

---

[5] See e.g., Lev. 20:27 and Deut. 18:9–13, although a major emphasis in these texts is on divination and necromancy. The same is true of Isa. 8:19–20, 19:3, and perhaps 65:2–4. Ezek. 13:17–23 may refer to sorcery but it is not entirely clear what was actually going on.

[6] Mal. 3:5.

[7] Yamauchi, 'Magic in the Biblical World', p. 181.

[8] C. E. Arnold, *Ephesians: Power and Magic* (Cambridge: Cambridge University Press, 1989), p. 18.

[9] Arnold, *Ephesians: Power and Magic*, p. 15.

Mesopotamia, about twelve miles south of Carchemish and a very long way from Balak, king of Moab. He is undoubtedly a paradoxical character. On the one hand, he identifies himself as a prophet of God. He declares that any response he may give to Balak must depend on what the Lord will say to him (22:8, 13, 18; 23:3, 12, 26; 24:12–13), implying that he knows and serves the God of Israel to whom he refers by his covenant name, *the LORD* – Yahweh himself. And this is the view that some commentators take of him: 'Balaam is depicted from the outset as a true prophet of Yahweh who is bound to declare the true word of God.'[10] However, the narrator of the story takes a rather more nuanced view of the man, and the ambiguous nature of Balaam's relationship with the Lord becomes especially clear in the account of his journey to Moab. As he travels *the angel of the LORD* comes as an adversary against him on three separate occasions, opposing his journey. It is clear that this professed prophet of the Lord is acting in contravention of the wishes of the Lord he claims to serve, who is indeed *very angry* with what he is about (22:22). Not only that, but while Balaam's donkey can clearly see the opposing angel and recoils from him, the 'prophet' remains blind to his presence. He beats the ass, which is in fact more spiritually perceptive than he and which finally turns on him and rebukes him for his obtuse brutality (22:28–30).

The reality is that Balaam is a practitioner of sorcery, a soothsayer or diviner, 'a numb-skulled, money-grubbing, heathen seer',[11] rather more than he is a prophet of the Lord. In the story he is a man known for his ability to manipulate words, accompanied perhaps by ritual acts,[12] in order to bring suffering on a named victim – which is precisely what a sorcerer does. At numerous points the text drives this home.

First, Balaam evidently had an established reputation for prowess in those very occult arts that are explicitly forbidden to God's people. The reason for which Balak, king of Moab, summoned him in the first place was not to bring the prophetic word of God into the situation he faced, but quite simply to curse Israel: *Now come and put a curse on these people because they are too powerful for me* (22:6). Balak selected Balaam precisely because he was notorious for the skill with which he could manipulate supernatural

---

[10] See e.g., P. J. Budd, *Numbers*, Word Biblical Commentary 5 (Waco: Word, 1984), p. 271. See too P. L. Day, *An Adversary in Heaven: śāṭān in the Hebrew Bible* (Atlanta: Scholars Press, 1988), pp. 50ff.

[11] G. J. Wenham, *Numbers*, Tyndale OT Commentaries (Leicester: Inter-Varsity Press and Downers Grove: InterVarsity Press, 1981), p. 164.

[12] See Yamauchi, 'Magic in the Biblical World', p. 186, on the much later use of small human figures in southern Palestine in cursing enemies.

powers to harm the enemies of his clients: *I know that those you bless are blessed, and those you curse are cursed* (22:6). Balak's words echo those of a member of the Zulu people, reflecting on the power of traditional Zulu herbalists: 'They heal with strength. But I tell you, they also kill with strength. Their medicines are very fearful.'[13]

Furthermore, Balaam's reputation as a sorcerer was clearly widespread. He was no mere local, village diviner responding to the petty fears and animosities of his neighbours, but an internationally acclaimed performer to the point that he was considered capable of drawing down a curse that might produce the destruction of a whole people. This is surely why Balak, king of Moab, knew of him despite the fact that the two men lived hundreds of miles from each other in a world connected only by the most basic means of communication. In short, Balaam was a superstar in the field of occult manipulation, and his assistance was sought out by the government of a significant people, much as some prestigious financial or economic consultant might be summoned for advice in our own day.

Third, and just like any such consultant, Balaam's expertise in the practice of sorcery commanded a hefty fee. On their initial visit to Pethor Balak's messengers took with them *the fee for divination* (22:7), and when Balaam declined their invitation Balak declared that he was ready to pay whatever was necessary to secure the services of one so renowned in his trade: *Do not let anything keep you from coming to me, because I will reward you handsomely and do whatever you say* (22:16–17).

And finally, the text indicates that on arrival in Moab Balaam initially employed the techniques of sorcery as he sought to carry out Balak's wishes. It was only when he realized that God would not permit him to curse Israel that he finally abandoned them, at which point the Spirit of God came upon him: *Now when Balaam saw that it pleased the LORD to bless Israel, he did not resort to sorcery as at other times . . . the Spirit of God came upon him and he uttered his oracle . . .* (24:1–2).

Balaam is mentioned in several of the later books of the Bible, but nowhere positively. He practised divination (Josh. 13:22); he was hired to call down a curse on Israel (Neh. 13:2); he loved the wages of wickedness and was rebuked by a donkey (2 Pet. 2:15–16).[14] By the unanimous consensus of Scripture, this man was no true prophet of the Lord.

---

[13] A.-I. Berglund, *Zulu Thought-Patterns and Symbolism* (London: Hurst and Cape Town and Johannesburg: David Philip, 1989), p. 290.

[14] See also Josh. 24:9–10; Mic. 6:5; Jude 11; Rev. 2:14.

2. Balaam and sorcery

The story of Balaam is a major episode in the book of Numbers, occupying three complete chapters. That the author accorded so much space to it indicates its importance to his narrative. When the incident took place Israel was close to entering the land of divine promise, and at the same time opposition was mounting from neighbouring peoples. The military aggression of Sihon and Og had failed and now, in desperation, Balak and his people determined to invoke supernatural power against Israel by means of a curse.

At stake in all this was the fulfilment of God's covenant with Abraham, and specifically his promise to turn back the curse of any who might attempt to bring a curse down upon Abraham and his descendants: 'and whoever curses you I will curse'.[15] This is the focus of the story: can the enemies of God's chosen people effectively bring a curse upon them? There is, however, an assumption underlying both that foundational promise and the story of Balaam itself. It is the assumption that a curse may indeed be successfully invoked against a specified victim such that real harm is done to them. The promise contained in God's original covenant with Abraham, as well as the lengthy drama of the Balaam story, would make little sense were this not the case. If all along cursing is by definition a futile activity, the promise would be rather meaningless and the story an empty one. This in turn raises the question of the attitude towards magic that emerges from Scripture, both in this text and elsewhere. It is a critical question. Most human societies for most of human history have believed in the efficacy of magic, and vast numbers of people still do. They seek supernatural protection by using charms and fetishes, pursue vendettas through sorcery, and consult diviners for answers to their dilemmas. As we have already noted, it is the scepticism of the West that is unusual rather than belief in such things as spirits, sorcery, divination and the like held by everybody else.

Magicians of various sorts appear from time to time in the pages of Scripture. Moses, for example, encountered the magicians of Egypt in Pharaoh's court, and they were initially able to reproduce the wonders that Moses had performed, turning their staffs into serpents, changing water into blood and making frogs come up on the land of Egypt (Exod. 7:11–12, 22; 8:7). Two things are noteworthy in the account. First, they did in fact carry out supernatural feats. There is no suggestion in the text that they were mere illusionists, accomplishing their wonders by sleight of hand. Second, the wonders they produced by their magic arts were to an ever greater extent

[15] Gen. 12:3.

overshadowed by those brought about by Yahweh, the Lord. The 'serpents' into which they turned their staffs were swallowed by Aaron's 'serpent'. By turning water into blood and bringing frogs up on the land, far from reversing the plagues that Moses and Aaron had produced, they were simply making them worse and in so doing furthering the purposes of God. And very quickly they were outpaced and could no longer replicate what Moses and Aaron were doing: 'The magicians said to Pharaoh, "This is the finger of God."'[16] Finally, with the sixth plague, 'the magicians could not stand before Moses because of the boils that were on them and on all the Egyptians'.[17]

The same pattern is found generally in the Bible. In the Old Testament, for example, Joseph was able to interpret Pharaoh's dreams while Pharaoh's own 'magicians and wise men' could not (Gen. 41); and Daniel could both recount and interpret Nebuchadnezzar's dream when the king's numerous 'magicians, enchanters, sorcerers and astrologers' found themselves out of their depth (Dan. 2). In the New Testament Simon the magician recognized the inferiority of his magic compared with the power of the Holy Spirit and tried to buy the latter (Acts 8:9–24), while Paul put the sorcerer Elymas to flight (Acts 13:8–12).

Moreover, various apocalyptic passages in the New Testament refer to miraculous signs and wonders that false end-time prophets and deceivers will carry out. The 'man of lawlessness' will come with 'all kinds of counterfeit miracles, signs and wonders',[18] and the beast who comes 'out of the earth' will perform 'great and miraculous signs'.[19] Jesus himself referred to the coming of 'false Christs and false prophets' who would 'perform great signs and miracles to deceive even the elect'.[20] Clearly, the Bible does not simply deny the reality of magic. It does, however, very loudly declare its absolute inferiority compared with the limitless power and wisdom of almighty God.

From a pastoral perspective there are two implications for believers troubled by the threat of hostile magic. First, the Christ they have come to know is infinitely more powerful than any magic they might fear, and they can trust in his 'incomparably great power for us who believe'.[21] As we have seen,[22] the powers that stand behind magic

[16] Exod. 8:19.
[17] Exod. 9:11.
[18] 2 Thess. 2:9.
[19] Rev. 13:11, 13.
[20] Matt. 24:24.
[21] Eph. 1:19.
[22] See pp. 19–22 above.

were created in, by and for Christ and, as we will see later,[23] God has now 'appointed him to be head over everything for the church'.[24] Second, in view of the utter subordination of all such powers to Christ, there is no reason for those who are 'in him' to attempt their own detailed research into the murky workings of the occult and demonic realm. It is enough to know that God rules over it all and has told us all we need to know; it is emphatically unwise and unhealthy to try to penetrate beyond what he has revealed about such matters. 'Our enemy works within the fog of war, and God does not explain all that goes on in the fog.'[25]

One further, closely related point demands brief reference. We have noted that in the thinking of many traditional peoples suffering is often attributed to the activity of witches. Such a belief has itself caused immense misery. At the very least, given that suffering is a more or less continuous experience in human life, the assumption that witches are responsible inevitably leads to constant suspicion among neighbours and family members, poisonously exacerbating the everyday strains of ordinary human relationships. Suspicion in its turn leads frequently to accusation and revenge, including the removal of 'witches' by their expulsion from the community or their execution. Meanwhile, human societies enslaved by such a belief fail to pursue the real causes of suffering and to seek out effective remedies for them. In response some theologians argue that there is no biblical justification for the belief that one human being can hurt another by occult means: 'Nowhere in Scripture do we find anyone attributing affliction or death to a human third party acting through evil occult means.'[26] Such a view needs to be assessed. On the one hand, it is certainly true that the identification of witchcraft as a generalized explanation of suffering has no biblical basis. 'Nowhere do the Scriptures suggest that witches and sorcerers are *major* or *pervasive* causes of human suffering.'[27] A view which identifies witchcraft as *the major* source of human grief is a devastating lie, one of the intellectual consequences of the fall and a foul offspring of

---

[23] See p. 152 below.

[24] Eph. 1:22.

[25] D. Powlison, 'The Classical Model', in J. K. Beilby and P. R. Eddy (eds.), *Understanding Spiritual Warfare: Four Views* (Grand Rapids: Baker Academic, 2012), p. 90. The point made here is more fully developed on pp. 6–7 and 154–155.

[26] R. Priest, quoted by R. Moon, 'Warning on Witches: Missionaries May Be Encouraging Witchcraft Accusations', *Christianity Today* (24 March 2011), at <http://www.christianitytoday.com/ct/2011/march/warningonwitches.html>, accessed 10 January 2015.

[27] K. Ferdinando, 'Evil and AIDS – an African Perspective', *Africa Journal of Evangelical Theology* 31.1 (2012), p. 79.

'the father of lies'.[28] It is a lethal poison that must be vigorously combated. On the other hand, however, to affirm that witchcraft is not a major cause of human suffering, or that there is no specific case in the Bible, does not mean that the very notion of witchcraft is total illusion. Balaam, as we have seen, was renowned for the power of his curse, and the biblical text does not at any point question the basis of his reputation. On the contrary, his ability to do what Balak invited him to do is a fundamental assumption of the text. The story of Balaam alone offers reason to suppose that within the vast array of human wickedness, use of occult, possibly demonic, means to harm other people may have a place.[29]

3. Balaam and God

Balaam was summoned, then, to curse those whom God had blessed. He was unable to do so, and in fact did the contrary: the proposed curse was turned into blessing (Deut. 23:5). This is the central point of the story. God takes control of the sorcerer and carries out his own purpose through him.

Although Balaam protests throughout that he can speak only what God allows him to say (22:8, 13, 18; 23:3, 12, 26; 24:12–14), the text indicates that his heart was otherwise inclined. Faced with Balak's first delegation Balaam had heard and obeyed God's answer to their request: *Do not go with them. You must not put a curse on those people, because they are blessed* (22:12). God had not only given an answer that was clear and decisive, but had also let Balaam know the reason for it: *they are blessed*. Balak's demand that Israel be cursed was the absolute contrary of God's purpose and determination to bless them, and God's will could scarcely have been more clearly expressed. The issue was surely closed: there was no ground for any further consideration of Balak's request. Nevertheless, when a second Moabite delegation appeared Balaam entertained them once again, declaring that he would find out what God would tell him overnight, as if God had not already spoken with sufficient clarity. Balaam's ambivalence faced with Balak's emissaries contrasts sharply with the categorical response God had earlier given. Perhaps he was flattered and seduced by the arrival of the second delegation of Moabite princes, *more numerous and more distinguished than the first* (22:15); doubtless he was attracted by the apparently limitless wealth on offer, itself hardly a quality of the true servant of God (22:17; 2 Pet. 2:15); maybe, indeed, he 'cherished the idea that he might be able to

[28] John 8:44.
[29] There is more discussion of this issue on pp. 154–155.

influence what Yahweh might say to him', and so he 'sought a dream, perhaps using some technique, in which God might say something "more" to him'.[30] Whatever the factors involved in his flirtation with Balak's reiterated offer, God was *very angry* when Balaam set off for Moab in the company of Balak's men (22:22).

However, God used Balaam to communicate his blessing upon his people. The prophet's recalcitrance became the occasion of an awesome demonstration of the Lord's overwhelming sovereignty even over spiritual powers of darkness. Despite Balaam's initial use of his usual occult methods, eventually abandoned when he at last realized that he could in no way manipulate the Lord through his divinatory techniques (24:1), the result was consistently and repeatedly the blessing of Israel. So Balaam announced that he foresaw *no misery* nor *misfortune* in Israel (23:21); he spoke of Israel's strength and invincibility (23:24; 24:8–9); and he reaffirmed the covenant promise given to Abraham (24:9; cf. Gen 12:3):

> *May those who bless you be blessed*
> *and those who curse you be cursed!*

Moreover the promises became richer and richer, culminating in the fourth oracle when he sees a coming king (24:17):

> *I see him, but not now;*
> *I behold him, but not near.*
> *A star will come out of Jacob;*
> *a sceptre will rise out of Israel.*
> *He will crush the foreheads of Moab,*
> *the skulls of all the sons of Sheth.*

On the one hand, far from cursing Israel on behalf of Moab, Balaam speaks here of the future devastation of Moab by a king of Israel. Beyond that, however, the words with which Balaam introduces the oracle, *Let me warn you of what this people will do to your people in days to come* (24:14), may refer more specifically to 'the final days', giving them a messianic tone.[31] Jewish and Christian interpreters have understood them in this sense, as a foreshadowing of Christ, 'the Root and the Offspring of David, and the bright Morning Star'.[32]

---

[30] J. N. Oswalt, 'Is Balaam's Donkey the Real Prophet (Numbers 24:1–4)?', in D. G. Firth and P. D. Wegner (eds.), *Presence, Power and Promise: The Role of the Spirit of God in the Old Testament* (Nottingham: Apollos, 2011), p. 209.

[31] See Wenham, *Numbers*, p. 178.

[32] Rev. 22:16. Wenham, *Numbers*, p. 179.

Perhaps most significantly for the present discussion, Balaam declared the futility of attempting occult aggression against Israel (23:23):

> *There is no sorcery against Jacob,*
> *no divination against Israel.*

And he gives the reason a few lines before (23:21):

> *The Lord their God is with them;*
> *the shout of the King is among them.*

Not only will a curse have no effect, but God does not even allow it to be uttered. He takes hold of the sorcerer and speaks through him to declare his words of blessing. There is no curse because the curser is overwhelmed by the power of the Almighty and can only do his will. Indeed, Balaam is the donkey. Just as God took hold of Balaam's ass and, contrary to its own nature, spoke through it to restrain 'the prophet's madness',[33] so he took hold of the sorcerer himself and, contrary to his moral and spiritual condition, spoke his own authentic word through him to declare the invincibility of his purposes for Israel and the uselessness of opposition to them, whatever its origin or nature.

4. Balaam and Israel

Israel was apparently unconscious of the drama being played out by Balaam and Balak on the Arnon border (22:36). Shortly afterwards, however, Israelite men had a calamitous encounter with Moabite women – and Midianite women too (Num. 25:6) – who *invited them to the sacrifices of their gods*, sacrifices which involved sexual immorality (25:1–2). The result was God's judgment of his people, including the death of their leaders and a plague in which 24,000 perished (25:4, 9). The apostasy with the Baal of Peor became proverbial for Israelite unfaithfulness (Deut 4:3; Josh. 22:17; Ps. 106:28; Hos. 9:10).

Balaam is not mentioned in the course of the narrative describing the apostasy. However, his role in the incident is made clear a little later when Moses rebuked the officers of Israel's army for allowing the women to live after Israelite forces had overcome Midian. Moses' words are telling: '"Have you allowed all the women to live?" he asked them. "They were the ones who followed Balaam's advice and

---

[33] 2 Pet. 2:16.

were the means of turning the Israelites away from the LORD in what happened at Peor, so that a plague struck the LORD's people." [34] Evidently the worship of the Baal of Peor and the associated sexual immorality were not occasioned by Israelite waywardness alone, but had been engineered on the advice of Balaam. It demonstrates both the essential wickedness of Balaam, and his perverse spiritual insight.

Near the beginning of the story of Cain and Abel there is a moment when God rebukes Cain for his anger, and urges him to master his sin. 'If you do what is right, will you not be accepted? But if you do not do what is right, sin is crouching at your door; it desires to have you, but you must master it.' [35] The term used for 'crouching' is the same as an ancient Babylonian word which referred to demons crouching threateningly at the door of a building, [36] but the words God addressed to Cain are something of a polemic against such an idea. It is not demons that lurk and endanger men and women, but rather their own sin which threatens to bring catastrophe upon them. [37] People are not mere victims of dark powers; they are rather rebels and as such themselves responsible for the adversities that fall upon them. Cain must master his sin. Balaam understood this. He had found that faced with the universal sovereignty of Israel's God he could not curse Israel and bring evil upon them by sorcery. But he understood that if Israel sinned God himself would judge them. Success lay in turning Yahweh himself against his own people. Accordingly Balaam advised Moab to seduce the Israelite men as a strategy far more potent than any sorcery.

The story of Balaam contains both encouragement and warning, as well as reorientation for believers in societies gripped by fear of sorcery, witchcraft, the curse and the evil eye. The people of God need not fear the sorcerer or the witch, supposed manipulators of evil powers. No human or supernatural power can withstand God's blessing of his people: *He has blessed, and I cannot change it ... There is no sorcery against Jacob, no divination against Israel* (23:20, 23). They must, however, beware of their own faithlessness and rebellion, and of their consequences. 'Above all else, guard your heart, for it is the wellspring of life.' [38]

---

[34] Num. 31:15–16.

[35] Gen. 4:7.

[36] *The NIV Study Bible* (London: Hodder and Stoughton, 1985), note on Genesis 4:7.

[37] G. J. Wenham, *Genesis 1–15*, Word Biblical Commentary 1 (Waco: Word, 1987), p. 106: 'Sin is personified as a demon crouching like a wild beast on Cain's doorstep.'

[38] Prov. 4:23.

Part 2
The warfare of the Son of God

Matthew 4:1–11
6. The testing of the Son of God

When Israel had crossed the Red Sea the people celebrated their deliverance in the 'Song at the Sea' (Exod. 15:1–18), proclaiming 'The LORD is a warrior; the LORD is his name'.[1] Neighbouring peoples also spoke of the warfare of their deities on their behalf but in more synergistic terms: their gods fought alongside them as they themselves engaged in battle. In Exodus, however, the Lord fights alone to save his people, and so the glory too belongs to him alone. The Song is a pivotal Old Testament text in this and other respects, acclaiming a victory which would be paradigmatic for all the divine warrior's later acts of salvation for his people, of which there were many. One or two of those later victories would begin to take on a cosmic dimension. Isaiah, for example, refers to the Lord's coming judgment of both human and heavenly powers: 'In that day the LORD will punish the powers in the heavens above and the kings on the earth below.'[2]

In the New Testament it is the incarnate Son of God who comes in person to engage the enemies of God and bring deliverance to his people. Implicit in Jesus' proclamation of the kingdom of God is the establishment of God's reign and the defeat of his foes. The war Jesus waged, however, was paradoxical in nature, which caused confusion for some, including John the Baptist who had prophesied impending judgment: 'His winnowing fork is in his hand to clear his threshing-floor and to gather the wheat into his barn, but he will burn up the chaff with unquenchable fire.'[3] Faced with something apparently quite different, John began to wonder, 'Are you the one who was to come, or should we expect someone else?'[4]

[1] Exod. 15:3.
[2] Isa. 24:21; cf. 27:1.
[3] Luke 3:17.
[4] Matt. 11:3.

Nevertheless, very clearly among the enemies Jesus fought were Satan and all the forces of darkness. So, when he was challenged regarding the means by which he drove out evil spirits he declared, 'but if I drive out demons by the Spirit of God, then the kingdom of God has come upon you'.[5] In his teaching the approach of God's kingdom meant many things, but among them was his own coming as divine warrior to engage Satan and the dominion of darkness. It was an element clearly expressed by the apostles. Jesus came 'to destroy the devil's work',[6] and in him God 'disarmed the powers and authorities . . . triumphing over them'.[7] In his warfare with the powers of darkness Jesus overcame the devil's temptations; he expelled demons from their victims; and he achieved the crowning victory of the cross.

1. The testing of God's Son

All three synoptic Gospels tell us that Jesus' public ministry was preceded by a solitary encounter with Satan in the Judean desert. In the contemporary imagination the desert was a haunt of demons, and it symbolized the power of Satan.

> In the OT blessing is associated with inhabited and cultivated land; the wilderness is the place of curse. In the wilderness there is neither seed nor fruit, water nor growth. Man cannot live there. Only frightening and unwanted kinds of animals dwell there . . . Jesus confronts the horror, the loneliness and the danger with which the wilderness is fraught when he meets the wild beasts. Their affinity in this context is . . . with the realm of Satan.[8]

Hence, Mark's brief observation, 'he was with the wild animals',[9] communicates something of that sense of sinister and foreboding menace, as wild animals 'frequently appear in league with the forces of evil'.[10] One might suppose that Jesus went into the desert to spend time fasting and praying in preparation for the ministry he was about to commence, and certainly both Matthew and Luke record that he fasted. However, there was much more to it than that. First, the

---

[5] Matt. 12:28.
[6] 1 John 3:8.
[7] Col. 2:15. See discussion of this text below in ch. 8.
[8] W. L. Lane, *The Gospel of Mark*, New International Commentary on the NT (Grand Rapids: Eerdmans, 1974), p. 61.
[9] Mark 1:13.
[10] R. A. Guelich, *Mark 1–8:26*, Word Biblical Commentary 34A (Dallas: Word, 1998), p. 38.

Gospels all affirm that it was the Spirit of God who, having just come upon Jesus at his baptism, now led him into the desert where he was tempted. Mark uses the strongest language. The NIV's rendering, 'at once the Spirit sent him into the desert',[11] does not fully capture the force of the verb, which is frequently used later in the Gospel for Jesus' expulsion of demons. The Spirit *impelled* Jesus to go into the wilderness – he *drove* or *thrust* him into the desert; the text conveys a sense of the urgency and necessity of what took place. His withdrawal from society was not, it seems, primarily motivated by a personal desire for spiritual retreat. Second, Matthew's account explains that the purpose for which the Spirit sent him into the desert was precisely that he should face testing: *Jesus was led by the Spirit into the desert to be tempted by the devil* (1). In other words, his presence in the wilderness was not a mere fortuitous circumstance that Satan was able to exploit for his own destructive ends. Rather it was God's unambiguous intent that his Son be tested by the devil, and he drove him into the desert for that very purpose. Later Jesus would tell his disciples to pray the Father that they should not be led into temptation (Matt. 6:13), but in his case the Father deliberately sent him to confront it.[12] He is sent into the desert just as he is sent into the world: the desert mission is an integral element in the redemptive mission – necessary indeed to its fulfilment, as we will see.

And so, powerfully impelled by the Spirit, Jesus took the fight to Satan in the wilderness, and there Satan tested the Son of God in accordance with the purpose of God.

2. The tests of God's Son

Mark's Gospel does not record the individual temptations. Matthew and Luke describe three, the same in each of the two Gospels although presented in slightly different sequences. Their accounts are brief and simple, but the meaning of each temptation and response remains always somewhat elusive. Clearly an intense struggle is taking place between Jesus and Satan, but there is a depth and mystery about it all and, perhaps inevitably, we struggle to identify where exactly the battle lines lay.

a. Tell these stones to become bread (3–4)

Both Matthew and Luke begin with the temptation to turn stones into bread: *If you are the Son of God, tell these stones to become*

---

[11] Mark 1:12.
[12] C. E. B. Cranfield, *Mark* (Cambridge: Cambridge University Press, 1959), p. 57.

bread (3). Jesus had already been fasting for forty days and was hungry, which is of course what gives the temptation its force. What, however, makes it a temptation as opposed to a merely reasonable, even innocent suggestion? At his baptism Jesus had indeed been declared Son of God and anointed with the Spirit. He was doubtless able to turn stones into bread, and would later multiply loaves and fish for thousands. His own body now longed for nourishment after weeks of fasting, and eating food is not sinful. Where is the problem?

It is Jesus' response that indicates the crux of the temptation. From the beginning he knew that the mission of the Son of God entailed suffering. This becomes explicit immediately after his disciples confess him as the Christ (Matt. 16:21), but in Mark's Gospel there is a clear suggestion of it rather earlier when Jesus refers to himself as the 'bridegroom' who will be *taken away*, so causing his followers to grieve: 'the time will come when the bridegroom will be taken from them, and on that day they will fast'.[13] In his statement Jesus picks up the verb[14] used twice in the Greek version of Isaiah 53:8 to describe the affliction of 'the servant of the LORD': 'By oppression and judgment he was *taken away*. And who can speak of his descendants? For he was *cut off* from the land of the living . . .' There is thus a clear echo of Isaiah's prophecy in Jesus' words, containing an equally clear allusion to an eventual violent death. In addition to that solitary text all the Gospel narratives indicate that from very early in his ministry Jesus faced opposition and suffering, which steadily escalated as the story moved forward. At the very heart of his own sense of messianic identity and divine sonship, therefore, was the conviction that God had sent him to suffer and die (John 12:27; Mark 10:45). He was the suffering servant of the Lord, and it was to carry out the servant's mission that he had been anointed.

In that context, the suggestion that he should use the power conferred on him as anointed Son of God to feed himself was, at the very least, inappropriate and incongruous. The meaning of his life, the goal of his ministry, the reason for his anointing, was to be the servant of the Lord, carrying out the will of the Father rather than serving himself. Hence Jesus responded as he did, quoting Moses' words to Israel: 'He humbled you, causing you to hunger and then feeding you with manna, which neither you nor your fathers had known, to teach you that man does not live on bread alone but on every word that comes from the mouth of the LORD.'[15] Jesus 'commits himself to the path of self-abasement that culminates at

---

[13] Mark 2:20.
[14] *apairō*.
[15] Deut. 8:3.

Calvary'.[16] He recognized the subtle deceitfulness of a temptation which invited him to satisfy a legitimate physical need, but to do so through a misappropriation – indeed a corruption – of all that he was and all that he had come to do as God's anointed Son. It is not so far from those Christian leaders in our own day who exploit their position to satisfy their own human appetites. And capitulation to the temptation would have meant the implosion of Jesus' mission no less surely than surrender to the challenge he would face later as he hung on the cross, also accompanied by the words, *if you are the Son of God*: 'Come down from the cross, if you are the Son of God!'[17] To be the anointed Son of God was not about food, nor at any point about himself and his personal well-being, but about obedience to the word and will of the Father wherever that might take him.

b. Throw yourself down (5–7)

Matthew's second temptation takes place at the temple where Satan urged Jesus to throw himself down from the summit. This time the tempter himself invoked the Scriptures with a quotation from Psalm 91: *'If you are the Son of God,'* he said, *'throw yourself down. For it is written: "He will command his angels concerning you, and they will lift you up in their hands, so that you will not strike your foot against a stone"'* (6). There is an undoubted shrewdness here as Satan clothes his temptation in the words of Scripture, giving it an apparent – albeit totally specious – plausibility. But what is he getting at? In the context it does not appear to be a suggestion that Jesus offer a sign to the Jewish people, for there is no reference to the presence of anybody other than Satan and Jesus.

Again, it is Jesus' answer that illuminates the issue: Satan is telling him to test God. The scripture that Satan refers to begins with an assurance of divine protection addressed to the faithful believer: 'If you make the Most High your dwelling – even the LORD who is my refuge – then no harm will befall you.'[18] Since God had just declared Jesus to be his beloved Son, surely Jesus fulfilled the condition and so could count on the promise. Accordingly Satan incites him to test the promise and, implicitly perhaps, to 'silence any lingering doubts about his relationship with God'.[19] It would, however, be a manipulative act of coercion, forcing God to intervene on behalf of his Son

[16] S. H. T. Page, *Powers of Evil: A Biblical Study of Satan and Demons* (Grand Rapids: Baker and Leicester: Apollos, 1995), p. 96.
[17] Matt. 27:40.
[18] Ps. 91:9–10.
[19] R. T. France, *Matthew*, New International Commentary on the NT (Nottingham: Inter-Varsity Press, 1985), p. 99.

in order to keep him from harm, and as such it would surely be fatally corrosive of Jesus' filial relationship with his Father. Any truly personal relationship is rooted in simple trust between those concerned, and a demand for gratuitous demonstrations of love can only undermine that trust. In this case the Father had spoken words of love and affirmation, and the Son had heard them. Subsequently to put the Father's promises to the test would necessarily be to question his faithfulness and his word; indeed, it would prematurely terminate the mission of the Son, deeply rooted as it was in the profound intimacy of his relationship with the Father, to which the Gospels bear abundant testimony. 'The Son of God can live only in a relationship of trust which needs no test.'[20]

Jesus cut across the devil's malevolent challenge by returning directly to the words of Scripture, again drawn from Deuteronomy, this time 6:16: *Jesus answered him, 'It is also written: "Do not put the Lord your God to the test"'* (7). He refused to debate on the devil's terms and instead reiterated his utter confidence in the Father's absolute trustworthiness. The sovereign God is not to be trifled with, nor is his word to be the subject of facile and immature experimentation. It is simply to be believed and acted upon.

This is not quite, however, the end of the story. In Luke's Gospel the temptation to test God is the final one and it is followed immediately by the account of Jesus' rejection when he preached in the synagogue of Nazareth (Luke 4:16–30). The climax of that incident occurs when those he had addressed took him to the brow of a hill in order to throw him down the cliff. 'But he walked right through the crowd and went on his way.'[21] By juxtaposing the temptation with the attempted murder of Jesus Luke points out that God does indeed intervene most promptly to protect his Son when such action is truly appropriate.[22]

c. Bow down and worship me (8–10)

The third temptation is the most audacious and flagrant of the three. Satan offers to give Jesus the kingdoms of the world on one condition: *All this I will give you . . . if you will bow down and worship me* (4:9). Luke's version is fuller, especially with the devil's claim that the world had been given to him and was his to dispose of: 'I will give you all their authority and splendour, for it has been given to me, and I can give it to anyone I want to. So if you worship me, it will all be yours.'[23]

[20] Ibid., p. 99.
[21] Luke 4:30.
[22] See Page, *Powers of Evil*, p. 97.
[23] Luke 4:67.

Such a blatant proposition seems to be very much at variance with the preceding tests. Satan abandons all subtlety and goes direct to the very heart of all temptation. But why would he suppose that Jesus might accept such an obvious act of betrayal? There are two issues involved. On the one hand, Satan is apparently offering Jesus what he had come to regain – indeed, 'exactly what his Father had commanded him to recover'.[24] More significantly, however, he is offering it without pain. The potential appeal of the proposal lay in the suggestion that the fulfilment of Jesus' purpose might be achieved without a cross. The agony of Jesus' coming sufferings, expressed not only in the physical torment he would endure but much more in the overwhelming experience of abandonment by his Father (Matt. 27:45–46), must have cast an oppressively heavy shadow back across his entire life and ministry. He knew a day would come of 'well-nigh unsustainable awfulness', when his intimacy with his Father, never before interrupted even for a moment, would be broken; when there would be 'no sense of his own divine sonship, no sense of God's love and no sense of the Father's approval'; and when under the anger of God his identity would be 'contracted to the point where the whole truth about him was that he was the sin of the world'.[25] In that context, Satan was offering an alternative, pain-free means to achieve the end for which Jesus had come. The temptation was surely powerfully attractive, and one to which 'Israel had fallen . . . again and again'.[26]

Jesus saw, however, the underlying absurdity of the proposition. First of all, 'the father of lies' was simply lying again, since the kingdoms of the world were not his to give. He certainly exercised power over rebellious humanity as 'prince of this world',[27] 'god of this age',[28] the one under whose control the whole world lies,[29] but he did so as a despotic usurper, parasitically exploiting the sin of men and women in order to tyrannize them. He had the right neither to rule nor to bestow rule on another, for 'the earth is the LORD's, and everything in it, the world, and all who live in it'.[30] Second, the kingdom of God could come and Jesus' mission be accomplished only by dealing with sin and expelling Satan, which in turn could be achieved uniquely through the cross (John 12:31). In large though

[24] A. Begg and S. B. Ferguson, *Name above All Names* (Wheaton: Crossway, 2013), p. 118.
[25] D. Macleod, *Christ Crucified: Understanding the Atonement* (Nottingham: Inter-Varsity Press, 2014), pp. 48–49.
[26] France, *Matthew*, p. 99.
[27] John 12:31; 14:30; 16:11.
[28] 2 Cor. 4:4.
[29] 1 John 5:19.
[30] Ps. 24:1.

certainly not total measure Satan was himself the problem Jesus had come to address, and the notion that *worshipping* him and thereby acknowledging his despotism would enable Jesus to achieve his mission was an absolute nonsense. Third, however, the really crucial issue was that of obedience. To transfer to Satan the worship owed to God would be the ultimate act of disobedience and betrayal. 'And this is what all temptation involves: whatever form it takes, temptation is an invitation to give one's allegiance to someone or something other than God.'[31] In short, regardless of any attraction the proposal may conceivably have held for him, Jesus saw with total clarity the wickedness and futility of Satan's invitation, and in full obedience he again responded in words drawn from Deuteronomy 6:13: *Away from me, Satan! For it is written: 'Worship the Lord your God, and serve him only'* (10).

Once again, there is a most significant aftermath to the temptation. At the end of Matthew's Gospel, when Jesus had died and risen from the grave, he announced to his disciples, 'All authority in heaven and on earth has been given to me'.[32] What Satan had deceitfully offered, Jesus had truly secured by his absolute obedience to the Father – and so much more! For it was not only authority on earth that had been given to him, but authority in heaven too, including authority over the tempter himself and all the forces of darkness.

God's purposes can only be achieved by God's means, which invariably include servanthood, suffering, persecution, and 'not by triumphant self-assertion, not by the exercise of power and authority'.[33] This same theme runs throughout Jesus' temptations. Paul too recognized the impossibility of using Satan's devices to do God's work when he rejected 'the hidden things of shame'[34] in the exercise of his own ministry: 'We have renounced secret and shameful ways; we do not use deception, nor do we distort the word of God. On the contrary, by setting forth the truth plainly we commend ourselves to every man's conscience in the sight of God.'[35]

Through the centuries churches, Christian organizations and individual believers have not always been so perceptive. Too often they have been persuaded by the devil's offer of growth or dominance through turning human power structures to their own purposes while avoiding the way of the cross. Examples are not hard to find: Charlemagne's forcible conversion of the Saxons in eighth-century

---

[31] Page, *Powers of Evil*, p. 97.
[32] Matt. 28:18.
[33] D. A. Hagner, *Matthew 1–13*, Word Biblical Commentary 33A (Dallas: Word, 1998), p. 70.
[34] *ta krypta tēs aischynēs.*
[35] 2 Cor. 4:2.

Germany; the brutal persecution of independent Christian congregations by church and state in sixteenth- and seventeenth-century Europe; and the complicity of some missions with the colonial interests of Western governments in order to gain advantage. As Cardinal Lavigerie reminded the White Fathers he sent to Africa, 'Nous travaillons aussi pour la France' (We are also working for France).[36] The history of 'Christianity' contains so many cautionary tales, but by God's grace there are innumerable stories too of those who faithfully took up the cross and followed Jesus. How vital to pursue that profound understanding of God's word which he himself demonstrated in the desert if we are to be alert to Satan's schemes (2 Cor. 2:11).

3. The victory of God's Son

But why did God send his Son *to be tempted by the devil* (1) in the first place? It is not so difficult to understand why Satan would seize the opportunity to tempt Jesus; as enemy of God his desire was to derail the mission of God's Son, and indeed to do so when it had scarcely begun. Satan was not, however, the initiator of the encounter. Indeed, as the account reminds us, even when he tempts Satan can act only subject to God's sovereign purpose – as also in the cases of Job (Job 1:12; 2:6) and Peter (Luke 22:31). But for what purpose would God actually initiate this encounter between his Son and the devil? The answer is that in the desert two totally central Old Testament narratives are being played out again, both of them of absolute importance.

First, when Jesus encounters Satan it is as the second Adam, representative and head of a new humanity, and there is a recapitulation of the confrontation between Adam and the serpent in Eden. The second Adam theme is particularly explicit in Paul's writings,[37] but it lies behind the temptation narratives too, especially in Luke's version. Between his accounts of the baptism and the temptations of Jesus Luke places his genealogy, which he lists in reverse order such that it concludes with 'Adam the son of God'.[38] There is thus a deliberate parallel with the language of Luke's first temptation as well as his third, 'If you are the Son of God'.[39] In the garden of Eden Adam, the first 'son of God', had been tested, and now Jesus, the

---

[36] D. Bosch, *Transforming Mission: Paradigm Shifts in Theology of Mission* (Maryknoll: Orbis Books, 1991), p. 304.

[37] Rom. 5:12–21; 1 Cor. 15:20–22.

[38] Luke 3:38.

[39] Luke 4:3. C. A. Evans, 'Typology', in J. B. Green and S. McKnight (eds.), *Dictionary of Jesus and the Gospels* (Downers Grove: InterVarsity Press, 1992), p. 864.

Son of God and second Adam, is also being tested, but this time in a desert. Details of the location are indeed significant. While Adam had confronted the serpent in a garden rich in food-bearing vegetation and inhabited by animals obediently subject to his authority, Jesus must come to a hostile, barren wilderness occupied by wild animals, harsh evidence of the serpent's malignant handiwork. 'Jesus, the Last Adam, had to conquer in the context of the chaos the first Adam's sin had brought into the world.'[40]

More important than the location, however, is the act of testing. As Paul points out in Romans, the result of Adam's testing was his disobedience and the consequent condemnation and death of the whole race which he represented (Rom. 5:15–19). We are all lost in Adam. The issues at stake were the same as the drama was replayed, with Jesus the second Adam facing the same tempter in spiritual combat. He came as representative and head of a new humanity which God purposed to create both in and through him, and to succeed in his mission he had to overcome Satan at the very point at which Adam had failed. Mere annihilation of the devil would not do it. Satan's power over human beings is grounded in their own rebellion, and Jesus could overcome Satan and free lost men and women only by offering to God that perfect obedience which Adam had failed to bring. And this he did in the desert, pursuing a process of redemption which would ultimately impact the whole of creation and, indeed, bring life back to the barren wilderness itself: 'The desert and the parched land will be glad; the wilderness will rejoice and blossom.'[41]

Second, Jesus faced Satan as a new Israel – a new people of God. There are undoubted echoes of the early experience of Israel, also God's son (Exod. 4:22; Hos. 11:1), in the temptation story. Most obviously, forty days and nights spent in the desert prior to beginning his ministry recall the forty years that Israel spent in the desert prior to entering Canaan. More significantly, Jesus' repeated use of Deuteronomy in his replies to the tempter recalls Israel's repeated disobedience. So, Israel too had been hungry and thirsty in the barren wilderness, but had responded with grumbling instead of learning to trust in God's word (Exod. 16:2–3; 17:1–3; Num. 11:1–6). Israel had put God to the test with their complaints, demanding, for example, that he provide water in the desert (Exod. 17:1–7), while Jesus refused to force God's hand by throwing himself down from the temple. Israel had made and worshipped the golden calf (Exod. 32:1–6), and in their later history had repeatedly 'renounced their

[40] Begg and Ferguson, *Name above All Names*, p. 27.
[41] Isa. 35:1.

exclusive loyalty to God for the sake of political advantage',[42] while Jesus rejected the path of idolatry and compromise. Jesus, therefore, confronted the devil as the embodiment of a renewed people of God, a true Israel. He offered God a faithfulness and obedience that the old Israel had failed to give from the very beginning of its history. Here there is a new beginning, once again in a desert, once again in a context of harsh testing.

The twin themes – second Adam and renewed Israel – intersect and coalesce. In the Lord Jesus Christ a new humanity and a restored people of God are coming into being. But this is one reality and one people rather than two, as Old Testament themes are realized in him, and move forward to their end-time fulfilment.

Jesus overcame the tempter in the wilderness. His victory was crucial but not yet final, and temptations continued throughout his ministry. While Matthew and Luke refer to the devil's departure at the end of the desert testing (Matt. 4:11; Luke 4:13), Mark 'does not record any triumphant conclusion to the temptation – for him the opposition of evil did not cease'.[43] Indeed, the narratives of Matthew and Luke similarly indicate the continuing testing which Jesus would have to face. Most strikingly Jesus recognized in Peter's dismissal of his coming humiliation and trials the very same voice of temptation that he had heard in the desert, seeking yet again to divert him from the way of the cross: 'Get behind me, Satan! You are a stumbling-block to me; you do not have in mind the things of God, but the things of men.'[44]

The wilderness testing is, indeed, representative of the ongoing, unrelenting, crushing pressure that Jesus would have to face throughout his ministry. With all his might Satan sought to suffocate the new creation at the moment of its inception just as he had smothered the first: 'the force and relentless nature of Satan's temptations against Christ surely surpassed anything Satan has ever done to anyone else'.[45] For it was through the Saviour's obedience to the point of death that his redemptive mission would be accomplished. It was his righteousness that would be imputed to his people, and it was his righteousness that would qualify him to die for their sins, 'the righteous for the unrighteous'.[46] By his hard-won obedience he destroyed the devil's work (1 John 3:8).

---

[42] France, *Matthew*, p. 99.

[43] L. Morris, *New Testament Theology* (Grand Rapids: Academie Books, 1986), p. 97.

[44] Matt. 16:23.

[45] B. A. Ware, *The Man Christ Jesus: Theological Reflections on the Humanity of Christ* (Wheaton: Crossway, 2012), p. 85.

[46] 1 Pet. 3:18.

Mark 5:1–20
7. Releasing the oppressed

John Nevius served for forty years as a Presbyterian missionary to China and made significant contributions to missionary thinking. Doubtless his most influential contribution was the book, *The Planting and Development of Missionary Churches*, written in 1885 just a few years before his death in 1893.[1] Less well known is his *Demon Possession and Allied Themes: Being an Inductive Study of Phenomena of Our Own Times*.[2] Initially sceptical about the stories of 'possession' which he encountered in China, Nevius became increasingly aware both of the prevalence of such cases and of the remarkably close similarity of the symptoms involved with those displayed by possessed persons in the synoptic Gospels. He also noted that relatively new and untaught Chinese Christians were able to bring release to those so afflicted by praying and invoking the name of Jesus. Nevius recognized that he was witnessing not only the same affliction that he had read about in the New Testament, but also the same liberating power of the Lord Jesus Christ.

1. The Gerasene's affliction

The Western terminology of demonic 'possession' does not quite correspond to that used by the synoptic writers, although that does not necessarily make it misleading. The evangelists employ a somewhat different range of expressions to describe the experience of those who were afflicted by demons or spirits. All of them, and especially Matthew, refer to such people as being 'demonized';[3] Mark

---

[1] J. L. Nevius, *The Planting and Development of Missionary Churches* (New York: Foreign Mission Library, 1899).

[2] J. L. Nevius, *Demon Possession and Allied Themes: Being an Inductive Study of Phenomena of Our Own Times* (Chicago: F. H. Revell, 1894).

[3] Matt. 4:24; 8:16, 28, 33; 9:32; 12:22; 15:22; Luke 8:35; Mark 1:32; 5:15–16, 18. The Greek verb is *daimonizomai*.

and Luke also speak of them as 'having a demon';[4] in Mark alone and on two occasions victims are said to be 'in an unclean spirit',[5] which Cranfield calls 'a thoroughly Jewish expression';[6] and Luke alone refers to those who were troubled or harassed by unclean spirits.[7] Nevertheless, comparison of the various expressions in their contexts suggests that they are more or less interchangeable and that all of them have the same phenomenon in view. Accordingly, Mark describes the man whom Jesus encountered in *the region of the Gerasenes* both as being 'in an unclean spirit' (2) and as 'demonized' (15, 16, 18). But what does it all mean?

The New Testament tells us very little about demons, especially when compared with non-biblical Jewish literature or with the non-Jewish world of the time, apart from the fact that they 'demonize' people.[8] Nor does the Old Testament contribute a great deal on the matter. They are clearly immaterial spirits, but possessed of intelligence, speech and will and, therefore, like Satan himself, not merely impersonal forces. Thus the demons that afflicted the Gerasene man spoke through him to Jesus (9), initially attempted to resist Jesus (7), pleaded with him (10) and finally resorted to negotiation (12). Moreover, as we shall see, they are somehow bound to Satan himself and the afflictions they bring reflect that.

Nowhere does the New Testament offer an abstract definition of 'demonization' but the Gospels do indicate a range of symptoms, many of them evident in our text. First, the Gerasene apparently lived in isolation from ordinary human society. So, when Jesus got out of the boat the man came to him from *the tombs* where he was living, a place associated with demons and desolation. Possibly he had been driven there by his neighbours or, perhaps impelled by the spirits, he had himself repudiated human companionship. A common feature of possession in the African context has been a flight from society into the untamed bush. Second, his behaviour was bizarre, even deranged or psychotic, suggesting 'perhaps schizophrenia or a manic-depressive disorder'.[9] Living in a cemetery is one indication of this, but even more so Mark's report that *night and day among the tombs and in the hills he would cry out and cut himself with stones* (5). He was also naked, Luke telling us that 'for a long time this man

[4] Mark 7:25; 9:17; Luke 4:33; 8:27; Acts 8:7; 16:16; 19:13.
[5] Mark 1:23; 5:2.
[6] C. E. B. Cranfield, *The Gospel According to St Mark* (Cambridge: Cambridge University Press, 1959), p. 74.
[7] Luke 6:18; Acts 5:16. The Greek verbs used in the two references are only very slightly different: *enochleō* in Luke and *ochleō* in Acts.
[8] Cranfield, *Mark*, p. 74.
[9] S. H. T. Page, *Powers of Evil: A Biblical Study of Satan and Demons* (Grand Rapids: Baker and Leicester: Apollos, 1995), p. 150.

had not worn clothes',[10] which is also implied in Mark's reference to the fact that when the locals came to see him after his deliverance they found him *in his right mind* and *clothed* (15).

Third, there is a tendency towards self-destruction in his behaviour: he *cut himself with stones* (5). The drowning of the pigs whom the demons took over after leaving the man indicates their essentially murderous character and intent. In a similar way the boy whom Jesus delivered later in Mark's narrative was thrown into fire and water by the afflicting spirit, which tried to kill him (Mark 9:22; cf. Matt. 17:15). Related to this, some of the synoptic Gospels also occasionally refer to various disabilities associated with demonization. Once again, the boy whom Jesus delivered appears to have had symptoms of epilepsy. The father's description of episodes of possession suggests a grand mal seizure: 'Whenever it seizes him, it throws him to the ground. He foams at the mouth, gnashes his teeth and becomes rigid.'[11] The point, of course, is not that epilepsy indicates possession, but rather that *in this case* the spirit inflicted symptoms of epilepsy on the child. The boy was also unable to talk, as was another possessed man referred to by Matthew (9:32–33), who also speaks elsewhere of 'a demon-possessed man who was blind and mute'.[12] All of these symptoms, social, behavioural and physical, indicate the fundamentally destructive nature of possession: 'the purpose of demonic possession to distort and destroy the divine likeness of man according to creation is made indelibly clear'.[13]

Fourth, the Gerasene was exceptionally strong: *no one could bind him anymore, not even with a chain. For he had often been chained hand and foot, but he tore the chains apart and broke the irons on his feet. No one was strong enough to subdue him* (3–4). The remarkable strength was doubtless attributable to his supernatural empowerment by the spirit. In the same way, without being told he simply knew Jesus' true identity as *Son of the Most High God* (7), as did other possessed individuals (Mark 1:24, 34; Luke 4:34).

Finally, the spirit spoke through the person it demonized, who thus became its host. When Mark refers to the Gerasene's hostile reaction to the presence of Jesus (7), he makes it clear that it is actually the spirit who is responding to Jesus' efforts to expel it: *For Jesus had said to him, 'Come out of this man, you evil spirit!'* (8). When Jesus then asked for the spirit's name, *they* responded *My name is Legion . . . for we are many* (9).

---

[10] Luke 8:27.

[11] Mark 9:18. J. Wilkinson, 'The Case of the Epileptic Boy', *ExpT* 79 (1967–8), p. 42.

[12] Matt. 12:22.

[13] W. L. Lane, *The Gospel of Mark*, New International Commentary on the NT (Grand Rapids: Eerdmans, 1974), p. 182.

It was presumably on the basis of such symptoms that the phenomenon was quite easily diagnosed. When the Syro-Phoenician woman pleaded with Jesus to deliver her possessed daughter, who was not present during the encounter (Mark 7:24–30), Jesus apparently accepted her diagnosis unquestioningly without himself having seen the girl. It is, however, the final symptom which is conclusive in enabling us to move towards an understanding of the meaning of possession. It is the domination of a person by an unclean spirit. It seems that there is in human beings a mechanism which under certain circumstances enables an alien will to seize control of an individual. This is what takes place when people are hypnotized and also in cases of demonization, as the individual loses control of his or her own self which falls under the command of another intelligence.[14] In that sense 'possession' is an appropriate identification of the phenomenon.

Some other features of demon possession also emerge from this and other New Testament narratives. First, there is no indication here or elsewhere in the New Testament that possession is a consequence of sin. Not only do the narratives not attribute it to sin, but those afflicted are not called on to repent of sin; they are simply delivered or healed. Moreover, very young people might suffer possession, including the boy who had suffered demonization from childhood (Mark 9:21), which 'it is scarcely possible to ascribe . . . to moral causes'.[15] In the same way, human sin is never attributed to the influence of a possessing spirit. The biblical response to sin is always a call to repentance, never the expulsion of a demon of anger or adultery or whatever else.

Second, possession may be continuous or intermittent. The Gerasene seems to have suffered continuous possession: *night and day . . . he would cry out and cut himself* (5). However, the boy brought to Jesus' disciples by his father apparently suffered sporadically: 'whenever it seizes him, it throws him to the ground'.[16]

Third, the affliction may be more or less severe, the severity being contingent both on the number of spirits involved and on their character. The Gerasene was possessed by numerous spirits, which doubtless contributed to the extreme nature of his symptoms: *My name is Legion . . . for we are many* (9). Mary Magdalene had been possessed by seven spirits before Jesus cured her (Luke 8:2), and

[14] R. Kampling, 'Jesus von Nazaret – Lehrer und Exorzist', *BZ* 30 (1986), p. 238; J. M. Nicole, *Précis de Doctrine Chrétienne* (Nogent-sur-Marne: Éditions de l'Institut Biblique, 1983), p. 99.

[15] A. Edersheim, *The Life and Times of Jesus the Messiah*, vol. I, 7th edn (London: Longmans, Green and Co., 1892), p. 480.

[16] Mark 9:18.

Jesus' parable of the restless demon refers to possession by multiple spirits and to the spirits' varying degrees of wickedness (Matt. 12:43–45; Luke 11:24–26).

Finally, while in the Gospels possession is an involuntary phenomenon, the sole case described in Acts, that of the Philippian slave girl possessed by a spirit which enabled her to tell the future (Acts 16:16), was apparently voluntary. Voluntary possession is when the presence of a possessing spirit is actively embraced and turned to the financial or social profit of its victim, enabling him or her to become a diviner, shaman or member of a spirit cult, and the phenomenon has been very widespread across cultures.[17] For Israel evaluation of possessing spirits was so totally negative that the only conceivable response to them was expulsion. In Gentile societies, however, where they might be viewed more positively, the response could be to negotiate an ongoing relationship with a possessing spirit with a view to benefiting from it.

2. Jesus' ministry of expelling demons

The synoptic Gospels contain numerous references to Jesus' expulsion of unclean spirits from those afflicted with them. He was unquestionably renowned for delivering the possessed during his earthly ministry. First, the synoptic Gospels contain four separate accounts of his ministry to specific individuals: the 'possessed' man he encountered in the synagogue at Capernaum;[18] the Gerasene or Gadarene demoniac(s);[19] the daughter of the Syro-Phoenician or Canaanite woman;[20] and the boy with apparently epileptic symptoms.[21] The same Gospels record other miracles that Jesus carried out – giving sight to the blind and hearing to the deaf, restoring the paralysed and cleansing the leprous, raising the dead – but there are more accounts of his liberation of the demon-possessed than of any other single category. Second, the Gospels periodically give summaries of Jesus' ministry, and the expulsion of demons appears regularly in them. So, for example, on the evening of the day on which he healed the demoniac in the synagogue at Capernaum, he also carried out many other miracles, including the driving out of demons from other victims of possession: 'The whole

[17] See T. K. Oesterreich, *Possession: Demoniacal and Other among Primitive Races, in Antiquity, the Middle Ages and Modern Times* (London: Kegan Paul, Trench, Trubner & Co. Ltd), 1930.
[18] Mark 1:21–28; Luke 4:31–37.
[19] Matt. 8:28–34; Mark 5:1–20; Luke 8:26–39.
[20] Matt. 15:21–28; Mark 7:24–30.
[21] Matt. 17:14–21; Mark 9:14–29; Luke 9:37–43.

town gathered at the door, and Jesus healed many who had various diseases. He also drove out many demons, but he would not let the demons speak because they knew who he was'.[22] Third, even during his lifetime Jesus' name was being invoked by others, including those not apparently belonging to his own circle of disciples, who were trying to expel demons from their possessed victims: '"Teacher," said John, "we saw a man driving out demons in your name and we told him to stop, because he was not one of us."'[23] The invocation of a power source, the name, for example, of a spirit or a god, was a regular part of the technique of contemporary exorcists in Jesus' day. That his own name should be invoked by others, and that during his own lifetime, was quite extraordinary and testifies to his reputation as one who could successfully deliver those suffering from demons. Fourth, so remarkable was Jesus' ministry of expelling demons in both its extent and its success that his enemies were unable to deny it. Rather they were obliged to advance a slanderous interpretation of his activity. According to them, what Jesus did was accomplished by the power of Satan: 'And the teachers of the law who came down from Jerusalem said, "He is possessed by Beelzebub! By the prince of demons he is driving out demons."'[24] The very use of such an accusation was in itself a powerful if perverse testimony to the effectiveness of Jesus' ministry of deliverance, coming as it did from bitter opponents. And finally, all of this very substantial testimony contrasts sharply with the fact that there is little evidence from this period of others with anything approaching the impact and success that Jesus had in his ministry.[25]

Furthermore, not only was the scale of his ministry extraordinary, but also the way in which Jesus drove out demons was quite different from the more or less magical techniques employed by contemporary exorcists. Typically they would attempt to bring the demon under their control by forcing it to speak and reveal its name and then binding it; they used a special vocabulary, incantations and rites that had to be followed to the letter; and they invoked the name of a power source, a god or spirit. Jesus did none of this. There is no evidence in the Gospels, including the expulsion of the demons from the Gerasene man, that Jesus even prayed when he drove out spirits. Indeed, in the case of the Gerasene it is ironically the demons who try to bind Jesus by means of a typical exorcistic adjuration in order to protect themselves from him. They use Jesus' own name in

[22] Mark 1:33-34; cf. Matt. 8:16; Luke 4:40-41. See also summaries in Matt. 4:23-25; Mark 1:39; 3:11.
[23] Mark 9:38; cf. Luke 9:49.
[24] Mark 3:22; cf. Matt. 12:24; Luke 11:15.
[25] Kampling, 'Jesus von Nazaret', p. 240.

'a desperate attempt to gain control over him',[26] followed by the verb
'to adjure' (*horkizō*) which Jesus never used, and then the invocation
of a named power source, God himself: '*What have you to do with
me, Jesus, Son of the Most High God? I adjure you by God, do not
torment me*' (7, ESV).[27] On the other hand, while Jesus asks the
demons for their name he does not use it when he expels them; and
in the other recorded incidents, far from making demons speak, he
orders them to be silent. Indeed, in the case of the Gerasene the
demons recognize his vastly superior power from the outset and,
after their initial forlorn attempt at resistance, they submit to his
command. He uses no incantation, no meaningless magic word, no
rite, no named power source. He merely commanded the demons
to leave with the everyday verb 'come out' (*exerchomai*): '*Come out
of this man, you evil spirit!*' (8).[28] Indeed, in every case he 'drove
out the spirits with a word'.[29]

It was this very simplicity and the total absence of the usual
terminology and ritual nonsense that astonished those who witnessed
his works and gave him such a reputation: 'He even gives orders to
evil spirits and they obey him!'[30] Moreover, it is probably for this
reason that the synoptic writers never refer to him as an exorcist,
although the word exists in Greek.[31] The way in which he drove out
unclean spirits, not to mention the meaning of the expulsions he
carried out, was so different from the contemporary practice of
exorcism with its magical overtones that use of the word in his case
would convey an utterly false impression.[32]

3. The meaning of Jesus' ministry

Not only do the synoptic Gospels underline the remarkable nature
of Jesus' ministry of delivering those possessed by unclean spirits,
but they also indicate its theological significance.

a. Terminology

First, as noted above, the synoptic Gospels consistently avoid the
contemporary language of exorcism in their descriptions of Jesus'

[26] Lane, *Mark*, p. 183.
[27] The NIV translation does not capture the force of the demons' words of adjuration:
horkizō se ton theon, mē me basanisēs.
[28] See also Mark 1:25; 9:25; Luke 4:35.
[29] Matt. 8:16.
[30] Mark 1:27.
[31] *exorkistēs*.
[32] W. W. Everts, 'Jesus Christ, No Exorcist', *BS* 81 (1924), pp. 355–362.

expulsion of unclean spirits. Instead they use a quite different and highly significant vocabulary of their own. The verb *epitimaō*,[33] normally translated 'rebuke', is often used to describe Jesus' encounters with demons.[34] It corresponds to a Semitic equivalent[35] which 'conveys the sense of bringing under control a hostile power',[36] and in certain contexts represents God's own sovereign word of command 'by which evil powers are brought into submission'.[37] The synoptists' use of such a term is, therefore, consistent with the idea that Jesus' acts of delivering possessed people from demonic affliction were not simply extraordinary miracles or deeds of compassion, although they were undoubtedly both of those things, but that in them the divine warrior himself was 'bringing under control' those powers of darkness which were ravaging his creation.

Similarly, the act of expelling a demon is invariably communicated by a verb, *ekballō*,[38] not used outside the synoptic Gospels with that particular meaning. In the Septuagint, however, *ekballō* is 'used mostly in the context where an enemy, frustrating or standing in the way of God's fulfilling his purpose for his chosen people, is "cast out" so that God's purpose may be fulfilled'.[39] Use of such a verb by the synoptic authors would again point towards their understanding of the theological significance of Jesus' expulsion of demons, and one consistent with the use of *epitimaō*.

As well as the use of a distinctive vocabulary, however, there are two passages which bring clearly into focus Jesus' own understanding of what was taking place in the expulsion of demons.

b. Plundering the strong man

The first is the occasion on which he was accused of being himself possessed by Beelzebub, and of driving out demons 'by the prince of demons'.[40] The name, Beelzebub, is not found elsewhere in Jewish writings but the exchange here between Jesus and his adversaries indicates quite clearly that it was a synonym for Satan. In his reply,

---

[33] Admonish, charge, rebuke.

[34] Matt. 17:18; Mark 1:25; 3:12; 9:25; Luke 4:35; 9:42.

[35] Heb. *gā'ar* and Aramaic *ge'ar*.

[36] H. C. Kee, *Medicine, Miracle and Magic in New Testament Times* (Cambridge: Cambridge University Press, 1986), p. 24.

[37] H. C. Kee, quoted by R. A. Guelich, *Mark 1–8:26*, Word Biblical Commentary 34A (Dallas: Word, 1998), p. 57. See e.g., 2 Sam. 22:16; Job 26:11; Pss 80:16; 104:7; 106:9; Zech. 3:2.

[38] Drive out, throw out, expel, send away.

[39] G. Twelftree, *Christ Triumphant: Exorcism Then and Now* (London: Hodder and Stoughton, 1985), p. 105. Cf. Exod. 23:30; Deut. 33:27–28.

[40] Mark 3:22; Matt. 12:24; Luke 11:15.

therefore, Jesus assumes first of all that there is a solidarity between Satan and demons such that to attack them is to attack him, the one who is their 'prince'. There is thus an absurdity in the accusation that he drives out demons by Beelzebub, for it would mean that Satan was attacking his own – indeed, himself. Second, again implicit in Jesus' reply is the assumption that there are really only two possible means by which he might expel demons. On the one hand there is the power of Beelzebub, but that is ruled out as an absurdity. The only possibility remaining is that he acts by the 'Spirit of God'[41] or the 'finger of God'.[42] That being the case, God himself is assaulting the strongholds of Satan through these acts of deliverance.

What is occurring should not, therefore, be understood merely as a series of isolated attacks on a few scattered demons but rather as part of a full-scale assault on Satan himself and his entire 'house'. The 'prince of demons' is being expropriated. Accordingly, it is God's Spirit and no other spirit who is at work through the Lord Jesus Christ, and Jesus is thereby revealed as the servant of the Lord and his long-awaited anointed one (Isa. 42:1; 61:1). Moreover, as Jesus points out, this must also mean that the promised end-time kingdom of God has come in power, as the Spirit moves to defeat God's enemies and deliver those they have oppressed.[43]

There is more than a suggestion here that Jesus is echoing Isaiah's description of the Lord who overcomes and plunders Israel's foes and applying it to himself, with obviously immense Christological implications:[44]

> Can plunder be taken from warriors,
>   or captives rescued from the fierce?
> But this is what the LORD says:
> 'Yes, captives will be taken from warriors,
>   and plunder retrieved from the fierce;
> I will contend with those who contend with you,
>   and your children I will save.'[45]

Further, the words Luke records, 'But if I drive out demons by the finger of God, then the kingdom of God has come to you',[46] recall those spoken by the Egyptian magicians when they could no longer

[41] Matt. 12:28.
[42] Luke 11:20.
[43] Luke 11:20; Matt. 12:28.
[44] See T. Longman III and D. G. Reid, *God Is a Warrior* (Grand Rapids: Zondervan, 1995), pp. 111–112.
[45] Isa. 49:24–25.
[46] Luke 11:20.

reproduce the signs that God was carrying out in Egypt through Moses: 'The magicians said to Pharaoh, "This is the finger of God."'[47] The reference to 'the finger of God' indicates, therefore, that now through Jesus a new exodus is taking place, the very salvation of the last days, as men and women oppressed by Satan experience God's sovereign act of liberation from their bondage, while their enemy suffers decisive defeat. The description of the drowning of the demon-possessed pigs after the Gerasene's deliverance may be making a similar point. 'It recalls the drowning of Pharaoh, the god-king, in the sea',[48] and so draws attention both to the deeper significance of the expulsion of the spirits from their victim, and to the utter finality of the deliverance achieved.

c. Satan's fall from heaven

The second passage is Jesus' brief exchange with the seventy-two disciples after their return from the mission on which he had sent them (Luke 10:17–20). When they declare, 'Lord, even the demons submit to us in your name', Jesus replies, 'I saw Satan fall like lightning from heaven.' The response is enigmatic and has been interpreted as a reference either to a primeval fall of Satan or to an eschatological fall. However, the words must make sense in the context of the dialogue, and should be seen as a comment on the disciples' report. In that light Jesus is explaining the significance of the demons' submission to his disciples. As demons submit to them, something much greater is taking place than the liberation of a few individuals. Indeed, each expulsion represents the collapse of Satan's empire. The disciples are themselves, therefore, participating in the coming of the kingdom of God through Jesus, and he wants them to see the eschatological and cosmic significance of what is taking place through his name. 'What is happening is not simply the expulsion of random demons that they might come across in their travels but the beginning of the complete overthrow of Satan's rule.'[49] This means, of course, that the point he makes here coincides with what he said to those who accused him of casting out demons by the power of Beelzebub. However, he takes it a step further. Not only do the demons submit to the disciples, but Jesus gives them authority 'to overcome all the power of the enemy; nothing will harm you'. When in Jesus' name they will very shortly take the good news of the kingdom of God into the world, they will continue to see it

[47] Exod. 8:19.
[48] Longman and Reid, *God Is a Warrior*, p. 116.
[49] D. E. Garland, *Luke*, Zondervan Exegetical Commentary on the NT (Grand Rapids: Zondervan, 2012), p. 429.

overcome the forces of darkness that oppose it, and God will preserve them too.

4. Making the connections

There is much to be learned from the story of the Gerasene's liber-ation, and indeed from those of the many other people similarly oppressed by unclean spirits but rescued by Jesus. Three points demand particular attention.

a. Deliverance ministries

First, should believers encounter demonized people, the simplicity that characterized Jesus' approach should similarly characterize theirs. Jesus counselled prayer (Mark 9:29) and his followers invoked his name (Luke 10:17; Acts 16:18). That is all. There is no biblical case for elaborate rituals; for forcing a demon to speak and reveal its name; for binding it as the Gerasene man sought to bind Jesus; and certainly not for physical violence and brutality. Believing prayer in the name of Jesus is the 'method'.

b. Deliverance of Christians

A frequent question is whether demons can possess Christians. The standard response would probably be to deny such a possibility, as Frederick Leahy does. 'In the light of Scripture we are compelled to reject the view that the Holy Spirit and an evil spirit can co-exist in the same person. Attempts to prove the contrary on the basis of observations are valueless.'[50] Not all agree, however. According to Martyn Lloyd-Jones, 'Christians in certain circumstances may become possessed . . . If we open the door to evil powers we can be possessed by them.'[51]

There are, nevertheless, solid grounds for retaining the traditional approach. First, from a theological perspective, the New Testament identifies Christians as temples of the Holy Spirit (1 Cor. 6:19), and it must be problematic to suppose that a Christian who is indwelt by God's Spirit could at the same time be 'possessed' by a demon. Second, a Christian is somebody who by definition has been freed from the dominion of darkness. Demonic possession might be seen

---

[50] F. Leahy, *Satan Cast Out: A Study in Biblical Demonology* (Edinburgh: The Banner of Truth Trust, 1975), p. 95.

[51] D. M. Lloyd-Jones, *Healing and Medicine* (Eastbourne: Kingsway Publications, 1987), p. 162. See also, for example, M. F. Unger, *What Demons Can Do to Saints* (Chicago: Moody Press, 1977).

as one of the most extreme expressions of Satan's tyranny over human beings. It seems implausible to suppose that an individual might be freed from the dominion over which Satan holds sway while remaining a victim of possession.

Third, the Bible itself offers no support for the idea that Christians can be possessed. The numerous New Testament epistles cover a wide range of pastoral issues, but nowhere do they respond to difficulties in the Christian life by suggesting that the expulsion of a demon would be the answer. Insofar as believers experienced problems in their lives, the answer was invariably repentance, obedience, faithfulness, perseverance, the filling of the Holy Spirit and so on, but nowhere the expulsion of demons.

Fourth, there is the issue of experience. As Leahy implies in the quotation above, many have claimed that in practice – in experience – deliverance from possession has helped some particular Christians in one way or another. Such an approach raises larger issues, and especially whether questions of Christian faith and practice should be determined by the word of God or by human experience. It is certainly clear that the *meaning* of an experience may be ambiguous such that experiences can often be interpreted in more than one way. On this particular issue, there are cases of believers who have experienced sufferings which might well have been identified as possession, but which have, in fact, been resolved by approaches quite other than the expulsion of invading demons. On the other hand, there are those who have gone through a procedure which apparently delivered them from demonic possession, only for the effects of the deliverance to have lasted but a brief period before the symptoms reappeared. It is indeed possible to ask whether some 'exorcisms' may in reality be hypnotic episodes which persuade victims that they have been delivered, and in that sense effect a cure. The issue is clearly not simple.[52]

Finally, there is the critical danger of minimizing sin. Human depravity can ruin lives, including Christian lives. There is a risk of attributing to demons what should in fact be attributed to sin, and to pursue the expulsion of demons when it is repentance that is really called for. Nowhere does the Bible explain human sin in terms of demonic possession. Similarly, if somebody is ill, the biblical response is prayer and confession rather than deliverance from demonic attack (Jas 5:14–16).[53]

[52] For a much fuller discussion of this issue see D. Powlison, *Power Encounters: Reclaiming Spiritual Warfare* (Grand Rapids: Baker, 1995).

[53] The content of this section is largely drawn from K. Ferdinando, *The Battle Is God's: Reflecting on Spiritual Warfare for African Believers* (Bukuru: African Christian Textbooks, 2012), pp. 107–109.

c. Wider implications

Finally, the incidents of demonic expulsion recorded in the Gospels have a significance far beyond specific questions about the deliverance of possessed people. For just as 'devils fear and fly' at Jesus' name,[54] so every force that opposes his sovereign redemptive purposes must yield. This was the assurance Jesus gave the seventy-two as he drew out the implications of what they had been seeing during the mission they had been engaged in: 'I have given you authority . . . to overcome all the power of the enemy.'[55] It is the same promise he addressed to the Eleven as he sent them out again: 'All authority in heaven and on earth has been given to me. Therefore go . . .'[56] Jesus Christ will build his church and use his people to do so, and neither Satan nor demons will hinder him.

[54] C. Wesley, 'Jesus, the name high over all', *Hymns and Sacred Poems*, 1749.
[55] Luke 10:19.
[56] Matt. 28:18–19.

Colossians 2:13–15
8. Disarming the powers

John's Gospel contains no report of the expulsion of demons by Jesus. It is a remarkable omission given the prominence of that aspect of Jesus' ministry in the other Gospels, and has been variously explained.[1] What John does refer to, however, is Jesus' announcement of his own imminent expulsion of Satan from the world of which he is 'prince'. 'Now is the time for judgment on this world; now the prince of this world will be driven out.'[2] Especially striking here is the word translated 'driven out'. It is *ekballō*, the verb regularly used in the synoptic Gospels of Jesus' expulsion of demons: Jesus drives them out.[3] Here in John, then, the focus is not on the driving out of demons from individual men and women, but rather the expulsion from the world itself of the one who is both 'prince of demons' and 'prince of this world'.

Jesus goes on to show how this will be accomplished. His repeated use of the adverb 'now' is especially important, for a little earlier in the passage he has announced, 'the hour has come for the Son of Man to be glorified'.[4] Previously the 'hour' was always 'not yet' (John 2:4; 7:30; 8:20). In the context of the Gospel narrative, therefore, the announcement that at last the 'hour' has come means that Jesus' death, resurrection and exaltation – understood as a single event of being 'glorified' or 'lifted up' – is close at hand. And 'now', when the 'hour' has come, it is through that lifting up of the Son of Man that Satan will be 'driven out'. 'When Jesus was

---

[1] See the summary in W. H. Salier, 'Deliverance without Exorcism? Jesus and Satan in John's Gospel', in P. G. Bolt (ed.), *Christ's Victory over Evil: Biblical Theology and Pastoral Ministry* (Nottingham: Apollos, 2009), pp. 83–88.

[2] John 12:31.

[3] See p. 91 above.

[4] John 12:23.

glorified, "lifted up" to heaven by means of the cross, enthroned, then too was Satan dethroned.'[5]

The following verse then speaks of the result of Satan's expulsion: 'But I, when I am lifted up from the earth, will draw all men to myself.'[6] As Jesus is lifted up on the cross to die and then lifted up in glorious new resurrection life, Satan's power over humanity is broken – he is 'driven out' – and 'all people without distinction, Jews and Gentiles alike'[7] are drawn to the Son of Man as they are freed from Satan's tyranny.

In these few verses, then, Jesus very clearly declares that his death is also the very moment at which Satan experiences decisive defeat. In the synoptic Gospels the liberation of possessed people indicated that Satan's power was crumbling,[8] but each act of deliverance was only an anticipation of what would take place once and for all at the cross. 'Casting out unclean spirits was the minor skirmish that antici-pated this great moment when the prince of this world would be cast out.'[9] Nevertheless, there is profound paradox here. Normally in human affairs the death of a combatant implies their defeat; here, however, it is Jesus who dies and Satan who loses. Somehow, the cross does not signal Jesus' own downfall but that of Satan, who was himself instrumental in bringing it about.[10] How does it all work? Paul explains very succinctly in Colossians 2:13–15.

1. Dead in sins

The situation which Paul addresses in his letter to the Colossians has already been discussed.[11] The verses we consider here are absolutely central to his argument, for it is here that he explains the total suffi-ciency of Christ's work for the salvation of his people. In 2:9–12 Paul has affirmed that in Christ 'all the fullness of the Deity lives' and the Colossian believers 'have been given fullness in' him. Moreover, he reminds them that Jesus is 'head over every power and authority', echoing his insistence in the first chapter that even the creation of the principalities and powers was 'in', 'by' and 'for' him (1:16). Therefore, they do not need to look elsewhere for the completion of their salvation, including their security from dark spirits, as if

[5] D. A. Carson, *The Gospel According to John*, Pillar NT Commentary (Leicester: Inter-Varsity Press and Grand Rapids: Eerdmans, 1991), p. 443.
[6] John 12:32.
[7] Carson, *John*, p. 444.
[8] Matt. 12:29; Mark 3:27; Luke 10:18–19; 11:21–22.
[9] P. G. Bolt, 'Towards a Biblical Theology of the Defeat of the Evil Powers', in Bolt (ed.), *Christ's Victory over Evil*, p. 78.
[10] Luke 22:3; John 13:2, 27.
[11] See pp. 15–17 above.

Christ was somehow inadequate. He then goes on to summarize the Colossians' Christian experience as one of union with Christ: circumcised in Christ, buried with Christ in baptism, raised with Christ, the one whom God has raised from the dead. Briefly, in Christ and him alone they have all they could ever need.

One might suppose that this would bring his argument to a close, but Paul has more to say and he pushes the argument in new directions, two of which should be mentioned at the outset. First, in the section 2:13–15 the subject changes from 'you' to 'God'. This picks up on the last clause of 2:12 where God is also the subject: 'who raised him from the dead'. So, just as God brought about Jesus' resurrection, so Paul now focuses on God's sovereign action in bringing new life to the Colossians, thus underlining from a different perspective the total sufficiency of their salvation. At the same time he still emphasizes that it has all been brought about *with Christ* (13) and *in Christ* (15).[12] Second, he reframes his exposition of salvation in order to push the argument a major step further, allowing him to highlight the impact of God's work in Christ on the *powers and authorities* (15) in a climactic conclusion.

The first step in this part of Paul's exposition is his insistence on the hopeless spiritual and moral state of the Colossians before God intervened: *you were dead in your sins and in the uncircumcision of your sinful nature* (13). In their pagan past the Colossians had been spiritually dead, meaning that they were alienated from God. Eternal life is found in knowing him through Jesus Christ his Son (John 17:3), and the Colossians did not know him. On the contrary, as Paul explains in Romans, their condition of spiritual death was characterized by hostility to God and an inability both to submit to him and to please him (Rom. 8:7–8).

Paul attributes their condition to two factors. First, it was because of their life of 'transgressions'.[13] The term is 'one of several words for sin which particularly emphasizes the deliberate act of disobedience with its fateful consequences'.[14] Paul uses it of specific acts of rebellion, and quite frequently in his discussion of Adam's primal act of disobedience in Romans 5:15–19. Second, he speaks of

---

[12] The NIV has *by the cross* at the end of v. 15 but the word so translated is a pronoun rather than a noun which could equally refer to Christ. The translation *by the cross* assumes that Christ has become the subject in vv. 14 and 15 which then makes 'by him' impossible. However, the flow of this whole section suggests that the pronoun 'him/it' at the end of v. 15 refers to Christ as it does repeatedly from v. 11.

[13] The word is *paraptōma*, which the NIV translates as *sins* although it uses 'transgressions' for the same word in Eph. 2:1.

[14] P. T. O'Brien, *Colossians, Philemon*, Word Biblical Commentary 44 (Dallas: Word, 1982), p. 122.

the uncircumcision of your sinful nature (13)[15] which, unlike 'trans-gressions', refers not to specific sins but rather to the rebellious disposition which gives rise to them. As Gentiles the Colossians were of course uncircumcised in the physical sense but, following on from verse 11, Paul is using the term 'uncircumcision' metaphorically here to say that prior to God's transforming intervention their profoundly sinful nature had not been dealt with. On the contrary, it was rampant and it spelt death for them.

So, Paul begins this section by stressing the helplessness of his readers before they encountered the gospel. They were alienated from God – dead and lost – both because of what they *were* as fallen and corrupt human beings, and because of the countless sins which they inevitably *did* as a result of that fallenness.

2. Made alive in Christ

But God made the dead Colossians live. Paul highlights the absolute primacy of the divine initiative in bringing this about. By definition Colossian pagans could not deliver themselves from their state of death, and what brought them to life was God's sovereign act. Paul stresses, however, that God did not do this independently of Christ: it was **with Christ**, whom God had raised from the dead, that God made the Colossians alive (13). They rose *with him* in *his* resurrection (2:12). 'It is only in union with him that death is vanquished and new life, an integral part of God's new creation, is received.'[16]

It was not, however, simply an act of divine power. The reason for which the Colossians had been in a state of death was their trans-gressions and sinful nature. The disease that afflicted them was a moral and spiritual one, and only by dealing with that could they be made alive. At the heart of their reception of new life, therefore, was the fact that God *forgave us all our sins* (13). It was in this way alone that dead sinners could be made alive. The details of Paul's language are vital here. First, while earlier he spoke of 'you' – 'God made you alive' – here he associates himself with the Colossians as one equally forgiven by God. There is no distinction between Jew and Gentile, for salvation is focused in the same act of divine forgiveness irrespect-ive of every human difference. Second, the forgiveness is total: *all our sins*. Sins of thought, word and deed, sins heinous and – in human terms – minor, sins past, present and future, all are included in the one all-embracing act of forgiveness. Consequently, all human effort,

---

[15] The word Paul uses is 'flesh', *sarx* in Greek, but it has a moral rather than a physical sense here, and refers to the fallen condition of human nature.

[16] O'Brien, *Colossians, Philemon*, p. 123.

human merit and human boasting are necessarily excluded. 'Nothing in my hand I bring.'[17] Third, therefore, and most important, it is grace alone that stands behind God's forgiveness. This is made explicit by the verb that Paul uses here for 'forgive', *charizomai*, which is related to *charis* – the Greek noun for 'grace': 'God has graced us all our sins.' His forgiveness is an act of utter and totally undeserved grace towards dead, helpless, hopeless sinners.

That grace, however, is itself rooted in the work of Christ. In Scripture divine forgiveness is never an arbitrary and passive decision to dispense with justice: there is never any 'cheap' grace on God's side. Rather it is costly beyond human words and understanding, for God takes the full requirements of his own righteousness upon himself. To explain this Paul introduces a novel metaphor for atonement, which is focused on the word *cheirographon*, which is translated *written code* in the NIV. It is a term unknown elsewhere in the New Testament, but it was widely used in both Jewish and Greco-Roman society to refer to a '"note of indebtedness" written in one's own hand as a proof of obligation'.[18] In Philemon 19 Paul himself gives an example of a *cheirographon*, although not using the word itself: 'I, Paul, am writing this with my own hand. I will pay it back . . .' In short, then, it was a written IOU, a bond of debt, and Paul uses it figuratively to represent the debt which sin entails. He goes on to qualify it in two ways. First, he mentions the *regulations* which accompany it. These are no doubt the legal demands of God's law, the transgression of which is the very reason why the IOU comes into being in the first place. Second, there is what seems to be a somewhat repetitious allusion to the negative testimony of the *cheirographon*: *that was against us and that stood opposed to us* (14). The two phrases are not necessarily tautological, however. The first of them, *that was against us*, may signify the simple fact of indebtedness, while the second, *that stood opposed to us*, underlines 'the active hostility produced by this fact'.[19] In other words, the IOU not only tells us that we are in debt, but it also pronounces condemnation upon us for the debt we have incurred.

But God has dealt with the *cheirographon*, and Paul's description of what he has done is a climactic moment in this whole section, 2:13–15. For the IOU testifies to those sins which bring death to sinful men and women; God makes such people alive by forgiving

---

[17] A. M. Toplady, 'Rock of Ages', 1763.

[18] O'Brien, *Colossians, Philemon*, p. 124. The word was also used in other senses, and for a summary of interpretations of *cheirographon* in its present context see e.g., N. T. Wright, *Colossians and Philemon: An Introduction and Commentary*, Tyndale NT Commentaries (Leicester: Inter-Varsity Press, 1986), pp. 111–112.

[19] O'Brien, *Colossians, Philemon*, p. 126, quoting M. J. Harris.

their sins; and he does so by personally settling their debts against himself. Paul indicates how God achieves that in three ways, the very repetition underlining the totality and absolute finality of his act. First, God has simply cancelled the IOU – he has destroyed it or wiped it out; it has been 'literally "smeared out", "obliterated", as writing on wax was smoothed away'.[20] The verb here translated 'cancelled' is similarly used in Acts 3:19: 'so that your sins may be wiped out'. God has effaced the writing on the bond of debt so that it can no longer bear its hostile, condemnatory testimony. Second, he totally removes it. Literally, Paul says that he has lifted it 'from the midst'. Previously it was simply there as *the* defining and inescapable reality – *the* great elephant in the middle of the room – which utterly determined the lives and destiny of men and women, which indeed rendered them *dead*. But now God has simply picked up the bond and got rid of it: it has just completely disappeared from the scene. It is, however, the third point that brings us right to the heart of it all: *nailing it to the cross* (14). Symbolically Paul represents God as taking up the sinner's bill of indebtedness himself, and nailing it to the cross of Jesus. There in Christ, his own Son, he made a full and final settlement of all the debts of his own people; for 'God was reconciling the world to himself in Christ, not counting men's sins against them'.[21] There is grace to sinners because Christ 'died for our sins', 'the righteous for the unrighteous to bring you to God'.[22] The IOU is cancelled and removed because the IOU has been paid, and paid with the precious blood of the Son of God.

3. Delivered from the powers and authorities

The cancellation of the bond of indebtedness at the cross looks very much like the triumphant conclusion of Paul's argument. There can surely be nothing he can add which could come even close to surpassing what he has just said. Through the cross God has raised to new life men and women previously dead in their sins. Indeed, there is a close parallel with the flow of thought in the first verses of Ephesians 2 where Paul similarly speaks of the spiritual deadness of his readers which was brought mightily to an end through the mercy of God: 'But ... God, who is rich in mercy, made us alive with Christ even when we were dead in transgressions.'[23] Here in Colossians, however, Paul evidently wishes to push the argument a

---

[20] C. F. D. Moule, *The Epistles to the Colossians and to Philemon* (Cambridge: Cambridge University Press, 1957), p. 98.

[21] 2 Cor. 5:19.

[22] 1 Cor. 15:3; 1 Pet. 3:18. Cf. Rom. 5:6, 8; 2 Cor. 5:14–15; 1 Thess. 5:10.

[23] Eph. 2:4–5.

step further and show his readers the implications of the atonement achieved by Christ for the *powers and authorities*. A central concern of his letter is indeed to deal with the Colossian believers' insecurity and fear of spiritual powers, and their failure to grasp the absolutely total sufficiency of Christ for their salvation. In Colossians 1, therefore, Paul has already shown them that such beings were made 'in', 'by' and 'for' Christ, and are therefore subject to him as creatures before their creator.[24] Here he goes on to explain that through Christ God not only dealt with the debt of human sin but also, *by so doing*, has simultaneously broken the power they once held over sinful human beings.

Paul uses a series of three military metaphors to make his point, the repetition again serving to underscore the decisiveness of his triumph. First, God has *disarmed the powers and authorities* (15).[25] The image is drawn from the battlefield where the defeated army is deprived of its weapons and rendered impotent, unable to resume the conflict and so totally subject to the victor. There is, moreover, deep irony here, 'for while the centurions had stripped Jesus and exposed him as powerless before the crowd (Mark 15:20), Paul says that it was the "rulers and authorities" who were being truly stripped of their power'.[26] Second, God has *made a public spectacle of them* (15). Having disarmed them he has exposed their humiliating powerlessness before the cosmos and the devastation of all their ambitions. Finally, he has triumphed over them. The verb used here recalls the procession that was accorded to a victorious Roman general, allowing him to parade through Rome and display before the masses the riches gained from his conquest as well as his vanquished enemies, now naked and in chains, who were being led to the place of their execution. Even so God triumphs over the powers. 'Their period of rule is finished; they must worship and serve the victor.'[27]

The critical issue, though, is that of identifying the relationship between this verse and the argument that precedes it. Where is the logical connection? The flow of Paul's narrative indicates that it is in fact through Christ's death for the sins of men and women that God also achieved the victory just described over the *powers and authorities*. When he wiped the bond of debt clean, removed it from the midst, nailed it to the cross, by that very act he broke the power

[24] See pp. 19–25 above.
[25] The translation of the opening words of 2:15, and especially the way in which the 'disarming' is to be understood, has been much disputed. The issue is discussed in the commentaries.
[26] J. R. Treat, *The Crucified King: Atonement and Kingdom in Biblical and Systematic Theology* (Grand Rapids: Zondervan, 2014), p. 117.
[27] O'Brien, *Colossians, Philemon*, p. 129.

that they held. If this is his thinking, it must also mean that the tyranny that these beings exercise over humanity is itself rooted in human sin. They are in fact parasites, deriving their malevolent power – and most especially the 'power of death' spoken of in Hebrews 2:14 – from the rebellion of those very beings whom they deceive, oppress and seek ultimately to destroy. As Smeaton says: 'Sin was the ground of Satan's dominion, the sphere of his power, and the secret of his strength; and no sooner was the guilt lying on us extinguished, than his throne was undermined, as Jesus Himself said (John xii.31).'[28]

Moreover, this explains and illuminates Paul's use in this passage alone of the word, *cheirographon*, the IOU or bond of debt. At the end of verse 14 Paul says that God has eliminated it, and then immediately afterwards at the start of verse 15 he announces the disarmament of the powers. The clear implication is that it is the *cheirographon* itself of which the *powers and authorities* have been disarmed. This is not necessarily to say that they somehow held it in their own hands, and Paul is of course using metaphorical language here, but that it was there, in the midst as Paul says, a constant testimony to the sin of those whom they tyrannized and sought to destroy. Now God has dealt with it and there is no such testimony because there is no sin; when the debt is paid the IOU is torn up. And so the powers of darkness have lost the very basis of their power. Not only so, but the cosmos as a whole has witnessed what has happened. All the invisible powers, good or otherwise, know that a massive reversal has taken place in the spiritual realm. By the unimaginable, unbelievable sacrifice of his own beloved Son God has completely outwitted and outmanoeuvred the enemy and laid waste to all his purposes. And the day will come when humanity as a whole will know it too. Meanwhile, the *powers and authorities* themselves, now chained and led captive by their conqueror, are on the way to their own certain and final judgment.

4. Salvation and Satan

Paul's exposition defines the nature of the human malady as one of spiritual death brought about by the sin of men and women. God, however, makes them alive by totally forgiving their sins and pays the debt himself through the atoning sacrificial death of Jesus Christ his Son. The immediate and primary object of the cross is that the

---

[28] G. Smeaton, quoted in S. Ferguson, 'Christus Victor et Propitiator: The Death of Christ, Substitute and Conqueror', in S. Storms and J. Taylor (eds.), *For the Fame of God's Name: Essays in Honor of John Piper* (Wheaton: Crossway, 2010), p. 184.

penalty of sin should be paid so that human beings might be brought from death to life. However, by the very act of atoning for sin God also overcame Satan and the powers. He disarmed them, both of the basis on which they keep men and women in bondage, and also of the grounds on which they hold 'the power of death'.[29]

Many of the great normative affirmations of the gospel throughout the New Testament, including Paul's own writings, focus on the fact of Christ's death for sins. It was this, for example, 'as of first importance', that Paul had communicated to the Corinthian believers – 'that Christ died for our sins'.[30] Here in the Colossian letter he moves beyond that to the implications of the cross for the *powers and authorities* because of the particular concerns and fears of his intended readers. In their case they especially needed to understand not only that they were forgiven but also that they were freed from the tyranny of the *powers and authorities* which they so much feared.

There are some important implications of Paul's argument here.

a. Forgiveness and liberation

The atonement that the Lord Jesus Christ made for sins and the victory he gained over the devil have sometimes been seen as totally distinct – even mutually opposed – ways of understanding his death. The truth is, however, that there is a profound complementarity and unity between the procurement of forgiveness and the defeat of Satan. Both are achieved through the cross, and the one flows out of the other as its necessary and logical consequence: in dying Christ dealt with sin and *by so doing* also triumphed over Satan. 'The atonement, which terminates on God (in propitiation) and on man (in forgiveness), also terminates on Satan (in the destruction of his sway over believers). And it does this last precisely because it does the first two.'[31]

b. Sinners, not victims

The primary problem of men and women is not that they are victims, but that they are sinners. This is not to deny the power of Satan and his massive and terrifying malevolence and tyranny. Satan undoubtedly blinds minds and deceives, but it is the minds of 'unbelievers' that he blinds (2 Cor. 4:4). The human malady is first of all a horrendous inner disease of moral and spiritual corruption rather than an

---

[29] Heb. 2:14.
[30] 1 Cor. 15:3. See also, for example, John 1:29; Rom. 3:21–26; 2 Cor. 5:21; 1 Pet. 2:24; 3:18; 1 John 4:10; Rev. 5:5.
[31] Ferguson, 'Christus Victor et Propitiator', p. 185.

external problem of dark powers. We go seriously wrong if we fail to appreciate the awful depth of sin in the human heart, the horrors that it can produce and its dread final and eternal consequence. The powers attach themselves to that sin like parasites, they tyrannize the sinners and pursue their utter destruction, but the great problem lies in *us*. Barrett expresses this very clearly in speaking of Adam's fall.

> Man upset the balance of God's creation by reaching for that which was above him, for which he had not been made and was not fitted. Out of this imbalance arise both the anthropological and cosmic malaise of the universe: man attempts to live independently of his Creator, treating himself as his own god, and thereby not only ceases to be truly himself but also loses control of what should have been under his dominion *and falls under the control of demonic powers.*[32]

Christ therefore died 'for our sins', and by repentance and faith, acknowledging their own sin and guilt, men and women may receive forgiveness and, at that same moment, find also liberation from the powers of evil.

c. Tempter, accuser, murderer

The text also helps us to see the connections between the various names and activities that the Bible attributes to Satan. At the beginning of both creation and new creation Satan tempts. In Eden, disguised as a serpent, he tempts the woman and her husband to disobey God's word. Matthew describes him as 'the tempter' in his account of the temptation of Jesus at the outset of his public ministry.[33] And at numerous points in Scripture he acts or is expected to act in the same way.[34] The point, however, is that he tempts in order to entice his prey to sin, which is the source of his power over them and the means by which he purposes to bring them to destruction.

The Scriptures also identify him as the accuser. In Job 1 – 2 he accuses Job of hypocrisy in his worship of God. In Zechariah 3:1 he stands beside Joshua, Israel's high priest, to accuse him. Most significant, in Revelation he is identified as 'the accuser of our brothers, who accuses them before our God day and night'.[35] His accusations have sometimes been understood subjectively as

[32] C. K. Barrett, *From First Adam to Last: A Study in Pauline Theology* (London: A & C Black, 1962), pp. 92–93, my italics.
[33] Matt. 4:3.
[34] See e.g., 1 Chr. 21:1; John 13:2; 1 Cor. 7:5; 1 Thess. 3:5.
[35] Rev. 12:10.

addressed to the consciences of believers in order to discourage them. The relevant texts, however, indicate that it is rather before God himself that he accuses men and women, indicting them indeed of those sins he himself tempted them to commit. Once again, he does so because the sin he accuses them of is the source of his power over them as well as the means by which he kills.

Satan's ultimate goal is the destruction of those he tempts and then accuses. He is the murderer (John 8:44), his temptations and accusations always carried out with a view to the destruction of God's own creation. The wages of sin is always death (Rom. 6:23), and Satan tempts to sin and accuses of sin. He tempted Adam and Eve to an act of disobedience whose consequence was death. This also explains the only reference to Satan in Hebrews as 'the one who holds the power of death'.[36] Like everything else death falls under the invincible rule of God; nobody dies outside his sovereign will. However, by temptation to sin and accusation Satan seeks to bring men and women under the judgment of death and so, in that sense, exercises 'the power of death'.

Satan is tempter, accuser, murderer, and there is an evident unity in that triple identification. The three roles belong together. But when Christ dies in the place of sinners, and the bond of debt which testified against them is nailed to the cross, then Satan and all the powers of evil are disarmed. Sin is forgiven and removed. Accusation therefore becomes baseless, for the sinners have been acquitted by the supreme judge on the basis of Christ's saving work: 'Who will bring any charge against those whom God has chosen? It is God who justifies . . .'[37] And the penalty of death is no longer applicable, having been paid by another. 'Since the children have flesh and blood, he too shared in their humanity so that by his death he might destroy him who holds the power of death – that is, the devil – and free those who all their lives were held in slavery by their fear of death.'[38]

d. Disarmed, but not yet destroyed

The *powers and authorities* were disarmed at the cross of that which gave them power over humanity and enabled them to pursue the destruction of God's creation. They were not themselves destroyed, however, because their destruction would be irrelevant to the real issue which is human sin. Their downfall was a moral and spiritual one rather than the defeat of annihilation. It means, therefore, that

[36] Heb. 2:14.
[37] Rom. 8:33.
[38] Heb. 2:14–15.

they continue to exist and to remain active in the world. Moreover, they are now venomously hostile to God's people, forgiven and made alive and so the living and visible embodiment of the powers' own utter humiliation, frustration and hopelessness. But Satan and his angels do not surrender. On the contrary they attack the church in every way they know, but always conscious of the ultimate futility of their efforts and of the inevitable judgment to come.

The defeat of the principalities and powers at the cross is the climactic moment in God's conflict with cosmic rebellion and wickedness. It is the decisive moment in his spiritual warfare, the moment at which his word of prophecy to the serpent at the very beginning of human history is fulfilled: 'he will crush your head, and you will strike his heel'.[39] It is such an astonishing event and victory. There are cases in human history of outstandingly brilliant and creative generalship when the tactics of soldiers such as Hannibal or Napoleon take their enemies totally by surprise and bring them to utter defeat – great victories that are then endlessly studied and compared over the future centuries. The victory of God at the cross is totally beyond compare. Not only was Satan so out-generalled that he was complicit in his own defeat – through his inspiration, for example, of Judas' act of betrayal; but also, in the greatest of all paradoxes, he was overcome by the very death of the enemy whom he thought to destroy. It was through the *death* of Jesus that God saved sinners and defeated his enemies.

And the gospel continues to advance through the cross. So often the church of Jesus Christ has failed to understand, and has pursued power in one or other of its many forms in order supposedly to carry out the mission God gave it. But its true warfare is always a warfare of the cross. It is always and only when 'a grain of wheat falls into the ground and dies' that it produces 'many seeds'.[40] It is always those who 'did not love their lives so much as to shrink from death' who overcome the accuser.[41]

[39] Gen. 3:15.
[40] John 12:24.
[41] Rev. 12:11.

Revelation 12:1–17
9. The dragon hurled down

The drama of the book of Revelation has challenged Christian readers almost from the beginning. Understanding the book was no doubt much easier for its first-century readers, but not at all straightforward two thousand years later when the literary genre to which it belongs is quite alien to us. Revelation is the almost unique New Testament example of apocalyptic literature, to which the Old Testament prophecy of Zechariah and the second half of Daniel also belong, as does a good deal of ancient non-biblical Jewish literature. The difficulty with apocalyptic lies primarily in its very heavy use of symbolism. Revelation itself is permeated by symbols to the point that 'the essence of the book is figurative'.[1] 'Elaborate and sometimes bizarre symbolism depicts past, present, and future events in a way that requires a careful decoding of the elements of the text.'[2] As L. P. Hartley might have said, 'The past is a foreign country: they write things differently there.'[3]

At the centre of the book's narrative there is a *war in heaven*, which we discuss in this chapter. It is a war in which *Michael and his angels fought against the dragon and his angels* (7) and hurled them down. On the face of it the brief story is straightforward and describes a celestial defeat of Satan. The problem is working out what exactly that defeat signifies, which means deciphering the symbols. We need to know, for example, what Satan was doing in heaven in the first place, what sort of battle it was and when it took place, and

[1] A. Bandy, 'The Hermeneutics of Symbolism: How to Interpret the Symbols of John's Apocalypse', *Southern Baptist Journal of Theology* 14.1 (2010), p. 49.
[2] W. W. Klein, C. L. Blomberg and R. L. Hubbard, *Introduction to Biblical Interpretation* (Dallas: Word, 1993), p. 371.
[3] L. P. Hartley, *The Go-Between* (London: Penguin, 1997 [1953]), p. 5. What he actually wrote was, 'The past is a foreign country: they do things differently there.'

what Satan's expulsion meant for him and, indeed, for generations of later Christian readers of the story.

1. Two signs (12:1–6)

In the narrative flow of Revelation 12 the war in heaven is preceded by two 'signs', neither of which should be understood literally. The 'signs' are *a woman* (1) and *a dragon* (3), and the story that John tells is the classic tale of 'an evil usurper who is doomed to be vanquished by a yet unborn prince', and who 'tries to escape his destiny by killing the prince when he is born'.[4]

a. A woman (1–2, 5)

Essentially the woman symbolizes the entire community of God's chosen people across all of time and space and both before and after Christ's coming. The twelve stars represent the patriarchs from whom the tribes of Israel are descended and, linked as they are here with the sun and moon, there is an echo too of Joseph's dream (Gen. 37:9). That she is clothed with the sun indicates the woman's glory and righteousness, while the crown of twelve stars that she wears and the moon that forms her footstool allude also to the reign of God's people.

In the vision, however, there is pain as well as glory, for the woman is experiencing childbirth. At this point the symbolism deepens. On the one hand, the woman of the vision points back to the first woman, Eve 'the mother of all the living', from whom the seed or offspring would be born who would crush the head of the serpent (Gen. 3:15).[5] It is that offspring to whom she is giving birth here in John's vision. It is clear, however, that the woman is much more than Eve alone but symbolic also of her collective offspring, the entire community of God's chosen people from Abel onwards, including of course the faithful of Israel. It is from that people that the child will come and, as they wait for him, they experience the pains of childbirth, an image drawn from the Old Testament where it is frequently used to describe the sufferings of Israel.[6] Here in Revelation those pains symbolize the centuries of anguish that God's people have endured at the hands of the dragon as God's purpose of redeeming them moves slowly towards its fulfilment.

Finally, however, the child is born (5), but in John's narrative the sufferings of the woman continue (13–17). No longer is this because

[4] G. K. Beale, *The Book of Revelation*, New International Greek Testament Commentary (Grand Rapids: Eerdmans and Carlisle: Paternoster, 1999), p. 624.

[5] See the discussion in ch. 3 above.

[6] In Isa. 26:17–18; 66:7–8; Mic. 4:10; 5:3, for example.

the dragon hopes to frustrate God's saving purpose but rather because, in hopeless and vindictive fury, he rages against the woman, now revealed as the redeemed people of Jesus Christ. Ultimately, however, in the final denouement of Revelation her sufferings will end in glory when she appears as the new Jerusalem, 'coming down out of heaven from God, prepared as a bride beautifully dressed for her husband'.[7]

b. A serpent (3–4)

While the woman cries out in childbirth *an enormous red dragon – another sign* – appears. Use of the word, 'dragon', evokes Old Testament allusions to the mythical sea monster, Rahab or Leviathan, which symbolizes those who oppose and persecute God's people with Egypt especially in view.[8] In Ezekiel 29:3 Pharaoh himself is the great 'dragon': 'you great monster lying among your streams'. Here, however, the dragon is not the symbol of a historical enemy but is shortly to be unmasked as the devil himself: *the great dragon was hurled down – that ancient serpent called the devil, or Satan* (9; see also Rev. 20:2). The identification is significant in bringing together the various names of Satan found through the Scriptures and confirming that they all denote a single being. The dragon's colour symbolizes its wickedness, echoing the colour symbolism of Isaiah 1:18: 'Though your sins are like scarlet, they shall be as white as snow'; the great prostitute who appears later will similarly be clothed 'in purple and scarlet'.[9] The horn is a symbol of strength and so the dragon's *ten horns* speak of its power and recall the ten-horned beast which appears at the climax of Daniel's vision: 'terrifying and frightening and very powerful'.[10] Meanwhile the seven heads may refer to the creature's vitality and seeming indestructibility as it faces the church: 'No sooner is it defeated in one place than it breaks out elsewhere.'[11] Moreover, they are crowned, representing 'the devil's false claims of sovereign, universal authority in opposition to the true "King of kings and Lord of lords," who also wears "many diadems."'[12] Finally, the stars that the dragon's tail sweeps from the sky and flings to the earth, echoing Daniel 8:10, likely refer to Satan's

---

[7] Rev. 21:2. It is this whole history of the woman that indicates that she cannot simply be identified with Mary the mother of Jesus.
[8] Pss 74:13–14; 89:10; Isa. 30:7; 51:9; Ezek. 29:3; 32:2; etc.
[9] Rev. 17:4.
[10] Dan. 7:7, 24.
[11] L. Morris, *Revelation: An Introduction and Commentary*, Tyndale NT Commentaries (Nottingham: Inter-Varsity Press, 1987), p. 154.
[12] Beale, *Revelation*, p. 635.

inspiration of angelic rebellion, in which case it gives an idea of the scope of that rebellion.[13]

The main point of the *sign*, however, is the dragon's purpose, which was to destroy the woman's child. Once more Satan is identified as 'murderer from the beginning',[14] and the immense scope of his murderous ambition is disclosed. Having brought death to the original creation in Eden, his aim now is to destroy the new one at the moment of its birth by devouring the second Adam, Jesus Christ the Son of God and seed of the woman. It is here that the enmity between the serpent and the woman's offspring (Gen. 3:15) reaches its climactic moment, as the serpent stands ready to strike first in order to prevent the offspring from striking at all. It offers an explanation of much Old Testament history, including moments at which God's people faced annihilation, as a result of Egyptian and Persian inspired genocide or Assyrian and Babylonian deportations, for example, and indeed much else besides. In the New Testament it might comprise both physical attack, such as Herod's massacre of the boy toddlers of Bethlehem, and spiritual onslaught including that to which the devil subjected Jesus in the desert. Indeed, it seems likely that Satan's inspiration of Jesus' crucifixion was motivated by the utterly misguided idea that such a death would terminate his mission.[15] It was, after all, only following the resurrection that the mystery of God hidden through the ages was finally made fully known (see Eph. 1:9; Col. 1:26; etc.).

c. A child (5–6)

What follows is enigmatically expressed. The woman gives birth to a child who, in language drawn from Psalm 2:8–9, is identified in messianic terms: *who will rule all the nations with an iron sceptre*. The child is then immediately *snatched up to God and to his throne*, with no explicit reference to the course of his earthly career. However, the messianic purpose of the child's birth is clearly fulfilled, for he *will rule all the nations*. Further, the survival and exaltation of the child obviously mean that the murderous intention of the dragon has been frustrated and that it has suffered a decisive defeat.

[13] P. E. Hughes, *The Book of Revelation*, Pillar NT Commentary (Leicester: Inter-Varsity Press and Grand Rapids: Eerdmans, 1990), p. 136; S. H. T. Page, *Powers of Evil: A Biblical Study of Satan and Demons* (Grand Rapids: Baker and Leicester: Apollos, 1995), p. 214. The throwing down of the stars may alternatively refer to the dragon's persecution of God's people, see Beale, *Revelation*, pp. 635–637.

[14] John 8:44.

[15] W. Hendriksen spends some time discussing the meaning of the dragon's intended devouring of the child in *More Than Conquerors: An Interpretation of the Book of Revelation*, 2nd edn (Grand Rapids: Baker, 1962), pp. 137–140.

Nevertheless, following the child's departure its mother needs protection and God prepares a place of refuge for her *in the desert*. Having failed to eliminate the Christ, the dragon has turned its attention to his people.

2. The heavenly battle (12:7–9)

And there was war in heaven (7).

There are two principal protagonists in the war. *Michael* is evidently leader of the angels of God: *Michael and his angels*. There is scarcely any suggestion of an angelic hierarchy in Scripture, but Michael uniquely is identified as an archangel (Jude 9). He is also associated elsewhere with conflict against the enemies of God, whether the princes of Persia and Greece (Dan. 10:13, 21) or Satan himself (Jude 9). And in Daniel 12:1 he has the role of guardian of Israel: 'the great prince who protects your people'.

Against Michael there stands *the dragon* who is similarly leader of *his angels*. The narrator lists his various biblical titles: he is the *serpent* who tempted Adam and Eve in Eden; *the devil* (*diabolos*), literally the slanderer, who accuses the people of God; and *Satan*, adversary of God and of his people, who accused and afflicted Job (Job 1 – 2), also accused Joshua the high priest (Zech. 3:1–2), and tempted David (1 Chr. 21:1). Further, he is the one *who leads the whole world astray*, a characterization found several times in the New Testament,[16] and which especially recalls Jesus' identification of the devil as a liar (John 8:44). Indeed, this whole chapter illustrates the truth of Jesus' summary of Satan's character in terms of two dominant traits: liar and murderer. In verses 1–6 the dragon seeks to devour the child; here in verses 7–12 he is identified as the liar; and in verses 13–17 he is once again the murderer, seeking to destroy the woman and her offspring.

The war takes place *in heaven*. Subsequently, indeed, the dragon will make war on the woman and her offspring *on earth* as it tries to destroy the church spread throughout the world. Given the context of the book of Revelation the author doubtless has the physical persecution of the church very much in mind, but the language does not exclude attacks also of a moral, spiritual or doctrinal kind. The war in heaven, however, is different in nature, and the fact that Satan and his angels *lost their place in heaven* (8) and were *hurled down* (9) suggests that in some sense it was their access to the presence of God himself that was being contested. Further, the war was apparently initiated by *Michael and his angels*. They fought to deprive the

---

[16] See e.g., 2 Cor. 4:4; Eph. 2:2; 1 John 5:19; Rev. 20:3.

dragon of its *place in heaven* – of a position, or role, or opportunity which it had previously possessed – and although the dragon *fought back* (7) it did not prevail.

The language employed stresses the significance, scale and conclusiveness of its defeat. It is indeed *the great dragon* that is overcome, and the Greek word order emphasizes its power.[17] The listing of its various biblical titles similarly draws attention to the fact that it is that very enemy of God – serpent, devil, Satan – that had for so long sought to bring about total devastation by its lies and accusations that was now, at last, decisively dealt with. And the simple fact of the expulsion is proclaimed three times with a steadily increasing insistence: ... *they lost their place in heaven* ... *The great dragon was hurled down* ... *He was hurled to the earth, and his angels with him*. So, beginning with the simple fact that the dragon had lost its place, John then adds that it was in fact forcibly evicted, and then again, and yet more comprehensive, that it was thrown down to the earth with all its forces. The writer is determined to impress upon hard-pressed Christian readers that, powerful though he undoubtedly is, the great enemy of God and his people through the long centuries of human history, the one, indeed, who stood behind the persecutions and trials that those readers themselves were experiencing at that very moment, had now suffered a shattering defeat of cosmic significance from which there could be no return.

3. The heavenly interpretation (12:10–12)

But what does the 'hurling down' of the dragon actually signify, especially given that he remains active and as malignant as ever, perhaps even more so (v. 12)? And when did it take place? The meaning and timing of the war in heaven have long been debated. Various interpretations have been proposed, but the key to understanding it is the way it fits into the whole narrative of Revelation 12.

a. The big picture

Three features of the passage show that the story of Satan's downfall is an integral part of the storyline of the chapter as a whole. First, there is clearly a relationship between the war in heaven and the preceding story of the woman and child. Obviously the war follows immediately on the birth and exaltation of the child, but there are also parallels between the two events. In both stories there is antagonism between the dragon on the one hand and God's purposes and

---

[17] *ho drakōn ho megas.*

agents on the other. Moreover, in both the dragon suffers frustration or defeat.

Second, the constant repetition of the word 'and' links the successive events described throughout the chapter, including the *war in heaven* (7–9), the signs of the *woman* and the *dragon* which precede it (1–6) and the hymn that follows (10–12).

> *And a great sign appeared in heaven* (1) . . . *and another sign appeared in heaven* (3) . . . *and she gave birth to a son* (5a) . . . *and her child was snatched away* (5b) . . . *and the woman fled into the desert* (6) . . . *and there was war in heaven* (7) . . . *and I heard a loud voice* (10) . . . *and when the dragon saw that he had been hurled to the earth* (13) . . .[18]

Third, and most significant, the hymn which follows the war in heaven (10–12) interprets the 'hurling down' of the dragon, and does so in a way which indicates that it is the Lamb himself – the one who is also the child born to the woman – who has brought it about. It is his coming and exaltation which stands behind the victory of Michael and his angels. This is the vital clue to the meaning of the *war in heaven* and to its timing.

b. The hymn of victory (10)

Then I heard a loud voice in heaven (10). The *loud voice* which speaks the hymn is probably that of saints already in heaven. In the hymn they proclaim the coming of God's kingdom and salvation, and they explain it in terms of the hurling down of *the accuser of our brothers*. Without a doubt they are referring back to the war in heaven just described when the dragon *was hurled to the earth and his angels with him* (9). The hymn celebrates Michael's victory and the dragon's defeat. What is especially significant is the double, insistent reference in the hymn to the dragon's role as accuser: *the accuser of our brothers, who accuses them day and night before our God, has been cast down* (10).[19] The hymn is indicating that the dragon has been thrown down from heaven *precisely in his role as accuser of our brothers*, the 'brothers' accused being themselves fellow believers with those who speak from heaven.

The hymn also defines the nature of the dragon's accusations, and does so in two ways. First, the dragon accuses the brothers before God. These are not accusations experienced in the consciences of the

---

[18] My translation. See also the allusion to the continuity in Beale, *Revelation*, p. 650.
[19] *ho katēgōr tōn adelphōn hēmōn, ho katēgorōn autous.*

believers themselves, but accusations brought before the one who is ruler and judge of the whole earth. They are accusations which seek the condemnation and death of those accused. This is not to say that the accuser is in some way an official prosecutor, God's servant charged with opposing the wrongdoer.[20] Nowhere in the Bible is such a role ever attributed to Satan. Nor are they the accusations of an aggrieved plaintiff demanding justice for himself. Human sin, real though it is, does not harm Satan but furthers his cause. These are rather accusations rooted in the unmitigated malice of the one who is 'murderer from the beginning' and pursues the destruction of those he accuses.

Second, they are incessant, *day and night*. Constantly and obsessively the dragon pursues 'our brothers' before the throne of God with a view to their destruction. He insists on the imposition of the death which sin brings. Accordingly, when Michael hurls him from heaven he is removed from the presence of the one before whom he remorselessly accuses his victims. The meaning of his defeat in the battle is just this: *he can no longer accuse*. It is not a victory achieved by superior power in the usual sense, for Satan's 'force resides in the rightness of his accusations'[21] and simply annihilating him would not remove the basis of those accusations. His defeat lies rather in the cancellation of sin, and so the impossibility of accusation. It is this which cuts the ground from under Satan's feet, and it is in this sense that salvation has come.

c. The blood of the Lamb (11)

How is it, though, that Satan can no longer accuse? After announcing that the accuser has been hurled down, the hymn turns to the ways in which the 'brothers' overcame him, of which there are three.[22] It is the first which is especially relevant here: *They overcame him by the blood of the Lamb*.

In terms of New Testament witness in general and the book of Revelation in particular, the blood of Christ was shed as a sacrifice for the remission of sins. In the introduction to Revelation John's words of worship reflect that: 'To him who loves us and has freed us from our sins by his blood.'[23] Later on the great multitude standing before the throne of God are identified as those who 'have washed

---

[20] G. B. Caird, *Principalities and Powers* (Oxford: Clarendon Press, 1956), pp. 31–32.
[21] H. Blocher, '*Agnus Victor*: The Atonement as Victory and Vicarious Punishment', in J. G. Stackhouse, Jr (ed.), *What Does It Mean to Be Saved? Broadening Evangelical Horizons of Salvation* (Grand Rapids: Baker, 2002), p. 83.
[22] This text is discussed more fully in ch. 21 below.
[23] Rev. 1:5.

their robes and made them white in the blood of the Lamb'.[24] In other words, the death of Christ has made atonement for the sins of his people, who are now forgiven and clothed with his righteousness. Returning to the hymn in 12:11 then, the brothers have overcome Satan because by virtue of Christ's blood shed for them Satan has no longer any ground of accusation against them. In metaphorical terms he has been hurled down from heaven where he brought his accusations because the death penalty which the brothers indeed merited has been carried out in full. It was when Christ was crucified and by means of his crucifixion that the dragon was defeated.

d. The role of Michael

Finally, though, why is it Michael rather than Christ who actually drives the dragon from heaven? The primary work that Christ accomplished through the cross and resurrection was to make an atonement for sins; the dragon's expulsion from heaven is the result of that. Accordingly, in terms of the narrative of Revelation, Satan's expulsion from heaven takes place when Christ is still on earth. 'Christ's redemptive work on earth unleashes the effect in heaven of Michael's victory.'[25] Or, in the words of G. B. Caird,

> Some commentators express surprise that it should be Michael and not Christ who is God's champion. The point is, however, that, when this victory is won in heaven, Christ is on earth, on the Cross. Because He is part of the earthly reality He is not part of the heavenly symbolism. The heavenly chorus . . . explains that the victory has been achieved 'by the sacrifice of the Lamb' . . . Michael, in fact, is not the field officer who does the actual fighting, but the staff officer, who is able to remove Satan's flag from the heavenly map because the real victory has been won on Calvary.[26]

4. The trials of the woman (12:13–17)

The trials of the woman, however, are not at an end.

The phrase, 'the inhabitants of the earth',[27] is used several times in Revelation as a technical term 'for unbelieving idolaters'.[28] Here in Revelation 12:12, the hymn concludes with a summons addressed to *you heavens and you who dwell in them* to rejoice at Satan's defeat.

[24] Rev. 7:14.
[25] Beale, *Revelation*, p. 652.
[26] G. B. Caird, 'On Deciphering the Book of Revelation', *ExpT* 74 (1962–3), p. 13.
[27] *hoi katoikountes epi tēs gēs.*
[28] Beale, *Revelation*, p. 290. See e.g., 3:10; 6:10; 8:13; 11:10.

The phrase which the NIV translates 'you who dwell in them [the heavens]',[29] although it uses a different verb, is an antithetic parallel to 'the inhabitants of the earth' and refers to the faithful, those who worship God. Accordingly, while the summons to rejoice doubtless applies to those actually in the very presence of God including angels and departed saints, it is also addressed to Christians physically located on earth. Because of salvation already achieved they have boundless reason to rejoice. However, being still present in the world they live where the dragon is active, which means that they will also experience his furious venom as it is vented upon the whole earth. And, as the following verses show, a critical dimension of this is that they must face his attacks on the church itself.

A number of points emerge from this. First, while Satan has been defeated he nevertheless remains active and venomous. Indeed, the frustration of his ultimate ambition, through the death of Christ, goads him to cause as much destruction as he can while he can and by whatever means remain available to him. Thus the eschatological tension which believers experience in most aspects of their salvation is true also of the defeat of Satan and of their deliverance from him. They are *already* freed from bondage to him, but *not yet* removed from the earthly sphere of his activity.

Second, Christians should not allow the havoc that Satan causes on earth to mislead them. The destruction that he brings to the world, including the activities of the beasts which he inspires (Rev. 13), might easily lead them to suppose that Satan is lord and is winning. In fact the contrary is true. His present fury is not the expression of victory but comes from the frustration of utter defeat. His grand strategy has irretrievably failed, and in hatred and malice he rages simply in order not to do nothing.

Third, therefore, Satan's ongoing savagery highlights the futility of evil. *He knows that his time is short* (12) and that nothing but final judgment awaits him, and yet uselessly and hopelessly he continues to murder and destroy. Rather like the Nazi Third Reich, fighting on after successive crushing defeats in both east and west and causing untold bitter suffering even to its own people, the devil rages on in utter pointlessness, for it is all in vain *and he knows it.*

Finally, the sovereign God protects his people. This does not mean that they do not suffer at Satan's hand, for indeed they do. However, God limits the period during which Satan is permitted to operate. The reference to the shortness of Satan's time links with the *1,260 days* or the *time, times and half a time* during which the woman is protected in the desert (6, 14) – a period also referred to in Revelation

---

[29] *hoi en autois skēnountes.*

as forty-two months (11:2–3). For Jewish people the time reference undoubtedly recalled the 1,260 days of Judas Maccabeus' struggle against Antiochus Epiphanes' brutal attempt in the second century BC to impose his Greek paganism on the Jewish people and wipe out the worship of Yahweh. Readers of Revelation saw it, therefore, as symbolic of a period of immense pain and suffering for the faith, but one also of decidedly limited duration between Christ's accomplishment of salvation and defeat of Satan on the one hand, and his return and final condemnation of Satan on the other. So, believers are assured that the period of Satan's present onslaught is limited – indeed they are but 'light and momentary troubles' compared with the 'eternal glory' to come.[30]

Moreover, they are also assured of God's protection through that period. He prepares a place of safety for the woman, enables her to reach it and provides for her there (6, 14); and he prevents the dragon from sweeping her away (16). The point is not that the people of God do not face severe trials that may indeed seem to threaten their very existence, but that God preserves them through those trials for the glory to come. For he has already seated them 'in the heavenly realms in Christ Jesus',[31] a place of total security.

5. Complementary narratives

Although John uses a very different metaphor, his account of the 'war in heaven' speaks of the same reality as Paul's description of the disarming and defeat of the 'powers and authorities' in Colossians 2:15. In both cases the defeat of evil powers is the result of the death of Christ for sins. It is the *blood of the Lamb* (Rev. 12:11) and the nailing to the cross of the fatal bond, the *cheirographon* (Col. 2:14), that effects their downfall. Human sin empowers them, but once it is cancelled, their power evaporates.

Jesus' words in John 12:31 speak also of the same event. In Jesus' declaration 'the prince of this world' is driven from the world which he tyrannizes rather than from heaven. However, in the context of the text it is still the cross that brings that about, and Jesus speaks of Satan's being driven from earth because his particular emphasis is on the liberation of human beings from Satan's grip rather than on the termination of his accusations in heaven. And so, after announcing the imminent expulsion of Satan, Jesus declares, 'But I, when I am lifted up from the earth, will draw all men to myself.'[32] In fact,

[30] 2 Cor. 4:17.
[31] Eph. 2:6.
[32] John 12:32.

expulsion from heaven and expulsion from earth are both metaphors representing two sides of the same reality: through Jesus' death Satan can no longer accuse before God in heaven, and in consequence human beings are freed from his tyranny here on earth.

The same theme is also present in Hebrews 2:14: 'Since the children have flesh and blood, he too shared in their humanity so that by his death he might destroy him who holds the power of death – that is, the devil.' It is the only verse in Hebrews where the devil is mentioned, and the author speaks of him simply to declare that he is 'destroyed' by the death of Christ. Elsewhere in Hebrews the cross is a sacrifice for sin (Heb. 9:14, 15, 26, 28), and so, here again, the writer is implicitly telling his readers that Christ's destruction of the devil is brought about by his death which is *for sin*. Once more, the power of Satan is rooted in human sin and it is atonement for sin that breaks it.

And finally, Peter's enigmatic reference to Christ's proclamation 'to the spirits in prison'[33] moves in the same direction. It would take too long to analyse the passage in detail,[34] but the spirits in question are most likely the fallen 'angels, authorities and powers' referred to a little later in the passage (1 Pet. 3:22), and the content of Christ's announcement to them is news of their defeat. What is especially significant, however, is that immediately preceding his reference to Christ's proclamation to these spirits Peter has very concisely summarized his atoning work: 'For Christ died for sins once for all, the righteous for the unrighteous, to bring you to God.'[35] Now, following his death and in his resurrected state, he brings to the spiritual powers of darkness news of their defeat. The implication, once again, is that it is specifically as a result of his death, which is a death *for sins*, that the spiritual forces of darkness have been overcome.

A vital and repeated dimension of the New Testament testimony to the gospel of Jesus Christ is that by his death and resurrection Jesus defeated Satan and all the hosts of evil. He has done so in the most utterly paradoxical way, by giving up his life as an offering for sin and so cancelling the debt of those for whom he died. It is this which breaks Satan's power over them because it is their sin which empowers him and which he exploits to bring about their destruction. And so

---

[33] 1 Pet. 3:19.
[34] See, however, R. T. France, 'Exegesis in Practice: Two Examples', in I. H. Marshall (ed.), *New Testament Interpretation* (Exeter: Paternoster, 1977), pp. 252–279; or K. Ferdinando, *The Triumph of Christ in African Perspective* (Carlisle: Paternoster, 1999), pp. 347–351.
[35] 1 Pet. 3:18.

Jesus overcame him and all the spiritual powers of darkness by offering himself to God as an atoning sacrifice. In their different ways, and using diverse metaphors, John and Paul, Peter and the unknown author of Hebrews all bear consistent testimony to this absolutely crucial dimension of Christ's saving work. The crucified Christ is the mighty conquering Christ – he is *Christus Victor*.

Revelation 20:7–10
10. The last battle

Hopes that the First World War would be a 'war to end all wars' were quickly disappointed by the events which followed. Human history is, indeed, a long tale of warfare, unendingly symbolized by John's vision of the white horse and its rider riding out 'as a conqueror bent on conquest'.[1] Nevertheless, the book of Revelation does look forward to a final 'war to end all wars', a climactic battle at the end of earth's history following which the great murderer and destroyer himself will be finally and eternally punished.

1. The thousand years

At the beginning of Revelation 20 Satan is seized, bound and imprisoned in the abyss by an angel from heaven (20:1–3). The last battle takes place when the thousand years of Satan's imprisonment come to an end and he is released. Detailed analysis of the meaning of these thousand years and what takes place during them is beyond the scope of the present discussion but, as is true throughout Revelation, it is vital to recognize the symbolic nature of the language used and to be careful in identifying its meaning. Clearly the seizure of the dragon, its binding and confinement in the abyss which is 'locked and sealed … over him' speaks of a defeat of Satan, albeit one that is not final, in that at the end of the 'thousand years' he will be released from the abyss.[2] On the basis of other biblical references to Satan's defeat there are good grounds to suppose that this account too probably refers to what happened to him as a result of the death and resurrection of the Lord Jesus Christ.

Two texts point particularly clearly in this direction. First, there is Jesus' own announcement of the imminent expulsion of 'the prince

[1] Rev. 6:2.
[2] Rev. 20:2–3, 7.

122

of this world' from his domain (John 12:31); and, second, there is the account of Satan's expulsion from heaven by Michael (Rev. 12:8–9). In rather different terms both these references allude to the impact of Jesus' death and resurrection on the devil,[3] and both connect with the binding and imprisonment of Satan here in Revelation 20:1–3. According to this latter text, the explicit purpose of throwing Satan into the abyss and locking it 'over him' is 'to keep him from deceiving the nations any more until the thousand years were ended'.[4] So, it is with reference to his capacity as 'the father of lies', whose work of deception began in Eden and has spread across the earth, that Satan is bound and confined. Meanwhile, in Revelation 12 the dragon who is expelled from heaven is similarly identified not only as the serpent, the devil and Satan, but also as the one 'who leads the whole world astray'. The flow of the text suggests that at least part of the meaning of Satan's expulsion from heaven lies in his defeat precisely *as* the great father of lies: 'And the great dragon was thrown down . . . the deceiver of the whole world – he was thrown down to the earth'.[5] More clearly still, when Jesus speaks of the expulsion of the prince of this world, he immediately goes on to speak of the result of that event for human beings: 'But I, when I am lifted up from the earth, will draw all men to myself.'[6] For Jesus, therefore, the impact of Satan's expulsion would be visible in Jesus' own drawing of an immense multitude of men and women to himself. In other words, the consequence of the cross and resurrection of Jesus would be that Satan would deceive the nations no more.

From this perspective, then, the thousand years of Satan's imprisonment in the abyss refer in fact to the present period, a period of great length though not literally one thousand years,[7] beginning with the first coming of the Christ and ending close to the moment of his return. Prior to this period knowledge of the one true God, maker of heaven and earth, was largely if not exclusively confined to Israel, while the nations were deceived by the great liar. However, now that Christ has come and made a perfect and complete atonement for sin, the gospel has spread across the earth and the nations – the Gentiles – respond. They are undeceived. It is, therefore, the time during which God's covenant promise to Abraham is realized: 'all

---

[3] See the discussion in ch. 9 above.

[4] Rev. 20:3.

[5] Rev. 12:9, ESV. The NIV breaks the flow of thought in the text with a full stop.

[6] John 12:32.

[7] See discussion in G. K. Beale, *The Book of Revelation*, New International Greek Testament Commentary (Grand Rapids: Eerdmans and Carlisle: Paternoster, 1999), pp. 1017–1021.

peoples on earth will be blessed through you';[8] when Isaiah's prophecy is fulfilled: 'in that day the Root of Jesse will stand as a banner for the peoples; the nations will rally to him, and his place of rest will be glorious';[9] and when, in the language of Paul, new branches are grafted into the olive tree (Rom. 11:17–21). As mediator of salvation, all authority 'in heaven and on earth' has been given to Jesus, and through his heralds he summons the nations to repentance and submission to that authority (Matt. 28:18–19). Satan can deceive them no more.

This does not mean that he is inactive through the thousand years. His wickedness is still evident and he continues to lie and destroy as he has always done. All that the devil now does, however, is the expression of his frustration and fury as he sees a people of God – a new humanity – being created from the nations and yet is powerless to stop it (Rev. 12:17). It is that powerlessness in the face of the fulfilment of God's invincible purpose through Christ which constitutes his imprisonment in the abyss.[10]

2. Deceiving the nations (20:7–9a)

When the thousand years are over, Satan will be released from his prison and will go out to deceive the nations (7).

John foresees a moment towards the end of the present age when Satan will be freed such that he is once again able to deceive the nations. Clearly the text indicates that Satan does not free himself and somehow escape the constraint imposed upon him by the angel. The author's use of the passive voice, *Satan will be released* (7), indicates divine agency. Satan's liberation and final period of activity take place, as is true of everything he does, in the context of God's sovereign decree. God liberates him and allows him once more to deceive the nations.

a. Deceiving the nations

The text suggests that there are two dimensions of Satan's renewed activity. First, he *will go out to deceive the nations in the four corners of the earth* (8). The range of his activity is the entire world and all nations are touched; he will be able to deceive them just as he had done before the coming of Christ. The words indicate a closing down of the gospel age as materialism and hedonism, false gods and secular

---

[8] Gen. 12:3.
[9] Isa. 11:10.
[10] For a much fuller discussion of the issues raised in this section see the commentaries, e.g. Beale, *Revelation*, pp. 972–1021.

ideologies, and the various emasculated forms of Christianity take hold of the minds of men and women. At the same time those movements of God's Spirit which have characterized and revitalized the church across the centuries come to an end. Given the power, the reach and the increasing pervasiveness of modern means of communication, it is not difficult to imagine how Satan might inspire the spread of utter godlessness and the smothering of gospel truth.

Nevertheless, Satan's apparent victory is not absolutely universal, for a remnant of faithful believers remains, *the camp of God's people, the city he loves* (9). This is not to be understood as a literal city or camp, but as a reference to the church, God's own chosen people, small in number but faithful. The language used – *the camp of God's people* – recalls the Israelites crossing the desert as they progressed to the Promised Land, a people who 'do not have [here] an enduring city, but . . . are looking for the city that is to come'.[11] And so too, they are in themselves the city God loves – not constituted of buildings but of his own redeemed people later to be revealed in all their glory and beauty as the new Jerusalem (Rev. 21:1 – 22:5).

b. Gathering the nations for battle

Accordingly, second, not only does Satan deceive the nations but he also gathers them for battle against the camp and the city which it is ever his purpose to destroy. He is still intent on making war against the woman and her offspring (Rev. 12:17), and this is the final act of the drama. The reference to Gog and Magog recalls Ezekiel 38 – 39; Gog is king of Magog and both here and in apocalyptic writings they are symbolic of the nations and their rulers in their opposition to God and his people, and so essentially identical with the beast from the sea (Rev. 13:1-8).[12] The picture presented in Revelation 20, then, is one of immense massed forces physically gathered together by Satan from the whole earth in preparation for pitched battle with *the camp of God's people, the city he loves*. Although the language is that of conventional military warfare, what is being described is rather the onslaught of satanically inspired human power structures against the church which exists in their midst. What distinguishes it from former persecutions is that this time the attack is truly worldwide and there is universal participation. No state remains to take in Christian refugees fleeing persecution, or even to defend freedom of religion and speak up for the beleaguered people of God.

---

[11] Heb. 13:14.
[12] L. Morris, *Revelation: An Introduction and Commentary*, Tyndale NT Commentaries (Nottingham: Inter-Varsity Press, 1987), p. 227.

Meanwhile, all the means of modern media facilitate the carrying on of this battle at the level of the mind, while Gog and Magog utilize state power to impose their will and crush all resistance. Governments pass legislation outlawing every authentic expression of faith; their judicial systems impose increasingly restrictive and punitive laws against the church and its members; and participation in both society and economy becomes ever more problematic for those who seek to maintain a faithful witness to Christ.

The vision that Revelation presents here, of a final and apparently overwhelming eruption of godlessness and persecution in which Satan seems at last to have won, reflects ideas found elsewhere in the New Testament and with roots indeed in the Old. In his first epistle John speaks of a coming Antichrist, echoes of whom were already present in his own time: 'Dear children, this is the last hour; and as you have heard that the antichrist is coming, even now many antichrists have come. This is how we know it is the last hour.'[13] Similarly, Paul speaks of 'the man of lawlessness' who must come before the return of the Lord Jesus Christ, who will himself destroy him:

> That day will not come until the rebellion occurs and the man of lawlessness is revealed ... He will oppose and will exalt himself over everything that is called God or is worshipped ... whom the Lord Jesus will overthrow with the breath of his mouth and destroy by the splendour of his coming.[14]

And, of course, the Lord Jesus Christ himself spoke of 'false Christs and false prophets' performing signs and miracles 'to deceive even the elect – if that were possible', and of 'the distress of those days' immediately prior to his return.[15]

3. The final battle (20:9b–10)

There is a striking anticlimax at the heart of John's description of the battle. In verses 7–9 he conveys a picture of the steady and apparently overwhelming build-up of Satan's huge forces for the final annihilation of God's people. It conjures up images of Alexander moving across Asia or Hitler preparing the invasion of Russia, a deployment of force unbelievably awesome in extent and terrifying to behold. Surely, the climax of such a massive mobilization will be a great battle

---

[13] 1 John 2:18.
[14] 2 Thess. 2:3–4, 8.
[15] Matt. 24:24, 29.

with huge manoeuvres and stratagems, alongside individual tales of conflict and heroism. But it is not like that at all. God simply destroys those who conspire to destroy his people, and the extreme brevity of John's description, especially noticeable in a book filled with imagery and graphic description, underlines the comprehensiveness – and indeed the utter effortlessness – of the total victory that takes place. *But fire came down from heaven and devoured them* (9b): that is all it took. It is a supreme act of absolute, transcendent and effortless divine sovereignty. It is equally the climactic biblical portrayal of Satan's ultimate powerlessness in the face of the omnipotence of the Lord God Almighty.

Moreover, the whole chapter makes this same point. At the beginning of Revelation 20 it is an angel and not God himself who seizes, binds and imprisons Satan, just as in Revelation 12 it is an angel, Michael, who expels him from heaven. 'The final unimportance of Satan is perhaps indicated in the fact that it is not the Father who deals with him, nor the Christ, but only an unnamed angel.'[16] Then, as we have noted, Satan does not escape from his confinement but it is God who liberates him and allows him to engage in one final explosion of rebellion. This vision of the end, therefore, reminds the hard-pressed readers of Revelation that final victory is absolutely assured. God directs the events of time, and Satan's activities never for a moment move beyond divine control. Even the total mobilization of all the forces of evil, both human and demonic, is as nothing in the face of him who reigns in glory. 'The One enthroned in heaven laughs; the LORD scoffs at them.'[17]

So, in literal terms, what actually happens? The apocalyptic nature of the language forbids precise definition but the picture is one of ever-increasing pressure on the church, probably not unlike the massive empire-wide persecution of Christians in the Roman Empire in the second half of the third century, especially under Diocletian (284–305) and Galerius (305–11). Nor will it be unlike what is taking place in our own time as we witness the persecution of Christian believers on a huge global scale. 'Christians are the single most widely persecuted religious group in the world today.'[18] This need not mean that we are even now living through Satan's final deception; throughout its history the church has been subject to recurrent waves of persecution. Nevertheless, the sufferings of twenty-first-century Christians because they are Christians is

[16] Morris, *Revelation*, pp. 223–224.
[17] Ps. 2:4.
[18] P. Marshall, L. Gilbert and N. Shea, *Persecuted: The Global Assault on Christians* (Nashville: Thomas Nelson, 2013), p. 4.

'massive, widespread, increasing and still underreported'.[19] A recent article in *The Spectator* drew attention to the situation. 'According to the Pew Forum, between 2006 and 2010 Christians faced some form of discrimination, either de jure or de facto, in a staggering total of 139 nations, which is almost three-quarters of all the countries on earth.'[20] At worst they are 'tortured, raped, imprisoned or killed'. Alternatively they may suffer 'more bureaucratic methods of abuse' including denial of access to jobs or education. And their church buildings may be bulldozed, burned down or simply seized.[21]

> Orissa was the scene of the most violent anti-Christian pogrom of the early 21st century. In 2008, a series of riots ended with as many as 500 Christians killed, many hacked to death by machete-wielding Hindu radicals; thousands more were injured and at least 50,000 left homeless . . . An estimated 5,000 Christian homes, along with 350 churches and schools, were destroyed.[22]

And examples could be multiplied: Nigeria, Burma, North Korea and so on.[23]

The text of Revelation suggests an ever-growing intensity of persecution, and a gathering or focusing of forces to strike the final blow: *They marched across the breadth of the earth and surrounded the camp of God's people . . .* (9). It is at this point when persecution has reached an apparently overwhelming crescendo that God intervenes. On the one hand his intervention is about the deliverance of his own people. Apparently faced with imminent obliteration from the face of the earth, they are rescued. On the other hand, the immense forces arrayed against them are brought to nothing – indeed, they are brought to judgment. It is certainly the moment of the return of Christ and his visible and physical assumption of sovereignty over the whole earth. Which raises further questions.

4. A double narrative

In Revelation 19:11–21 the Lord Jesus Christ comes with 'the armies of heaven' to do battle. His purpose is to strike down the nations which he will rule 'with an iron sceptre', a reference to Psalm 2 which at the same time recalls the mission of the child who was born to the

---

[19] Marshall et al., *Persecuted*, p. 9.

[20] J. L. Allen, 'The War on Christians', *The Spectator* (5 October 2013), at <http://www.spectator.co.uk/2013/10/the-war-on-christians/>, accessed 29 February 2016.

[21] Marshall et al., *Persecuted*, p. 7.

[22] Allen, 'The War on Christians'.

[23] See Marshall et al., *Persecuted*, passim.

woman in Revelation 12:5. Indeed, he comes in judgment, to 'tread the winepress of the fury of the wrath of God Almighty'.[24] The nations, however, determine to resist him, and 'the beast and the kings of the earth and their armies'[25] gather to make war against him. But they are rapidly and easily overcome.

Accordingly, each of chapters 19 and 20 records a judgment of God or Christ against those who oppose them; in Revelation 19 it is the beast and the nations and then in Revelation 20 it is Satan and, again, the nations. These are often seen as two different moments, the first preceding and the second following the 'thousand years' when Satan is bound in the abyss. Such a view has plausibility, assuming as it does that the narrative of Revelation is essentially linear with the events described succeeding one another in chronological progression. There is good reason, however, to suppose that the text of Revelation is constructed rather more subtly than that, and that the author frequently employs a cyclical structure rather than a linear one. For example, the three series of seven – the seven seals, the seven angels with their seven trumpets, and the seven angels with their seven plagues – can readily be seen as parallel to one another rather than successive, each of them spanning 'the entire gospel age' and each climaxing with scenes of final judgment.[26]

In the same way, there are numerous similarities between the two accounts of the judgment of God's enemies in Revelation 19 and 20, which suggest that these two narratives may also be parallel rather than consecutive. First, and obviously, both record a divine act of judgment against the enemies of God, both human and supernatural. Second, in both cases the nations are involved in rebellion and suffer defeat. Third, in Revelation 20 Satan inspires the nations in their rebellion, while in Revelation 19 it is the beast who does so, but this beast is itself Satan's creature which, earlier in Revelation, he had called forth from the sea: 'And the dragon stood on the shore of the sea. And I saw a beast coming out of the sea.'[27] Fourth, in Revelation 19 the 'false prophet', which first appears in Revelation 13 as the beast 'coming out of the earth',[28] uses signs to delude 'those who had received the mark of the beast and worshipped his image';[29] in the context these people must surely be identified as the nations that are being led out to battle. Meanwhile, in Revelation 20 it is Satan himself

[24] Rev. 19:15.
[25] Rev. 19:19.
[26] See e.g., W. Hendriksen, *More Than Conquerors: An Interpretation of the Book of Revelation* (Grand Rapids: Baker, 1962), p. 17.
[27] Rev. 13:1.
[28] Rev. 13:11.
[29] Rev. 19:20.

who deceives the nations. Fifth, in both chapters the writer describes a massive build-up before the battle and then, in both cases, the conflict is all over in an instant when the nations and their leaders are overthrown in a single mighty act of divine sovereignty, exercised either by Christ or from heaven. And sixth, in both cases the inspirers of rebellion are finally thrown into 'the fiery lake of burning sulphur'.[30] There are therefore very substantial grounds for supposing that the two accounts describe the same event although with differing emphases and detail. The sequence would not, then, be a chronological one, but a sequence of visions rather than of events, with each vision bringing its own contribution to an understanding of one single event, the great and final eschatological battle.[31]

Accordingly, the vision of Revelation 19 emphasizes the role of Christ in the battle. It is his coming – his return and parousia – which precipitates the closing stages of this present age and the final defeat of all the enemies of God and his people. And he comes to the battle as the great mediator of salvation, with robes dipped in a blood which is surely his own (Rev. 19:13) and which signifies his right and his worthiness (cf. Rev. 5:9) to perform the culminating act of the salvation which he accomplished at the cross.[32] In his coming he subjugates the rebellious nations and establishes his messianic rule over them 'with an iron sceptre' (Ps. 2:9; Rev. 12:5). He also defeats for ever the beast and the 'false prophet', the two beasts of Revelation 13. The identity of these beasts has been exhaustively discussed over the centuries. Both are creatures of Satan. The beast from the sea is apparently a representation of the violence of state power, brutally and apparently irresistibly turned against God's people (Rev. 13:2–7), while the beast from the earth – the false prophet – inspires worship of the beast from the sea (Rev. 13:12). They may best be understood as a repeated manifestation of the opposition to God and his people from the state, on the one hand, and its religious or ideological machinery, on the other; at the time John was writing, Rome and the religious support it enjoyed were the obvious visible embodiments of the beasts. They will come to climactic expression, however, with the release of the dragon from his thousand-year imprisonment. As we noted above, in his first epistle John speaks similarly of the coming of the Antichrist, anticipations of which were, however, already visible in his own day (1 John 2:18).

Meanwhile, the vision of Revelation 20 emphasizes the absolute transcendence of the divine victory, viewing it as an act of sovereign

[30] Rev. 19:20; 20:10.
[31] See Beale, *Revelation*, pp. 974–976.
[32] C. Rowland, *The Open Heaven* (London: SPCK, 1982), p. 434.

judgment carried out from the very throne of God. It focuses on the defeat of Satan himself as the ultimate instigator of the rebellion of the nations, rather than on the beasts as the earthly vehicles by which that rebellion is brought about. And it identifies the divine victory over evil as being also the moment when God's people, surrounded by the immense forces raised against them by Satan, experience a definitive and complete deliverance from all their enemies.

5. Eternal punishment

Finally, the devil and the two beasts are thrown all three *into the lake of burning sulphur* (20:10; 19:20). In their rebellion they had set themselves up as a trinity of evil, a hideous parody of Father, Son and Holy Spirit, and as such had deceived humanity into offering to themselves the adoration which is due to the triune God alone.[33] It is therefore as deceivers – and Satan, especially, as 'a liar and the father of lies' from the moment of his first appearance in Eden at the very beginning of history – that they experience final punishment. The notion of throwing a spirit such as Satan into a lake of burning sulphur must of course be understood figuratively, but the reality signified by this *lake of burning sulphur*, a reality which is doubtless beyond human experience and language, is clearly a terrible punishment and one consistent with the unspeakable treachery and malignity of the devil and of all the forces of wickedness he deployed. Moreover, John explicitly affirms that such condign punishment must last for ever: *day and night, for ever and ever* (10). Satan and the beasts are not destroyed or annihilated. With their total defeat in the last battle they are indeed unable further to challenge the sovereignty of Almighty God, to trouble his people and to deceive the nations, but they are also condemned to eternal conscious punishment. One might see a problem here with regard to the beasts, which we have understood as structures and institutions, but those institutions were themselves 'composed of people, so what an institution suffers, that also the people composing the institution will suffer'.[34] Satan and the beasts he raised up to do his will never cease to exist and to experience the dire consequences of their rebellion.

And in all of this God is glorified. Finally, through the work of the Son the whole cosmos is reconciled in that all is brought, willingly or unwillingly, into submission to the Creator. 'At the name of Jesus

---

[33] See e.g., G. R. Beasley-Murray, *Revelation*, 2nd edn (London: Marshall, Morgan and Scott and Grand Rapids: Eerdmans, 1981), p. 207.

[34] Beale, *Revelation*, p. 1029. See also D. A. Carson, *The Gagging of God: Christianity Confronts Pluralism* (Leicester: Apollos, 1996), p. 527.

every knee' will bow and 'every tongue confess' that he is Lord.[35] At the same time divine justice is at last totally vindicated. From a frail and finite human perspective the 'mills of God' may indeed 'grind slowly' but at the end of the story the outcome is one of perfect justice. And not only is justice accomplished but salvation is completed as God's people experience total deliverance from the enemy of their souls and all his works. For in the new heaven and new earth there is 'no longer any sea'.[36] In Ancient Near Eastern mythology the sea was perceived as a force of chaos and evil. While the biblical account of creation categorically repudiates such an idea, John exploits the symbolism to declare that in the new creation no evil nor any source of evil can be found – whether Satan, demons, beasts or rebellious humanity. The victory of the Lamb is complete.

> In that day,
> the LORD will punish with his sword,
>   his fierce, great and powerful sword,
> Leviathan the gliding serpent,
>   Leviathan the coiling serpent;
> he will slay the monster of the sea.
>
> In that day –
> 'Sing about a fruitful vineyard:
>   I, the LORD, watch over it;
>   I water it continually.
> I guard it day and night
>   so that no one may harm it.'[37]

[35] Phil. 2:10–11.
[36] Rev. 21:1.
[37] Isa. 27:1–3.

132

Part 3
Liberated and liberating

Colossians 1:13–14
11. Delivered from the darkness

The Slavery Abolition Act passed through the British House of Commons in the summer of 1833. It emancipated some 800,000 slaves throughout most of the British Empire at the huge cost of 20 million pounds to the national exchequer.[1] It was a hugely significant moment, a massive step towards the correction of unspeakable injustices and cruelty that had been perpetrated and sustained over centuries.

The point Paul makes in Colossians 1:13–14 is that in Christ God has brought about the emancipation of his people from the spiritual slavery they had experienced, an act vastly more momentous than anything a merely human government could achieve and, what is more, carried out at infinitely greater cost. He rescued them *from the dominion of darkness*.

1. Giving thanks

Normally the letters Paul wrote to churches begin with an account of his prayers on their behalf, in which he expresses both his gratitude for what God had already accomplished among them and his requests for their ongoing growth to maturity. In Colossians, having thanked God for the faith and love of the believers, Paul goes on to ask him to give them a knowledge of his will so that they might live worthily of him and please him 'in every way'. Using four participles

---

[1] The 2015 equivalent of £20,000,000 would obviously be much higher but over such a length of time the calculation is not simple. At its highest, in terms of economic power relative to the total output of the economy, it would be worth over 80 billion pounds. A simple standard of living equivalent would be closer to 1.7 billion pounds. See 'Five Ways to Compute the Relative Value of a UK Pound Amount, 1270 to Present', at <http://www.measuringworth.com/ukcompare/>, accessed 27 November 2015.

he specifies four particular ways in which such God-pleasing lives should be evident:

> Bearing fruit in every good work, growing in the knowledge of God, being strengthened with all power according to his glorious might so that you may have great endurance and patience, and joyfully giving thanks to the Father, who has qualified you to share in the inheritance of the saints in the kingdom of light.[2]

The concern of the final petition, 'joyfully giving thanks', reverberates throughout the epistle.[3] The Colossian believers should be thankful people just as Paul was. However, it is here in his prayer report that Paul explains what in particular the Colossians should be thankful for, namely that God had qualified them 'to share in the inheritance of the saints in the kingdom of light'. And in verses 13–14 he goes on to tell them how God did that: *For he has rescued us from the dominion of darkness and brought us into the kingdom of the Son he loves, in whom we have redemption, the forgiveness of sins.*

The frequency of encouragements to thankfulness throughout Colossians, its inclusion here in Paul's prayer and the many references to it in his other letters[4] all indicate how important the theme was in his thinking and theology. The reason is that gratitude is the indispensable counterpart of any true experience of grace – it is 'the flip side of a key Pauline theological claim: that Christians are saved by and live in grace'.[5] So here, the reason for which the Colossians should thank God is his mercy in rescuing them from darkness and bringing them into the kingdom of his Son. From beginning to end it is all God's doing through Christ, and brought about at infinite cost to himself. As such the only possible response on the part of his people must be one of sheer rejoicing gratitude. The authors of the Heidelberg Catechism (1563) captured the significance of this theme in their identification of the three things that a Christian must know in order to enjoy the comfort of the gospel: 'The first, how great my sins and miseries are; the second, how I may be delivered from all my sins and miseries; the third, how I shall express my gratitude to God for such deliverance.'[6] The first and

---

[2] Col. 1:10–12.

[3] Col. 1:3, 12; 2:7; 3:15, 16, 17; 4:2.

[4] E.g. Rom. 6:17; 1 Cor. 1:4; 10:16; 15:57; 2 Cor. 2:14; 9:12, 15; Eph. 5:20; Phil. 1:3; 1 Thess. 2:13; 3:9; 5:18; etc.

[5] D. J. Moo, *The Letters to the Colossians and to Philemon*, Pillar NT Commentary (Grand Rapids: Eerdmans, 2008), p. 100.

[6] R. F. Lay, *Readings in Historical Theology: Primary Sources of the Christian Faith* (Grand Rapids: Kregel, 2009), p. 227.

then the constant response of every believer to the experience of salvation is to give thanks to its author. 'Thanks be to God for his indescribable gift!'[7]

2. The dominion of darkness

Christians give thanks, then, first of all because they have been rescued *from the dominion of darkness*. There is a powerful echo here of Exodus 6:6–8 where God rescues his people from the land of slavery and oppression, also by redeeming them, and then brings them into the land promised to their forefathers.[8] Paul is speaking, then, of a new exodus, but one that has taken place at an altogether different level. It is not from one earthly realm to another, but from the *dominion of darkness* where evil, sin and Satan dominate, to 'the kingdom of light' where God's own Son is king.[9]

a. The dominion of darkness in heavenly places

The *dominion of darkness* embraces all that resists God and is characterized by wickedness, falsehood and folly. Implicit in the phrase there is also the suggestion of tyranny and of the consequent enslavement of human beings held captive by it. It consists first of all of those whom Jesus referred to as 'the devil and his angels',[10] and Paul identifies as 'the spiritual forces of evil in the heavenly realms'.[11] The Bible gives little detail, however, about the nature of this dominion of 'spiritual forces of evil' and we should be wary about imagining it in terms of some 'highly complex organizational structure'.[12] Peter Bolt argues, indeed, that there is no reason to suppose the evil powers would have 'a high degree of organization at all': 'God is the god of order, but why wouldn't Satan's domain be totally chaotic, random and directionless?'[13]

The New Testament testimony suggests, however, that this may be overstating the case. When Jesus responded to those who accused him of driving out unclean spirits by Beelzebub, 'the prince of demons', he implicitly confirmed their assumption that Satan is indeed 'prince' of a demonic realm. Far from denouncing the idea,

---

[7] 2 Cor. 9:15.
[8] Moo, *Colossians and Philemon*, p. 103.
[9] Col. 1:12.
[10] Matt. 25:41.
[11] Eph. 6:12.
[12] P. G. Bolt, 'Towards a Biblical Theology of the Defeat of the Evil Powers', in P. G. Bolt (ed.), *Christ's Victory over Evil: Biblical Theology and Pastoral Ministry* (Nottingham: Apollos, 2009), p. 64.
[13] Bolt, 'Towards a Biblical Theology of the Defeat of the Evil Powers', p. 65.

he pointed out its logical implication ('How can Satan drive out Satan?'); and he went on to speak in terms of a kingdom: 'if a kingdom is divided against itself, that kingdom cannot stand'. His words indicate that Satan is indeed ruler of a kingdom of unclean spirits, such that the possession of a human being by a demon is in reality an act of Satan, and that the oppression and suffering which demons inflict comes ultimately from him (Mark 3:23–27).[14]

So, while evil by its very nature may no doubt possess an inherently violent, warring and divided quality, the 'darkness' nevertheless constitutes a single entity under a single head. As with the fragmented world of men and women it is no doubt drawn together by Satan's power and guile, but much more than that it is united by a common hatred towards the great enemy against whom it wars, the Lord God Almighty. Just as 'the kings of the earth take their stand and the rulers gather together against the LORD and against his Anointed One',[15] divided and mutually hostile though they invariably are, even so do the spiritual powers of darkness also 'take their stand and . . . gather together' against the Lord God and his Christ. It is this above all which gives to the darkness both on earth and in heaven its nature as a single 'dominion of darkness' – literally 'the authority of darkness',[16] despite the bitter internal hatreds and wars that characterize the men and women, peoples and nations and, no doubt, powers and demons that belong to it.

b. The dominion of darkness on earth

For the *dominion of darkness* consists not only of evil and rebellious spiritual powers. In Pauline terms human sin itself – the 'flesh' – is an existential power which also holds its prisoners captive: 'the sinful mind [literally, 'the mind of the flesh'] is hostile to God. It does not submit to God's law, nor can it do so'.[17] Indeed, in Ephesians 5:8 Paul even tells his readers that they themselves were 'once darkness' – not just that they were in darkness; they represented 'that dominion in their own persons'.[18] For sin brings the loss of full humanness for men and women and enslaves them. It is not just that they do bad things. Made to live in communion with the God who is source of all life, rebellion and the alienation it brings mean that their humanity itself – their very nature as human beings – is grievously diminished

---

[14] See also Luke 10:17–18 and discussion above on pp. 93–94.
[15] Ps. 2:2.
[16] *hē exousia tou skotous.*
[17] Rom. 8:7.
[18] P. T. O'Brien, *The Letter to the Ephesians*, Pillar NT Commentary (Grand Rapids: Eerdmans and Leicester: Apollos, 1999), p. 367.

and disfigured. Although by common grace they still enjoy many of the blessings of creation (Matt. 5:45; Acts 14:17), their experience is one of darkness characterized by enslavement to 'all kinds of passions and pleasures',[19] as well as to Satan and to the mind of the fallen world. At the very heart of their being sinful men and women are indeed darkness.

The 'world' too, humanity as a whole united in rebellion against its creator, forms part of the darkness as men and women blindly 'follow the ways of this world'[20] and are gripped by its godless values, lusts and ambitions (1 John 2:15–17). And repeatedly the New Testament declares that Satan, the lord of darkness, exercises rule over the world of rebellious humanity. In Acts 26:17–18, speaking of his call to apostleship, Paul expresses this through two parallel phrases which indicate an equivalence between the 'darkness' and the 'power of Satan': 'I am sending you to them to open their eyes and turn them from darkness to light, and from the power of Satan to God.'[21] Meanwhile, in the words of Jesus Christ Satan is 'the prince of this world';[22] for Paul he is 'the god of this age',[23] 'the spirit who is now at work in those who are disobedient' and the one whom they follow;[24] and John tells his readers that 'the whole world is under the control of the evil one',[25] the one 'who leads the whole world astray'.[26] 'The power of darkness is the power of Satan, and the apostle's language [in Col. 1:13] reminds us that the dark and satanic not only influence, but control us.'[27]

So, the Colossians, and Paul himself before his encounter with Christ, had been part of this *dominion of darkness* – the darkness constituted by their own sins with all that that entails in terms of pain, despair and death; the darkness of an instinctive solidarity in rebellion with the rest of fallen humanity; and the darkness of subjection to the tyranny of Satan – the liar, tempter, accuser and murderer – and all the spiritual forces of 'darkness'. It is a bleak picture and a hopeless one but for the intervention of God.

---

[19] Titus 3:3.

[20] Eph. 2:2.

[21] Page points out how close the language here is to that of Col. 1:13–14. S. H. T. Page, *Powers of Evil: A Biblical Study of Satan and Demons* (Grand Rapids: Baker and Leicester: Apollos, 1995), p. 134, n. 170.

[22] John 12:31; 14:30; 16:11.

[23] 2 Cor. 4:4.

[24] Eph. 2:2.

[25] 1 John 5:19.

[26] Rev. 12:9.

[27] D. Macleod, *Christ Crucified: Understanding the Atonement* (Nottingham: Inter-Varsity Press, 2014), p. 225.

3. Rescue

But God had rescued them, doing what they were totally unable to do for themselves – unable, indeed, even to recognize that it needed to be done. Paul writes that the rescue consisted in a transfer to *the kingdom of the Son he loves*, to which we return later; and then, finally and very briefly, explains how it was brought about: *in whom we have redemption, the forgiveness of sins* (14).

As he clarifies the nature of God's deliverance the words Paul uses are few but rich in meaning. First, the Colossians' emancipation from the *dominion of darkness* is an act of rescue. They had been imprisoned but now God has freed them. He has sprung them from the prison in which they were held. Second, the nature of that rescue is one of redemption. The notion of redemption is found throughout the Bible and for its first-century readers it would suggest the liberation of a slave or prisoner from servitude by means of the payment of a ransom. So God too rescues those enslaved to darkness by redeeming them with a ransom. But, third, that word *redemption* is immediately followed by the phrase *the forgiveness of sins*, which defines its nature. Their redemption consisted in having their sins forgiven by the one against whom those sins had been committed. And then, finally, Paul identifies Christ – *the Son he loves* – as the one in whom all this had taken place. He is the sin-bearer in whom the Colossians had found the forgiveness which constituted their redemption and consequent rescue.

a. Implications

Numerous implications flow from Paul's brief explanation. First, clearly it was their own sins that had bound the Colossians in the dominion of darkness. If they are freed from the darkness by the forgiveness of their sins, then it was evidently those sins which caused their enslavement in the first place and made them part of the darkness where Satan holds sway. Once again, therefore, men and women are not just unhappy victims of Satan and spiritual beings too strong for them, but they are themselves responsible for the bondage which they suffer. Second, the ruler of the dominion of darkness and his accomplices are therefore able to enslave and tyrannize humanity only as a result of their own sins. They are parasitic, exploiting the guilt of a fallen human race in order to oppress and ultimately destroy them, which is indeed the real and final goal of the darkness. Third, then, the forgiveness of sins made possible through the death of Christ not only deals with the sinners' guilt and condemnation, but also rescues them from bondage to the spiritual rulers who feed off those sins.

Finally, however, it must be noted that the ransom Christ paid by his own atoning death, which brings about the deliverance of sinful men and women, is by no means paid to Satan and the powers as was argued by some in the early church. The death of Christ was not a payment that they received – 'a price in some sense taken by Satan'[28] – but a defeat that they suffered (Col. 2:15). They are rebellious usurpers without rights, claims or legitimacy, and under the divine curse (Gen. 3:14); it is inconceivable that God would pay them off with the sacrifice of his Son. Not only that but, according to the Gospels, far from pursuing a ransom Satan is 'intent on opposing the solemn resolve of Christ to give his life as "a ransom for many"'.[29] God vanquished Satan, not by paying him a ransom, but 'by removing the guilt and dominion of sin that made his reign possible'.[30] The removal of that sin and the liberation of the sinners certainly took place at vast cost to God, but 'he pays it to himself, because it is to himself that the debt is owed'.[31]

All of this ties up, of course, with Paul's explanation of the defeat of the 'powers and authorities' later in the epistle.[32] There Paul describes how at the cross the bond (*cheirographon*) which testified to the sinners' debt was effaced, removed and nailed to the cross, as a result of which the powers were disarmed of that which had empowered them and thereby defeated. There the great act of redemption from Satan's power was accomplished – the battle was won. But now, here in Colossians 1:13–14, Paul explains how that one great and unrepeatable act of redemption at Calvary had been worked out in the lives of these particular Colossian believers – and, indeed, of himself. To put it another way, here in Colossians 1:13–14 Paul reminds the Colossians of what happened in their own personal lives and experience when they were rescued; in Colossians 2:13–15 he explains rather more fully how the work of Christ had brought that rescue about.

[28] N. Dimock, *The Doctrine of the Death of Christ in Relation to the Sin of Man, the Condemnation of the Law, and the Dominion of Satan*, 2nd edn (London: Elliot Stock, 1903), p. 127. While recognizing that some of the church Fathers did not express themselves well on the matter, Dimock claims that there is some truth in the idea that a ransom was paid to Satan and argues the case.

[29] S. B. Ferguson, 'Christus Victor et Propitiator: The Death of Christ, Substitute and Conqueror', in S. Storms and J. Taylor (eds.), *For the Fame of God's Name: Essays in Honor of John Piper* (Wheaton: Crossway, 2010), p. 178.

[30] Ibid., p. 183.

[31] Macleod, *Christ Crucified*, p. 235.

[32] Col. 2:15. See ch. 8 above.

b. Galatians and Ephesians

There are clear echoes of the theme of Colossians 1:13–14 elsewhere in Paul's writings too. In Galatians 1:4, for example, the Lord Jesus Christ 'gave himself for our sins to rescue us from the present evil age, according to the will of our God and Father'. Implicit here is the notion of the two ages, of which the present age is evil and subject to Satan, himself 'the god of this age',[33] and to all the powers of darkness. Thus, 'the present evil age' in Galatians 1:4 equates closely to the *dominion of darkness* in Colossians 1:13. And Paul assures his Galatian readers that Christ had rescued them from it by giving himself 'for our sins'. Again, rescue from this age, of which Satan is the god, is secured by Christ's giving himself – dying – for our sins, because it is those sins which have brought about the enslavement to this age in the first place.

The argument of Ephesians 2:1–10 echoes the same thinking. Here Paul explains that human beings are dead in *their own* 'transgressions and sins', and are 'children of wrath' (ESV) because of the gratification of *their own* sinful natures. Accordingly salvation consists in God's making such people alive with Christ, 'even when we were dead in transgressions'. However, Paul also speaks here of Satan's power over lost human beings: he 'is at work in those who are disobedient' and the Ephesians themselves formerly 'followed the ways . . . of the ruler of the kingdom of the air'.[34] It is that very condition of disobedience that gives Satan his opportunity to be 'at work' in rebellious, godless humanity, as he exploits their fallen spiritual and moral state and so brings them into servitude to himself. Therefore, Paul also tells his readers that when God makes sinners alive with Christ, at that very same moment he also frees them from Satan. He explains that the risen Christ is now seated 'far above all rule and authority, power and dominion',[35] and then that God has also 'seated us with him in the heavenly realms in Christ Jesus'.[36] In other words, redeemed sinners share in Christ's own triumph over Satan and the powers; they have been liberated from them by virtue of their redemption from sin in Christ. As they are no longer in a state of 'disobedience', they are freed from Satan's grasp.

---

[33] 2 Cor. 4:4.

[34] The phrase, 'the ruler of the kingdom of the air', is another title for Satan. The 'air' was seen as the 'dwelling place of evil spirits', and so equates with 'the heavenly realms' in Eph. 6:12. See O'Brien, *Ephesians*, p. 160.

[35] Eph. 1:21.

[36] Eph. 2:6. See below, pp. 151–154.

4. The kingdom of the Son he loves

Believers are redeemed *from* the darkness, but it does not stop there. They are also brought *into* the light: *he has ... brought us into the kingdom of the Son he loves* (13). Redemption is not merely a negative cancellation of sin and all its consequences, but also the entry into a whole new reality.

a. A new identity

The first thing that Paul's language underlines is the truly radical change that takes place in the life and identity of those whom God has rescued, as they undergo a transfer from darkness to light. The utterly fundamental character of the transformation is expressed throughout the New Testament in a number of striking antitheses. Conversion is the passage from death to life (Eph. 2:1–6), from blindness to sight (2 Cor. 4:4–6) and, of course, from darkness to light (Col. 1:12–13; Eph. 5:8). It is a wholly new identity, for 'once you were not a people, but now you are the people of God; once you had not received mercy, but now you have received mercy';[37] it means that 'if anyone is in Christ, he is a new creation; the old has gone, the new has come!'.[38] Perhaps the strongest expression of the antithesis is John's distinction between 'the children of God' and 'the children of the devil'.[39] These are polar opposites between which there is no continuity, no point of convergence, no fellowship. Indeed, 'what fellowship can light have with darkness?'[40] One obvious missiological implication is that non-Christian religions and philosophies can scarcely be seen as preparation for the gospel,[41] as if followers of Christ have merely moved rather further along a road they were already treading before their conversion. The appalling situation of human beings without Christ, and so 'without God and without hope in the world',[42] demands radical rescue and redemption which can only be known through the cross of the sin-bearing Son of God.

b. A new freedom

Transfer into *the kingdom of the Son* also brings freedom to those so redeemed. Of course, they are now God's own possession, bought

---

[37] 1 Pet. 2:10.
[38] 2 Cor. 5:17.
[39] 1 John 3:10.
[40] 2 Cor. 6:14.
[41] *Praeparatio evangelica*.
[42] Eph. 2:12.

by him at the price of the blood of his Son (1 Cor. 6:19–20), but that means restoration to what God created them for. They become fully *human* beings, with a humanity restored to what God intended it to be. Their profound inner alienation and dislocation, their blindness, their spiritual lostness and hopelessness, the darkness, are all gone. Transfer to the kingdom of the Son restores fellowship with the Father out of which alone a truly *human* life can flow. It means that redeemed human beings are freed from enslavement to their own sinful natures, and the marred and ravaged image of God which they bear is progressively renewed as they are 'conformed to the likeness of his Son'.[43] The great commandments, to love God and neighbour, are no longer threat and condemnation but promise and possibility. They are liberated from darkness to live truly human lives in willing and delighted submission to the Lord Jesus Christ, the king of the kingdom and head of a new humanity. As God's new creation they are able to resist Satan and the world. They do not yet enjoy sinless perfection but they have been set free from the slavery that sin and Satan imposed. All things have become new, and they 'may live a new life'.[44]

c. A new imperative

Redemption from darkness and into light brings with it an obligation. The new being – the new identity and freedom of believers – must become a reality in the totality of their lives. Although the kingdom of God's Son has come, and those he has rescued are already a part of it, the dominion of darkness remains a potent presence. The rescue of the redeemed from its power and their transfer to the kingdom of God's Son does not mean physical removal from the sphere in which it operates. They live still in a fallen world, in pagan cities like Ephesus, Corinth and Colosse, and so their daily lives continue to be carried on in the presence of that very darkness they had been freed from. They face the constant determination of Satan to undermine their Christian lives and witness. And there is an ongoing and bitter struggle with the sinful pull of the old nature which remains active even though defeated. The epistle to the Colossians and much of the rest of the New Testament were in large part written to exhort believers to live out in practice the life of *the kingdom of the Son* into which they had been transferred.

Later in his letter, therefore, Paul urges his readers to be active in putting 'to death . . . whatever belongs to your earthly nature'.[45] He

[43] Rom. 8:29.
[44] 2 Cor. 5:17; Rom. 6:4.
[45] Col. 3:5.

144

then goes on to tell them, 'as God's chosen people', to clothe themselves with those virtues which belong to the light (Col. 3:12–14). Both the negative and positive sides of the redemption they had experienced, rescued *from* the darkness and brought *into* the kingdom of the Son, demanded corresponding action on their part as they sought to eradicate all in themselves that had belonged to the darkness and actively embrace the character and deeds of the light. It is a bitter struggle, 'the hardest thing in the world because blinding darkness clings so closely'.[46] Nor is that all, for the world too seeks to coerce them into conformity to its beliefs and values and lifestyle, whether through the subtle social and cultural pressure that it exerts, or more directly by means of outright hostility, exclusion and persecution. Citizens of the kingdom of God's Son have become exiles and strangers in the world from which they were rescued, but which remains the everyday environment in which they live and can easily seem 'normal' to them. The daily, unremitting challenge is deliberately to embrace the life of the stranger (1 Pet. 1:1, 17; 2:11). So Paul warned the Colossian believers that the legalistic religious practices and asceticism they had been adopting actually represented a capitulation to the world from which they had been rescued and so a denial of the freedom they had found in Christ: 'Since you died with Christ to the basic principles of this world, why, as though you still belonged to it, do you submit to its rules?'[47] And behind all of this, whether the world or the flesh, stands Satan, luring, tempting, deceiving, persecuting – operating alternately as an angel of light (2 Cor. 11:14) or as the beast come from the abyss of hell (Rev. 11:7).

The reality of present Christian experience is characterized by a good deal of tension and struggle. Christians have, indeed, received already blessings beyond calculation, but at the same time they are confronted by the old age, the dominion of darkness, which threatens. They feel the heat – the fragility and too frequent waywardness of their own hearts, the pressure of a world that wants to steer them back into the ways of the darkness, and all the subtlety and guile of the tempter. Sometimes they doubt and fear and fail, but all the time they can be confident in hope, 'because the darkness is passing and the true light is already shining'.[48] And they belong to that light: for God *has rescued us from the dominion of darkness and brought us into the kingdom of the Son he loves.*

---

[46] D. Powlison, 'The Classical Model', in J. K. Beilby and P. R. Eddy (eds.), *Understanding Spiritual Warfare: Four Views* (Grand Rapids: Baker Academic, 2012), p. 98.
[47] Col. 2:20.
[48] 1 John 2:8.

Ephesians 1:19b – 2:7
12. Seated with Christ

However they may try to hide the fact, human beings are fearful creatures who battle constantly with a vast range of anxieties and insecurities – illness, death, bereavement, accident, redundancy, failure, homelessness, abandonment. And the list represents only the most obvious tip of a massive iceberg. Human fear is in fact one of the consequences of the fall. Alienated from their creator, men and women live out their short, uncertain lives in a universe that can be unpredictable and hostile, while simultaneously belonging to a race characterized by violence at every level from verbal to genocidal. They have reason to fear.

And in some ways the causes to fear apparently multiply for those who become people of God. As such they are rendered strangers and exiles in a world that lives in rebellion against him (1 Pet. 1:17; 2:11; Heb. 13:14), and become particular objects of the animosity of the 'dominion of darkness' from which they have been rescued (Col. 1:13). It is for this reason that the Bible again and again addresses the words, 'do not fear', to God's people. The first person to whom God spoke them was Abram, some time after he had fought the armies of four eastern kings when they captured his nephew, Lot: 'Do not be afraid, Abram. I am your shield, your very great reward.'[1] It was a word of encouragement to a man who had left his home and people at God's command, and who daily faced the insecurities and dangers of a semi-nomadic existence in the midst of potentially hostile neighbours, exemplified indeed in the recent conflict. Sometimes Abram's response to his own fears landed him in difficulties, but on this occasion the Lord himself assured him of protection and then sealed his promises of coming blessing with a solemn covenant (Gen. 15:17–21) and

[1] Gen. 15:1.

one unique in the Scriptures, 'a promissory oath made by God alone'.[2]

When Paul wrote his epistle 'to the saints in Ephesus' one of his major concerns was to allay the fears of those who had trusted God and, in their case particularly, ongoing fear of the powers of darkness.

1. Ephesus and the powers

An initial question is whether the epistle was in fact sent to the church of Ephesus alone, or whether it was a circular letter. The evidence suggests that it was probably the latter, 'written for churches in this province [Asia], perhaps in and around Ephesus, or on the road to Colossae'.[3] Nevertheless, Ephesus would unquestionably have been the most significant of the various locations to which the letter may have been sent. It was one of the greatest cities and ports of the Mediterranean world, with a population of perhaps a third of a million people, and correspondingly economically and culturally dominant in the vicinity in which the letter was being circulated.

There are other solid grounds to infer an Ephesian background to the letter. The city was well known for the magic arts. 'Of all ancient Graeco-Roman cities, Ephesus, the third largest in the Empire, was by far the most hospitable to magicians, sorcerers, and charlatans of all sorts.'[4] As evidence of such renown the famous 'Ephesian Letters' (*Ephesia grammata*) 'were six magical words (or names) used in spoken charms or inscribed on amulets'[5] and first mentioned 'as early as the fourth century B.C. in a Cretan tablet'.[6] They were used particularly to ward off harmful demons, as well as for other purposes, including the pursuit of success in some venture. The cult of the Ephesian goddess Artemis was also strongly associated with magic. She was 'called upon repeatedly in the invocations of magical texts', not only to help her suppliants but also 'to effect curses'.[7] One text appeals to her to kill an enemy: 'Draw out her breath, Mistress (κύρια), from her nostrils.'[8] The cult of Artemis was widespread throughout the province of Asia; indeed

[2] G. J. Wenham, *Genesis 1–15*, Word Biblical Commentary 1 (Waco: Word, 1987), p. 333.

[3] P. T. O'Brien, *The Letter to the Ephesians*, Pillar NT Commentary (Grand Rapids: Eerdmans and Leicester: Apollos, 1999), p. 49.

[4] B. M. Metzger, in C. E. Arnold, *Ephesians: Power and Magic* (Cambridge: Cambridge University Press, 1989), p. 14.

[5] C. E. Arnold, *Ephesians*, Zondervan Exegetical Commentary on the NT (Grand Rapids: Zondervan, 2010), p. 35.

[6] Arnold, *Ephesians: Power and Magic*, p. 15.

[7] Arnold, *Ephesians*, p. 35.

[8] Ibid.

there were local Artemis cults modelled on that of Ephesus far beyond Asia itself.[9]

Although magic and sorcery are not explicitly mentioned in Paul's epistle, there is good reason to believe that one of his purposes in writing it was precisely to respond to such concerns. In particular, he quite frequently uses a terminology that echoes the language of magic. Most notably, when he refers to Jesus' exaltation *far above all rule and authority, power and dominion* (1:21), the Greek terms he uses (*archē, exousia, dynamis, kyriotēs*) are those also employed in sorcery to invoke the aid of supernatural beings or to ward off their attacks.[10] That Paul had such manipulation of principalities and powers in mind is further implied by his reference to *every name that is named* (1:21, ESV) or 'invoked'.[11] 'The naming of names was foundational to magic; knowing the right names (ὀνόματα [*onomata*]) and invoking them was the means for harnessing the power and service of the beings represented by their appellations.'[12] Significantly, the only other New Testament passage that speaks of naming a name is the reference in Acts to itinerant Jewish exorcists who sought to name the name of Jesus himself in order to empower their magic: they 'tried *to invoke the name of the Lord Jesus*[13] over those who were demon-possessed'.[14] Paul uses the vocabulary of 'principalities and powers' quite frequently in Ephesians (Eph. 1:21; 3:10; 6:12), and there are other terms too that also suggest he is addressing the issue of magic and sorcery.[15]

On the one hand, then, the powers Paul speaks of in Ephesians would have been seen by his readers as potential protectors, even benefactors, whose names were named with magic rites and words in the interests of those who invoked them. On the other hand, they might be identified as vindictive and cruel oppressors, perceived either as capriciously attacking hapless victims from pure spite or as being magically invoked to injure the enemies of the sorcerer or of

---

[9] Arnold, *Ephesians: Power and Magic*, p. 20.

[10] Arnold, *Ephesians*, p. 112. The same is true of the 'world rulers' (*kosmokratores*) mentioned in Eph. 6:12.

[11] *kai pantos onomatos onomazomenou*. The 2011 revision of the NIV translates it as 'every name that is invoked'.

[12] Arnold, *Ephesians*, p. 114.

[13] *Onomazein . . . to onoma tou kyriou Iēsou*.

[14] Acts 19:13, my italics. Arnold, *Ephesians*, p. 114.

[15] In Eph. 1:19, for example, the word *hyperballon* ('incomparably' in the NIV) is not found in the Greek Old Testament but is 'used in a number of inscriptions from Ephesus and in the magical papyri'. See Arnold, *Ephesians*, p. 109. Similarly in 1:21 Paul speaks of Christ as 'far above' (*hyperanō*) the 'principalities and powers', which were typically spoken of as dwelling in the world or the realm 'above' (*ho anō kosmos* or *ho anō chōra*): Arnold, *Ephesians*, p. 111.

his or her paying clients. In short, for the pagan inhabitants of Ephesus and, indeed, far beyond, *rule and authority, power and dominion* (1:21) constituted a dark and ambiguous realm of constantly menacing terror which had to be endlessly negotiated and renegotiated by means of magic rites and incantations.

2. Conversion and the powers

During Paul's own stay in Ephesus there was a moment when large numbers of Christians who had formerly practised sorcery 'brought their scrolls together and burned them publicly'.[16] The scrolls in question were undoubtedly magic texts and Luke estimates their value at 50,000 drachmas, a huge sum when just one drachma constituted a whole day's wages.[17] The event surely indicates that very many members of the church in Ephesus had been actively involved in magic before their conversion, and that up to that point they had not yet totally severed their links with their former occult practices.

Throughout the world and for much of its history a very large proportion of those who respond to the gospel have similarly come from more or less animistic backgrounds in which magic is widely practised as a means of manipulating or warding off spirits. In Africa, for example, much like Ephesus and the whole first-century Mediterranean world, people have tended to use charms to protect themselves against unseen forces which they fear would do them harm, including spirits and ancestors, witches and sorcerers. For such people conversion inevitably brings the dilemma of whether they should continue to use their traditional means of protection against such threats. The Ephesian Christians who finally burned their scrolls may well have been keeping them as a prudent measure *just in case* they might have need of them for some future emergency. In much the same way many observers have noted that all too often 'the usual resort of the African Christian in crisis situations is a reversion to traditional African religious practices'.[18]

In the case of African believers, at least some of the responsibility for their continued reliance on charms lies paradoxically with those who brought the gospel to them in the first place. While their total commitment to Christ and the gospel is not at all in question, they nevertheless too frequently failed both to understand the profound fears of those they served and to appreciate the rich implications of the gospel of Jesus Christ with regard to those fears. At this point

[16] Acts 19:19.

[17] C. E. Arnold, *Powers of Darkness* (Leicester: Inter-Varsity Press, 1992), p. 33.

[18] O. Imasogie, *Guidelines for Christian Theology in Africa* (Achimota, Ghana: Africa Christian Press, 1993), p. 11.

149

they had few answers to the questions of their converts because they had never asked those questions themselves. The increasingly secular West from which most of them came had long since largely ceased to trouble itself with spirits and sorcerers. So, in the words of Paul Hiebert, 'When tribal people spoke of fear of evil spirits, they denied the existence of the spirits rather than claim the power of Christ over them.'[19] But mere denial was not enough for Christians whose world view was permeated with a deep sense of the reality of an unseen world of menace, and so many new believers continued quietly to deal with the problem as they always had. They consulted diviners and traditional healers, and they used protective magic and fetishes. They did not know that the gospel of Christ actually spoke very powerfully to their fears, and a significant part of their daily experience remained therefore untouched and unredeemed by it.

In his epistle to the Ephesians, however, and as a crucial part of his missionary proclamation, Paul explains to his readers the supreme power that Christ has over every hidden threat, and the security that his people therefore possess in him.

3. Christ and the powers

It is particularly in his prayer for his readers that Paul begins to respond to their fears of the unseen world. In Ephesians 1:18–19 he prays that they might grasp three things: first, their hope; second, 'the riches of [God's] glorious inheritance in the saints'; and finally, God's 'incomparably great power in us who believe'. The conjunction of the petitions is significant. The Ephesians might indeed understand the hope to which they had been called and their glorious identity as God's own inheritance, but what seems to have troubled them were the unseen powers that, in their eyes, threatened to harm or even destroy them before they could take possession of that hope. Paul therefore goes on to unpack in some detail the total sufficiency of God's power on their behalf, and he does so in two primary ways.

a. Risen

First, he defines it as *the working of his mighty strength, which he exerted in Christ when he raised him from the dead* (1:19–20). God's power is a resurrecting power. In New Testament terms the resurrection of Jesus from the dead is an event of cosmic significance, the pivotal moment in the unfolding of God's purposes. Of course,

---

[19] P. G. Hiebert, 'The Flaw of the Excluded Middle', *Missiology* 10.1 (1982), p. 44.

the Bible tells stories of other people who came back from death, including those raised by Elijah and Elisha (1 Kgs 17:17–24; 2 Kgs 4:18–37), and indeed by Jesus himself, including Lazarus, Jairus' daughter and the widow of Nain's son (John 11:1–44; Mark 5:21–43; Luke 7:11–15). Each of them demonstrates emphatically the mighty power of the sovereign God. However, Paul has in mind something far greater still, for in each of the cases just mentioned those who were raised remained frail and mortal and went on to die again later.

Jesus' resurrection was of a totally different order. He not only rose from the dead but he overturned death itself and the reign of death. With his resurrection the remorseless tyranny of universal death to which all humanity is subject in consequence of Adam's disobedience has gone into reverse; death itself has been overwhelmed and forced to yield up its prey. For when Jesus was raised from the dead a totally new age began through him, and he rose with a body radically different from the one that died on the cross, a body belonging to that new age – imperishable, glorious, powerful and attuned to the realm of the Spirit of God (1 Cor. 15:42–44). And so, in Ephesians Paul tells his readers that here and now that same almighty power that ushered in a new age through Jesus' resurrection, bringing about the transformation of the whole cosmos, is at work 'for us who believe'.[20] Among other things this means that the powers of darkness, which by definition belong to the old age and whose driving purpose is to inflict death on men and women, have suffered and continue to experience utter and irreversible defeat. They may still be operating, but glorious resurrection power has cut the ground from under their feet.

b. Reigning

Second, Paul proclaims the reign of the risen Christ and he does so twice, first to establish the extent of his reign and then to identify its purpose.

First, he declares that Jesus is now seated at God's *right hand in the heavenly realms* (1:20). The statement is drawn from Psalm 110:1, an Old Testament text more often cited or alluded to by the authors of the New Testament than any other, some thirty-three times in total:[21] 'The LORD says to my Lord: "Sit at my right hand until I make your enemies a footstool for your feet."' It is a

[20] Eph. 1:19a.

[21] D. M. Hay, *Glory at the Right Hand: Psalm 110 in Early Christianity* (Nashville: Abingdon Press, 1973), p. 15.

prophetic affirmation of the fundamental confession of New Testament believers that 'Jesus is Lord' (Rom. 10:9; 1 Cor. 12:3). Significantly, however, Paul draws out the meaning of Christ's lordship specifically in terms of his absolute superiority with regard to the unseen powers: *far above all rule and authority, power and dominion, and every title that can be given, not only in the present age but also in the one to come* (1:21). Paul's argument is that if Christ is exalted to God's right hand, then all such beings without exception are necessarily inferior to him. Moreover, in case some pedantic reader of his letter might claim that there were far more powers than Paul had explicitly identified, he supplements his already lengthy list of names with the words, *and every name that is invoked, not only in the present age but also in the one to come* (1:21, NIV 2011).

Paul then proclaims the reign of the risen Christ a second time, this time alluding to a different psalm (Ps. 8:6): *And God placed all things under his feet and appointed him to be head over everything for the church* (1:22). While the point is nearly identical to the one he has already made in 1:20–21, he moves the argument forward in two directions. First, this time 'the powers are not simply inferior to Christ; they are also subject to him'.[22] The psalm Paul quotes originally spoke of God's subjection of 'all things' to men and women, to whose stewardship he had entrusted the world in which he put them. However, Paul declares that it finds its real and ultimate fulfilment in the incarnate Son of God, the second Adam now exalted: 'You made him ruler over the works of your hands; you put everything under his feet.'[23] Moreover, while the original focus of the psalm was on the subjection of animals, fish and birds, Paul sees beyond that to its implications for Christ's rule over the powers of darkness as well. It is these in particular which are now *under his feet*. Second, the subjection of all things to Christ is *for the church*, a phrase which echoes what Paul said earlier about God's 'incomparably great power *for us who believe*'.[24] Of course, as second person of the eternal Trinity the Son has always reigned along with the Father and the Spirit. Here, however, Paul declares that he now reigns specifically as mediator of the salvation of those he has redeemed. The Father has *appointed him to be head over everything* precisely *for us who believe* and *for the church*. So Christ not only reigns over the powers, but he does so in the interests of his people whose salvation he is bringing about.

---

[22] O'Brien, *Ephesians*, p. 145.
[23] Ps. 8:6.
[24] Eph. 1:19a.

4. Christians and the powers

There is, however, a further stage in Paul's argument. He wants to drive home the implications of what he has said, and show that the resurrection and reign of Christ are not just remote facts but integrally and intimately related to the new reality that his readers were presently experiencing as Christians. Accordingly, at the beginning of Ephesians 2, after describing the state of spiritual death which had defined his readers' existence before they became Christians, he explains how God had transformed their situation through their union with Christ and consequent participation in his resurrection and exaltation. The compound verbs that Paul uses alone make the point very powerfully: make alive *with*, raise *with*, seat *with*.[25]

> *But because of his great love for us, God, who is rich in mercy,* **made us alive with** *Christ even when we were dead in transgressions – it is by grace you have been saved. And God* **raised us up with** *Christ and* **seated us with** *him in the heavenly realms in Christ Jesus* (2:4–6).

So, it is not just that Christ is risen and now reigning. In addition, those whom God has saved through Christ have also been raised *with Christ*, and they too are seated *with him* and *in Christ Jesus* in the heavenly realms (2:6). *In Christ*, then, believers have experienced the same power that raised him from death. It has made them spiritually alive, raised them up, and so also made them participants in the new age which Christ's resurrection brought into being. It is an age in which the powers that had tyrannized them and which they feared have neither place nor power. Not only that, but with and in Christ Christian believers are now seated at God's right hand, far above the reach of those same powers. Paul's desire is that they would grasp the new reality God has brought into being, and then live out its implications.

For Paul's readers, that would mean that they should never again succumb to the temptation to reach for the magic books which belonged to their life in the old age – before they were raised with Christ and seated with him *in the heavenly realms*. The gospel responds to fear of the powers and all their works by delivering from their oppression all who are in Christ, and giving them security in him. It is unutterably good news for men and women redeemed in contexts of animistic belief, in which fear of ancestors, spirits and witches dominates the spiritual horizon. The sovereign power of the

---

[25] *syzōopoieō, synegeirō, synkathizō.*

living God and the redemption he has accomplished in Christ bring deliverance from fear of all such things.

There are, however, important qualifications to make.

a. Christians and magic

First, in all of this it is significant that Paul does not explicitly address the issue of magic, though it was certainly there in his readers' background and thinking. He speaks of *rule and authority, power and dominion*, the spirits which were invoked in the occult activity with which his readers were so familiar, and certainly accepts their reality. Indeed, later on he will speak of God's revelation to them of his own 'manifold wisdom' 'through the church';[26] and later still he describes the struggle of God's people 'against the rulers, against the authorities, against the powers of this dark world and against the spiritual forces of evil in the heavenly realms'.[27] However, he neither confirms nor denies the substance, the specific content, of his Ephesian readers' fears of magic itself. He does not attempt to penetrate the 'fog of war' within which Satan operates.[28] To be more exact, he does not comment on the ways in which they might have conceived of the spirit world and of how it impinged on the lives of human beings; nor does he comment on the efficacy or otherwise of human attempts to manipulate spirits and powers, whether for purposes of self-protection and self-advancement or of aggression. He does not belittle their beliefs and fears, nor does he endorse them, but simply proclaims that whatever may go on in the spiritual domain, Christ is superior to all the powers and sovereign over them. Rephrasing Hiebert's observation quoted above, in the face of his formerly pagan readers' concerns about magic and spirits, he neither denied nor affirmed the content of their beliefs but proclaimed the power of Christ over all that they feared. He gave them a vision of reality radically different from their own.

The point is important. Conceptions of the spirit world and of the activities of witches and sorcerers vary widely across cultures and can at times take the most bizarre forms, and without much – or any – biblical support, especially given the Bible's reticence about this whole area. Paul's approach to the issue sidesteps the need to engage in detailed argument regarding the validity or otherwise of such beliefs, argument which may in fact be counterproductive as it tends

---

[26] Eph. 3:10.
[27] Eph. 6:12. See ch. 20 below.
[28] D. Powlison, 'The Classical Model', in J. K. Beilby and P. R. Eddy (eds.), *Understanding Spiritual Warfare: Four Views* (Grand Rapids: Baker Academic, 2012), p. 90.

paradoxically to promote an ongoing fixation with the very phenomena which engender fear rather than bringing about liberation from it. Instead, whatever the belief, however bizarre or terrifying or foul, Paul's response is to proclaim Christ – Christ risen, Christ reigning, Christ exalted far above all. In the light of these great truths God's redeemed people should turn their regard away from the dark powers they fear, and fix it upon the Saviour lifted up to the Father's right hand.

b. Christians and trials

Second, Paul's words do not mean that believers are freed from satanically inspired trial and suffering, which may take many forms, some of them extremely painful and perplexing. To be sure Paul's emphasis in Ephesians is on the realized dimension of Christian eschatology in which Christians are *already* raised from the spiritual death brought about by their sins, *already* enthroned with Christ and *already* part of the new age. Elsewhere in his writings, however, the other 'unrealized' dimension of his eschatology is more to the fore as he responds to believers who have exaggerated notions of their present situation in Christ. This is so, for example, in the decidedly ironic tone of his response to the Corinthians: 'Already you have all you want! Already you have become rich! You have become kings – and that without us! How I wish that you really had become kings so that we might be kings with you!'[29]

The fact is that until Christ's return believers still have the feeble, perishable bodies of the old creation; while belonging to the new age, they must continue to live out their mortal lives as strangers in the midst of the old one; and, that being the case, although redeemed from the powers that dominate the old age, they remain exposed to their hostility. Accordingly, close to the end of Ephesians Paul speaks of conflict against 'the rulers, against the authorities, against the powers of this dark world and against the spiritual forces of evil in the heavenly realms'.[30] The context indicates that he understands this conflict largely in terms of the attempted spiritual seduction of God's people, which will most often be expressed through temptation to moral sin, doctrinal deviation and apostasy.[31] However, in pursuit of his objectives Satan also incites the physical persecution of the church with a view to its destruction, either through the apostasy of its members or through their literal, physical annihilation. In Revelation

[29] 1 Cor. 4:8.
[30] Eph. 6:12.
[31] See pp. 245–246 below.

13 the dragon calls up the beast from the sea, a creature that symbolizes political power hostile to God and his people and that is, indeed, almost an exact mirror image of the dragon itself (Rev. 12:3; 13:1). He gives it 'his power and his throne and great authority',[32] and it goes on to blaspheme God and his people and 'to make war against the saints and to conquer them'.[33] Christ's letter to the Ephesian church earlier in Revelation suggests that they had themselves experienced pressure of this sort: 'You have persevered and have endured hardships for my name, and have not grown weary.'[34]

How, then, is such experience of persecution, inspired as it is by the powers of darkness, compatible with Paul's confidence that believers are even now risen with Christ and seated with him *in the heavenly realms, far above all rule and authority, power and dominion*? The answer is this.

First, nothing can happen to those who are risen and reigning with Christ outside his will and purpose, for he reigns. Significantly the description of the furious onslaught of the beast in Revelation 13 is itself communicated through a series of verbs in the passive voice which indicate that ultimately it is God alone who enables the beast to pursue its venomous career, and that only for a very limited period. 'The beast *was given* a mouth to utter proud words and blasphemies and to exercise his authority for forty-two months . . . He *was given* power to make war against the saints and to conquer them. And he *was given* authority over every tribe, people, language and nation.'[35]

Second, God has made Christ *head over everything for the church, which is his body* (1:22). As he exercises his rule, his purpose at every point and through every circumstance, including even the most painful of them, is to bring his people to the full experience of their salvation – redeeming them, sanctifying them, enabling them to persevere, bringing them to glory. Paul makes the point in Romans 8:28–30: in God's providence everything his people go through works together for their good, because in *everything* he is progressively effecting their salvation, from its beginning in his eternal electing love right up to its glorious consummation. 'In all things God works for the good of those who love him, who have been called according to his purpose. For those God foreknew he also predestined . . . called . . . justified . . . glorified.'[36]

Third, therefore, despite all the hatred and venom of the enemy nothing can frustrate God's purpose in the salvation of his people.

[32] Rev. 13:2.
[33] Rev. 13:7.
[34] Rev. 2:3.
[35] Rev. 13:5, 7.
[36] Rom. 8:28–30.

Those who are in Christ may be despised and persecuted in this age, prisoners, refugees, fugitives, deprived of their possessions and separated from their families, but unknown to their tormentors, they are in Christ, and from the perspective of eternity God has already raised them up with him and seated them with him in the heavenly realms (Eph. 2:6). They are eternally safe, and their Saviour assures their security. 'I give them eternal life, and they shall never perish; no one can snatch them out of my hand. My Father, who has given them to me, is greater than all; no one can snatch them out of my Father's hand.'[37]

[37] John 10:28–29.

Matthew 28:18–20
13. Moving out

The work that God accomplished through the mission of his Son is one that has to be proclaimed, and Jesus gave responsibility for that task to his disciples. Near the end of John's Gospel he tells them, 'as the Father has sent me, I am sending you',[1] and there is a similar commission at the end of each of the Gospels (Matt. 28:18–20; Mark 16:15–16; Luke 24:45–49) as well as the beginning of Acts (Acts 1:8). God's people are a missionary people, co-workers with God in his redemptive purpose. He redeems them out of the world, and then sends them back into the world as heralds of the good news of salvation in Christ. Mission to the peoples of the earth is, therefore, no mere appendix to the life of the church, nor just one among many activities that Christians might usefully engage in, but rather *the great task* which it is called to carry out in this present age. The church comes into being through mission, and it is then sent out in mission.

1. New Testament mission

In Matthew's Gospel Jesus' purpose in calling men to follow him is made clear from the outset: '"Come, follow me," Jesus said, "and I will make you fishers of men."'[2] And then, at the end, those whom he called to be his disciples are finally sent into the world to carry out the task they had been called to. As Carson says, 'there is a straight line from this commission [in Matt. 4:19] to the Great Commission'.[3] Indeed, the very placing of the 'Great Commission' in Matthew is significant. It is there right at the conclusion of the

[1] John 20:21.
[2] Matt. 4:19.
[3] D. A. Carson, 'Matthew', in *The Expositor's Bible Commentary*, vol. VIII, 1st edn (Grand Rapids: Zondervan, 1984), pp. 119–120.

Gospel, its closing word, the endpoint to which the whole story leads. It answers the 'so what?' question. It tells its readers that in view of Jesus' life, death and resurrection, those who confess him as Lord can do nothing other than make disciples of all nations, just as Jesus had made disciples of them. This is their Lord's parting and authoritative word to his people. And it is extraordinary.

For what then took place constituted a new and revolutionary movement in the history of salvation. Although God's covenant with Abram had declared 'all peoples on earth will be blessed through you',[4] it was a promise rather than a command. There is in fact little evidence in the Old Testament of 'any concern that the people of Israel should go out and share their knowledge of the one true God with the other nations'.[5] At best there was some limited incorporation into Israel of Gentiles such as Ruth the Moabitess or Ebed-Melech the Cushite (Jer. 38:7–13; 39:15–18), coupled with the expectation of an ingathering of Gentiles in the last days.[6] The prophecy of Isaiah concludes, however, with a vision of God sending out messengers to summon the nations and so actively bringing that ingathering to pass:

> I will send some of those who survive to the nations – to Tarshish, to the Libyans and Lydians (famous as archers), to Tubal and Greece, and to the distant islands that have not heard of my fame or seen my glory. They will proclaim my glory among the nations. And they will bring all your brothers, from all the nations, to my holy mountain in Jerusalem as an offering to the Lord.[7]

It is this movement out to the nations which Jesus' command initiates, and it is the worldwide vision and the going out of his heralds to the peoples of the earth that is so utterly novel and unique. 'Jesus' missionary commission to the disciples initiated a new phase in the history of God's people: the universal and international dimension of God's history with the world that Israel had expected for the last days.'[8] Indeed, it was a radically new departure not only in the history of salvation, but in the history of the whole human race. Nothing like this had ever happened before. Violent rulers and their armies had

---

[4] Gen. 12:3.

[5] A. J. Köstenberger and P. T. O'Brien, *Salvation to the Ends of the Earth: A Biblical Theology of Mission* (Leicester: Apollos and Downers Grove: InterVarsity Press, 2001), pp. 34–35.

[6] Ibid., pp. 36, 41–42.

[7] Isa. 66:19–20.

[8] E. Schnabel, *Early Christian Mission*, vol. I, *Jesus and the Twelve* (Leicester: Apollos and Downers Grove: InterVarsity Press, 2004), p. 385.

certainly gone out to the nations time and again to conquer and to colonize, and they still do, but never before had preachers gone out peacefully, humbly and sacrificially with a message of good news from the creator of all the world and a summons to respond to him. 'The mission of the early Christians was unique.'[9]

2. Mission and spiritual warfare

Nevertheless mission does entail conflict, and inevitably so. This is not because the messengers use physical force to impose their message – or at least not if they are faithful to the message they speak and to its divine originator – for they go armed simply with the word of God and in the power of his Spirit.[10] It is rather that as they bring a message of redemption to men and women, they face bitter hostility from the dominion of darkness which holds those people captive. For when human beings respond in obedience to the gospel, Satan is despoiled of his possessions and so he resists, as does the rebellious world to which the hearers of the good news belong. Proclaiming the gospel of grace and truth is itself, therefore, an act of spiritual warfare, both provocative and dangerous, and messengers must be alert to that fact. Accordingly, when Jesus sent the Twelve out to preach good news to the 'lost sheep of the house of Israel', he warned them over and over again of the hostility and persecution they would surely face:

> Be on your guard against men; they will hand you over to the local councils and flog you in their synagogues . . . All men will hate you because of me . . . When you are persecuted in one place, flee to another . . . Do not be afraid of those who kill the body but cannot kill the soul . . . do not suppose that I have come to bring peace to the earth.[11]

The great commission which concludes Matthew's Gospel both assumes and addresses that reality.

a. All authority

First of all, Jesus' commission begins with an assertion of the universal authority he has received from the Father. As God's Messiah, crucified but now risen from the dead, he declares that

[9] Köstenberger and O'Brien, *Salvation to the Ends of the Earth*, p. 71.
[10] It is of course true that there have been lamentable episodes in the history of Christianity when the sword has been used in one way or another to impose 'Christian' faith.
[11] Matt. 10:17, 22, 23, 28, 34.

Daniel's prophecy of the bestowal of authority on 'one like a son of man' has been fulfilled in himself: 'There before me was one like a son of man, coming with the clouds of heaven. He approached the Ancient of Days and was led into his presence. He was given authority, glory and sovereign power; all peoples, nations and men of every language worshipped him.'[12] It is on this basis that his command to go and make disciples is founded: *All authority in heaven and on earth has been given to me. Therefore go and make disciples . . .* (18–19). The Son of Man sends his envoys to summon 'all peoples, nations and men of every language' to come under the authority that he has received.

There is, moreover, an obvious parallel here with Paul's declaration in Ephesians, that God has 'placed all things under his feet and appointed him to be head over everything *for the church*'.[13] The authority referred to in Matthew is equally given to Jesus as mediator of the salvation of his people. As eternal Word and Son of the Father, the Lord Jesus Christ never at any point ceases to have universal authority, but what he has now received is a mediatorial reign specifically *for the church*, because its purpose is precisely to 'make disciples of all the nations' through the mission of those he sends. They go as his representatives through whom he will build his church (Matt. 16:18).

Further, in order that their task should be accomplished, his authority extends to both heaven and earth. In Jesus' declaration there is a significant echo of the temptation he had faced at the beginning of his ministry when the devil showed him all the kingdoms of the world: '"All this I will give you," he said, "if you will bow down and worship me."'[14] Jesus had rejected the devil's proposal and he carried out the mission his Father had given him in the way the Father had commanded, the way of the cross, from which the devil's temptation was intended to divert him. As a result of his total obedience to God's will not only did he now possess all that the devil had claimed to be able to offer him there in the wilderness, but far more than that, for God had given him all authority not only on earth but *in heaven* as well. So the human, earthly realm was now subject to him, along with the spiritual, heavenly realm too, including Satan himself and all the kingdom of darkness. Again there is an echo of Paul's declaration of Christ's enthronement 'in the heavenly realms, far above all rule and authority, power and dominion'.[15] In

---

[12] Dan. 7:13–14. R. T. France, *Jesus and the Old Testament* (London: The Tyndale Press, 1971), pp. 142–143.

[13] Eph. 1:22, emphasis mine.

[14] Matt. 4:9.

[15] Eph. 1:20–21.

consequence, the dominion of darkness is unable to withstand the rescue from its power of those it has enslaved, however much it may seek to strike down the messengers and devastate their mission, and whatever the means it may use to do so. Neither can the rebellious peoples of earth prevent the advance of the gospel and the making of disciples from among their own number.

When the seventy-two[16] returned from the mission on which Jesus had sent them he gave then an assurance very similar to the one here. 'I have given you *authority* to trample on snakes and scorpions and to overcome all the power of the enemy; nothing will harm you.'[17] Once again there is Jesus' assertion of his authority, and it is on the basis of that authority that the disciples will be able to 'overcome all the power of the enemy'. Given the immediate context as well as the later unfolding of the story in Acts, Luke is clearly referring to the mission he gives his disciples to take the gospel to lost men and women, and he assures them that neither Satan nor all the resources he disposes of will hinder the fulfilment of their task. Moreover, although they face Satan's hostility he will not be able to 'harm' them. Given that Luke records Jesus' numerous warnings of the persecution his disciples will face (Luke 6:22–23; 9:23–27; 12:4–5, 11; 21:12–17), the assurance can hardly mean that they will avoid physical suffering. Rather he is telling them that they have an eternal security which Satan cannot touch.

b. All nations

The disciples' task of making disciples *of all nations* is a profoundly subversive one. These are the nations which have long been deceived by Satan (Rev. 12:9; 20:3) and blinded by him (2 Cor. 4:4), and which in consequence lie under his control (1 John 5:19). They belong to a fallen world and in their various and innumerable ways they worship the beast and carry its mark (Rev. 13:8, 16–17). Moreover Satan regards them as his possession. In Luke's version of the temptations Satan shows Jesus 'all the kingdoms of the world' and then he says, 'I will give you all their authority and splendour, for it has been given to me, and I can give it to anyone I want to.'[18] The mission of the disciples repudiates the claim and in their going they declare that the earth belongs to Christ.

All of this is expressed in Paul's words as he recalled the commission he had himself received from the risen Lord some time after

---

[16] Or seventy, according to some manuscripts.
[17] Luke 10:19.
[18] Luke 4:6.

that recorded in Matthew 28: 'I am sending you to them to open their eyes and turn them from darkness to light, and from the power of Satan to God, so that they may receive forgiveness of sins and a place among those who are sanctified by faith in me.'[19]

Consequently, messengers of Christ face hostility and savage opposition. In their own way they are like agents of a state that is at war with its neighbour, and who quietly infiltrate the enemy's territory. Once there they summon its peoples to revolt against their rulers and to adopt and live out goals and policies that their rulers abominate. For their subversion such men and women are hunted down and, when caught, suffer the most extreme penalties of the law. Accordingly, in the Acts of the Apostles persecution of those who proclaim the gospel begins in Jerusalem and intensifies as the message is brought to the nations. James and Stephen are put to death; on various occasions the leaders of the church in Jerusalem are arrested, threatened and beaten; and Saul hunts down Christians and extends the pursuit as far as Damascus. Then Paul, along with his companions, is chased from town to town; he is regularly threatened, maligned, stoned, flogged, imprisoned, mocked, assaulted. His own summary says it all:

> I have . . . been in prison more frequently, been flogged more severely, and been exposed to death again and again. Five times I received from the Jews the forty lashes minus one. Three times I was beaten with rods, once I was stoned . . . in danger from my own countrymen, in danger from Gentiles . . .[20]

And he acknowledges, 'I only know that in every city the Holy Spirit warns me that prison and hardships are facing me.'[21] Such incidents are repeated over and over again down through the centuries as missionaries take the gospel of Christ to nations that know nothing of him and summon them to submit to him. What is striking, however, is that even though barriers may be raised to prevent the spread of the gospel to the nations, and the messengers themselves may be persecuted and struck down, still the gospel advances and the church is built.

c. All I have commanded you

So those whom Jesus sends summon the nations to conversion – to an absolute change of allegiance by becoming *disciples* of Jesus.

---

[19] Acts 26:17–18.
[20] 2 Cor. 11:23–26. See also 1 Cor. 4:11–13; 2 Cor. 4:7–12; 6:4–10.
[21] Acts 20:23.

According to the great commission this change is expressed in two ways.

First, they must be baptized *in the name of the Father and of the Son and of the Holy Spirit* (19). Baptism is an act filled with meaning, but at heart it expresses submission to the triune God and entry into fellowship with him by union with Christ. It is a positive statement of faith and commitment, which acknowledges a new Lord and the necessity of a transformed life. This means that it is also, at the same time, an act by which the baptized repudiate the false gods, ideologies and beliefs that had controlled their hearts and lives previously. In so doing they forsake the world and the devil which stand behind all worship that is not addressed to the one true God. In the early church this was sometimes made explicit with a verbal renunciation of Satan at the time of baptism.[22] So Tertullian wrote: 'When we are going to enter the water, but a little before, in the presence of the congregation and under the hand of the president, we solemnly profess that we disown the devil, and his pomp, and his angels.'[23] Such an act means that by virtue of their proclamation, heralds of the gospel defy the dominion of darkness by calling men and women to renounce it in the name of Christ. They engage in spiritual warfare.

Second, they teach new disciples *to obey everything* Christ has commanded. Those who have been baptized into the name of the triune God need to know the implications of what they have done. What does the Lord Jesus Christ require of them, and how are those requirements to be lived out in daily practice? Again, in so doing Jesus' disciples teach redeemed men and women to live according to the ways of a kingdom radically different from that of this world and its ruler. Among many other things they teach them to live as strangers and aliens in the world (1 Pet. 1:1, 17; 2:11); to refuse to conform to it (Rom. 12:2); to go 'outside the camp' as they look forward to 'the city that is to come' (Heb. 13:13–14). Their teaching is subversive of the values, priorities and idols of this world, indeed of its very heart and soul, and of the authority of its ruler.

It is clear that in all of this the ministry Jesus' disciples exercise is fundamentally a ministry of the word. They announce Christ, they call men and women to respond positively to the message of Christ, they baptize them and they teach them. The New Testament con-stantly emphasizes the centrality of the proclamation of the gospel as the means by which God saves and transforms people. In the narrative of Acts the gospel repeatedly advances through the word –

---

[22] C. E. Arnold, 'Early Christian Catechesis and New Christians' Classes in Contemporary Evangelicalism', *JETS* 47.1 (2004), p. 52.
[23] Arnold, 'Early Christian Catechesis', p. 52, n. 44.

through preaching (Acts 2:14; 4:31; 8:4; 8:35; 9:19–20; 28:30–31). It was clearly at the centre of Paul's conception of his own ministry. So he says 'we preach Christ crucified',[24] and again, 'we do not preach ourselves, but Jesus Christ as Lord'.[25] In Acts time and again he preaches, experiences persecution, moves on to another place, and then simply preaches again and the cycle repeats itself. The summary of his ministry that he himself gave to the Ephesian elders repeatedly stresses the communication of God's message: preaching (Acts 20:20), declaring (20:21), testifying (20:24), proclaiming (20:27). It is the word of truth that alone exposes the lies of the devil and brings redemption and freedom to those who are deceived, blinded and enslaved by them. At the heart of mission there is a message to be proclaimed, a truth to be believed. It is at this level that conflict with the dominion of darkness takes place.

At the same time mission does *not* involve direct engagement with Satan and demons by means of a so-called 'strategic-level' spiritual warfare or deliverance. A quite large body of recent literature has emphasized the role of territorial spirits – 'high-ranking principalities and powers'[26] – in hindering the spread of the gospel, and the consequent need to engage them as an integral element of Christian mission. In this view, engaging them might include identifying the names of the spirits involved, perhaps by speaking to other spirits; 'mapping' the areas over which they exercise authority; 'identificational repentance', which means unmasking past sins in the territory concerned and confessing them; 'prophetic declarations to demonic rulers and authorities'[27] and prophetic acts; driving the spirits out by 'warfare intercession', prayer walks, prayer journeys, and so on. The approach is based very heavily on ambiguous anecdotal evidence along with speculative exegesis of the various biblical texts cited in support, and all suffused with more than a tinge of animistic thinking.

The book of Daniel does indeed refer to the 'prince of Persia' and the 'prince of Greece',[28] evidently demonic protectors of the empires of Persia and Greece who resisted the implementation of God's purpose. These were not in fact specifically 'territorial' spirits but political, associated with empires which themselves had shifting territorial boundaries. Indeed, the actual territories occupied by Persia and Greece were very much coterminous as Greece overcame Persia

[24] 1 Cor. 1:23.

[25] 2 Cor. 4:5. See also Rom. 10:17; 1 Cor. 15:2; 2 Cor. 4:2; Eph. 6:17; 2 Tim. 4:2.

[26] C. P. Wagner and R. Greenwood, 'The Strategic-Level Deliverance Model', in J. K. Beilby and P. R. Eddy (eds.), *Understanding Spiritual Warfare: Four Views* (Grand Rapids: Baker Academic, 2012), p. 179.

[27] Ibid., p. 188.

[28] Dan. 10:13, 20.

and took control of its lands.[29] Accordingly, the revelation Daniel received certainly confirms the malign involvement of spiritual forces in human politics, but Daniel himself does not directly engage them, nor is he called to do so. In the narrative of the book what he does is to communicate God's message to *human* emperors, including Nebuchadnezzar and Belshazzar, and pray to God. Similarly in the New Testament Jesus' disciples simply pray and preach in the power of the Holy Spirit. Jesus commands them to go and declare the gospel on the basis of a universal authority which has already been given to him. It is *because* he has that authority that they are able to go, not *in order* to establish it. Accordingly there is no suggestion in the great commission itself nor at any point in the New Testament that the spread of the gospel depends on their own preliminary skirmishes with 'territorial spirits': 'we do not need to defeat Satan. Christ has defeated him already, and will one day destroy him'.[30] And so, in the one New Testament book that describes the earliest advance of the gospel, the Acts of the Apostles, we find no trace of 'strategic-level' spiritual warfare, nor in the missionary practice of the church in the centuries following. 'Strategic-level spiritual warfare has no biblical precedent or warrant – the Bible simply does not go there.'[31]

d. Always

The injunctions of the great commission are framed by two declarations which bring assurance to those who are commissioned. At the beginning they are assured of Jesus' authority. They cannot go to any place where he is not already the Lord who holds total authority. At the end of the commission they are assured of his constant presence with them: *And surely I am with you always, to the very end of the age* (20). The promise is powerfully expressed. First, the initial word, *surely*, 'captures the force'[32] of the Greek[33] and underlines the trustworthiness and the importance of the promise that follows. As they contemplate the vastness of the task they have just been given and their own inadequacy, this is something they absolutely need to know. Further, Jesus emphasizes that it is indeed *he* who will be with them and not some deputy sent by him; it is as

[29] C. Lowe, *Territorial Spirits and World Evangelisation* (Fearn: Mentor/OMF, 1998), p. 34.
[30] Ibid., p. 144.
[31] D. Powlison, 'Response to C. Peter Wagner and Rebecca Greenwood', in J. K. Beilby and P. R. Eddy (eds.), *Understanding Spiritual Warfare: Four Views* (Grand Rapids: Baker Academic, 2012), p. 206.
[32] Carson, 'Matthew', p. 599.
[33] *idou.*

if he were to say 'And surely I, I myself, I am with you . . .'[34] He may be about to return to the presence of the Father but he does not abandon those whom he sends. Third, the promise echoes the meaning of his name, Immanuel, which Matthew cites at the beginning of his Gospel when he quotes Isaiah's prophecy: 'All this took place to fulfil what the Lord had said through the prophet: "The virgin will be with child and will give birth to a son, and they will call him Immanuel" – which means, "God with us".'[35] The one who came into the world as *God with us* continues with his disciples as *God with us* through all the generations to come until the very end of the age – and so to the completion of his and their mission on earth. Not only that, but even as they go to nations far beyond the land of promise and the location of the temple and move among peoples who know nothing of the God of Israel, Christ is with them and there is no fear of ever moving beyond his reach. Even in the darkest place, he is there. There are echoes, indeed, of the assurance David expresses in Psalm 139:

> . . . if I make my bed in the depths, you are there.
> If I rise on the wings of the dawn,
>   if I settle on the far side of the sea,
> even there your hand will guide me,
>   your right hand will hold me fast.[36]

Fourth, the expression he uses, translated *always* in English Bibles, is an unusual one found nowhere else in the New Testament, which really means 'the whole of every day'[37] – 'each day as we live it'.[38] At every single moment without exception, whatever the circumstances of the day and the trials they may be facing at that very instant, the disciples can count on the presence of the Lord who sends them.

The final point of the promise, however, is to encourage and sustain the disciples *in their mission*, as with similar promises to Moses and Joshua (Exod. 3:12; Josh. 1:5). 'Jesus' disciples experience the presence of the risen Lord precisely as they are sent and as they go.'[39] They go to a whole world that is lost and over which Satan holds sway, in order to call rebellious men and women, hostile to God and to his purposes, to be baptized and to obey all that God's Messiah has commanded. Far from their natural homes they will face

---

[34] *kai idou egō meth' hymōn eimi.*
[35] Matt. 1:22–23.
[36] Ps. 139:8–10.
[37] C. F. D. Moule, quoted by Carson, 'Matthew', p. 599.
[38] Carson, 'Matthew', p. 599.
[39] E. Schnabel, *Early Christian Mission*, p. 367.

hostility, persecution and death but, as they go, they will never face these things alone – nor Satan, nor all the powers of darkness. Christ has conquered, Christ is Lord, Christ is with them – always and everywhere.

Acts 13:4–12
14. Facing the foe

When the Spirit of God told the 'prophets and teachers' of the church at Antioch to set Saul and Barnabas aside 'for the work to which I have called them',[1] it was not the beginning of Saul's missionary activity. At that point he had already been preaching the gospel for a period of about twelve years following his encounter with the risen Christ in AD 31/2.[2] During that time he had ministered in Damascus (Acts 9:19–25) and Jerusalem (Acts 9:26–29), including a visit into Arabia, 'the Nabatean kingdom east of the Jordan River'.[3] Most of those years, however, had been spent in Syria and Cilicia (Gal. 1:21–22), including the cities of Tarsus (Acts 9:30) and Antioch (Acts 11:25–26).[4] So, when Paul took ship at the port of Seleucia along with Barnabas and John Mark, he was already in many ways a seasoned missionary. Nonetheless, we have very little detail about his ministry during those early years, but from Acts 13 onwards Luke provides a remarkably detailed account of Paul's missionary activity. 'We possess more information about the twelve years of Paul's missionary work on Cyprus, in Galatia, Macedonia, Achaia and in the province of Asia in the years A.D. 45–56 than about any other period in the history of the early church in the first century.'[5]

1. Paul's missionary journey

Moreover, the narrative that begins in Acts 13 is significant not only because of the amount of information Luke provides, but for other

---

[1] Acts 13:1–2.
[2] E. Schnabel, *Early Christian Missionm*, vol. II, *Paul and the Early Church* (Leicester: Apollos and Downers Grove: InterVarsity Press, 2004), p. 1031.
[3] Gal. 1:17. Schnabel, *Early Christian Mission*, p. 1032.
[4] Ibid., p. 1047.
[5] Ibid., p. 1073.

important reasons too. On the one hand the church of Antioch is itself actively involved in initiating the mission of Saul and Barnabas. It is not a merely individual activity but one in which the people of God are themselves implicated through their leaders who act under the direction of the Holy Spirit. Luke's narrative describes 'the first piece of planned "overseas mission" carried out by representatives of a particular church, rather than by solitary individuals, and begun by a deliberate church decision, inspired by the Spirit, rather than somewhat more casually as a result of persecution'.[6] It underlines the fact that mission is the responsibility of God's people as a whole, as one body united in Christ and *together* sent out with good news.

Further, as the mission advances it also becomes clear that Paul and his colleagues are not moving randomly from place to place but pursuing a strategy and intentionally moving into 'regions beyond' those already reached with the gospel – places 'where Christ was not known'.[7] To a significant extent they focused on major urban centres like Pisidian Antioch and Iconium, although sometimes including less important places such as Lystra as well. In the case of Cyprus they landed at Salamis in the east of the island and moved steadily *through the whole island until they came to Paphos*, the provincial capital, at the western end.

And it seems certain that in each place they came to they focused initially on ministering *in the Jewish synagogues*, wherever there was one, as they did in *Salamis* at the beginning of their work in Cyprus (5). Theological principle was involved in this, for Paul recognized the special place of the Jewish people in God's purposes and their prior right to hear the gospel as those to whom the covenant promises had been made (Acts 13:46–47). Further, from a more pragmatic perspective these were people who were already waiting and eager for news of the coming of the Messiah, people to whom Jewish missionaries like Paul and Barnabas had easy access – at least at the first contact, and people in whose synagogues Gentile 'God-fearers' could invariably be found, attracted as they were by the God of Israel and frequently very open to the gospel.

In this context, and somewhat out of the blue, when they reached Paphos Paul and Barnabas were called to appear before *Sergius Paulus*, the Roman *proconsul* or governor of Cyprus. There is no explicit indication in the text that they had been actively ministering among Gentiles but Sergius Paulus had evidently heard about their activities on the island. It is possible that as ruler of Cyprus he felt

---

[6] I. H. Marshall, *Acts: An Introduction and Commentary*, Tyndale NT Commentaries (Nottingham: Inter-Varsity Press, 1980), pp. 227–228.
[7] 2 Cor. 10:16; Rom. 15:20.

it necessary to check out what Paul and Barnabas were saying and doing in order to make sure that their message presented no threat to public order and security.[8] The text of Acts suggests rather, however, that his concern was more personal and spiritual: he sent for the two missionaries because *he wanted to hear the word of God*, which at face value suggests a simple desire to hear at first hand the message Paul and Barnabas were preaching without any ulterior motive (7). Evidently he had learned something of their activities, perhaps through Jewish acquaintances or Gentile God-fearers who had heard them speaking in the synagogues and told him about it. However that may be, his interest was aroused – perhaps indeed a spiritual hunger – and he summoned the two men. It was a moment of immense significance, an opening to bring the good news into the heart of pagan society and the seat of political power on the island and, as a result, the possibility of an entry to circles in Paphos which would otherwise have been inaccessible.

2. A Jewish sorcerer

The focus of the account is, however, on the proconsul's *attendant* rather than on the proconsul himself. Named *Bar-Jesus* or *Elymas* Luke introduces him ahead of Sergius Paulus, and the narrative of Paul's audience with Sergius Paulus is mainly concerned with Elymas' opposition to Paul's testimony. Luke identifies him as *a Jewish sorcerer and false prophet* (6).

On numerous occasions the Old Testament forbids any involvement of God's people with magic.[9] Nevertheless, its condemnations 'did not prevent some Jews from making illicit use of such measures'[10] and by the first century AD contemporary sources indicate that 'there was widespread Jewish involvement in magic, witchcraft and sorcery'.[11] Luke himself refers later to itinerant Jewish exorcists in Ephesus who evidently used standard exorcistic procedures to expel demons (Acts 19:13–16). Though not Christians they seized on the name of Jesus as yet one more power source to be added to the names of the numerous spirits they already invoked for the binding and expelling of demons. Jewish exorcists and magicians of this sort were by no means uncommon. 'Many Jews throughout the Mediterranean world adopted and even further developed these occult practices of their pagan neighbours. In fact Jewish magic gained a notoriety of

[8] Schnabel, *Early Christian Mission*, p. 1086.
[9] Exod. 22:18; Lev. 19:26, 31; 20:6; Deut. 18:9–14; Isa. 47:9, 12; Jer. 27:9; Ezek. 12:24; etc.
[10] E. M. Yamauchi, 'Magic in the Biblical World', *Tyndale Bulletin* 34 (1983), p. 171.
[11] C. E. Arnold, *Powers of Darkness* (Leicester: Inter-Varsity Press, 1992), p. 32.

its own in antiquity.'[12] The result was a syncretistic 'folk Judaism', reflecting the constant attraction of animistic practices for those living in cultures imbued with powerful beliefs in demons and sorcerers.

Accordingly, despite his Jewish origin Elymas was a *sorcerer*, and Luke also describes him as *a false prophet*, 'one who claims falsely to be a medium of divine revelation'.[13] As a Jew he presumably claimed to speak in the name of the God of his people, but the oracles he communicated were not the authentic 'word of the Lord' such as the Old Testament prophets had announced but derived rather from the divinatory techniques of magic. In this sense he was not perhaps so very different from Balaam. The latter was admittedly no Israelite but he claimed nevertheless to be a servant of the God of Israel while using divinatory techniques to produce his oracles, at least until he became conscious of their uselessness against Israel (Num. 24:1). Moreover, like Balaam Elymas used his expertise in the service of power and probably with a view to profit. Balaam was, of course, available for hire to whoever had the means to pay his fees, something indeed of a freelance sorcerer and diviner with his own private practice. Elymas, on the other hand, was apparently attached to the Roman proconsul as his personal *attendant* (7), effectively functioning as 'court astrologer and magician'.[14] So, when Paul was invited to come and explain the gospel to his employer he certainly had a good deal to lose in terms of job, status, prestige and income, and he reacted accordingly.

3. Elymas and Paul

Elymas' opposition to Paul and Barnabas was, however, more than a merely personal matter. In terms of Luke's narrative the encounter with him is the first major incident of these missionary journeys, whose purpose was to take the gospel to the Gentiles and so 'to open their eyes and turn them from darkness to light, and from the power of Satan to God'.[15] From that perspective the summons to appear before Sergius Paulus constituted an opportunity to do exactly what God had chosen and sent Paul and Barnabas to do. Rather like the

[12] Arnold, *Powers of Darkness*, p. 71.

[13] F. F. Bruce, *The Acts of the Apostles: The Greek Text with Introduction and Commentary*, 3rd edn (Grand Rapids: Eerdmans and Leicester: Apollos, 1990), p. 296.

[14] D. G. Peterson, *The Acts of the Apostles*, Pillar NT Commentary (Grand Rapids: Eerdmans and Leicester: Apollos, 2009), p. 380.

[15] Acts 26:18. S. R. Garrett, 'Light on a Dark Subject and Vice Versa: Magic and Magicians in the New Testament', in J. Neusner, E. S. Frerichs and P. V. M. Flesher (eds.), *Religion, Science and Magic: In Concert and In Conflict* (New York and Oxford: Oxford University Press, 1989), p. 143.

Greeks who had wanted to see Jesus (John 12:21), Sergius Paulus also *wanted to hear the word of God* (7) and so sent for his spokesmen. God was opening up access to one who in his position as proconsul represented that very Gentile world which he had sent Paul and Barnabas to penetrate with the good news of Christ. It was a momentous occasion, an extraordinary opportunity, and it provoked a reaction.

a. Elymas' opposition

A spiritual conflict took place, then, as the gospel with its call to repentance and faith was presented to the proconsul, and Paul and Barnabas sought to bring him 'from darkness to light'. Elymas' opposition represents the resistance of the darkness and, accordingly, in Luke's narrative he is 'closely linked with Satan'.[16] Paul makes the link explicit when he calls Elymas *a child of the devil*. He then goes on to describe him as *an enemy of everything that is right* and adds, *you are full of all kinds of deceit and trickery* (10). The language echoes one of the ways in which Paul speaks of Satan in his epistles. In Ephesians, for example, he refers to 'the devil's schemes',[17] the word he uses[18] making 'clear that the devil . . . employs cunning and wily stratagems'.[19] Elsewhere, Paul says, 'we are not unaware of [Satan's] devices',[20] and again his terminology[21] suggests wiles and plots. Elymas' deceit and trickery identify him, therefore, as a true child of his father.

Not only that, but in his efforts *to turn the proconsul from the faith* (8) Luke presents Elymas as one who does the work carried out by Satan in Jesus' parable of the sower.[22] There the seed that fell on the path is 'trampled on, and the birds of the air ate it up'. Jesus explains that the birds represent the devil 'who comes and takes away the word from [the hearers'] hearts, so that they may not believe and be saved'.[23] Of the three synoptic accounts of the parable Luke alone uses the words 'that they may not believe and be saved' to describe Satan's purpose, and his reference in Acts 13 to Elymas' attempt *to turn the proconsul from the faith* attributes precisely that role to him.[24]

[16] Garrett, 'Light on a Dark Subject', p. 153.
[17] Eph. 6.11.
[18] *methodeia*.
[19] A. T. Lincoln, *Ephesians*, Word Bible Commentary 42 (Dallas: Word, 1990), p. 443.
[20] 2 Cor. 2:11.
[21] *noēmata*.
[22] Garrett, 'Light on a Dark Subject', p. 153.
[23] Luke 8:5, 12.
[24] Garrett, 'Light on a Dark Subject', pp. 153–154.

Finally, Paul's question, *Will you never stop perverting the right ways of the Lord?* (10), reinforces Luke's description of Elymas as a *false prophet*. In his Gospel Luke introduces John the Baptist as 'a voice of one calling in the desert, "Prepare the way for the Lord, make straight paths for him"'.[25] John is the true prophet who calls on his hearers to make 'straight paths' for the Lord;[26] by contrast Elymas is a false prophet who perverts the *right ways of the Lord.*[27] His negative relationship to the fulfilment of the plans and purposes of God establishes his true identity.[28]

b. Paul's response

Paul responded to Elymas' opposition, *filled with the Holy Spirit* (9). In the same way Luke records that Peter too, 'filled with the Holy Spirit', addressed the Jewish rulers following his and John's arrest in the temple (Acts 4:8). In both cases introduction of the phrase at the critical moment of confrontation with forces hostile to the gospel – the very point when Peter and Paul had to respond – indicates that the two men received a special endowment of divine power for the challenge they faced exactly when they needed it. There is a fulfilment here of Jesus' promise to his disciples that in such situations they would be given the words to speak:

> . . . you will be brought before kings and governors, and all on account of my name. This will result in your being witnesses to them. But make up your mind not to worry beforehand how you will defend yourselves. For I will give you words and wisdom that none of your adversaries will be able to resist or contradict.[29]

And, indeed, both Peter and Paul, 'filled with the Holy Spirit', immediately *spoke* to their opponents. Not only that, however, but the words also reveal that the confrontation taking place was not simply one between Paul and Elymas but that, as they faced each other in the presence of Sergius Paulus, the evil one and the Holy Spirit of God were also facing each other. 'The confrontation between Bar-Jesus and Paul is also a confrontation between the Holy Spirit and Satan.'[30] The place of gospel proclamation had become a place

[25] Luke 3:4.
[26] *eutheias poieite tas tribous autou.*
[27] *tas hodous kyriou tas eutheias.*
[28] Garrett, 'Light on a Dark Subject', p. 154.
[29] Luke 21:12–15.
[30] Garrett, 'Light on a Dark Subject', p. 154.

of spiritual combat between God and Satan, and at issue in the battle was the proconsul's salvation.

The effect of the Spirit's renewed anointing of Paul was visible in several ways. First, he demonstrated an obvious courage and confidence as he *looked straight at Elymas* (9) and denounced him. The same had been true earlier of Peter and John before the Sanhedrin, 'when they saw the courage of Peter and John'. Then, when Peter and John were finally released after being seriously threatened not to continue preaching in the name of Jesus, and they returned 'to their own people', the church prayed for boldness to continue to speak God's word and 'they were all filled with the Holy Spirit and spoke the word of God boldly'.[31]

Second, Paul was able to see beyond the merely human animosity of a man whose livelihood was in danger of being lost, and to recognize the deeper spiritual dimension of what was taking place: *You are a child of the devil . . . an enemy of everything that is right . . . full of all kinds of deceit and trickery . . . perverting the right ways of the Lord* (10). In Ephesians 6:12 he makes the same distinction between a simply human and physical confrontation and the underlying struggle with invisible powers of darkness: 'For our struggle is not against flesh and blood, but against the rulers, against the authorities, against the powers of this dark world and against the spiritual forces of evil in the heavenly realms.'

Third, he tells Elymas that the Lord's hand is *against* him, which is made visible in a judgment of temporary blindness. The text makes it clear that this is no act of personal vengeance on Paul's part, because it is *filled with the Holy Spirit* that he speaks God's word and declares God's judgment. The forthrightness and severity of Paul's message recalls Peter's condemnation of Simon the sorcerer in Samaria: 'You have no part or share in this ministry, because your heart is not right before God . . . I see that you are full of bitterness and captive to sin.'[32] In both cases the challenge presented by practitioners of the magic arts was speedily and unequivocally dealt with.

For Elymas the result was immediate. As a *child of the devil* he belonged to the darkness and so he was symbolically consigned to physical darkness. His opposition was thereby swiftly terminated and he was reduced to helplessness, groping about and *seeking someone to lead him by the hand* (11). His experience recalls that of the magicians of Egypt who began by reproducing the signs that Moses carried out (Exod. 7:22; 8:7); who then quickly found themselves out of their depth and unable to replicate them, telling Pharaoh,

---

[31] Acts 4:13, 23, 31.
[32] Acts 8:21, 23.

'This is the finger of God'; and who were finally afflicted by the plague of boils along with everyone else and could no longer 'stand before Moses'.[33] In the same way after God's word of judgment Elymas could not stand before Paul and Barnabas, and the emptiness and futility of his magic were laid bare.

4. Belief and encounter

a. Believing the word

The proconsul *believed* (12). This is what the whole confrontation had been about – the response of Sergius Paulus to the gospel. Wherever and whenever the good news of Christ is communicated spiritual conflict takes place, not necessarily in the way it occurred here but in some form or other. Most often in Acts opposition came from unconverted Jews, but sometimes from vested commercial interests or from traditional pagan religion. It is for this reason that Jesus assured the Eleven that all authority in heaven and on earth had been given to him before he sent them out to make disciples (Matt. 28:18), and that he gave them authority 'to overcome all the power of the enemy'.[34] Satan resists the advance of the gospel, but all authority belongs to Christ.

Luke links Sergius Paulus' belief to two factors: he *saw what had happened* and *he was amazed at the teaching about the Lord* (12). The combination of the two is significant. On the one hand, before sending for Paul and Barnabas Sergius Paulus had clearly been captivated by magic to the point that he had kept his own personal sorcerer at his side as an attendant. Many rulers right up to the twenty-first century have behaved in much the same way and sought wisdom or security by employing fetishists, diviners or mediums. 'African leaders – especially in West Africa – have their spirit mediums and marabouts close at hand and consult them regularly.'[35] For Sergius Paulus, however, the blinding of Elymas and his reduction to a state of humiliating helplessness displayed the total uselessness of magic when confronted with the *hand of the Lord* (11) and so eliminated a major obstacle to his coming to faith in Christ.[36] On the other hand, however, it was the *teaching about the Lord* that was the object of his belief, and he believed because it amazed him. It was the gospel itself that took hold of him, as everywhere in Acts and throughout

---

[33] Exod. 8:19; 9:11.

[34] Luke 10:19.

[35] R. Dowden, *Africa: Altered States, Ordinary Miracles* (London: Portobello Books, 2008), p. 318.

[36] Peterson, *Acts*, p. 382.

the New Testament – the word of Christ crucified for the sins of lost human beings and risen again. It was this teaching that the proconsul had originally wanted to hear, that constituted the focus of Elymas' opposition, and that finally brought the proconsul to salvation.

b. Power encounter

Elymas was overcome by *the hand of the Lord*, indeed physically overcome, and thereby his opposition was abruptly quashed. It is an event that raises questions. The notion of a 'power encounter' has only been current in missiological thinking in recent years, although the phenomenon it refers to is found on a number of occasions in the Scriptures as well as in the subsequent history of the church's mission. The idea is very simple: 'A power encounter is a confrontation demonstrating that Jesus's power is superior to that of the old gods.'[37] The confrontation between Moses and the magicians of Egypt (Exod. 6:28 – 12:42), between Elijah and the prophets of Baal (1 Kgs 18:16–46) and between Jesus and the numerous demons he expelled might all be seen as power encounters. A similar event in church history would be the occasion on which the English missionary Boniface (680–754) defied the pagan gods by chopping down the sacred Oak of Thor before a large crowd at Geismar in Germany. And the moment when Paul and Barnabas faced the opposition of Elymas and overcame him by means of a physical judgment may be seen as another. It was not, of course, the power of 'the old gods' that was at stake here, but certainly that of sorcery and indeed of Satan himself.

The notion of 'power encounter', including this particular confrontation at Paphos, nevertheless needs some qualification. First, the book of Acts as a whole, Christian history in general and present experience do not lead us to suppose that demonstrations of this sort are the normal way in which people are brought to salvation. Where such events do occur they are often associated with the breaking down of major barriers to gospel progress, such as its entry into a new and unreceptive culture, or perhaps the conversion of a particularly significant figure, as here in Paphos where the proconsul's conversion doubtless opened doors for the gospel which might otherwise have remained closed.[38]

Second, the always central feature of authentic Christian mission is the communication of truth. Satan's defining characteristic is not

---

[37] C. Ott, S. J. Strauss and T. C. Tennent, *Encountering Theology of Mission: Biblical Foundations, Historical Developments, and Contemporary Issues* (Grand Rapids: Baker, 2010), p. 254.

[38] Peterson, *Acts*, p. 383.

his power, in which he is infinitely inferior to God, but his lies, and the gospel advances as the truth of Christ is proclaimed, the lies of Satan are thereby unmasked, and those enslaved by them are set free by the Son (John 8:36). 'If you hold to my teaching, you are really my disciples. Then you will know the truth, and the truth will set you free.'[39] Critical to the proconsul's conversion was his amazement at the *teaching about the Lord*, for that teaching – the truth, the good news of Christ – is itself amazing beyond whatever sign or wonder may accompany it. And the word of God wielded by the Spirit of God is itself powerful. In the Bible it is likened to a fire (Jer. 5:14; 23:29), a hammer (Jer. 23:29), a sword (Eph. 6:17; Heb. 4:12); and it unfailingly accomplishes the purposes of the God who speaks it (Isa. 55:10–11). Accordingly, while he certainly performed signs on many occasions – at Paphos, Lystra, Philippi, Ephesus and so on – what Paul did constantly and without fail, at every location, in every situation, to every person, was to preach the word of the gospel. And in his last epistle it was what he solemnly urged Timothy to continue: 'Preach the word.'[40]

Third, the power encounter can easily lead to a misunderstanding of the gospel as just another but more powerful form of magic, in some contexts producing new forms of animism. 'Those who choose Christ because they believe he is most powerful may also believe that they can manipulate him – as they tried to manipulate their old gods – to give them the benefits of power that they seek.'[41] Something of this is evident in the invocation of Christ's name by exorcists or sorcerers to energize their magic, as was the case with the 'sons of Sceva' (Acts 19:13–16). The 'power encounter' is not an end in itself, not the substance of salvation, but a means, a sign of the presence of the living God, and it 'must always be balanced with truth encounter'.[42] The act of power must be accompanied by a word of interpretation, as it is throughout the Bible.

Fourth, the 'power encounter' occurs in the context of God's sovereign will and purpose. Such moments are not at the disposal of the messenger of the gospel; they are not a tactic that may be employed at will as part of a predetermined strategy of 'power encounters'. Luke indicates in Acts 13 that Paul's powerful response to the sorcerer was inspired by the Spirit: *Then . . . Paul, filled with the Holy Spirit, looked straight at Elymas and said . . .* (9). Nowhere else do we read of him acting in this way although he faced opponents almost everywhere he went. At that moment, quite unexpectedly,

[39] John 8:31–32.
[40] 2 Tim. 4:2.
[41] Ott et al., *Encountering Theology of Mission*, p. 255.
[42] Ibid.

the Spirit took hold of the situation and used Paul to confound the sorcerer.

And, finally, the power of God may take many forms and not only that of miracles – indeed, not even primarily that of miracles. His power is manifested in transformed, gospel lives, in compassion and mercy, in service and supremely in sacrifice.[43] It is when 'the grain of wheat falls to the ground and dies' that it 'produces many seeds'.[44] The Lord Jesus himself triumphed in agony on a cross, that 'strangest victory'.[45] To be sure, 'Jews demand miraculous signs' – and not only Jews – 'but we preach Christ crucified . . . Christ the power of God and the wisdom of God'.[46]

[43] Ibid., p. 256.
[44] John 12:24.
[45] C. Idle, 'In silent pain the eternal Son hangs derelict and still', in B. Edwards et al. (eds.), *Praise! Psalms, Hymns and Songs for Christian Worship* (Darlington: Praise Trust, 2000), p. 428.
[46] 1 Cor. 1:22–24.

2 Corinthians 12:1–10
15. Strong in weakness

At the heart of the gospel there is a profound paradox which Paul expresses clearly in his first letter to the Corinthians: 'God chose the weak things of the world to shame the strong. He chose the lowly things of this world and the despised things – and the things that are not – to nullify the things that are, so that no one may boast before him.'[1] The paradox comes to expression from time to time in the Old Testament, as when God limited Gideon's army to a mere 300 men who then went on to defeat the thousands of Midianite oppressors (Judg. 7), or when he used the young David armed only with his sling to vanquish Goliath (1 Sam. 17). Indeed, it is evident in the very choice of Israel to be God's people: 'The LORD did not set his affection on you and choose you because you were more numerous than other peoples, for you were the fewest of all peoples.'[2] However, it is at the cross that the paradox is revealed to the highest degree, for there, in utter weakness and humiliation, Jesus Christ, eternal Word made flesh, triumphed over sin, death, hell and Satan. And as they follow their once-crucified master, Christian believers continue to live out the same reality as their lives and ministries are also characterized by the cross. 'We always carry around in our body the death of Jesus, so that the life of Jesus may also be revealed in our body.'[3] It is a central theme of the whole New Testament and one constantly apparent in church history through the centuries. Christian life and ministry are cross-shaped.

[1] 1 Cor. 1:27–29.
[2] Deut. 7:7.
[3] 2 Cor. 4:10.

1. Boasting

In 2 Corinthians 11 Paul begins to 'do a little boasting'.[4] He does so because his readers had evidently been captivated by the claims of certain unnamed 'super-apostles',[5] whom Paul identified as 'false apostles, deceitful workers, masquerading as apostles of Christ',[6] and even as servants of Satan (2 Cor. 11:14–15). The Corinthian church was, therefore, in serious danger of being 'led astray' from their 'sincere and pure devotion to Christ',[7] and in his letter Paul struggles to bring them to their senses. It is in that context that he 'boasts' to show that he is not 'in the least inferior' to these people (11:5; 12:11), but he hates doing so and repeatedly expresses his distaste: it is foolishness, it is not the way in which the Lord would speak, it is rather, indeed, what 'the world does'.[8] He felt it necessary, however, in order to 'cut the ground from under those who want an opportunity to be considered equal with us in the things they boast about'.[9] In brief, 'desperate situations call for desperate measures'.[10] For these were men who were trying to impose a more or less dictatorial authority over the Corinthian church, as Paul's sarcastic allusion to his readers' supine acquiescence makes clear: 'In fact, you even put up with anyone who enslaves you or exploits you or takes advantage of you or pushes himself forward or slaps you in the face.'[11] And they were doing so on the basis of their own triumphalistic boasting – about their Jewish ancestry, their service of Christ, the ecstatic experiences they had had and the like.

Paul begins to boast, therefore, by speaking of his own impeccable Jewish credentials (2 Cor. 11:22), but then he moves quickly on to his ministry and especially to all that he had suffered for Christ and the gospel:

> I have worked much harder, been in prison more frequently, been flogged more severely, and been exposed to death again and again . . . constantly on the move . . . in danger from rivers . . . from bandits . . . from my own countrymen . . . from Gentiles . . . in the city . . . in the country . . . at sea . . . from false brothers . . .

---

[4] 2 Cor. 11:16.
[5] 2 Cor. 11:5.
[6] 2 Cor. 11:13.
[7] 2 Cor. 11:3.
[8] 2 Cor. 11:17–18.
[9] 2 Cor. 11:12.
[10] R. P. Martin, *2 Corinthians*, Word Biblical Commentary 40 (Dallas: Word, 1998), pp. 395–396.
[11] 2 Cor. 11:20.

> Besides everything else, I face daily the pressure of my concern for all the churches.[12]

In all of this his whole attitude and approach is opposed to that of the false apostles. Far from arrogant boasting about his power he declares, 'If I must boast, I will boast of the things that show my weakness.'[13]

Nevertheless, at the start of chapter 12 Paul does boast of something other than his weaknesses, and writes of visions and revelations he had received. There is little doubt that he speaks in this way because the 'super-apostles' stressed their own ecstatic experiences as the source of their authority. This more than anything was the basis on which they sought to impose themselves and one that the Corinthians had accepted, and Paul, therefore, felt himself obliged to respond in kind.[14]

The New Testament actually refers to various visions Paul had received, notably when he was converted (Acts 9:3–6) and also when the Lord spoke to him at Corinth to encourage him to persevere with his ministry there (Acts 18:9–10).[15] The experience he describes here, however, was different from all of them. It had taken place fourteen years before he wrote this second letter to the Corinthian church (2 Cor. 12:2) which can be dated around AD 56 or 57. This would place the vision in about AD 42–3, several years after his conversion and possibly during the year he spent teaching the church in Antioch (Acts 11:26). More particularly it was not simply a vision or dream but an experience of rapture in which he himself was *caught up to the third heaven* or 'to paradise'. The verb Paul uses, which is translated 'caught up', is *harpazō* and the only other place in his letters where it is found is 1 Thessalonians 4:17 where he speaks of believers being 'caught up' to meet the Lord 'in the air' at the parousia. There has been a good deal of debate about the identification of the place Paul was *caught up* to but, as Hughes says, 'We may take it as certain that the Apostle ... was taken into the heavenly presence of the exalted and glorified Saviour.'[16]

Nevertheless, he writes of such matters with acute embarrassment and obvious reluctance. Throughout this brief section he uses the

---

[12] 2 Cor. 11:23–28.

[13] 2 Cor. 11:30.

[14] C. G. Kruse, *2 Corinthians: An Introduction and Commentary*, Tyndale NT Commentaries (Leicester: Inter-Varsity Press, 1987), p. 193.

[15] These were not the only ones. See also Acts 9:12; 16:9–10; 22:17–21; 23:11; 27:23–24.

[16] P. E. Hughes, *The Second Epistle to the Corinthians* (Grand Rapids: Eerdmans, 1962), p. 434.

third person as if to distance himself from what he is saying, although clearly he speaks of his own experiences:

> *I know a man in Christ who . . . was caught up to the third heaven . . . And I know that this man . . . was caught up to paradise. He heard inexpressible things . . . I will boast about a man like that, but I will not boast about myself, except about my weaknesses* (2–5).

Moreover, the terms he uses also move attention away from himself and towards the divine author of the experience. So, his repeated use of the passive voice (*was caught up . . . was caught up . . .*) indicates quite simply that this was something that was done *to Paul* rather than something that was achieved *by him*. 'What has happened has been done to Paul; he did nothing to obtain the vision.'[17] Further, Paul's self-identification as *a man in Christ* indicates why the experience was given to him. 'It was not by virtue of some natural psychic propensity or any acquired capacity for mystical experience that Paul was caught up in this way, but by virtue of his being, through grace, a "man-in-Christ."'[18] And finally, he refrains from disclosing what he heard, for these were inexpressible things *that man is not permitted to tell* (4). Even though he feels forced to *boast*, there is a limit to what he will say, in part because the experience was ineffable and in part because it was a sacred and personal gift from God to him alone, and one of which he only speaks at all under duress.

So, to conclude, while Paul 'boasts', he does so in such a way as to minimize his own role in what he had experienced fourteen years earlier and to ascribe it all entirely to God and his grace. Yet, at the same time what he had described would certainly put him 'on a level with the great heroes of faith, and by claiming such an experience Paul could completely outflank his opponents'.[19]

2. Hurting

And then Paul moves quickly back to his weaknesses again. In speaking of his experience of the *third heaven* he had briefly been arguing within a frame of reference dictated by the false apostles, but now he returns to his own perspective for, in his view, it is suffering rather than signs and wonders that constitutes the authentic mark of apostolic ministry. It is, indeed, through suffering that the

[17] Martin, *2 Corinthians*, p. 398.
[18] Hughes, *Second Corinthians*, p. 432.
[19] Kruse, *2 Corinthians*, p. 196.

gospel is brought to the nations (Col. 1:24) just as it was through Christ's suffering that there is a gospel to bring in the first place.

And so Paul speaks of *a thorn in my flesh, a messenger from Satan, to torment me* (7). As Martin observes, 'much scholarship has been devoted to this phrase, yet undeniably mystery and uncertainty remain'.[20] Clearly Paul refers to an affliction of some sort, and one that was evidently severe. The Greek word translated *thorn* (*skolops*) can indeed be understood as a stake or 'sharpened wooden staff',[21] and that may be the better translation.[22] Whatever Paul's exact intention, the image is emphatically 'of something sharp and painful which sticks deeply in the flesh and in the will of God defies extracting'.[23] It was an evil and unpleasant thing, and it was brought about by the agency of Satan himself. Some interpreters have suggested that the *messenger* (literally 'angel') *of Satan* should be understood in human terms, such that it would represent a human adversary or adversaries used by Satan to trouble the apostle. In the context, however, the *messenger of Satan* is probably best understood as a demon, which is surely how contemporary readers would most readily have taken the phrase.

Identifying the messenger as a demon would also be consistent with the view that the 'thorn' was a physical affliction, a malady of some sort. In other biblical texts Satan brings about physical suffering, sometimes through demonic activity and especially so in cases of demon possession, but also where possession was not involved. For example, in Luke's account of the woman who was 'crippled by a spirit' and 'kept bound' by Satan, resulting in severe curvature of the spine (possibly 'spondylitis ankylopoeitica'),[24] a demon was probably involved. The symptoms of possession found elsewhere in the Gospels were not, however, evident in her case, nor did Jesus deal with her as he habitually dealt with possessed people.[25]

Not all interpreters, however, see Paul's thorn in physical terms. Some argue that he may be using the word 'flesh' (*sarx*) in the ethical sense so that it was not necessarily his body that was afflicted. This would be consistent with the ethical purpose of the suffering:

[20] Martin, *2 Corinthians*, p. 412.

[21] Hughes, *Second Corinthians*, p. 447.

[22] D. E. Garland, *2 Corinthians*, New American Commentary (Nashville: B&H Publishing Group, 1999), p. 519.

[23] H. R. Minn, quoted in Garland, *2 Corinthians*, p. 519.

[24] Luke 13:10–17. The diagnosis proposed by J. Wilkinson, 'The Case of the Bent Woman in Luke 13v10–17', *EvQ* 49 (1977), pp. 196–200.

[25] So, for example, E. E. Ellis, *The Gospel of Luke* (London: Nelson, 1966), p. 186, who sees it as 'a purely physical effect caused by demonic power and not "demonic possession" of the personality'.

to keep me from becoming conceited (7). Accordingly the *thorn in my flesh* has been understood as an ongoing struggle with temptation which would keep him humble, or as the virulent Jewish opposition he had repeatedly to face, maybe even the opposition he encountered within some of the churches. It has also been seen as depression or demonic oppression and so on.[26] Nevertheless, none of these are quite convincing. In a fallen world temptation is a constant and it would hardly have begun to afflict Paul after his experience of rapture, though it is conceivable that he suffered especially intense satanic attack on his mind in the course of his ministry, as has sometimes been the experience of missionaries and evangelists. Similarly he faced Jewish opposition from the moment he began to preach the gospel in Damascus immediately after his conversion (Acts 9:23); and anyway, as we have noted, he regarded persecution as an integral part of his ministry and a crucial witness to its authenticity. Meanwhile, opposition *within* the churches seems to have come later. Nor do Paul's letters give the impression of a man depressed, although undoubtedly he had to deal with the stresses of his ministry including, as he says, his 'concern for all the churches'.[27] His epistles to the Corinthians are examples of this, as also his anguish over what was taking place in the Galatian church (Gal. 4:19–20) and his anxiety for the one in Thessalonica (1 Thess. 2:17 – 3:10). Nevertheless, such concerns do not amount to depression and, given the nature of his gospel ministry, he would scarcely have prayed that he should be relieved of them.

It seems, indeed, most likely that when Paul spoke of his *thorn in my flesh* he was referring to a physical affliction. So Hughes argues: 'The ethical sense is less likely here . . . since ordinarily Paul reserves it for a doctrinal-ethical context in which "the flesh" and "the spirit" are set forth as opposing forces.'[28] Among other suggestions it has been identified as an eye complaint, on the basis of Paul's reference to an illness he suffered while in Galatia (Gal. 4:13–15). There he speaks of a 'weakness of the flesh' (translated 'illness' in the NIV), so severe that it might well have provoked the 'contempt or scorn' of the Galatians themselves. However, quite to the contrary, Paul declares that 'if you could have done so you would have torn out your eyes and given them to me', which implies that he was suffering from a very severe and unpleasant ophthalmic condition. Moreover, his words near the end of the letter may perhaps suggest it was an

---

[26] J. Wilkinson, *Health and Healing: Studies in New Testament Principles and Practice* (Edinburgh: The Handsel Press, 1980), pp. 114–116. Martin, *2 Corinthians*, pp. 412–416, discusses the issue quite fully as does Hughes, *Second Corinthians*, pp. 443–446.

[27] 2 Cor. 11:28–29.

[28] Hughes, *Second Corinthians*, p. 448.

ongoing complaint: 'See what large letters I use as I write to you with my own hand!'[29]

William Ramsey very plausibly suggested that it may have been malaria which Paul could have caught in Pamphylia where it was endemic, following his arrival from Cyprus during his missionary journey with Barnabas. That would, indeed, explain how he came to be so ill during his ministry among the Galatians, and it more or less fits Paul's reference to the time of the onset of the problem, not too long after his experience of rapture. Moreover, it can be a recurrent disease, which coincides with what Paul says about the 'thorn'. 'In some constitutions malaria fever tends to recur in very distressing and prostrating paroxysms, whenever one's energies are taxed for a great effort. Such an attack is for the time absolutely incapacitating.'[30]

And there are certainly other theories. The fact is, however, that 'we will probably never know the truth (or, at least, never know for sure we have the truth)'.[31] Indeed, our very ignorance has advantages. 'The ambiguity about what Paul's thorn in the flesh might be allows others to identify their own personal "thorns" with Paul's and to appropriate the theological lessons.'[32] And we do at least know what Paul tells us. 'It was chronic and recurring, an embarrassment to his work, but not debarring from it. It was an individual and personal problem, and not such suffering as was the common lot of Christians.'[33]

3. Understanding

By his own admission, then, Paul believed himself to have been afflicted by *a messenger of Satan*. There is something unexpected and even perplexing in the fact that an apostle of Christ should suffer at the hands of a demon. Nevertheless, his experience is consistent with Job's and, in a somewhat different way, with that of the Lord Jesus Christ too whose betrayer was beguiled and ultimately possessed by Satan (John 13:2, 27). It indicates that while Jesus has given his disciples authority 'to trample on snakes and scorpions and to overcome all the power of the enemy',[34] he has not exempted them from all the physical torments that the enemy might seek to inflict. Satan may use human persecutors in his efforts to attack the church

[29] Gal. 6:11.
[30] W. M. Ramsay, quoted by Hughes, *Second Corinthians*, p. 445.
[31] Martin, *2 Corinthians*, p. 416.
[32] Garland, *2 Corinthians*, p. 521.
[33] C. J. Hemer, 'Medicine in the New Testament World', in B. Palmer (ed.), *Medicine and the Bible* (Carlisle: Paternoster, 1986), p. 79.
[34] Luke 10:19.

and frustrate its mission or, as with this *thorn in my flesh*, he may attack through demonic agents, or even do so directly himself. Whatever the case, he strikes back at those whom God has redeemed from the dominion of darkness and sent out with good news, *and the pain is real*. This fact echoes God's word of judgment to the serpent with the first promise of a seed of the woman who would bring deliverance from the serpent: 'he will crush your head, and you will strike his heel'.[35] While the disciples of that redeemer, sent out by him to announce to the nations the good news of his victory, will indeed trample on the enemy and overcome him, they will nonetheless also experience the savage venom of his hatred as Jesus did.

The point, however, is that God takes hold even of Satan's malice and turns it to his own good purposes. For the text shows that Paul understood his suffering not simply in terms of demonic aggression, but in the much greater context of God's all-encompassing sovereignty. Accordingly, first, as he speaks of his affliction he employs a passive verb to refer to the arrival of the *thorn in my flesh*: *there was given me*.[36] He does not identify the agent of the passive verb, but it is unlikely that it would be Satan as the verb 'to give' 'was usually employed to denote that God's favor had been bestowed'.[37] In other words, Paul is employing a *divine passive*, which implicitly identifies God 'as the hidden agent behind events and experiences in human lives'.[38] The act was truly Satan's, willed and carried out by him without any divine coercion, and motivated by his determination to attack those set free from his dominion and to hinder them as they announce the gospel of Christ. But through that act he unconsciously fulfilled God's purpose for Paul.

Second, Paul declares that there was a good and wise reason for his sufferings. For the experience he describes of being *caught up to paradise* and hearing *inexpressible things* was at once both glorious and dangerous. The nature of his still imperfect heart made him vulnerable to sins of pride and conceit which would seriously undermine his usefulness as an apostle of Christ. Paul was aware of this. He well knew that anything he might accomplish in the course of his ministry was achieved only by the grace of God and never in his own strength and wisdom. He expressed that, for example, when he compared his own labours with those of the other apostles: 'But by the grace of God I am what I am, and his grace to me was not without effect. No, I worked harder than all of them – yet not I, but

---

[35] Gen. 3:15.
[36] *edothē moi*.
[37] Martin, *2 Corinthians*, p. 412.
[38] Ibid.

the grace of God that was with me.'[39] No sooner does he speak of his own hard work than he immediately attributes it to God's grace. Earlier in 2 Corinthians he describes similarly the way God works through human weakness so that it may be totally clear that it is God's power that is at work (2 Cor. 4:7). And at the heart of it all there is the cross. God redeemed men and women through the cross of Christ, for Christ crucified is 'the power of God and the wisdom of God'.[40] And the advance of his kingdom is equally marked by the cross: 'God acts in the present in continuity with the way he acted in the past.'[41] A weak, despised, buffeted Paul is one through whom God may work, and partly for that reason he wants to know Christ 'and the fellowship of sharing in his sufferings, becoming like him in his death'.[42]

Paul came, therefore, to understand that the 'thorn' had been given by God to weaken and humble him, and so *to keep me from becoming conceited* (7) and self-sufficient. It forced him into a conscious dependence on God's grace rather than on his own strength, and so prevented him being a hindrance to the working of God's grace through him. The result was that he became more fruitful. *For when I am weak, then I am strong* (10). Moreover, in the context of his response to the 'super-apostles' in this part of the epistle, it meant that he could revert to weakness as the true criterion of authentic apostleship rather than echo his opponents' insistence on *visions and revelations*. It was not so much the experience of paradise that sustained his ministry, but rather the debilitating and humbling affliction which had been given to him to make room for the power of God: *my power is made perfect in weakness* (9).

Paul's understanding of his affliction is clearly drawn from God's response to his prayers: *but he said to me . . .* (9). It also reflects a knowledge of God that draws deeply from the testimony of Scripture. It is grounded, first, on an awareness of God's active and sovereign reign over all of his creation, including Satan himself and the whole dominion of darkness. It was not just that God permitted Satan to afflict Paul and then skilfully responded, redirecting what Satan did for his own purpose like some supreme grandmaster of chess. The 'thorn' was *given* by God: he was no mere observer of his adversary's moves but he actively ordained what took place. The same is true, of course, of the crucifixion. Sinful men brought about the death of the Lord Jesus Christ through their plotting and manoeuvring, and

---

[39] 1 Cor. 15:10.
[40] 1 Cor. 1:24.
[41] G. Tomlin, quoted in J. R. Treat, *The Crucified King: Atonement and Kingdom in Biblical and Systematic Theology* (Grand Rapids: Zondervan, 2014), p. 229.
[42] Phil. 3:10.

Satan had more than a hand in it all. The moments of arrest and trial, torture and crucifixion constituted the very hour when darkness reached its zenith: 'this is your hour – when darkness reigns'.[43] And yet it was all carried out by 'God's set purpose and foreknowledge';[44] through the actions of sinful men God himself 'fulfilled what he had foretold through all the prophets, saying that his Christ would suffer';[45] and so Pilate and Herod along with Jews and Gentiles did no more than what God's 'power and will had decided beforehand should happen'.[46] In Isaiah's prophetic words: 'It was the Lord's will to crush him and cause him to suffer.'[47] Unquestionably there is profound and inexplicable mystery in all this. God accomplishes his purpose through the malice of *a messenger of Satan*, the spinelessness of Pontius Pilate, the hatred of the Sanhedrin, and yet he remains totally untouched by their evil. As Paul says elsewhere, 'How unsearchable his judgments, and his paths beyond tracing out!'[48] Yet there is also immense encouragement for his people. In the spiritual conflict they face they know assuredly that God directs every circumstance and every actor, human or demonic, to accomplish perfectly his good and perfect will. Nothing escapes him. Satan never gets away with anything, never steals a trick, never slips in under the radar. The very wounds he inflicts on God's beloved children become blessing to them through the inscrutable logic of the cross, that 'strangest victory'.

Second, Paul speaks of a God who submits his children to affliction in order to protect them from sin and its consequences. What Paul experienced, whatever it may have been and whether seen as 'thorn' or 'stake', was painful, but it was *given* by God. That God should work in this way demonstrates quite clearly the gravity of the ongoing threat of sin in the lives of his people – its subtlety and deceitfulness; its insidious penetration of thoughts, attitudes and motives; and the way in which it is parasitic on what is good and able quickly to pervert even Paul's inexpressible experience of glory into an occasion of sinful and incapacitating pride. And so, as the ultimate Father, the God of all grace responds with a pre-emptive discipline which is painful and severe but which is yet born out of boundless mercy and a longing for the true and eternal well-being of his children and their usefulness to him. It was, indeed, a severe mercy, but a necessary one, the act of a God infinitely good but not

---

[43] Luke 22:53.
[44] Acts 2:23.
[45] Acts 3:18.
[46] Acts 4:28.
[47] Isa. 53:10.
[48] Rom. 11:33.

'safe'.[49] It illuminates the depth and the awesome fearfulness of his all-wise love which relentlessly and unfailingly works out the salvation of his children, preserving them from sin and bringing about that growing conformity 'to the likeness of his Son' for which they were predestined (Rom. 8:29).

4. Responding

Paul responded to the discipline he experienced in two ways, one following the other. First, he prayed; indeed, three times he *pleaded with the Lord to take it away from me* (8). In his praying he recognized that the 'thorn' was an evil thing and asked quite reasonably that it be removed. Ultimately all illness and pain are the result of sin and the work of the devil. The biblical response to them is not, therefore, one of passivity but of struggle. Jesus healed the sick; he wept at the grave of Lazarus and raised him from the dead; he was angry in the face of leprosy.[50] From the beginning Christian believers have therefore also been at the forefront of the struggle with disease, caring for the sick even at great risk to themselves and seeking remedies for their suffering.[51]

But then, as he prayed, Paul came to realize that God was not going to heal him and he saw his affliction in a different light. It was not that he ceased to perceive it as an evil. It was still the work of *a messenger of Satan* intended to harm him, but it was also given by God. At that point he embraced it positively as something which enabled Christ's power to rest on him (9). And the attitude he displays is not one of stoic acquiescence or grim resignation. He 'boasts' about his weaknesses and he *delights* in them – *in weaknesses, in insults, in hardships, in persecutions, in difficulties* (10). There is a joyous acceptance of God's providence in his life because he believes, he is firmly convinced, that in his infinite wisdom, goodness and power God is doing what is absolutely the best, painful though it may be. Even this ugly thing, this debilitating 'stake' inflicted by *a messenger of Satan* out of pure malice, is working for his good and for the good of the work God had entrusted to him. *For when I am weak, then I am strong* (10).

[49] The contrast comes from C. S. Lewis, *The Lion, the Witch and the Wardrobe* (Harmondsworth: Penguin, 1959), p. 75: 'Who said anything about safe? 'Course he isn't safe. But he's good. He's the King, I tell you.'

[50] Although the exegesis is debated, in Mark 1:41 when Jesus encounters a man with leprosy the variant *orgistheis* (angry) is probably to be preferred to *splagchnistheis* (moved with compassion), and it expresses Jesus' 'anger with Satan at his disfigurement of God's creature'. See C. E. B. Cranfield, *The Gospel According to St Mark* (Cambridge: Cambridge University Press, 1959), p. 92.

[51] See e.g., R. Stark, *The Rise of Christianity* (New York: HarperOne, 1996), pp. 82–88.

Part 4
Fighting in hope

Romans 12:1-2
16. Battle for the mind

'Your patient, thanks to Our Father below, is a fool.'[1] So, according to C. S. Lewis, did the senior devil Screwtape write to the junior tempter Wormwood shortly after the latter's anonymous 'patient' had become a Christian. There is an intimate relationship between sin and folly. Sin clouds and distorts the mental faculties of human beings. It does so because at its very root there is the perverse repudiation of the most foundational truth of all – that of the triune God himself – and in his place men and women put idols of their own imagining. As their conception of the absolutely ultimate reality is so utterly corrupted, so too are their thinking and reasoning and therefore also their very lives, and that at *every* level and not only with respect to specifically theological and spiritual matters. In many societies, for example, the prevalence of fatalism, belief in the notion of limited good, animistic thinking and bondage to fear of witchcraft and unseen powers contribute to a world view which sustains poverty and injustice. 'Physical poverty is rooted in a mindset of poverty, a set of ideas held corporately that produce certain behaviours.'[2]

Indeed, sin gained its first entry when Adam and Eve allowed their minds to be poisoned by the serpent's lies about their creator. In consequence they and the entire race they would engender were enslaved by sin and by the folly inseparably bound up with it. Paul expresses this at the beginning of his epistle to the Romans. Godless and sinful people 'suppress the truth' about God their creator, and that crucial denial means that 'their thinking became futile and their

---

[1] C. S. Lewis, *The Screwtape Letters* (London: Geoffrey Bles/The Centenary Press, 1942), p. 16.

[2] D. L. Miller, *Discipling Nations: The Power of Truth to Transform Cultures* (Seattle: YWAM Publishers, 1998), p. 67.

foolish hearts were darkened'.[3] Again, in Ephesians he speaks of how the Gentiles live, 'in the futility of their thinking. They are darkened in their understanding and separated from the life of God because of the ignorance that is in them due to the hardening of their hearts'.[4]

Enslavement to sin is, therefore, enslavement also to folly. Screwtape was right. When Satan seduces men and women to sin he makes them fools and, regardless of their IQ or the level of education and culture they may have attained, the minds of human beings are grossly disordered. The gospel, therefore, as it deals with sin also brings renewal to the mind, although not without determined resistance from Satan. This means that a critical theatre of the believer's spiritual warfare is the battle for the mind, and at the beginning of Romans 12 Paul focuses his readers' attention on its absolute importance.

1. Offering sacrifices (12:1)

Following his exposition of the gospel in Romans 1 – 11, Paul begins to draw out its implications: *Therefore, I urge you, brothers, in view of God's mercy, to offer your bodies as living sacrifices, holy and pleasing to God* (1). At the heart of the gospel there is God's mercy and Paul has been explaining it through all the preceding chapters. Its essence lies in 'God's abundant provision of grace and of the gift of righteousness',[5] as a result of which 'there is now no condemnation for those who are in Christ Jesus'.[6] It is this that makes it such utterly *good* news – news of total acquittal for people condemned and without hope! And Paul implores his readers to respond to that mercy by offering their bodies to God as living sacrifices.

Paul's challenge clearly recalls the language of Old Testament sacrifice but what he urges on his readers moves radically beyond the Jewish sacrificial system. First, the sacrifice he calls for does not involve animals but their own human bodies, by which Paul means 'their whole selves'.[7] As Calvin says, 'not only our skin and bones, but the totality of which we are composed'.[8] Further, it is not a merely passive sacrifice of themselves to which they submit as

---

[3] Rom. 1:18, 21.
[4] Eph. 4:17–18.
[5] Rom. 5:17.
[6] Rom. 8:1.
[7] C. G. Kruse, *Paul's Letter to the Romans*, Pillar NT Commentary (Grand Rapids: Eerdmans and Nottingham: Apollos, 2012), p. 461.
[8] J. Calvin, quoted by C. E. B. Cranfield, *The Epistle to the Romans, Volume II* (Edinburgh: T&T Clark, 1979), pp. 598–599.

victims, but one of which they are subject as well as object. *They* are to present *themselves*, very much as Jesus presented himself and laid down his life. Third, the sacrifice is to be living, holy and acceptable. The obvious meaning of 'living' is that it does not involve the physical death of the victims but rather their lives as lived day by day for God. In the context, however, Paul may be thinking rather of the 'new life' that the believer now lives in Christ (Rom. 6:4). 'It is a body alive from the dead that the believer is to present, alive from the dead because the body of sin has been destroyed.'[9] That same idea then continues with the word *holy*, which stresses the believers' separation *to* God and consequent separation *from* all that might defile. And such a sacrifice, living and holy, would therefore also be *pleasing to God*, one which 'is desired by God and which he will accept'.[10]

Finally, Paul adds, *this is your spiritual act of worship*. Earlier he used the word translated here as *act of worship* (*latreia*) of the temple worship (Rom. 9:4). It is also used three other times in the New Testament and frequently in the Septuagint always with reference to religious worship.[11] Paul is saying, then, that the worship of Christian believers is no longer focused on the temple cult but consists rather in the offering to God of their *bodies*. There is a totality about this worship: it embraces all of life, every aspect of 'their whole selves', every area in which their lives are carried on. It is then further qualified by a word (*logikos*) variously translated *spiritual* or 'reasonable'. The only other place where it is found in the New Testament is in Peter's reference to 'pure spiritual milk'.[12] With that sense 'your spiritual worship' might be a worship that stands 'in contrast with the externalities of Israel's temple worship'.[13] However, *logikos* is not the word usually employed in the New Testament to convey the notion of what is 'spiritual', while in Greek literature it means 'thoughtful' or 'rational'. This would fit well in the context, as Paul goes on to speak of the renewal of the mind. 'We give ourselves to God as his sacrifices when we understand his grace and its place in our lives. We offer ourselves not ignorantly, like animals brought to slaughter, but intelligently and willingly. This is the worship that pleases God.'[14]

[9] J. Murray, *The Epistle to the Romans* (London: Marshall, Morgan and Scott, 1974), p. 111. So too Cranfield, *Romans*, p. 600.

[10] Cranfield, *Romans*, p. 601.

[11] Kruse, *Romans*, p. 462.

[12] 1 Pet. 2:2.

[13] F. F. Bruce, *Romans*, Tyndale NT Commentaries (Leicester: Inter-Varsity Press and Grand Rapids: Eerdmans, 1963), p. 226.

[14] D. J. Moo, *Romans*, NIV Application Commentary (Grand Rapids: Zondervan, 2000), p. 395.

2. Not conforming (12:2a)

Paul continues, *And do not conform* . . . The word 'and' is omitted in the NIV but its presence indicates that what Paul says here continues the theme of the preceding verse. The positive worship of offering one's body demands a corresponding negative in terms of not conforming *to the pattern of this world* or, more literally, not conforming 'to this age'. In the New Testament 'this age' is one dominated by sin, and Satan is its god (2 Cor. 4:4); it is, therefore, an evil age but also one that is passing away. To a significant extent it finds tangible expression in human cultures and the world views which underlie them, which inevitably reflect something of the futile thinking and darkened, foolish hearts (Rom. 1:21) of those who fashion them.

a. The pressure to conform

Believers have already been rescued from this age by Christ's death for their sins (Gal. 1:4; Col. 1:13–14), and belong now to the age to come.[15] Nevertheless, although redeemed from this age they have not been removed from its presence but must live in its midst as strangers and exiles. They must, therefore, strive purposefully to live the life of the new age in the midst of the old, which constantly seeks to 'squeeze' them 'into its own mould'.[16] Much of the time it does so quietly and subtly, as believers are constantly exposed to the underlying non-Christian and anti-Christian 'noise' that permeates their cultures, and even more so in those with advanced and near inescapable technologies of communication. In societies more virulently hostile to the gospel pressure to conform may also be expressed violently. Whatever the case, confronted by an apparently overwhelming consensus against them, Christians may well question the plausibility of their own radically different beliefs and quietly conform to the thinking and way of life of 'this age'. Paul summons his readers to a purposeful, determined and unyielding refusal to do so.

Stott points out that Paul's words echo God's warning to Israel as they moved towards the land of promise: 'You must not do as they do in the land of Canaan, where I am bringing you. Do not follow their practices.'[17] The difference is that God also commanded Israel to remove the Canaanites from Canaan as they took possession of the land, so that they would not be drawn into their idolatrous

---

[15] See ch. 11 above.

[16] 12:2 as translated by J. B. Phillips, *The New Testament in Modern English* (London: Geoffrey Bles, 1960).

[17] Lev. 18:3. J. R. W. Stott, *The Message of Romans: God's Good News for the World*, Bible Speaks Today (Leicester: Inter-Varsity Press, 2001), p. 319.

worship and correspondingly corrupt lifestyle (Exod. 23:33; Deut. 7:16). Paul's readers would not be doing that – in their case the 'Canaanites' would stay. Paul is urging them to lead countercultural lives and to persist uncompromisingly in doing so.[18]

b. The practice of nonconformity

The implications of such a call are evident throughout the New Testament. For example, the Greek culture which prevailed throughout most of the eastern Mediterranean was characterized by an extremely liberal attitude towards sexual morality. In response Paul's letters contain repeated warnings to his readers not to conform to the sexual *mores* that were common in their towns and cities, and which in their own pre-Christian past they too had regarded as nothing other than normal and unremarkable. 'Among you there must not be even a hint of sexual immorality or of any kind of impurity.'[19]

Similarly both Paul and Peter urged their readers to live out the 'radical and profoundly liberating'[20] implications of the gospel in the context of their various social roles and relationships (Eph. 5:22 – 6:9; Col 3:18 – 4:1; 1 Pet. 2:18 – 3:7). They were to reflect God's creation order rather than the oppressive and dehumanizing attitudes towards women, slaves and children which characterized the societies they lived in. Accordingly,

> wives, children, and slaves are addressed equally with husbands, fathers, and masters (5:22; cf. 6:1,5,9). They have their own calling before the Lord, which is as responsible, honourable, and important as that of husband, parent, and master ... Those in authority have different roles with greater responsibility, but they are not *better* roles. The value, dignity, or worth of the members of the Christian household in a subordinate position is not less than that of those in authority.[21]

c. The price of nonconformity

Not conforming, however, comes at a price. At the lowest level there is the subjective sense of unease and alienation that arises from thinking and behaving differently from everybody else. Most people

---

[18] The present imperative Paul uses calls for a continuing refusal to conform.

[19] Eph. 5:3.

[20] M. Turner, quoted by P. T. O'Brien, *The Letter to the Ephesians*, Pillar NT Commentary (Grand Rapids: Eerdmans and Leicester: Apollos, 1999), p. 408.

[21] O'Brien, *Ephesians*, p. 408.

have a natural tendency to conform – a desire not to stand out but to be like everyone else. Cultures invariably permit a degree of variety in behaviour, but there is a point beyond which divergence from cultural norms becomes uncomfortable and leads to exclusion. In Revelation those who refused to bear the mark of the beast were excluded from buying and selling (Rev. 13:17). Some Corinthian believers continued participating at cultic feasts and the associated sacrifices in pagan temples as they had in the past, in order to avoid the social, economic and political disadvantages of absence (1 Cor. 8 – 10).[22] And ultimately nonconformity may lead to active persecution, including the loss of goods, liberty, and even life. Again, Revelation addresses those who faced those very challenges, some of whom were indeed conforming to the idolatries of imperial Rome, and urgently pressed them to a life of conscious separation no matter what the cost. 'Come out of her, my people, so that you will not share in her sins.'[23]

3. Being transformed (12:2b)

If they are to live nonconforming lives, however, Christians must be changed people. To suppose otherwise would be quite unrealistic, for people will inevitably live out what they most truly are. If the values of 'this age' remain embedded in their minds and hearts, then to 'this age' they will conform. So, Paul's negative call, *do not conform . . .* , is accompanied by a corresponding positive call, *but be transformed.*

Of course, the fact that they were Christians meant that Paul's readers had already experienced God's transforming work. They were born from above, and already a new creation (John 3:3, 6; 2 Cor. 5:17). However, the present imperative Paul uses here indicates that that vital, initial, regenerating act of God must be followed by a process of ongoing change. Like that first moment of new birth it too is a divine operation effected by the Holy Spirit, but now with the believer's active cooperation. Hence Paul addresses his readers with a command they themselves are responsible to obey: 'keep being transformed'. And the way in which transformation will come about is through *the renewing of your mind.*

a. Mind renewal

It is an absolutely vital point. As we saw above, at the beginning of the epistle Paul explained how human wickedness is tightly bound

---

[22] See below, pp. 232–233.
[23] Rev. 18:4.

up with suppression of the truth, futile thinking and folly (Rom. 1:18–22). Therefore, at the heart of that transformation which will enable his Roman readers to offer their bodies as sacrifices to God and to resist the pressure to conform to this age, there must be the renewing of minds. We are what we think: beliefs, attitudes, values, patterns of thought, assumptions – all the content and processes of the mind – are the source of human words, actions and whole lives. And despite the innumerable achievements of human intelligence, human minds are fallen minds, snared in folly, perverse and ignorant of all that really matters. Most crucially they are blind to God and utterly unable to respond to their own lost condition – unable, indeed, even to recognize it.

Redemption itself is therefore worked out through the liberating power of gospel truth as God miraculously opens eyes blinded by sin and the 'light of the knowledge of the glory of God in the face of Christ' shines in human hearts.[24] It is knowledge of the truth of Christ brought home to human minds by the Holy Spirit that sets free men and women enslaved by sin (John 8:32). He gives sight, awakens minds, disperses the fog. Nevertheless, that initial act of illumination must be followed by an ongoing work of God who progressively renews minds still soiled and disfigured with the detritus of sin, unbelief and folly. Meanwhile, Satan and this age remain active in their continuing efforts to contaminate and pollute. This is the battle for the mind. And if believers continue to think as they did, they will continue to act as they did. They will conform.

b. The word of God

In Eden the serpent supplanted the word of truth Adam and Eve had received from God with its own lies and by that means seduced them. The renewing of the mind means that by God's Spirit God's truth now progressively dislodges Satan's lies and restores a disordered mind to wholeness. On several occasions the New Testament emphasizes the revitalizing energy of God's word. Pre-eminently, in his prayer for his people Jesus asked that they would be made holy by God's word of truth: 'Sanctify them by the truth; your word is truth.'[25] When Paul wrote to the Ephesians he reminded them how the truth they had learned would make their minds new: 'You were taught . . . to be made new in the attitude of your minds . . .'[26] And the writer of Hebrews underlined the power of God's word to

[24] 2 Cor. 4:6.
[25] John 17:17.
[26] Eph. 4:22–23.

199

penetrate the human heart and unmask its deepest secrets and deceptions: 'For the word of God is living and active. Sharper than any double-edged sword, it penetrates even to dividing soul and spirit, joints and marrow; it judges the thoughts and attitudes of the heart.'[27]

Paul's summons calls, therefore, for the entry of God's truth into human minds. In practice it means nurturing a hunger for his word and developing also the spiritual facility of recognizing its implications. It means that all the furnishings of the mind – its assumptions, beliefs, values, priorities, ambitions and whatever else – must come under the penetrating scrutiny of the word and be reshaped by it. Diligent attention to preaching and teaching, to faithful and serious Christian literature, and especially to the reading of the Bible itself are clearly implied by all this. And with them a sincere and inquisitive willingness to change beliefs and patterns of thought according as the word demands. At heart it is about obedience and true worship, for the Lord God Almighty, creator of heaven and earth, has spoken. It is about truly hearing *him*. 'The lion has roared – who will not fear?'[28]

c. Rooting out the lies

In parallel with the positive assimilation of truth there is the elimination of lies. A major concern is the identification and repudiation of all the remaining debris of those false human religions or ideologies to which Christian believers adhered before they were saved. Paul praised the way in which the Thessalonian believers had 'turned to God from idols',[29] but the eradication of all vestiges of their former thinking would demand the ongoing renewing of their minds. To a significant extent it was in pursuit of that objective that he wrote his letters in the first place. Pre-Christian beliefs and values lurk in the still unredeemed assumptions and thought patterns of the past, until the light of God's word penetrates deep into 'the thoughts and attitudes of the heart'[30] to bring conviction and change. Nor is this true only of those converted from other religions, but also of the quasi-religious idols of modern secular and materialistic societies, idols such as wealth, consumption, sexual pleasure and social status. The problem is that the profound assumptions of world view, assimilated largely unconsciously from parents, friends, peers, schools, media and so on, are strongly resistant to change. This is why Paul faced so many challenges in his dealings with the Corinthian church,

---

[27] Heb. 4:12.
[28] Amos 3:8.
[29] 1 Thess. 1:9.
[30] Heb. 4:12.

for example; and also why the intentional pursuit of mind-renewal by word and Spirit needs to be taken so seriously. Nor was it a matter only for the churches Paul wrote to but an issue that needs urgently to be addressed in Western churches, which are also so readily 'squeezed into the mold of the pagan world around us', as evidenced by 'our preoccupation with material prosperity . . . our syncretistic and aberrant forms of worship . . . our refusal to obey the Lord's call to separation from the world . . . our divisiveness and competitiveness . . . our moral compromises . . .'[31] Behind it all there is that persistent assertion of human autonomy which is at the heart of sin, and ongoing resistance to the claims of the one who made us, defines us, owns us.

Moreover, not only is it a question of rooting out the lies already there, but also of filtering out the new ones trying to get in. In the Western world the secular, godless mind is powerfully disseminated by the media. The output of film producers and television programmers is never morally and spiritually neutral, even when it seems to be at its most innocuous. At the most basic level, the constant portrayal of human life with no reference at all to God subliminally and incessantly communicates the notion that he is a total irrelevance to human life and concerns, and that faith in him is little more than an archaic, psychological crutch for the inadequate. The visible result is the functional atheism of Western societies and the inevitable moral relativism that it produces. For Christians in the twenty-first century the renewing of the mind demands tireless monitoring and evaluation of the content of their viewing and, indeed, their reading too. Uncritically soaking up hours of visual output inescapably leads to the pollution of the mind by the god of this age. 'If we spend all our discretionary time watching network television, reading secular books, and listening to secular music, it will be a wonder if our minds are not fundamentally secular.'[32]

d. The knowledge of God himself

Above all else it is profound knowledge of God through his revelation of his very self that is essential to the renewing of the minds of Christian believers. In Eden the foundation of the serpent's temptation was rooted in the slanderous misrepresentation of God that he insinuated into the minds of Eve and Adam as he denied God's truthfulness, righteousness and goodness.[33] Their knowledge of God was

[31] D. I. Block, *Judges, Ruth*, New American Commentary (Nashville: B&H Publishing Group, 1999), p. 71.

[32] Moo, *Romans*, p. 399.

[33] See above, pp. 32–34.

corrupted by their acceptance of the serpent's words. And still, the ultimate source of all the garbage that human beings carry around in their heads lies in their profound ignorance of God, that is itself the fruit of those first demonic lies. 'The sinner deliberately reinterprets every fact and gives it a meaning that fits in with his denial of God.'[34]

This is why Calvin begins the *Institutes of the Christian Religion* as he does: 'Nearly all wisdom we possess, that is to say, true and sound wisdom, consists of two parts: the knowledge of God and of ourselves.'[35] True knowledge of the one and only God is absolutely fundamental to all other knowledge, and not least to a true knowledge of oneself; and a false conception of God entails the perversion of all other knowledge including, again, knowledge of oneself. 'That our idea of God corresponds as nearly as possible to the true being of God is of immense importance to us.'[36] It is knowledge of the living Creator God and Lord of all – eternally one in three persons, who has made himself known supremely in the eternal Word become flesh, crucified and raised from the dead – that brings renewal to minds corrupted by the lies of Satan.

4. Knowing God's will (12:2c)

One of the very many things that distinguishes biblical Christianity is its concern for the spiritual and moral maturity of all believers. It is this maturity that the renewing of their minds is intended to bring about as Paul states in the final clause of his exhortation: *so that you may discern what is the will of God.*[37] The verb *discern* or 'test' (*dokimazō*), is one Paul uses quite frequently 'where believers are told to exercise their discretion in testing and approving people and behaviour'.[38] Uniquely here, however, he uses it to speak of the believer's discernment with their own mind of the will of God himself. It is a mind now increasingly renewed as the Spirit delivers it from its fallen and disordered condition and refashions it in conformity with God's own words such that it becomes again a wholesome human mind.

The point is immensely significant. It means that as Christians seek to identify and carry out his will, God does not intend that they should be subject to the tutelage of a human priesthood nor to endlessly

---

[34] G. Goldsworthy, *According to Plan* (Leicester: Inter-Varsity Press, 1991), p. 42.

[35] J. Calvin, *Institutes of the Christian Religion*, ed. J. T. McNeill (Philadelphia: The Westminster Press, 1960), 1.1.1, p. 35.

[36] A. W. Tozer, in J. Sire, *Naming the Elephant: Worldview as a Concept* (Downers Grove: InterVarsity Press, 2004), pp. 128–129.

[37] New Revised Standard Version. The NIV obscures the flow of Paul's thinking by turning the purpose clause into a new sentence.

[38] Kruse, *Romans*, p. 465.

detailed manuals of rules and regulations. His purpose for his people is rather that they should be adults endowed with minds shaped by his word with which they are able to think truly *Christianly* for themselves. Their minds will be able to recognize the *good, pleasing and perfect* and distinguish it from the lies of the evil one, because they are minds renewed and refashioned in the image of the one who is in his own being the very measure of all that is *good, pleasing and perfect*.

More than once in his letters, therefore, Paul appeals to his readers to make their own judgment about some matter, or chides them for their inability to do so, or expresses God's purpose that they should be able to do so. He challenges the Corinthian believers to serious reflection: 'I speak to sensible people; judge for yourselves what I say',[39] and then soon after he does so again: 'judge for yourselves'.[40] A little later he rebukes them for their immaturity: 'Brothers, stop thinking like children. In regard to evil be infants, but in your thinking be adults.'[41] In Ephesians he declares his desire that by reaching unity in the faith and 'in the knowledge of the Son of God' his readers would 'become mature, attaining to the whole measure of the fullness of Christ. Then we will no longer be infants, tossed back and forth . . .'[42] To Timothy he says, 'Reflect on what I am saying, for the Lord will give you insight into all this.'[43] And in a similar way the author of Hebrews lamented his readers' slowness to understand and their consequent immaturity (Heb. 5:11–14), while Peter urged his readers to 'crave pure spiritual milk' so that they would 'grow up' in their salvation.[44]

As he expresses the purpose for which minds must be renewed, Paul's words recall the promise of the new covenant announced by Jeremiah.

> I will put my law in their minds
> and write it on their hearts.
> I will be their God,
> and they will be my people.
> No longer will a man teach his neighbour,
> or a man his brother, saying, 'Know the LORD,'
> because they will all know me,
> from the least of them to the greatest.[45]

[39] 1 Cor. 10:15.
[40] 1 Cor. 11:13.
[41] 1 Cor. 14:20.
[42] Eph. 4:13–14.
[43] 2 Tim. 2:7.
[44] 1 Pet. 2:2.
[45] Jer. 31:33–34.

As Paul calls, then, for the renewing of minds *so that you may discern what is the will of God*, there is an implicit recognition that believers should expect and pursue this as one of the rich blessings promised under the new covenant – minds reshaped by the fact that God's law has been written on them, minds which simply know God. The old covenant provided a law with considerable detail to guide the people of God. Now the new covenant has replaced the old through the mediation of the Lord Jesus Christ, and God refashions the minds and the hearts of his covenant people by his word and Spirit, and thereby transforms them. The fullest realization of the promise given through Jeremiah awaits the future, but believers can already know something of the reality now, even in the midst of 'this age'. They should pursue that; they should long for the liberation and maturity it brings; they should be transformed by the renewal of their minds.

James 3:13 – 4:10
17. Fighting and quarrelling

At 8:30 in the morning on Tuesday, September 5th, 2002, Mr. Kakani, the head nurse in the intensive care ward at Nyankunde Christian Hospital, had just finished early morning rounds. He was preparing to go to morning worship service when he heard sporadic gunfire and screaming. Looking out the open window, he saw dozens of women and children running towards the mission compound from the fields where they had been working since daybreak. Pursuing the field workers and heading directly towards the mission were an estimated 7000 soldiers, rebel militiamen from the neighboring Ngiti tribe. As Mr. Kakani watched in horror, the militiamen, with painted faces and rings of leaves on their head, brandishing rifles, bayonets, machetes and knives, started indiscriminately killing anyone in their path; women, children and the elderly . . . It is estimated that a thousand people died during the first few hours of onslaught; most brutally killed with machetes and knives.[1]

The incident described was just one of many brutal and horrifying moments in the ethnic conflict that took place in the north-east corner of the Democratic Republic of Congo around the beginning of the twenty-first century. In comparison with the savageries of the Rwandan genocide which had been carried out just eight years earlier and not very far away, the Congo conflict went relatively unnoticed but it was devastating for the countless numbers caught up in it. And the scars remain.

[1] Taken from a report of the attack on Nyankunde compiled shortly after the event by William Clemmer, an expatriate missionary in Oicha, DRC, September 2002. There is a full copy of the report under the title 'Massacre at Nyankunde', at <http://www.bereanpublishers.com/massacre-at-nyankunde/>, accessed 28 August 2015.

Violence is a dark and dominant thread that runs through the whole course of human history. It is, however, one to which the gospel of Christ responds as it brings about the creation of a new and reconciled humanity – God's own people – through the work of Christ. That community must strive to be in daily practice what it already is in Christ, but sadly the unity of Christ's body has all too often been compromised by conflict and division, as a watching world has been quick to notice.

> I have often wondered that persons who make boast of professing the Christian religion – namely love, joy, peace, temperance, and charity to all men – should quarrel with such rancorous animosity and display daily towards one another such bitter hatred, that this, rather than the virtues which they profess, is the readiest criteria (*sic*) of their faith.[2]

1. Human violence

Inevitably the Bible offers little glimpse of human society before the fall; indeed, at the beginning it comprised just one human couple. Nevertheless, God commanded them, 'Be fruitful and increase in number; fill the earth . . .',[3] and so clearly his purpose was that human community should develop and grow. This would, indeed, be consistent with, and even entailed by, his creation of humanity in his own image, for the triune creator exists eternally in the perfect fellowship of Father, Son and Spirit. Those who carry his image will also, therefore, as an integral and necessary dimension of their very nature as image-bearers, exist in community. At the most profound level human society – community – is basic to what we are as human beings.

As a result of the sin of Adam and Eve, however, it is terribly disfigured. The fall has scarred humanity at numerous points, the most devastating of which is alienation from the Creator himself with all that that entails. Closely associated with it is the alienation of fallen people from one another, bringing grievous fractures throughout human society. The evidence is there first of all in the fall narrative itself: when Adam and Eve heard 'the sound of the LORD God as he was walking in the garden in the cool of the day' they hid from him,[4] but even before that they had already taken measures to hide from one another by sewing fig leaves together to

---

[2] Benedict de Spinoza, quoted by D. J. Moo, *The Letter of James*, Pillar NT Commentary (Grand Rapids: Eerdmans and Leicester: Apollos, 2000), p. 181.
[3] Gen. 1:28.
[4] Gen. 3:8.

make 'coverings for themselves'.[5] There is alienation between the man and his wife.

And alienation leads quickly to conflict. It is visible for the first time when Adam blames Eve for their joint disobedience to God's command: 'The woman you put here with me – she gave me some fruit from the tree, and I ate it.'[6] Then it escalates to violence. In Genesis 4 Cain murders his brother, Abel, and a little later in the narrative his descendant, Lamech, kills 'a mere lad for a mere wound'.[7] He boasts of his crime in a poem (Gen. 4:23–24), and declares his determination that any injury he might suffer will be avenged seventy-seven-fold, brazenly revealing the violence and cruelty of his heart. Eventually the bloodlust that animated Lamech overwhelms the whole earth and brings God's judgment down upon it. For when the Genesis narrative speaks of the human wickedness, evil and corruption that prevailed in the years before the flood (Gen. 6:5, 11–12), the one specific sin it identifies is that of violence. 'Now the earth was corrupt in God's sight and was full of violence.'[8] And then, when after the flood God established his covenant with Noah, he spoke specifically of the punishment required for murder, responding to the problem of human violence which had brought about his judgment in the first place. Three times he says that he will demand an 'accounting' for the shedding of blood, and then he decrees,

> Whoever sheds the blood of man,
>   by man shall his blood be shed;
> for in the image of God
>   has God made man.[9]

Nevertheless, violence continues throughout the Old Testament, including violence among the people of God itself, and even at times of genocidal proportions (Judg. 12:1–6; 19 – 21). In addition there were constant wars with a whole list of neighbours as well as two plots to wipe Israel from the face of the earth (Exod. 1:15–16, 22; Esth. 3:5–15). Throughout human history the same unrelenting conflict and violence can be found in the life of every single people on earth, whether 'barbarous' or 'civilized', in wars and rebellions, in acts of genocide, oppression and imperial subjugation, and in the

[5] Gen. 3:7.
[6] Gen. 3:12.
[7] D. Kidner, *Genesis*, Tyndale OT Commentaries (Leicester: Inter-Varsity Press, 1967), p. 78.
[8] Gen. 6:11.
[9] Gen. 9:5–6.

petty hatreds, grudges and clashes of ordinary men and women in the course of their everyday lives.

When Paul concluded his demonstration of the universal sinfulness of humankind in Romans 3 he did so by citing a series of Old Testament texts drawn mostly from the psalms (Rom. 3:10–18). At the beginning and end he quotes verses that speak of humanity's rejection of its Creator: 'There is no one who understands, no one who seeks God . . . There is no fear of God before their eyes.'[10] In the middle, however, the focus is especially on the violence that human beings perpetrate against one another. First, the spotlight is on verbal violence: *throats* that are open graves, *tongues* that practise deceit, *lips* tainted with the poison of vipers, and *mouths* 'full of cursing and bitterness'.[11] Then Paul moves on to physical violence: 'Their feet are swift to shed blood; ruin and misery mark their ways, and the way of peace they do not know.'[12] After their repudiation of God himself, the sin that lies closest to the heart of human fallenness is the manifold violence that human beings remorselessly inflict on one another. Sin shatters human community, and human beings show only too clearly that they have truly become children of their father, the devil, who 'was a murderer from the beginning'.[13]

2. The gospel of peace

The gospel is rich and diverse in its implications, but at its very heart there is the provision of peace with God through Christ's atoning sacrifice for sins. At the same time he also reconciles those he redeems with one another in the body of Christ. There is, therefore, a double reconciliation which corresponds to the double alienation as well as to the two commandments of the law which Jesus identified as supreme: 'Jesus replied: "'Love the Lord your God with all your heart and with all your soul and with all your mind.' This is the first and greatest commandment. And the second is like it: 'Love your neighbour as yourself.'"'[14]

The church, then, is a new humanity of reconciled men and women which God has brought into existence through the work of his Son. In Christ God makes peace, a word which Paul uses four times in Ephesians 2 as he explains how God reconciles Jew and Gentile (2:14, 15, 17). For Christ has reconciled 'both of them to

[10] Rom. 3:11, 18.
[11] Rom. 3:13–14.
[12] Rom. 3:15–17.
[13] John 8:44.
[14] Matt. 22:37–39.

God through the cross', and by so doing not only brings about peace with God (2:16, 17) but also destroys the hostility that characterized their attitudes towards one another. Since it is *in Christ* that both are reconciled to God, being now both *in Christ* they are also at the same time reconciled to one another. Christ creates 'in himself one new man out of the two' – a reconciled new humanity in which the old divisions are totally relativized (2:15–16). 'For he himself is our peace, who has made the two one and has destroyed the barrier, the dividing wall of hostility.'[15] It is the blood of Christ (2:13), the cross of Christ (2:16), that brings this about. There is, therefore, no place for human divisions and conflicts at the cross: there all barriers are broken down, whether religious, ethnic, social, gender or whatever. 'There is neither Jew nor Greek, slave nor free, male nor female, for you are all one *in Christ Jesus*'.[16] So, too, at the Lord's Table the one loaf symbolizes the unity of God's one people: 'Because there is one loaf, we, who are many, are one body, for we all partake of the one loaf.'[17]

In a warring world the peace that should characterize God's people is fundamental to their Christian testimony. It is the love and grace they display towards one another that distinguish them most radically from the society that surrounds them and that should, beyond anything else, demonstrate the authenticity of the message they preach. 'By this all men will know that you are my disciples, if you love one another.'[18] Nevertheless, the visible practice of love, grace and peace in the church cannot be passively assumed. Believers must actively strive to realize in practice what God has already done for them in Christ: they must become what they are. Moreover, they must do so in defiance of a world that wants to conform them to its own divisive values; of the remains of sin in their own hearts; and of Satan's determination to undermine their testimony by fomenting animosity and division among them. This is why so soon after writing about the glory of the church in Ephesians 2 Paul implores his readers to do their utmost to maintain its unity: 'Make every effort to keep the unity of the Spirit through the bond of peace. There is one body . . .'[19] Churches mired in internecine conflict, as they so often are, merely mirror a warring world back to itself and in so doing visibly deny the power and truth of the gospel.

[15] Eph. 2:14.
[16] Gal. 3:28; cf. Col. 3:11.
[17] 1 Cor. 10:17.
[18] John 13:34–35; and cf. John 17:23.
[19] Eph. 4:3–4.

3. Warring churches (3:13 – 4:3)

James grapples with this problem in his letter; it was evidently an issue for his intended readers. There were *fights and quarrels* (4:1) in their churches and James' purpose was to bring about peace.[20] He was indeed a peacemaker and the same concern is evident in Acts where twice he serves the church in that way (15:13–21; 21:18–26). 'It is that same spirit which breathes through this passage, with its hatred of all that sunders and its evident delight in all that unites.'[21]

a. Wisdom (3:13–18)

James begins by speaking of *wisdom*. He has already affirmed the importance of wisdom for Christian living at the beginning of his letter: 'If any of you lacks wisdom, he should ask God . . .'[22] Now he asks, *Who is wise and understanding among you?* (13), and goes on to contrast two opposing types of wisdom which are differentiated according to their origin and their fruit. One is *from above*[23] (13, 17–18) and produces peacemakers; the other, which is clearly not true wisdom at all and is certainly not from above, is *earthly, unspiritual, of the devil* (15) and produces *disorder and every evil practice* (16).

The person with wisdom from above demonstrates it through a *good life* which consists in *deeds done in the humility that comes from wisdom* (13). Wisdom, then, is characterized by humility which becomes visible in corresponding deeds, attitudes and words. Humility or meekness was not appreciated in Greek society but James points out that it flows naturally from the wisdom God gives. Such wisdom consists in an understanding of one's own weakness, unworthiness and dependence before God's overwhelming greatness and holiness. It is visible, for example, in the 'prayer of Moses the man of God' (Ps. 90) which begins with a declaration of God's eternity and faithfulness and then moves on to an acknowledgment of human frailty and confession of human sinfulness.

James ironically contrasts this wisdom with a *'wisdom'* (15) which produces a very different fruit – that of *bitter envy and selfish ambition* (14). It is the very opposite of humility, focused as it is on envy of the possessions or position of others and the egotistic pursuit

---

[20] Moo, *Letter of James*, p. 168.
[21] J. A. Motyer, *The Message of James: The Tests of Faith*, Bible Speaks Today (Leicester: Inter-Varsity Press and Downers Grove: InterVarsity Press, 1985), p. 135.
[22] Jas 1:5.
[23] ESV. The word in 3:15 and 17 is *anōthen*.

of self-advancement. The word translated 'selfish ambition' (*eritheia*) was in fact used by Aristotle 'to describe the narrow partisan zeal of factional, greedy politicians in his own day',[24] and James is apparently suggesting that such attitudes were visible among some members of the churches he was writing to. Those who were motivated by them had, therefore, no grounds to make any claim to be wise but needed rather to acknowledge the sorry truth about themselves: the 'wisdom' they claimed to have did not come 'from above' – that is from God who alone gives true wisdom (1:5) – but from a totally different source, which James goes on to analyse.

First, it is *earthly*. The word he uses (*epigeios*) need not necessarily carry a negative sense but it certainly does here. Far from being 'from above' it is 'from below' and belongs to the rebellious world of humanity in all its pride, self-seeking and enmity. Second, it is *unspiritual*. The word is *psychikos* which in the New Testament is always 'placed in explicit opposition to "spirit" or "spiritual"'.[25] Accordingly James is saying that the Spirit of God has nothing to do with such a wisdom,[26] which comes rather from the vestiges of the old sinful nature. Finally, and most unambiguous of all, it is *of the devil* or 'demonic' (*daimoniōdēs*). It comes direct from him who is 'a murderer from the beginning'[27] and the ultimate source of division and violence, whose purpose is to disfigure and, if it were possible, to destroy God's new creation.

'In sum, then, this false wisdom, which does not lead to good works and humility (v. 13), is characterized by "the world, the flesh, and the devil."'[28] Its particular consequence is to destroy that communion among God's people which is brought about by the gospel, such that the church is drawn back into the world it was redeemed from in all its conflict and turmoil. For wherever there exists the *envy and selfish ambition* that James has spoken of (14), the result will necessarily be *disorder and every evil practice* (16). When people pursue personal interests and agendas, or form factions and parties to advance a cause, disharmony and conflict will result.

In response James explains the true wisdom which really does come *from heaven* or 'from above' (17). He does so in terms of qualities of character and behaviour quite different from those evident in the other type of wisdom: *first of all pure; then peace-loving, considerate, submissive, full of mercy and good fruit, impartial and sincere*. Commentators have noticed a correspondence between

---

[24] Moo, *Letter of James*, p. 171.
[25] Ibid., p. 173.
[26] P. Davids, *The Epistle of James* (Exeter: Paternoster, 1982), p. 152.
[27] John 8:44.
[28] Moo, *Letter of James*, p. 173.

211

James' list here and Paul's fruit of the Spirit (Gal. 5:22–23).[29] Both are 'from above' and summarize the fruits of a true work of God in the life of the believer.

First, wisdom 'from above' is marked by purity. The word refers to innocence, holiness and guilelessness, and so to a freedom from the ambition and jealousy which James has just spoken of. The following qualities spell out what such purity means, and especially emphasize how it produces Christian fellowship and harmony. So, second, it is *peace-loving* or peaceable (*eirēnikos*), as wisdom is also in Proverbs: 'all her paths are peace'.[30] Third, James continues with two traits that are 'probably subordinate to the first':[31] *considerate* and *submissive*. A peaceable person is considerate of the concerns and interests of others, and 'does not get angry, combative, or defensive even under provocation'.[32] He or she is submissive – not without convictions[33] but not insistent on their own rights.[34] There is an echo in Paul's words to the Philippians: 'Each of you should look not only to your own interests, but also to the interests of others.'[35]

Fourth, and particularly important, it is *full of mercy and good fruit*. James may be speaking of practical concern for the poor, which he talks about a good deal in the letter (1:27; 2:8–9, 12–13, 14–16; 5:1–6) and which produces an obvious and 'peaceable' fruit. However, he probably intends something other than this. Because no member of the church is ever perfectly pure, peaceable and so on, all members need to show mercy to one another just as Christ has shown mercy to them (Eph. 4:2, 32). Such mercy is a defining element of Christ's body, the fruit of the believer's consciousness of his or her own infinite indebtedness to God's grace in Christ. And it is essential to the maintenance of true fellowship. 'We live with each other in a full consciousness of the other person's neediness and helplessness.'[36] Its absolute importance is expressed in Paul's words to the Colossians: 'Therefore, as God's chosen people, holy and dearly loved, clothe yourselves with compassion, kindness, humility, gentleness and patience. Bear with each other and forgive whatever grievances you may have against one another. Forgive as the Lord forgave you.'[37]

[29] D. J. Moo, *James: An Introduction and Commentary*, Tyndale NT Commentaries (Leicester: Inter-Varsity Press, 1985), p. 139.
[30] Prov. 3:17.
[31] Moo, *Letter of James*, p. 176.
[32] Davids, *James*, p. 154.
[33] Ibid.
[34] Motyer, *James*, p. 136.
[35] Phil. 2:4.
[36] Motyer, *James*, p. 136.
[37] Col. 3:12–13.

Finally there is impartiality and sincerity. The word translated *impartial* (*adiakritos*) may mean either impartiality or undivided-ness. The latter would tie in with sincerity, meaning that the wisdom 'from above' is characterized by an absence of hypocrisy, a guile-lessness and transparency. Those in whom God has worked this wisdom are not faking a Christian profession, but there is a reality about them free from the hidden agendas of *envy and selfish ambition*.

James concludes that those who have this wisdom are true *peace-makers*. This is the vital point in his analysis. Serious conflict among the people of God, the *fights and quarrels* he goes on to refer to (4:1), is not occasioned merely by circumstances or differences of opinion on this or that issue. They stem from the *envy and selfish ambition* of human hearts (3:14, 16). It is the transforming power of the wisdom from above that produces peace in the church by changing human hearts. And the result is *a harvest of righteousness* – the visible righteousness of a Christian community that lives out the peace that the gospel creates.

b. Conflict (4:1–3)

The community James writes to, however, was not seeing such a harvest, and he moves on directly to respond to the conflicts his readers were experiencing. The language he uses suggests that the disharmony may even have involved physical violence, which would not be unknown in church history. However, even supposing – as may perhaps be more likely – that James' language is metaphorical, it nevertheless conveys his sense of horror at the awfulness of the bitter divisions within the church. These were Christian believers who had experienced God's grace and so become a new people in Christ, and James asks what could possibly have caused such dire discord among them. His immediate answer is that it arose from their *desires* (*hēdonē*), a word which suggests self-indulgent pleasures, which *battle within you*. There is an obvious echo of the *bitter envy and selfish ambition* he has already referred to (3:14, 16), and as James moves on that echo sounds ever more insistently, and especially so in the translation of 4:2 favoured in the ESV and elsewhere:

> You desire and do not have, so you murder.
> You covet and cannot obtain, so you fight and quarrel.[38]

---

[38] See Moo, *Letter of James*, pp. 182–183, for a substantial defence of this punctuation.

In each of the two parallel sentences James speaks of the wanting or coveting that his readers felt, of its frustration, and then of the resulting conflicts and violence that arose among them. The source of the conflicts within the community, he says, lies precisely in the condition of hearts whose sinful longings were not being satisfied (3:14).

James does not specify what the desires were. Moo suggests his readers may have been after positions of leadership, partly on the basis of James' earlier warning: 'Not many of you should presume to be teachers.'[39] At all events, James says that they *do not receive* because they *do not ask God*, and even when they do ask him the purpose of their prayers is the gratification of their own pleasures (3, *hēdonē* again, as in 4:1). They have no concern for God and his glory, nor for the health of his people, but pursue position and power for themselves from motives of *selfish ambition*.

4. A call to repentance (4:4–10)

What then is the answer? First James uses the strongest language to make his readers appreciate the enormity of what was taking place. The words, *you adulterous people* (4), echo the Old Testament language of spiritual infidelity which identifies God's wayward people as an unfaithful spouse. By using them James forthrightly condemns his readers for their unfaithfulness to God and to the covenant he has made with them. Underlying their envy and ambition and the consequent division of their community there is a friendship with the world, a tacit acceptance of its values and attitudes, that sets them at enmity with God. Their fighting and quarrelling do not mean a breach of fellowship on the horizontal plane alone but also, and far more seriously, a betrayal of God himself. James' repetition of the point – *don't you know that friendship with the world is hatred towards God? Anyone who chooses to be a friend of the world becomes an enemy of God* (4) – underlines the extreme gravity of what was happening. They were actually guilty of hatred towards God and had become his enemies, reconciled with him though they were through Christ! Nor was it something that had simply happened to them: through the attitudes they 'harboured' (3:14) they had actively *chosen to be a friend of the world* (4). Indeed, the barrenness and futility of their prayers was already a manifestation of how dire their spiritual condition had become (4:3).

James, therefore, goes on to call for repentance, but before getting there he asks a question which has been understood in more than

---

[39] 3:1. Moo, *Letter of James*, pp. 184.

one way.⁴⁰ *Or do you suppose it is to no purpose that the Scripture says, 'He yearns jealously over the spirit he has made to dwell in us'?* (5, ESV). The key to its interpretation is the metaphor he has just used, which identifies his readers' conduct as an act of spiritual adultery against the God who had betrothed them uniquely to himself. So, in 4:5 God is jealous because of their unfaithfulness: *He yearns jealously over the spirit he has made to dwell in us.* The word, spirit, may refer to the spirit he gives to all human beings by which they live (Gen. 2:7; 6:3) or to the Holy Spirit who indwells believers. However that may be, the point is clear: God longs with a holy and righteous jealousy for the wholehearted faithfulness of his people and their repudiation of the illicit friendship they have formed with the world. There is a hint of warning in the text: *do you think that Scripture says without reason . . . ?* James is recalling the frequent Old Testament allusions to the sin of unfaithfulness and he tells his readers they should not suppose that such repeated warnings and rebukes are mere empty threats. As Paul says, 'God cannot be mocked.'⁴¹ God's purpose, however, is not to judge them but rather to demonstrate grace and restore fellowship: *but he gives us more grace* (6). This is why James writes, to call them to repentance, which he does in the following sustained and passionate exhortation.

a. Humble yourselves (6)

At both beginning and end of his summons to repentance James appeals for humility on the part of his readers, quoting Proverbs 3:34 in support. It is the essential precondition of everything else he will call on them to do. The *envy and selfish ambition* displayed by his readers are rooted in pride, but if they are to know God's *grace* (6) and so be restored by him (10) they must humble themselves. It means confessing their rebellion and spiritual adultery, as well as the earthly, unspiritual and devilish condition of their hearts (3:15), and asking for mercy and restoration. It is, indeed, the course of wisdom (3:13), for to go in any other direction will bring God's judgment upon them.

b. Submit yourselves (7–8)

Such a humbling of themselves in repentance will be expressed in two principal ways. First they must *submit* to God and *come near*

⁴⁰ See discussions in Moo, *Letter of James*, pp. 188–191, and Davids, *James*, pp. 162–164, whose approach is followed here. R. P. Martin, *James*, Word Biblical Commentary 48 (Dallas: Word, 1998), pp. 149–151, takes a different line.
⁴¹ Gal. 6:7.

to him. This is the heart of repentance: coming back to the God from whom they have strayed. Their ambitions and conflicts are in reality sins against God which have brought about their alienation from him. But God is ready to respond immediately to their repentance, like the father of the prodigal son: *come near . . . and he will come near . . .* Such a reconciliation with God is the vital precondition of reconciliation among themselves.

Significantly, however, between the calls to submit to God and to draw near to him there is the command: *resist the devil and he will flee from you* (7). James is pointing out, first, that Satan has a significant role in the division of the Christian community, as he had already indicated earlier (3:15). He is the murderer and destroyer. His intent is to lay waste that unity of believers which Christ brought about through the cross, and which in a world of wars mightily testifies to the prodigious power of the gospel. Resisting his efforts to disrupt Christian unity is, therefore, a critical sphere of the church's spiritual warfare and one to which James' readers needed to be far more alert than they had been.

Second, the placing of the words suggests that submitting to God and resisting Satan are necessarily closely related to each other. On the one hand, there is no submission to God that does not entail a parallel resistance to Satan; it is only the double-minded person who would think otherwise (4:4, 8). On the other hand, believers are able to resist Satan precisely insofar as they submit to God and draw near to him; it is by availing themselves of God's grace as they pursue real fellowship with him that they are able to stand.

Finally, James' choice of the verb, *resist*, is significant. Neither Satan nor his demons have *possessed* these believers. They do not need to be driven out but resisted. In Scripture the response to sin is never one of deliverance from demonic or satanic possession, as some have supposed; it is always one of confession and repentance. James' readers may have been tempted and lured by Satan but they remain responsible for their sin which is their own: *they willed it themselves.* And in God's strength they will be able to resist Satan in the future.

c. Wash yourselves (8)

James also calls for change, and he does not spare his readers (8). Addressing them as *sinners* and *double-minded* he seeks to bring home once again the gravity of their spiritual state. The severity of his language is the more startling when compared with his more usual mode of addressing them as 'brothers' or even 'dear brothers'.[42]

---

[42] Moo, *Letter of James*, p. 194.

The contrast between hands and heart is drawn from the Old Testament and denotes 'both deed and disposition'.[43] So first, as sinners they must wash their hands. Quite simply they must cease from sinning – from the pursuit of selfish ambition, personal interests and the quarrels which result. Their behaviour must decisively change. More than that, however, there must be a fundamental change of disposition, for their sinful acts are the fruit of divided hearts. The word *double-minded* recalls their adulterous relationship with the world (4:4), and stands in contrast with the undividedness and sincerity that is an attribute of the wisdom from above (3:17). As double-minded they must therefore purify themselves by embracing a wholehearted, single-minded, undivided commitment to God and repudiating friendship with the world.

d. Grieve (9)

Finally, and again evoking the language of Old Testament prophecy, there will be genuine sorrow for their state, expressed in grief, mourning and wailing. James is not calling for some superficial display of distress from his readers, nor is he suggesting that forgiveness can be earned by tears. Rather he wants them to come to an awareness of the terrible seriousness of their sin as an act of adultery which they have committed against God himself, because only then will they actually turn from it. They need to reflect on what has become of them, and of the church to which they belong, and especially of their relationship with God himself. Most important of all, they need to see something of the immense and horrifying cost to God himself of their forgiveness. It is as that reality sinks in that they will repent with such grief and loathing for what they have done that their ability to continue in their sin will be seriously weakened. 'If you forget the costliness of sin, your prayers of confession and repentance will be shallow and trivial . . . We must be inwardly grieved and appalled enough by our sin – even as we frame the whole process with the knowledge of our acceptance in Christ – that it loses its hold over us.'[44] And when they do so, and see their *fights and quarrels* truly as sin – and indeed as *their* sin which they consciously own – then *he gives us more grace* (4:6). They had tasted utter spiritual defeat in conflict and division; it was in repentance alone that they would overcome. 'In repentance and rest is your salvation . . .'[45]

[43] Ibid.
[44] T. Keller, *Prayer: Experiencing Awe and Intimacy with God* (London: Hodder and Stoughton, 2014), p. 212.
[45] Isa. 30:15.

Christ died so that his people should be reconciled with God and reconciled with one another in his body, which is the church. The unity of that body, procured by his blood, is infinitely precious to him and a compelling testimony to the power of the cross. How terrible, then, the sin of dividing it; how urgent the summons to keep the unity of the Spirit. A part of our Christian warfare is earnestly to strive – against the world, the flesh and the devil – to guard the unity Christ has won for his people at such measureless cost.

1 John 2:12–17
18. The world and its lusts

For the New Testament as for the Old, God made the world (*kosmos*) and he made it good. The Bible utterly repudiates the cosmological dualism present in much Greek thinking, according to which the physical world, including the human body, is by nature evil. It is not. Nevertheless, New Testament writers use the word *kosmos* not only of the world as created by God and so good, but also of the world of humanity and so, by extension, of humanity united in a collective state of sinfulness: 'The life of human society as organized under the power of evil.'[1] John uses the word in that sense on several occasions, as when he exposes Satan as the one in whose power the world lies: 'We know that we are children of God, and that the whole world is under the control of the evil one.'[2] It is with that same meaning that Jesus tells his disciples that he has chosen them 'out of the world'[3] such that they are no longer 'of the world'.[4]

Nevertheless his disciples remain 'in the world'[5] and, indeed, Jesus sends them back 'into the world'[6] with the gospel (John 20:21). In consequence they will face the world's hostility (John 17:14) and experience 'trouble' in the world.[7] Not only that, but they also risk being contaminated by the world's values which they themselves had once shared. This is the issue that John confronts in this text. Those he writes to are believers who have been freed from the world,

[1] C. H. Dodd, quoted in J. R. W. Stott, *The Letters of John: An Introduction and Commentary*, Tyndale NT Commentaries (Leicester: Inter-Varsity Press, 1988), p. 102.
[2] 1 John 5:19.
[3] John 15:19.
[4] John 17:14, 16.
[5] John 17:11.
[6] John 17:18.
[7] John 16:33

but its rebellious orientation and its sinful mind remain an ongoing threat to them. They need, therefore, vigilantly to guard their still vulnerable hearts from love of the world and of *everything in the world* (15).

1. Celebrating salvation (2:12–14)

Before addressing the threat posed by the world, however, John writes words of encouragement and assurance. It is significant that he does so. These verses bring a remarkable pastoral balance to his teaching, standing as they do in juxtaposition both with the quite severe warning about hatred that precedes them ('whoever hates his brother is in the darkness . . .'), and with the admonition about the world which follows. In his earnest concern for the spiritual well-being of those he writes to, John wants them to grasp the profound moral and spiritual implications of fellowship with the God who is light and in whom 'there is no darkness at all'.[8] At the same time, however, he is convinced of the authenticity of their Christian profession and does not want his words of warning to make them doubt it.

John's words of assurance are expressed through a poetic structure with two series of three stanzas each, of which the second series largely echoes the first. Commentators have debated the identity of the *children*, *young men* and *fathers* to whom the various stanzas are individually addressed. However, what John actually says to each category would be true of all genuine Christians regardless of the supposed physical or spiritual maturity which the modes of address are sometimes taken to imply. Indeed, as if to prove the point, in the second series of stanzas John swaps around what he says to children and to fathers. The thing is that he is confident that his readers have indeed experienced forgiveness of sins; that they have come to know God the Father; that they have overcome Satan; and that they are strong and God's word lives in them. He writes to them because this is truly their experience, not because it is not; their profession of faith is a solid and convincing one. So, as he moves on to warn them of the danger posed by the world, he does not do so because he doubts their Christian profession; in fact, there would be little point in warning them about the world if they still belonged to it. Rather he wants them to be self-aware, especially with regard to the affections of their hearts, and alert to the pervasive and deceitful temptation posed by the world and its values.

[8] 1 John 1:3, 5.

2. The menace of the world (2:15)

John presents the threat of the world 'in three interlocking strophes, balancing the threefold structure' of the preceding verses, in which each strophe 'contains a "striking contrast"', as follows:[9]

(15) Love of the world   Love of the father
     ↓   ↓
(16) comes from the world   comes from the Father
     ↓   ↓
(17) the world passes away   the one who does God's will lives for ever.[10]

The concern John is expressing is not so much about the external pressure that the world might exert on believers to make them conform, whether through physical persecution or in more subtle ways. His focus is rather on the hearts of the believers themselves, and on the 'worldly' affections that once shaped their lives and still posed a potential threat to their faithfulness. And so he tells them, *Do not love the world or anything in the world.*

The verb he uses is *agapaō*, related to the noun *agapē*, which means love and which is sometimes incorrectly assumed to refer to some specifically Christian type of love – especially God's own love and then also the love of his children towards him or towards other Christians. This is not the case here, however, where John uses the verb to speak both of love of God and of love of the world. The point is that the lives of men and women are always directed in love towards some object which holds a supreme place in their affections. Here, with a negative present imperative (meaning literally 'do not go on loving'), John is telling his readers that they should not permit their lives to be driven by love of the world or of anything in it. Love for the world certainly characterized their pre-Christian past and John recognizes the danger that those same desires and longings might too easily beguile and seduce them again. Consciously and deliberately, therefore, they need to take responsibility for the orientation of their hearts. It is not a matter of the emotions but of the will, and John's exhortation echoes that of the writer of Proverbs: 'Above all else, guard your heart.'[11] It is a command – something to be *done*.

Nevertheless, John's words should not be misunderstood. First, he is not telling his readers that they may not enjoy the good things of

[9] S. S. Smalley, *1, 2, 3 John*, Word Biblical Commentary 51 (Waco: Word, 1984), p. 80.
[10] The diagram is from Smalley, ibid.
[11] Prov. 4:23.

creation. Certainly there is the danger of idolatry when the Creator's gifts usurp the place of the Creator in the affections of the recipients. The problem in such a case lies, however, with the sinful human heart rather than with the gifts themselves. When received with thanks and used for the glory of the giver, the innumerable blessings of creation are good, having been made, indeed, for human enjoyment (1 Tim. 4:4–5; 6:17). Second, John's exhortation is not in contradiction with the love that God has for the world and which is so often verbalized in Scripture: 'For God so loved the world that he gave his one and only Son.'[12] On the one hand, as Stott says, the world has different connotations depending on context. 'Viewed as people, the world must be loved. Viewed as an evil system, organized under the dominion of Satan and not of God, it is not to be loved.'[13] Here in John 2:15–17 it is the 'evil system' that is in focus rather than men and women in their lostness. On the other hand, the nature of the love is also somewhat different in each case, even though the same verb may be used. God's love of the world, and by implication that love of the world that should also characterize his people, 'signifies outgoing care and compassion. It is the kind of love which is concerned for the benefit of the person loved'.[14] By contrast, the love forbidden here is concerned with the pursuit of specifically sinful appetites for personal self-gratification.[15]

John gives two reasons for not loving the world. The second is in verse 17 and focuses on the transitoriness of the world. The first is found here in verse 15: *If anyone loves the world, the love of the Father is not in him.* The expression, *the love of the Father* clearly refers to love for the Father as it stands in contrast with love for the world. John is declaring that love for the Father and love for the world are mutually incompatible: nobody can love both. There is an obvious parallel with James – 'friendship with the world is hatred towards God';[16] and an even more striking continuity with Jesus' words of warning about the love of mammon: 'No one can serve two masters. Either he will hate the one and love the other, or he will be devoted to the one and despise the other.'[17]

There is an absoluteness in John's warning that demands an unequivocal response. God and the world are in polar opposition to one

---

[12] John 3:16.

[13] Stott, *Letters of John*, p. 104.

[14] I. H. Marshall, *The Epistles of John*, New International Commentary on the NT (Grand Rapids: Eerdmans, 1978), p. 143.

[15] C. G. Kruse, *Letters of John*, Pillar NT Commentary (Grand Rapids: Eerdmans and Leicester: Apollos, 2000), p. 94; Marshall, *Epistles of John*, p. 143.

[16] Jas 4:4.

[17] Matt. 6:24; Luke 16:13.

another and the human heart and its love can only be focused on one or the other. There is no place for compromise. Professing Christians whose love is in fact oriented towards the world do not know love for God. They are hypocrites. John's words are a call to a relentless refusal of the blandishments of the world, and to a heart undivided.

3. The content of the world (2:16)

John then defines more closely the content of the world and what he means by the 'things' – *anything* and *everything* (15, 16) – that are in the world. As he does so it becomes perfectly clear why love of the world and what is in it is so utterly incompatible with love of God.

He sums these 'things' up in terms of three qualities or dispositions. The 'things' are not physical things: the problem does not lie with the created world and the physical things in it, all of which God has made and made good, as we have noted. Nor is John speaking here of particular human activities, of situations or of places people might frequent. The rebellious world will undoubtedly assume tangible form through such things, but they are its product rather than its essence. Instead John is concerned here with the attitudes of the human heart – with such things as motives, values, priorities, ambitions. It is at this level that he defines *the world* of sinful men and women.

Accordingly, at the end of the paragraph (v. 17) he summarizes what is *in the world* (15, 16) with the one word *desire* or 'lust' (*epithymia*). He is referring to the disposition or orientation of the mind common to rebellious and fallen humanity in every age and place, and regardless of every distinction, whether ethnic, social, economic or whatever else. It is the desire which the world spawns and which exposes it as the rebellious, lost and hopeless thing that it is, united finally in sin alone. Further, it unequivocally demonstrates that the world is part of the dominion of darkness and enslaved to the purposes of the evil one.

a. The cravings of sinful man

The first two 'things' of which John speaks are expressed in closely parallel terms, which is somewhat obscured in the NIV translation: *the desire of the flesh* and *the desire of the eyes*. The word translated 'desire' (*epithymia* again) is used thirty-eight times in the New Testament, mostly with negative connotations.[18] The phrase 'desire

[18] Kruse, *Letters of John*, p. 95.

of the flesh' (or *cravings of sinful man* according to the NIV translation) should not, however, be misunderstood. In the New Testament the word 'flesh' (*sarx*) is used not only of the human body but frequently refers to humanity as a whole and then, more specifically, to humanity in its state of sinfulness and so to fallen human nature. Consequently when John speaks of the 'desire of the flesh' he is not referring only to what is 'fleshly' or physical in nature – sexual immorality, gluttony, drunkenness, debauchery and so on. He is rather speaking of desire that is expressive of human sinfulness – desire that is contrary to the holy character of God and to his purposes. 'Any and every desire of man in his rebellion against God is what is meant.'[19] This would of course include sins of a purely physical kind, but it goes very much further and encompasses all the sins of the mind such as pride, hatred, bitterness and so on.

John's brief expression, 'the desire of the flesh', actually draws attention to the sinfulness and folly of all human desire that springs from rebel hearts and is divorced from a true knowledge of God and pursuit of his glory. For God alone can be the final, ultimate object of human desire, and that for two main reasons. First, God alone can satisfy. All desire, including desire for what may in itself be good and appropriate, can find its true purpose and fulfilment only in the context of the ultimacy and supremacy of love for God himself. This is why the authors of Scripture occasionally express their desire for God in the most absolute terms. It is present for example in the words of Asaph: 'Whom have I in heaven but you? And earth has nothing I desire besides you.'[20] And then again it is there in the words of Psalm 84: 'My soul yearns, even faints, for the courts of the LORD; my heart and my flesh cry out for the living God.'[21] The psalmists' words do not deny the validity of other desires and longings – the desire for human companionship, security, intimacy, joy and so on. These are good things and among God's richest blessings to his human creation. The point, however, is that as human beings, creatures that are finite but also made in the very image of God himself, only knowledge of him will bring real fulfilment. No finite, created thing can do that for us; they can only bring true joy in the context of personal relationship with him. Bertrand Russell, celebrated philosopher and lifelong atheist, wrote a book entitled *Why I Am Not a Christian*. In a biography of her father, however, his daughter wrote this of him: 'Somewhere at the back

<hr/>

[19] Marshall, *Epistles of John*, p. 145.
[20] Ps. 73:25.
[21] Ps. 84:2.

of my father's mind, at the bottom of his heart, in the depths of his soul, there was an empty space that had once been filled by God, and he never found anything else to put in it.'[22] Russell himself wrote, 'Nothing can penetrate the loneliness of the human heart except the highest intensity of the sort of love the religious teachers have preached.'[23]

Second, and even more important, nothing and nobody but God can possibly be legitimate, worthy or good as the ultimate object of human desire and longing. To desire as one's definitive good anything else, however fine and valid it may seem in itself – perhaps family or country, children, achievement or whatever else – becomes idolatrous and expressive of the very heart of human rebellion, because that thing, whatever it may be, takes the place of the transcendent and infinite Creator in one's affections. 'The desire of the flesh' is, therefore, that desire which consists in the world's rejection of God and its 'desire' instead for something that is not God and is less than God – some aspect or other of his finite creation, one of the many gifts he has given, but not himself (cf. Rom. 1:25).

Such 'desire' is the very core and root of sin. It is there in the sin of Adam and Eve as they conspire together to dethrone their creator and 'desire' his place for themselves. And throughout its history the world of lost humanity, despite all its multiplicity, variety and division, is united in this one thing. In his letter John is strongly aware of the danger that the Christian readers of his epistle might be enticed by one or other of the manifold expressions of the 'desire of the flesh'. In the very last words of his epistle he therefore warns them once again, in the most tender terms: 'Dear children, keep yourselves from idols.'[24]

b. The lust of his eyes

The second 'thing' of which John speaks is *the desire* [NIV 'lust'] *of the eyes*. The phrase emphasizes the way in which people are so often and so readily seduced by the attractiveness of what they see. In the Bible the first example would be the way in which Eve 'saw that the fruit of the tree was good for food and pleasing to the eye'.[25] Achan's sin also began with his eyes: 'When I saw in the plunder a beautiful robe from Babylonia, two hundred shekels of silver and a

---

[22] K. Tait, quoted in R. A. Varghese, 'Preface', in A. Flew, *There Is a God: How the World's Most Notorious Atheist Changed His Mind* (New York: HarperOne, 2007), p. xxi.
[23] B. Russell, in Varghese, 'Preface', p. xxi.
[24] 1 John 5:23.
[25] Gen. 3:6.

wedge of gold . . .'[26] And so did David's adultery: 'From the roof he saw a woman bathing. The woman was very beautiful . . .'[27] In every case the things seen – the fruit, the robe and precious metals, the woman's body – were not in themselves evil. The problem lay rather in the person seeing and the nature of their seeing – in the disordered imaginations and longings of men and women who are so easily enticed by mere appearances that they turn the act of seeing into an occasion of sin. Jesus recognized the danger and warned his disciples of it: 'If your right eye causes you to sin, gouge it out and throw it away.'[28] And here as elsewhere, the insidious evil of sin is especially evident in the way in which it corrupts the use of human faculties which are themselves wonderful gifts of God.

There is, however, an even more perilous dimension of the 'desire of the eyes'. It lies in the fact that the things that are by far the most important are invisible to us. God himself is invisible, and the blessings of knowing him are not so obvious to the undiscerning human eye. The future resurrection of the body, the new heavens and the new earth, all the glory to come – none of these are visible. As Paul says, 'No eye has seen, no ear has heard, no mind has conceived what God has prepared for those who love him'.[29] And the problem is that our attention is so quickly drawn and our attitudes and values so easily shaped by what we can see and touch. We can be like children, mesmerized by baubles and indifferent or even hostile to far greater wonders because we do not see them.

The psalmist's words bring the issue into focus:

> But as for me, my feet had almost slipped;
>   I had nearly lost my foothold.
> For I envied the arrogant
>   when I *saw* the prosperity of the wicked.[30]

The visible reality around him challenged his faith in the invisible God and enticed him towards an idolatrous esteem for the all too obvious 'prosperity of the wicked'. He flirted with unbelief: 'Surely in vain I have kept my heart pure.'[31] What finally kept him from slipping over the edge was the moment when he moved beyond what was physically visible and contemplated the invisible but ultimate and eternal realities, specifically the final destiny of the wicked and the immeasurable

---

[26] Josh. 7:21.
[27] 2 Sam. 11:2.
[28] Matt. 5:29.
[29] 1 Cor. 2:9.
[30] Ps. 73:2–3 (my italics).
[31] Ps. 73:13.

worth of knowing God (Ps. 73:16–20, 23–26). In a similar way the purpose of John's vision of 'heaven opened' in the book of Revelation was to liberate his Christian readers from the 'desire of the eyes'. He wanted them to 'see' beyond their present trials and the obvious grandeur, power, wealth and *attractions* of the idolatrous society they lived in, and with eyes of faith to behold the throne from which God and the Lamb directed the course of history.

A defining characteristic of the contemporary Western world view is its functional atheism which brings an inevitable fixation with the material and the visible – the 'desire of the eyes' – because that is all there is. How easy it is to be seduced by its values and to set one's heart on the visible but transitory treasures of earth (Matt. 6:19–21). The response is deliberately to redirect our 'eyes' as the apostle Paul did. 'So we fix our eyes not on what is seen, but on what is unseen. For what is seen is temporary, but what is unseen is eternal.'[32]

c. The boasting of what he has and does

The third 'thing' John speaks of is *the boastfulness of possessions*. The word rendered 'possessions' is *bios*, which can be translated as 'life', but in the New Testament property or possessions is the principal meaning and John uses it with this sense in 1 John 3:17.[33] Meanwhile, the word translated 'boastfulness' (*alazoneia*) suggests not only that but also the arrogance of the boaster as well as 'a strong hint of the ultimate emptiness of boasting'.[34] The reference, then, is to human pride in position, power or wealth, the arrogance which it breeds, and the ultimate emptiness and futility of it all.

Again of course, the issue does not lie in the possessions themselves. God created all the things that human beings might own, and they are all good. In the Old Testament one expression of covenant blessing was the possession of sometimes very extensive riches, as with people like Abraham or Job. The problem lies rather in the disposition of the human heart towards possessions, and the ease with which wealth and the desire for wealth can corrupt, and indeed do so in many different ways.

First, there is the failure to recognize that God himself is the source of all possessions, and humbly to acknowledge and thank him for them. What indeed do we have that we did not receive from him (1 Cor. 4:7)? It is in the providence of God that the wealthy own

[32] 2 Cor. 4:18.
[33] Kruse, *Letters of John*, pp. 95–96.
[34] Marshall, *Epistles of John*, p. 145.

what they own, and the God who gave can equally take it all away. The rich fool was a fool not because he was rich but because of his totally godless and arrogant attitude towards his riches (Luke 12:13–23).

Second, not only do men and women frequently fail to thank God for their possessions, but they also make an idol of the things themselves. Paul identifies greed or covetousness as an expression of idolatry (Eph. 5:5; Col. 3:5), for an obsession with the accumulation and retention of things 'places at the centre of one's attention and devotion that which is not God'[35] and so becomes idolatrous. Moreover, that can be as true of the poor as of the rich, for it is not a question of the volume of possessions one has, but rather of the disposition of the heart towards them.

Third, and what John may have particularly in mind here, is the way in which the value of a human being is so widely estimated in terms of the quantity of his or her possessions. This can be seen in the often obsequious regard paid to rich people. James observed this in the churches he wrote to, and he doubtless saw it as an expression of being 'polluted by the world' which he had just warned against.[36] So he cautions, 'If you show special attention to the man wearing fine clothes and say, "Here's a good seat for you," but say to the poor man, "You stand there" or "Sit on the floor by my feet," have you not discriminated among yourselves and become judges with evil thoughts?'[37] And for the wealthy the possession of riches so easily breeds arrogance – 'the *arrogance* of possessions' as John's words might be translated. It is reflected in an attitude of entitlement and superiority along with a contemptuous disdain for those who possess relatively little. Ultimately the arrogance of the wealthy and the deference paid to them indicate again the way in which riches may corrupt, distort true values and become idols in human hearts.

All of these 'things', John concludes, come from the world. They define the depravity that characterizes fallen humanity as a whole; they are the dispositions which mark individual men and women as sinners and shape their lives. As such they have nothing to do with the Father. It is inconceivable, therefore, that those who love the Father would also love and participate in the things – the godlessness, the idolatry, the arrogance and pride – that characterize the world. And hence John's urgent insistence: *Do not love the world or anything in the world* (15).

---

[35] N. T. Wright, *Colossians and Philemon: An Introduction and Commentary*, Tyndale NT Commentaries (Leicester: Inter-Varsity Press, 1986), p. 134.
[36] Jas 1:27.
[37] Jas 2:3–4.

4. The destiny of the world (2:17)

John has told his readers that loving the world and loving God are incompatible (v. 15). Now in verse 17 he gives a second reason for not loving the world: *The world and its desires pass away, but the man who does the will of God lives for ever.* There are two complementary dimensions to what he says.

First, *the world and its desires* are passing away. The verb he uses is present tense and describes what is in the process of happening even as he speaks. Indeed, he has already said something almost identical in 2:8 when, using the same verb, he wrote, 'the darkness is passing'. In both cases John's words allude to the ending of the present age brought about by the coming of Christ and the Spirit. The age of sin and Satan and this world has been overthrown and the last days are already present: 'all that is antithetical to God and his grace is passing away; it is doomed'.[38] Meanwhile the new age has broken in and even now those who belong to Christ are part of it. It would, therefore, be total folly for John's readers to drift back and align themselves again with a world which is already under judgment and fast disappearing.

Then, in his second statement, John makes very much the same point but from the opposite perspective: while the world is disappearing the one who does God's will *lives for ever.* In contrast to what he says in verse 15, he does not speak here of Christians as those who love God but rather as those who do his will. The thrust of his words, however, is the same and the contrast between the two verses highlights the essence of both love and obedience. On the one hand, the person who truly loves God will certainly do his will; real love of God is not mere sentiment and emotion but issues in a desire to please him and a consequent outflow of obedience. On the other hand, the person who *truly* does God's will – as opposed to offering a merely legalistic and superficial obedience – does so out of a profound love of him. The two things, doing God's will and loving him, are therefore mutually indivisible – each absolutely demands the other and to speak of one is to speak of the other. 'This is love for God: to obey his commands.'[39] Meanwhile, the verb 'to do'[40] is again in the present tense, so that it speaks of one whose life is daily and constantly characterized by submission to God's will, who 'goes on doing the will of God'. In contrast with the world, then, which is even now passing away, *the one who does God's will* remains

---

[38] Kruse, *Letters of John,* p. 96.
[39] 1 John 5:3.
[40] John is using a present participle, *ho poiōn.*

into eternity. He or she will remain after the world has long since gone, for 'as the Father is eternal, so is the life which he gives to the believer'.[41] There could scarcely be a stronger motive for determined resistance to the enticements of the world.

In concluding, however, we should note again that even as John confronts his readers with the challenge presented by the world and 'the things that are in the world', he does so in the context of encouragement and assurance. It is not a bleak battle with a doubtful outcome that he is calling them to. On the contrary, they fight from a position of victory already secured for them by the Lord Jesus Christ. Through him *already* their *sins have been forgiven* (12), they enjoy communion with God and his word lives in them (13, 14), and they have *overcome the evil one* (13, 14). In brief, because of God's work in their lives, they are *strong* (14), and it is with confidence that John says to them, *Do not love the world or anything in the world.*

---

[41] Smalley, *1, 2, 3 John*, p. 88.

1 Corinthians 9:24 – 10:22
19. The snare of complacency

Complacency loses battles. In late 1990 Margaret Thatcher was facing a serious challenge to her leadership of the Conservative Party from one of many former members of her own government. The stakes could not have been higher, for if she lost the leadership she would have little choice but to resign as British Prime Minister. Running her campaign was her parliamentary private secretary, Peter Morrison. Kenneth Baker, at that time chairman of the Conservative Party, describes an encounter with Morrison during the contest: 'I went to see Peter Morrison one day and he was fast asleep in his chair. He was quite confident they were going to win. I said it was not my feeling at all. You are going to have to get out and persuade people. It was absurdly over-complacent.'[1] Margaret Thatcher went on to lose.

In Paul's letters to the Corinthians there are strong indications that he was dealing with believers who were deeply complacent about their own spiritual condition. The heavy irony of his rebuke early in 1 Corinthians certainly suggests it: 'Already you have all you want! Already you have become rich! You have become kings – and that without us!'[2] It is evident too in their attitudes towards sexual immorality, and in the approach some of them were taking towards participation in pagan worship, which Paul discusses very fully later in the letter.

1. Food sacrificed to idols

The issue of 'food sacrificed to idols',[3] to which Paul responds in 1 Corinthians 8:1 – 11:1, has been understood in numerous ways.

[1] J. Landale, 'Ten Days That Toppled Margaret Thatcher', at <http://www.bbc.co.uk/news/uk-politics-34673606>, accessed 30 October 2015.
[2] 1 Cor. 4:8.
[3] 1 Cor. 8:1.

One convincing approach is to see Paul as wrestling with two kinds of idolatry, subjective and objective.[4] *Subjective idolatry* takes place when a person deliberately takes part in an activity they judge to be idolatrous. If, however, somebody participates in an act or event they do not see as idolatrous, although in reality it is, that is *objective idolatry*. In Corinth some believers were engaging in objective idolatry by participating in feasts at pagan temples, even perhaps in the homes of non-Christian friends, during which a sacrifice or offering would be made to a pagan deity. They did not see it as an idolatrous act as they believed 'that an idol is nothing at all in the world and that there is no God but one'.[5] In their view all they were doing was eating with unconverted, Gentile Corinthians. However, that view was not shared by all Corinthian Christians and there was conflict on the matter. Moreover, by their example they risked leading some members of the church into what would for them be subjective idolatry.

Of course, the simple solution would be for all believers to agree to steer clear of pagan temples altogether, but against that there were compelling practical reasons for continuing attendance at the feasts. The obvious one was the opportunity to eat meat, but there was more to it than that. In places like Corinth temples were not just places of worship to gods and goddesses; as well as that the cultic feasts and sacrifices were 'intensely social occasions for the participants' and an accepted part of normal social life. 'For the most part the Gentiles who had become believers in Corinth had probably attended such meals all their lives.'[6] Accordingly non-participation would at the very least give rise to a keenly felt sense of social exclusion. More than that, it might also mean exclusion from civic life since religion and politics 'were indivisible in Ancient Hellenistic city life';[7] and it might even cause serious economic disadvantage. Individuals engaged in the same trade often associated together in guilds, members of which met together at temples for a meal accompanied by sacrifice. 'To have nothing to do with such gatherings was to cut oneself off from most social intercourse with one's fellows.'[8] Consequently, regardless of their Christian faith, some Corinthian believers were rationalizing their ongoing

[4] R. E. Ciampa and B. S. Rosner, *The First Letter to the Corinthians*, Pillar NT Commentary (Grand Rapids: Eerdmans and Nottingham: Apollos, 2010), p. 369.

[5] 1 Cor. 8:4.

[6] G. D. Fee, *The First Epistle to the Corinthians*, New International Commentary on the NT (Grand Rapids: Eerdmans, 1987), p. 361.

[7] D. E. Garland, *1 Corinthians* (Grand Rapids: Baker, 2003), pp. 347–348.

[8] L. Morris, *1 Corinthians: An Introduction and Commentary*, Tyndale NT Commentaries (Leicester: Inter-Varsity Press, 1985), p. 122.

participation in such occasions. They reasoned that while their attendance at the feasts and accompanying sacrifices might look like idolatry, in their case it was not. They were certainly physically present but claimed that they were totally unengaged in any worship because they knew that 'an idol is nothing at all' and so they could scarcely be involved in worshipping one. Indeed, no real spiritual transaction could take place when the object of the sacrifice was 'nothing at all'.

Paul took issue with the reasoning from the outset, and identified an underlying intellectual arrogance in those putting it forward (1 Cor. 8:1–2). On the one hand they were failing to consider the implications of their argument, and of the behaviour it ostensibly supported, for other believers who did not understand idols as they did. More seriously, the argument was as such unsound in that it failed to recognize the very real spiritual transactions that did indeed take place when sacrifices were offered to idols. The truth was that those who were putting it forward did not yet know as they ought to know (8:2), and the result of their ignorance was a startling and potentially lethal complacency regarding the spiritual dangers they were running by dabbling in pagan religious activity.

2. Self-discipline (9:24–27)

Paul's total response is long and detailed as he examines the issue from several perspectives. He comes to the crux, however, in 1 Corinthians 9:24–27, when he starts to raise the specific issue of complacency, initially speaking of himself. Some commentators have seen this brief paragraph as a conclusion of the discussion about foregoing one's rights for the sake of the gospel (9:1–23). However, it is not obviously linked to that theme and can more convincingly be understood as an introduction to the lesson Paul wants to draw from Israel's experience in the desert in 10:1–13: 'The Israel of the exodus . . . is comparable with the athlete who does not persevere in the hard discipline which leads to success.'[9]

Paul challenges the complacency of his readers first with an illustration from the games which would be very familiar to them. In a race all the runners compete but only one wins (v. 24). Although they were not in competition with one another, the Corinthians should run with that same determination to win, and all the more so as the prize they were pursuing is eternal as opposed to the merely transitory reward of the athlete. What that means is *strict training* and self-discipline (25): it is here that the point of the illustration lies.

---

[9] C. Senft, quoted in Ciampa and Rosner, *First Corinthians*, p. 433.

It is about serious spiritual self-discipline in the face of the challenge of living worthily of the gospel in a pagan environment.

Paul then applies his illustration to himself (vv. 26–27). In his own Christian conduct he is like a runner, and as such he does not jog along aimlessly but runs purposefully with a goal in view. In a parallel illustration he turns to the boxer: Paul fights seriously too, not just throwing his arms around, *beating the air*, and failing to connect with his opponent. Again, he has a goal in view, he is focused, and in order to succeed he follows a strict training regime: *I beat my body and make it my slave* (27). The point is that he exercises a ruthless spiritual and moral self-discipline, not just with respect to his physical body, although that is certainly included, but his whole self, and what motivates him to do so is *the prize* – he is looking to the final judgment. Five times in the paragraph he mentions *the prize* or the *crown* he wants to win: it is that hope which keeps him persevering.

In contrast, the Corinthians' problem was the laxity and self-indulgence they displayed in so many areas but specifically here in their pragmatic and self-serving approach to pagan worship. They failed to appreciate the utter seriousness of a life of disciplined and sacrificial Christian discipleship. A major factor may have been a certain indifference to the realities of Christ's return, the final judgment and the prize to be won. New Testament Christianity is throughout permeated and motivated by a strong focus on the parousia, but the Corinthians seem somehow to have concluded that God's final reign had already begun and they were already reigning with him.[10] Very likely this is the reason for Paul's ironic rebuke earlier in the epistle, 'Already you have all you want! Already you have become rich! You have become kings – and that without us!'[11] The belief that they had already received the prize would certainly explain their complacency, as well as Paul's repeated emphasis on the need to keep striving for it, including his reference to the danger of disqualification even for one like himself who had preached to so many others. Their complacency arose from a preoccupation with the things of this world in part because the glory to come – and the danger of failing to attain it – had so small a place in their thinking and theology.

3. A warning from Israel (10:1–13)

Paul turns from contemporary sporting illustrations to one drawn from Israel's experience in the desert. He introduces it with the word

[10] Fee, *First Corinthians*, pp. 172–173.
[11] 1 Cor. 4:8.

for: he is going to give an Old Testament basis for his warning of possible disqualification.[12] And there is a clear parallel with the sporting metaphor: 'All the runners run but not all win; so also, all the Israelites experienced the blessings of the exodus and divine provision, but not all made it to the Promised Land.'[13] In both cases, starting out, whether on the race or the journey, is not enough; the important thing is finishing, which demands faithfulness, perseverance, self-discipline. A spirit of complacency, a presumption of entitlement, will surely bring failure and irretrievable loss, as it did in the case of Israel's wilderness generation.

a. Our forefathers' blessings (1–4)

Paul describes the Israelites as *forefathers* of his Corinthian readers. In doing so he signals the underlying continuity of the one covenant people of God, and so establishes the validity for the Corinthians of the principle he wants to establish from their distant predecessors in the faith. He then points out the analogies between their experience and that of the Corinthian believers.

First, the Israelites had undergone a baptismal experience by being *under the cloud* and passing *through the sea*. The combination of the two ideas signifies God's sovereign redemption of his people: his saving presence was made visible in the cloud and enabled them to pass through the sea. Moreover, God worked through a mediator of salvation then as now into whom the Israelites can be said to have been baptized. The point is that like the Corinthians they experienced a mighty salvific work of God at the moment of their deliverance from bondage.

Second, they were also supernaturally sustained by God's provision of manna and water. Paul identifies these as *spiritual food* and *drink*, meaning that they were given by the Spirit of God, which in turn underlines the analogy between them and the bread and wine which the Corinthian believers received at the Lord's Table. Further, he also identifies the *rock* from which God gave them water with Christ and says that it accompanied them through the desert. He is probably using a Jewish tradition that the rock did indeed follow Israel through the desert, but more than that he is recalling the image of God as rock of his people, which is found repeatedly in the Song of Moses (Deut. 32:4, 15, 18, 30, 31). It was God, himself the rock, who remained with Israel continually throughout their desert wanderings and constantly provided for them. And Paul transfers

---

[12] D. E. Garland, in Ciampa and Rosner, *First Corinthians*, p. 445.
[13] Ciampa and Rosner, *First Corinthians*, p. 443.

the title to Christ. The rock from which the water flowed is, then, symbolic of God, the true source of that water, and so a symbol of Christ too.

b. Our forefathers' rebellion (5–10)

Verses 1–4 form one long sentence. It is immediately followed by a relatively brief sentence which vividly depicts an abrupt and shocking reversal of the immense blessings Israel had known: *Nevertheless, God was not pleased with most of them; their bodies were scattered over the desert* (5). Despite all that Israel had experienced, including even 'the presence of Christ to "nourish" them with "spiritual drink"',[14] because of their sin almost all of them, apart from Joshua and Caleb, failed to enter the Promised Land. Paul's purpose is to shock his readers into an awareness of the gravity of complacency and carelessness in their relationship with the holy God of Israel.

Accordingly, he stresses the fact that what took place is not of merely historic interest. *These things* are *examples*, and the word rendered 'example' is *typos*[15] which might cautiously be translated as 'type'. Paul is suggesting that there is a typological significance in the episode. 'Israel, as "our fathers," who had their own form of baptism and Lord's Table, genuinely prefigures "us." It was Christ who gave them their "spiritual drink," just as he does ours.'[16] From that perspective Israel is a 'type' of Christian believers. More than that, although Paul does not want what *happened* to Israel to prefigure what will happen to his Corinthian readers, he is telling them that if they set their hearts *on evil things* (6) as Israel did, then they can expect to fall under God's displeasure as Israel did. Baptism and the Lord's Table will not shield them just as they did not shield Israel. Further, moving on to verse 11, it was God's *intention* that the events that took place in the desert should serve as a 'type'. It is not just that Paul looked back and saw a parallel which he took advantage of, but rather that the experience of Israel was *intentionally* anticipatory and prophetic: 'there was typological significance in the events as they took place'.[17] God himself had 'woven the prefigurement into these earlier texts for the sake of his final eschatological people'.[18] The judgment Israel experienced happened in the first

---

[14] Fee, *First Corinthians*, p. 449.

[15] In 10:11 Paul uses the related adverb, *typikōs*.

[16] Fee, *First Corinthians*, p. 452.

[17] D. J. Moo, 'The Problem of *Sensus Plenior*', in D. A. Carson and J. D. Woodbridge (eds.), *Hermeneutics, Authority and Canon* (Leicester: Inter-Varsity Press, 1986), p. 196.

[18] Fee, *First Corinthians*, pp. 458–459.

place, therefore, precisely to warn future generations of God's people to guard their hearts, and so to keep them from disaster.

Paul goes on to define the nature of the sin which brought about Israel's judgment with allusions to four specific incidents. First, he refers to the idolatry and *revelry* that took place at the foot of Sinai when Aaron made the golden calf (Exod. 32:1–6). Clearly the description contained in the particular verse he quotes, especially its reference to eating, bears an uncomfortably close resemblance to what the Corinthians were doing in pagan temples, and his readers could scarcely fail to draw the obvious inference. Second, there is the sexual immorality that took place with Moabite women at Shittim on the plains of Moab (Num. 25:1–9). Significantly, it was also associated with participation in the offering of idolatrous sacrifice, this time to the Baal of Peor. Third, Paul mentions the occasion at Mount Hor when the people became impatient and grumbled about their 'miserable food' (Num. 21:4–9). His use of the verb *test* is suggestive here. It is not used in the Old Testament narrative but it links the incident with the way in which the Corinthians were testing God by participating in pagan sacrifices. The final incident is less specifically identified. Paul may be referring to Israel's grumbling refusal to enter the Promised Land when God declared that that whole generation would fall in the desert (Num. 14:20–38). Another possibility would be Numbers 11 which begins with a reference to the people's grumbling and goes on to speak of fire breaking out in the camp (11:1) and then later of a severe plague after the Israelites had again craved 'other food' (11:33–34). Or the reference could be to the grumbling which followed God's judgment of Korah's rebellion (Num. 16:41–50).

Each of the incidents parallels the situation in Corinth in one way or another: the participation in idolatry in two of the four; sexual debauchery also in two of them; and craving for food in one or two, while participation in an idolatrous feast was of course involved in the worship of the golden calf. And in each of them there was the testing of God and the judgment of death that it led to: *their bodies were scattered over the desert* (5).

c. The lesson of our forefathers (11–13)

In concluding this part of his argument Paul makes two substantial points.

First, he again reminds his readers that the judgments under which Israel had fallen were written as a warning for the benefit of those living in the last days: 'ultimately the whole OT has been pointing towards its eschatological fulfilment in God's new people'.[19] As part of that new people, the Corinthians should take to heart the experience of Israel and apply it to their own situation, and Paul helps them to do so.

In verse 12, then, he recognizes that in their own opinion they might well think they were *standing firm*. After all, they had been baptized and they were enjoying the blessings of the Lord's Table; but so had Israel (10:1–4)! Their participation in idolatry put them in danger and, although they might have rationalized their involvement in pagan sacrifice to their own satisfaction, their reasoning demonstrated a complacent disregard of the explicit expression of God's mind in Scripture. They needed to re-examine their position in the light of God's word, which Paul had just expounded to them. The experience of Israel indicated clearly and repeatedly that their situation was as grave as it could possibly be, and that a casual continuation in the course they had adopted would be disastrous to them.

Second, he points out that they can resist temptation; they are not powerless victims. The temptation to attend idolatrous feasts in pagan temples for whatever reason – nutritional, economic, social, political – was not irresistible. They were not facing an extraordinarily new temptation, nor one that was coming at them with unprecedented force. Indeed, in faithfulness to his covenant God would not permit his people to be tempted beyond their capacity to resist. Quite to the contrary, he would provide a way for them to stand. He might move them beyond the reach of unbearable temptation; he might provide strength to resist. Whatever the case, trusting in God the Corinthians could say 'no!' *Therefore*, Paul says, they should do so: *flee from idolatry* (14).

4. Fellowship with idols or with God (10:14–22)

Paul supports that categorical, unequivocal imperative with a final and conclusive argument. As we have noted, some of the Corinthians believed that because 'an idol is nothing at all' nothing of any consequence takes place when sacrifices are made to a pagan god or goddess. There is, after all, nothing there to receive the sacrifice. Paul now shows them that the claim is terribly wrong and confronts them with the reality of what actually takes place at a pagan sacrifice.

As he begins, he achieves a subtle and sensitive pastoral balance. First, his exhortation, *flee from idolatry*, communicates urgency with a suggestion of extreme danger.[20] For the Corinthians this is the *way*

---

[19] Fee, *First Corinthians*, p. 459.
[20] Ciampa and Rosner, *First Corinthians*, p. 470.

out of temptation (13), as indeed it always is (1 Cor. 6:18; 1 Tim. 6:11; 2 Tim. 2:22), and they need to take it. Second, however, it is expressed in the most tender terms: *my dear friends.* The expression is not a common one,[21] and in so speaking Paul reveals the attitude of his heart. These are not enemies to be browbeaten and brought under control, but beloved fellow believers who are in serious spiritual danger. It is because he loves them that Paul is striving so hard to bring them willingly back to an obedience to God's will. Third, alongside the imperative Paul appeals to them to think matters through for themselves. Some commentators see the words, *I speak to sensible people,* as irony or flattery, but neither is likely. If the Corinthians had suspected he was being ironic in calling them sensible it would hardly have helped them heed the substance of his argument, while the use of flattery would suggest a manipulative approach which would be both uncharacteristic and unworthy of Paul (cf. 2 Cor. 4:2). Rather, by speaking in this way he affirms them without guile as intelligent fellow believers who can indeed judge for themselves if they will. They are not simply to be commanded like immature children, but rather encouraged to think for themselves as adults. Moreover, in making such an appeal Paul is recognizing that true and heartfelt obedience cannot come from external imposition but only from personal conviction of the truth. The Corinthians must indeed judge for themselves what he is saying and reach their own conclusion if any substantial change is to take place. Paul then presents the argument that they are to judge.

a. Participation in Christ (16–18)

He speaks first of the Lord's Table. He describes it in terms of *participation* in both the body of Christ and the blood of Christ, using the word *koinōnia* which is more usually translated 'fellowship' or 'communion'. At the Lord's Table, then, believers have a true and profound fellowship with Christ in his death: they share in its blessings. They encounter him, receive him and experience his grace and mercy as they truly participate in the cup and the bread. This is why Paul describes the cup as, literally, *the cup of blessing which we bless* (16, ESV); for the cup depicts the utter indebtedness of those present at the table to the blood of Christ by which they receive all the blessings of salvation, and the consequent centrality of thankfulness in that act of participation.

Further, Paul points to the communal dimension of the Lord's Table. There is only *one loaf* at the table (17), symbolizing the one

[21] Morris, *1 Corinthians*, p. 142.

body of the Lord Jesus Christ. The very fact that all believers partake of that *one loaf* – that one Saviour – makes them one people, and eating the one bread symbolizes the fact.[22] Their fellowship, then, is not only with Christ but also, because of him, with one another. In his own body and through his own blood he makes the church, and it is therefore an inescapable reality for those who participate in his body and blood. It is for this reason that a little later Paul so strongly rebukes the divisions that were evident when the Corinthians assembled, which totally contradicted the very meaning of the Table (1 Cor. 11:17–34).

Paul then supports what he has been saying by referring to the sacrifices offered by *the people of Israel*. The expression he actually uses is 'Israel according to the flesh',[23] by which he may be distinguishing Israel in its physical, national reality from the true Israel,[24] those who are children of Abraham by faith. However that may be, he is speaking of the Jewish sacrificial system of his day and saying that those who eat the meat that has come from the altar have, in virtue of that fact, taken part in the sacrifice that put it on the altar. If they eat it they cannot claim to be uninvolved in the act of worship which the meat represents. They 'participate in the altar' (1 Cor. 10:18) just as Christians participate in the blood and the body of Christ.

b. Contamination (19)

And so he moves on to the implication of what he has been saying for the central issue of sacrifices offered to idols. Initially, however, in something of a parenthesis he agrees with one important point that the Corinthians were making. A sacrifice offered to an idol is, in itself, nothing. It remains no more than meat; no spiritual or ethical quality has been added to it and in itself it has no spiritual significance. This is why, a little later, Paul tells the Corinthians they can eat anything sold in the market 'without raising questions of conscience'.[25] If *a sacrifice offered to an idol* was in fact 'something' – tainted in some way by its use at the altar – then a Christian customer would definitely need to be asking questions about the provenance of any cut of meat they were proposing to buy. Similarly, an idol remains a merely physical object, made of wood or stone or whatever, again with no spiritual element superadded.

---

[22] T. Schreiner, *Paul, Apostle of God's Glory in Christ: A Pauline Theology* (Downers Grove: InterVarsity Press and Leicester: Apollos, 2001), p. 380.

[23] *ho Israēl kata sarka.*

[24] Morris, *1 Corinthians*, p. 144.

[25] 1 Cor. 10:25.

In his approach Paul reflects, albeit in a very different context, the radical change of perspective that the gospel brings regarding Old Testament laws on the transmission of uncleanness and contamination. Wenham suggests that the original intention of the laws was to bear witness in an essentially symbolic way to God's character as the 'God of life and health and normality'[26] by requiring his people to separate themselves from all that suggested death and disease, such as those suffering from leprosy, women with discharges, human corpses and dead animals. Throughout his ministry, however, Christ touched lepers, the sick and the dead, and in doing so brought such people cleansing, healing and new life. His saving ministry demonstrated that God's redeeming grace is immeasurably more powerful than disease and death, making obedience to the Old Testament laws of purity obsolete. 'God's character as the giver of life, wholeness and normality that the Old Testament law declared is not abolished. Rather it is demonstrated dynamically in our Lord's saving ministry.'[27]

The point is important in other contexts. In animistic religion objects may often be seen as the carriers of spirits or malevolent power, and such notions have penetrated some strands of missiological thinking, leading to more or less syncretistic approaches to spiritual warfare. However, Paul's words make it quite clear that physical objects do not carry demonic contagion or, indeed, any sort of spiritual contamination. 'Paul denies that physical contact with a physical object, previously dedicated to an idol, carries with it any intrinsic danger.'[28]

Similar, but further removed from the Corinthian situation, is the notion that the guilt and consequences of particular past sins may pass down through the generations as a sort of genetic disease or contagion and be experienced by later generations in the form of a curse. Of course, in an obviously natural way one generation may indeed have to face the consequences of the sins of its predecessors. A later generation may, for example, have to sort out the environmental neglect or fiscal irresponsibility of those who went before. The argument for the generational transmission of the 'curse' of sins is not, however, simply one of natural cause and effect. It is rather that in some spiritual and invisible way guilt and the penalty attached

---

[26] G. J. Wenham, 'Christ's Healing Ministry and His Attitude to the Law', in H. H. Rowdon (ed.), *Christ the Lord: Studies in Christology Presented to Donald Guthrie* (Leicester: Inter-Varsity Press, 1982), p. 125.

[27] Wenham, 'Christ's Healing Ministry', p. 125.

[28] R. J. Priest, T. Campbell and B. A. Mullen, 'Missiological Syncretism: The New Animistic Paradigm', in E. Rommen (ed.), *Spiritual Power and Missions: Raising the Issues* (Pasadena: William Carey Library, 1995), p. 63.

to it may be passed on like some sort of spiritual DNA such that, in the words of one exponent, 'it is not our personal sins that hold us but it is the iniquities of the ancestors'.[29] Accordingly the process of transmission must be halted by an act of 'identificational repentance' made by descendants on behalf of the sins of their forebears. The whole concept has scarcely any biblical basis and God's word to Ezekiel repeatedly and emphatically refutes it: 'The son will not share the guilt of the father, nor will the father share the guilt of the son.'[30] Paul's letter to the Corinthians points the same way. The 'curse' of sin is not transmitted, whether by means of objects, bloodline or whatever else. Sin's penalty is not a parcel transferred from person to person or generation to generation until repented of. Guilt is incurred by the perpetrator of sin alone. 'The soul who sins is the one who will die.'[31]

c. Participation with demons (20–22)

In the context, however, the issue of potential contamination from eating meat sacrificed to idols was not Paul's central concern and he moves on to the culminating point in his whole argument. What the Corinthians have neglected is the problem of their involvement in the actual performance of sacrifice. The issue is not the physical objects involved but what is happening in the *act* of worship, and Paul declares that demons are present in pagan idolatry. They do not infest the meat or the idol, but the sacrifice that is offered is in reality offered to them and not to God. Paul is again quoting from the Song of Moses[32] where Moses records Israel's idolatry in the desert: 'They made him jealous with their foreign gods and angered him with their detestable idols. They sacrificed to demons, which are not God . . .'[33] Moses goes on to speak of God's anger and rejection of his people who had rejected him who was their Rock: 'You deserted the Rock, who fathered you; you forgot the God who gave you birth. The LORD saw this and rejected them.'[34]

Paul's application to the Corinthians of Moses' indictment of Israel has devastating implications for them. Demons stand behind the

---

[29] N. Grbich, *Repentance: Cleansing Your Generational Bloodline* (Helderkruin, SA: Ariel Gate International Kingdom Communications, 2009), n.p. (Kindle edition). Ms Grbich herself apparently sees the generational transmission of guilt as a sort of parallel to the transmission of DNA.

[30] Ezek. 18:20.

[31] Ezek. 18:4, 20.

[32] He quotes the first five words of Deut. 32:17 exactly apart from modifying the tense: Ciampa and Rosner, *First Corinthians*, p. 481.

[33] Deut. 32:16–17.

[34] Deut. 32:18–19.

pagan sacrifices at which Corinthians believers had been present: 'they co-opt the worship and sacrifices intended for the idols, and thereby bring the idolater under a demonic sphere of influence'.[35] Through their involvement the Corinthians had themselves become participants with those demons; the word translated 'participants' is *koinōnoi*, meaning that they had joined in actual 'fellowship' with the demons, just as at the Lord's Table they had joined in actual fellowship with Christ. Consequently, if eating at the table of the Lord was no mere empty event but one of real spiritual substance, so too was eating at the altar of a pagan idol. Paul thus brings his Corinthian readers face-to-face with the utter horror of what they had done: their involvement at pagan sacrifice was an act of unfaithfulness to the one who had saved them – an act indeed of spiritual adultery. By their participation in such sacrifices they were implicitly rejecting the God who had saved them, as Israel did, and risked falling under his wrath, as Israel had. For that reason, and in terms that are understated but all the more powerful for that, Paul says to them, *I do not want you to be participants with demons* (20). And then he concludes with a statement and a warning.

Using synonymous parallelism for emphasis, Paul tells them that they must choose – between *the cup of the Lord* and that of demons, and between the table of the Lord and that of demons. There is no room for compromise: continuing participation at pagan sacrifices would mean that they were choosing demons and rejecting God. But the consequences of such a choice would be dire, and Paul warns his readers by yet again echoing the words of the Song of Moses: 'They made me jealous by what is no god and angered me with their worthless idols.'[36] Like Israel they are God's people bound to him by covenant, and the continuing unfaithfulness of their involvement in idolatry would surely provoke his jealousy. A double rhetorical question therefore asks them whether they are so foolish that they would intentionally provoke him, and so strong that they could then withstand the wrath they had provoked. *Are we trying to arouse the Lord's jealousy? Are we stronger than he?* (22). It is 'a frightening threat of judgment upon those Corinthian Christians who provoke God to jealousy'.[37] There is no room for complacency.

The issues that Paul discusses in these chapters may seem remote for most modern, especially Western, readers, who are doubtless unlikely to participate in sacrifices to idols. Nevertheless, the implications of

---

[35] D. Strange, *'For Their Rock Is Not as Our Rock': An Evangelical Theology of Religions* (Nottingham: Apollos, 2014), p. 266.
[36] Deut. 32:21.
[37] Ciampa and Rosner, *First Corinthians*, p. 484.

Paul's words are multiple. In the context of mission what he says raises some hard questions for advocates of approaches to the contextualization of Christian faith for Muslim-background believers, which encourage them to remain within the mosque and perhaps even to continue participating in corporate Islamic worship.[38] They are not, however, the only ones who need to grapple with Paul's words. Much more widespread is the worldliness that menaces all believers and feeds off the sort of complacency that was evident in the church at Corinth. At its root the issue is that of an attachment to the Lord Jesus Christ which is indifferent at best, while pursuit of other 'gods' determines the dominant priorities and goals of life – gods of money or status, perhaps of family or country. Such things are not bad in themselves, just as the Corinthian believers' desire to eat meat and to maintain social and economic contacts with their non-Christian Corinthian neighbours was not bad in itself. The problem, however, lies not with them but with the one who 'idolizes' them and fails truly to grasp the basic truth that the one true God, unique Creator and Redeemer, is alone worthy of our heart's worship. Complacency is the presumption that it doesn't really matter, and that everything will be all right in the end. It is found in the words of the German poet Heinrich Heine: 'Of course God will forgive me; that's his job.'[39] It is a fatal, monumental error, for God is a jealous God who tolerates no rivals. Our spiritual warfare is always so much with our own hearts – so easily divided, so skilled at rationalizing their idolatries, so blindly complacent, so foolish. But God can change hearts, and he does so. It is for us to pray, 'Thou and thou only the first in my heart . . . naught be all else to me, save that thou art.'[40]

---

[38] See e.g., the brief survey in A. S. Moreau, G. R. Corwin and G. B. McGee, *Introducing World Missions: A Biblical, Historical and Practical Survey* (Grand Rapids: Baker, 2004), pp. 298–299.

[39] Attributed as last words; see <https://en.wikiquote.org/wiki/Heinrich_Heine>.

[40] Hymn 'Be thou my vision', ancient Irish, tr. Mary E. Byrne, versified Eleanor Hull, 1912.

Ephesians 6:10–20
20. The weapons of our warfare

Finally . . . , Paul says, or more literally, 'for the rest . . .'[1] He has come to the last section of his letter to the Ephesians but what he writes is no mere wrapping up of the discussion. He does not just summarize what he has been saying to them in the previous chapters, nor does he share a few concluding exhortations or encouragements. Rather 'the paragraph pulls together everything that Paul has already been saying and puts a sharp point on it'.[2]

'It is a stirring call to battle . . . Do you not hear the bugle, and the trumpet? . . . We are being roused, we are being stimulated, we are being set upon our feet; we are told to be men. The whole tone is martial, it is manly, it is strong.'[3]

1. For the rest . . .

The opening words indicate, then, that a new section of Ephesians is beginning, but the essential continuity of the argument should not be missed. Paul is not opening up a wholly new theme, but is rather putting the exhortations and warnings of the preceding chapters in a deeper and broader perspective. At the beginning of the lengthy exhortatory section of his epistle he has urged his readers to 'live a life worthy of the calling you have received'.[4] Among many other things it is a call to work hard at maintaining their unity as God's people (4:1–16); to live as children of light in the midst of the darkness

[1] *tou loipou.*
[2] D. Powlison, 'The Classical Model', in J. K. Beilby and P. R. Eddy (eds.), *Understanding Spiritual Warfare: Four Views* (Grand Rapids: Baker Academic, 2012), p. 92.
[3] D. M. Lloyd-Jones, quoted in J. R. W. Stott, *God's New Society: The Message of Ephesians*, Bible Speaks Today (Downers Grove: InterVarsity Press, 1979), p. 262.
[4] Eph. 4:1.

which surrounds them – avoiding sexual immorality, working honestly, speaking truthfully and so on (4:17 – 5:21); and to please God in the varied relationships of life – as spouses, parents, children, masters and slaves (5:22 – 6:9). Now he tells them that as they seek to do those things, they will face the opposition of Satan and the forces of darkness. Although defeated, as Paul has already explained (1:19–23), they are still active, and their purpose is to drag Christian believers back to the ways of sin from which they were redeemed. Paul brings into focus the depth and breadth of the spiritual conflict his readers must face as Christians wanting to live holy lives and do the works of God. If they are to live worthily, they must fight.

In so writing there is also an implicit reorientation of his readers' thinking. As we have seen, Ephesus was a centre of magic.[5] The *rulers . . . authorities . . . powers of this dark world and . . . spiritual forces of evil in the heavenly places* (12) were seen as powerful and ambivalent spirits which brought physical suffering to human beings but which could also be manipulated for the purposes of sorcerers or of those who used their services. Paul indicates, however, that by far the greatest threat that the spirits pose is moral and spiritual rather than merely physical. They tempt and seduce with a view to undermining the witness of Christians and their churches, and thereby sabotaging their mission. Consequently, the appropriate response is not to negotiate with them by magic in order to turn them to personal advantage, nor to procure mystic protection from their attacks through amulets and the like. Such approaches are mere foolishness as they are irrelevant to what Satan is really about and, indeed, simply play into his hands. The powers of darkness can only be resisted in the strength found in God himself and by putting on the armour he provides. A critical issue is once again that of the mind. The perception of the menace posed by the powers which was prevalent in Ephesian culture was fundamentally wrong; the error needed to be addressed with truth so that the believers could deal with the powers appropriately and effectively. This is part of what Paul is doing here.

2. Our strength

a. Be strong

First, Paul speaks of the resources Christians possess as they face the devil's malignity. Much earlier in the letter he has already prayed that his readers would know the power of God, the invincibility of which is demonstrated both in the resurrection of Jesus Christ and in his

[5] See pp. 147–149 above.

enthronement at God's right hand 'far above all rule and authority . . .'[6] Paul also taught them that God had already raised them with Christ and seated them both 'with him' and 'in him' 'in the heavenly realms'.[7] The resources they need to face the foe are, therefore, fully available to them now as those who are *in Christ*. In their struggle, therefore, they need to live out the reality of what they already are and have in Christ. Being *in Christ* they can and should be *strong in Christ: be strong in the Lord and in his mighty power*. It is language which recalls significant moments in the Old Testament: God's words to Joshua at the beginning of his ministry (Josh. 1:6, 7, 9); David's response to a severe crisis in his early life when he 'found strength in the LORD his God';[8] and God's promise to the returned exiles, 'I will strengthen them in the LORD'.[9] Moreover, the insistent vocabulary of power in Paul's imperative underlines the total sufficiency of the resources his readers have access to in the Lord: *be strong, might, power*.[10] At heart it is about guarding their relationship with him, and Paul's writing reflects Jesus' words to his disciples: 'remain in me, and I will remain in you'.[11]

b. Put on the full armour of God

Paul amplifies his meaning further as twice he says, *put on the full armour of God* (11, 13). The repetition of his exhortation underlines its significance, and powerfully reinforces what he said immediately before in verse 10. The strength that Christians need is not found in themselves. It is theirs *in Christ* and in the form of an armour that God provides. Paul again echoes the Old Testament, this time Isaiah, who more than once depicts God as the divine warrior accoutred in his armour (Isa. 11:4–5; 59:17). So, as we read the passage 'the soldier we are to imagine is not Roman but divine and messianic. We are to imagine the Lord God in person'.[12] The armour Christians must put on is that in which God himself does battle and which he gives to his people so that they may fight as he does, all of which underlines the utter seriousness of the conflict.[13] It is expressed in a single word, *panoplia*, translated *full armour* in the NIV, which refers to 'a complete

---

[6] Eph. 1:21.

[7] Eph. 2:6.

[8] 1 Sam. 30:6.

[9] Zech. 10:12. P. T. O'Brien, *The Letter to the Ephesians*, Pillar NT Commentary (Grand Rapids: Eerdmans and Leicester: Apollos, 1999), p. 461.

[10] *endynamoō, kratos, ischys*.

[11] John 15:4.

[12] Powlison, 'The Classical Model', p. 94.

[13] A. T. Lincoln, *Ephesians*, Word Bible Commentary 42 (Dallas: Word, 1990), p. 442.

set of instruments used in defensive or offensive warfare'.[14] It is the whole *panoplia* and, indeed, nothing other than the *panoplia*, that is needed for the fight if God's people are to prevail. And believers must actively put it on, just as they must consciously and deliberately *be strong in the Lord.* The divine provision of strength and armour does not exclude their personal responsibility to make use of it.

c. Stand

Believers put on the armour of God so that they may *stand*, a verb which Paul uses four times in the passage (6:11, 13, 14).[15] He summons his readers to stand, to stand firm, to stand their ground. Such language may suggest that Paul is largely focusing on the defensive dimension of spiritual warfare, with the possible exception of his references to *the gospel of peace* (represented by the soldier's boots, 15) and the *word of God* (*the sword of the Spirit*, 17).[16] Such a view, however, reads too much into Paul's use of the one verb *stand*[17] and, more seriously, implies that God's people fight constantly on the back foot rather like nervous batsmen helplessly pinned down by a ferocious and unrelenting attack. As Powlison suggests, 'this gets the major emphasis exactly backwards'.[18] It is certainly not how God and his Messiah fight in the Isaianic texts from which the imagery is drawn (Isa. 11:4–5; 59:17). In the context of the victory Jesus Christ has already achieved and the certain advance of the gospel as he sends his church into the world, the reality must surely be otherwise:

> Spiritual warfare arises because God is carrying out his invasion, piercing the darkness with light. We who were formerly darkness have been made part of the light that he brings – and every photon of faith and love illumines and destroys darkness. Ephesians envisions a war in which the fighting is hot but the initiative and conquering power are on our side.[19]

This does not imply some false triumphalism, like that of the health and wealth gospel, in which Christians do not get hurt but

[14] J. P. Louw and E. A. Nida, quoted in O'Brien, *Ephesians*, p. 462.

[15] *histēmi* and its cognate *anthistēmi*.

[16] So, for example, C. E. Arnold, *Powers of Darkness* (Leicester: Inter-Varsity Press, 1992), p. 154.

[17] Cf. C. H. Talbert, *Ephesians and Colossians*, Paideia Commentaries on the New Testament (Grand Rapids: Baker, 2007), p. 161, who argues after some discussion, 'The idea of standing, then, is by itself neither strictly defensive nor strictly offensive in a military context.'

[18] Powlison, 'The Classical Model', p. 96.

[19] Ibid.

fly above the storm. The true church of Christ goes always the way of its Lord, bearing a cross, and filling up 'what is still lacking in regard to Christ's afflictions, for the sake of his body'.[20] But as it does so it perseveres in faithfulness and witness, and through its very sufferings spreads the fragrance of the knowledge of Christ (2 Cor. 2:14).

3. Our struggle

It is important to know the enemy. Doctors and nurses learn about the diseases they have to fight. In the early 1940s the British General Montgomery had a photograph of the German commander Erwin Rommel in his command caravan as he fought him across North Africa. In the same way Paul teaches his readers about the spiritual enemy they must contend with.

a. Not against flesh and blood

Paul tells his readers what the enemy is *not*: it is not *flesh and blood* (12). Of course he knows that men and women can seek to obstruct the gospel and in various ways do damage to believers. They can obviously be sources of temptation, deception and persecution. The so-called new atheism, the normalization of promiscuity and homosexuality by the media and discriminatory anti-Christian legislation are all expressions of human opposition to Christ and the gospel and there are countless other expressions of it too. Nor are these things to be ignored; believers are indeed to contend for the gospel (Phil. 1:27; 4:3; Jude 3). Paul's point, however, is that behind such things there lies the scheming and venom of invisible spiritual forces, 'who cannot be wounded or vanquished like human beings'.[21] And only God's strength and armour are sufficient to engage them.

Focusing on the merely human adversary is like treating the symptoms of a disease while ignoring its underlying causes. Worse than that, it encourages us to suppose that our spiritual combat is a humanly manageable enterprise. It will likely blind us, therefore, to the critical importance of the weapons God alone can give us, such things as faith, truth and righteousness, and even trick us into waging war as the world does and using its weapons – sarcasm, scorn, half-truth or downright lies, even perhaps brute force and coercion. Wily and scheming as he is, this is of course exactly how Satan would like

[20] Col. 1:24.
[21] R. Schnackenburg, *The Epistle to the Ephesians* (Edinburgh: T&T Clark, 1991), p. 273.

God's people to fight. By contrast, recognizing that the battle is *not against flesh and blood* '"lowers the temperature" amid human conflicts, the church's many failures, and the stubbornness of our own sin'.[22] And ultimately the men and women who oppose – *flesh and blood* – are themselves enslaved by the world, the flesh and the devil as we all once were. They desperately need to experience the power of the gospel itself rather than be pummelled into unwilling submission.

b. The devil and the powers

Paul refers to the enemy against whom the armour must be deployed first as *the devil* (11) and then as *the rulers . . . the authorities, . . . the powers of this dark world and . . . the spiritual forces of evil in the heavenly realms* (12). *Rulers* and *authorities* are among the terms he regularly uses to describe the spiritual powers of darkness,[23] but the other two expressions appear only here. The first of them is literally 'the world rulers of this darkness'.[24] 'World rulers' may refer to the spiritual powers which stand behind pagan deities such as Artemis goddess of the Ephesians, while 'of this darkness' identifies them with the present evil age from which believers have been delivered.[25] The phrase, *spiritual forces of evil in the heavenly realms*,[26] is probably a comprehensive, generic reference to 'all classes of hostile spirits'.[27] Evidently the devil and these various spiritual powers are all on the same side, united in the common cause of waging war against God and his people if in little else.[28] Further, the individual mention of the devil suggests his leadership in the whole enterprise. Using his own distinctive terminology of 'principalities and powers' Paul is speaking here of what the author of Revelation terms 'the dragon and his angels'.[29]

They are a formidable and fearsome enemy and the battle is clearly not to be taken lightly. The titles Paul uses, *rulers . . . authorities . . . world rulers . . . forces of evil*, all indicate power, while his repetitious phrase, *against . . . against . . . against . . . against . . .*, focuses the readers' attention on the relentlessness of their hostility.[30] Paul does not want the Ephesian believers to underestimate the strength

---

[22] Powlison, 'The Classical Model', p. 96.
[23] See above, p. 21.
[24] *hoi kosmokratōres tou skotous toutou.*
[25] O'Brien, *Ephesians*, p. 467.
[26] *ta pneumatika tēs ponērias en tois epouraniois.*
[27] O'Brien, *Ephesians*, p. 467.
[28] See above, pp. 137–138.
[29] Rev. 12:7, 9.
[30] O'Brien, *Ephesians*, p. 466, n. 112.

of the enemy, who is, indeed, far stronger than they are as mere human beings. Further, the word he uses to describe the conflict (*palē*), translated *struggle* (12) and found only here in the New Testament, similarly suggests the severity of the conflict. It derives not from the vocabulary of warfare but rather from the sport of wrestling, and in using it Paul's intention is probably 'to heighten the closeness of the struggle with the powers of evil'.[31] His readers must know that the warfare they are engaged in involves bitter and arduous combat, the spiritual equivalent of intense hand-to-hand fighting.

Nevertheless, Paul is writing from the perspective of the death and the resurrection of the Lord Jesus Christ which brought about the defeat of these beings. They may be stronger than his readers but Christ has conquered them. There is, therefore, a confidence running through the passage, that in Christ's strength and clothed with God's armour believers will indeed stand even in the face of such a foe, fighting as they do from the vantage point of victory already secured by their Saviour. 'The entire passage is suffused with a spirit of confidence and hope, and the reader is left, not with a feeling of despair, but with the sense that Satan can be defeated.'[32]

c. The devil's schemes

Clothed in their armour believers can take their stand against *the devil's schemes* (11). The expression somewhat echoes Paul's warning to the Corinthians, 'we are not unaware of his schemes',[33] and suggests the multiplicity and variety of the means that the devil employs. It also draws attention to his subtlety and guile, which were especially visible when the serpent led Eve step by step into disobedience. The devil seeks a foothold in the lives of believers by which to re-establish the tyranny broken at the cross, and he gains it through their sin. It might be unbridled anger, as Paul suggests earlier in the epistle (Eph. 4:27). It might also be 'falsehood (4:25), stealing (v. 28), unwholesome talk (v. 29)'[34] or any number of other things. The powers of darkness exploit those specific weaknesses that are particular to each one of us. They infiltrate into our minds patterns of thought hostile to God's truth. They exploit our illnesses, disappointments and failures to undermine faith. They work through the institutions of this world: its governments, laws, media,

[31] Arnold, *Powers of Darkness*, p. 153.
[32] S. H. T. Page, *Powers of Evil: A Biblical Study of Satan and Demons* (Grand Rapids: Baker and Leicester: Apollos, 1995), p. 187.
[33] 2 Cor. 2:11.
[34] O'Brien, *Ephesians*, p. 464.

businesses, structures of education. They exploit even the good in us, so we become unbalanced, extreme and judgmental over the very things we are right about, once again fighting the Lord's battles with the enemy's weapons. As one commentator points out: 'Evil rarely looks evil until it accomplishes its goal; it gains entrance by appearing attractive, desirable, and perfectly legitimate. It is a baited and camouflaged trap.'[35]

d. The day of evil

The text speaks enigmatically of *the day of evil* (13). The phrase occurs three times in the Old Testament and speaks there of coming judgment – 'the day of disaster'.[36] Paul does not use it elsewhere but in Galatians he speaks of 'the present evil age' and earlier in Ephesians he tells his readers to be careful how they live and to seize every opportunity 'because the days are evil'.[37] The reference is probably in part to the fact that now, day by day, believers live in an age of which Satan is god (2 Cor. 4:4) and in which they must therefore expect to face diverse trials. Further, and more specifically, there will be times when the struggle feels especially intense: a time of severe and persistent temptation, perhaps, or of bereavement, disappointment, loss, sickness, accident. Sometimes such a 'day' may arise in the life of the church as it grapples with false teaching among its members, or schism, or some severe moral lapse within its leadership. Then there are periods when Satan seems to hold his fire, which too easily breed complacency and so leave believers sluggish and unprepared on 'the day of evil'. They need to be constantly alert, clothed in their armour and strong in Christ, like soldiers in the trenches always ready for the enemy's next big push.

e. After doing everything

For there is a relentlessness about the struggle. It goes on throughout this age – every day and every minute of every day. There is no vacation, no weekend, no sabbatical, no home leave, no tea break. In a neglected rewriting of early British history Goscinny and Uderzo suggest that Julius Caesar's military success in Britain came about by exploiting the natives' refusal to fight during weekends as well as after five o'clock every afternoon when they took a break to

---

[35] K. Snodgras, quoted in O'Brien, *Ephesians*, p. 464.
[36] Jer. 17:17, 18; Obad. 13.
[37] Gal. 1:4; Eph. 5:16.

drink a cup of hot water.[38] The idea is obviously whimsical but it makes a point. The intensity and utter seriousness of the hostility Christians must face demands a corresponding commitment on their part. It is not a pastime, a game or a hobby, but total warfare, and Satan does not respect our times of relaxation but exploits them. Christians need to do all that the conflict requires and then, having done all things (13), they will stand.

4. Our armour

Paul describes piece by piece the armour which he has told his readers to put on. The force of the metaphor he uses lies largely in the thing signified by each piece, *faith* for example, or the *gospel*, or the *word of God*, and not so much in the images themselves, whether helmet, belt or whatever. Indeed, in 1 Thessalonians 5:8 he refers more briefly to the Christian's breastplate and helmet, but the signification of the two pieces is not identical with that in Ephesians 6.

Here Paul speaks of six pieces, each of which must be worn if the believer is to be equipped with *the full armour of God* and so can be said to have done all things. The identification of these pieces, the things signified, indicates that the struggle is primarily moral and spiritual and therefore that 'the battlefield lies within the hearts and lives of Christians'.[39] By clothing themselves in the qualities signified they will live as light in the darkness and so bring conviction of the gospel's truth and power.

a. The belt of truth

Paul does not refer specifically to a belt but simply says, 'having fastened truth around your waist'. Clearly, though, some sort of belt is assumed but probably not that of the Roman soldier, which was 'a leather apron which hung under the armour and protected the thighs'.[40] The point here is rather to fasten loose clothing tightly round the waist so that it should not get in the way, which 'made rapid movement easier and was vital preparation for any vigorous activity'.[41] The image surely comes from Isaiah's 'depiction of the coming Messiah . . . : "He shall be girded with righteousness around

[38] R. Goscinny and A. Uderzo, *Asterix in Britain*, tr. Anthea Bell and Derek Hockridge (London: Hodder Dargaud, 1970 [1966]), p. 6. According to the authors it was Asterix the Gaul who inadvertently brought tea to Britain, thereby enabling the ancient Britons to brew up.
[39] Page, *Powers of Evil*, p. 189.
[40] O'Brien, *Ephesians*, p. 473.
[41] Lincoln, *Ephesians*, p. 447.

the waist . . . and bound with truth around the sides" (Is 11:5)'.[42] Truth here may be the objective truth of God and his word which the Spirit uses in the sanctification of believers (John 17:17; 2 Tim. 3:16–17; Heb. 4:12). Alternatively, it may more likely refer to a subjective inner truth – the truth of integrity, guilelessness, transparency.[43] The glory of the incarnate Word of God himself was visible in that he was full of 'grace and truth'.[44] Understood in this way Paul is saying that to stand in the struggle there must first of all be a reality and truth about Christian believers and their profession. It is the sort of total integrity that he saw especially in Timothy, his co-worker: 'I have no one else like him, who takes a genuine interest in your welfare. For everyone looks out for his own interests, not those of Jesus Christ.'[45] The hypocrite will not be able to stand in the conflict, and neither will the person of divided heart or the believer who enjoys friendship with the world (Jas 4:4). Of course, there is a sense in which the objective and subjective meanings of truth ultimately coincide: as the word of God takes hold of a believer's life it will surely produce 'truth in the inner parts'.[46]

b. The breastplate of righteousness

The *breastplate* was widely used in Paul's time and not by the Roman army alone. Once again, however, he is probably drawing the image from Isaiah, and this time his portrayal of the Lord: 'He put on righteousness as his breastplate.'[47] As with the *belt of truth*, Paul may be speaking of the objective righteousness imputed by faith to the believer by which he or she is justified. In that case it would be parallel to 'the blood of the lamb' which does indeed overcome the accuser by dealing with the sin of those he accuses (Rev. 12:11).[48] In the context of this whole section of Ephesians, however, it probably refers to that righteousness which should characterize the believer's daily life, like the 'weapons of righteousness' Paul refers to in 2 Corinthians 6:7. His exhortation to put on *the breastplate of righteousness* would then be parallel to his reference earlier in Ephesians to putting on 'the new self, created to be like God in true

---

[42] C. E. Arnold, *Ephesians*, Zondervan Exegetical Commentary on the NT (Grand Rapids: Zondervan, 2010), p. 451.
[43] F. Foulkes, *Ephesians: An Introduction and Commentary*, Tyndale NT Commentaries (Leicester: Inter-Varsity Press, 1989), p. 179.
[44] John 1:14.
[45] Phil. 2:20–21.
[46] Ps. 51:6.
[47] Isa. 59:17.
[48] See below, pp. 264–265.

righteousness and holiness'.[49] So, as well as pursuing inner truth Christians also pursue outer righteousness in all the dealings of their daily lives: in their homes, work, relationships, conversation, church. There are implications for the church too, which must put on righteousness not only by discipling its members but also sometimes by the discipline of the wayward.

c. Feet fitted with the readiness that comes from the gospel of peace

There may well be a reference here to the studded boots of the Roman soldier, the purpose of which was to give a solid footing, but the language used also strongly echoes Isaiah 52:7: 'How beautiful on the mountains are the feet of those who bring good news, who proclaim peace.' There is, however, some debate about the exact meaning of the phrase.[50] The *gospel of peace* is undoubtedly the good news of reconciliation with God and with one another which Paul had expounded earlier in the letter (2:11–22). It is the notion of fitting the feet *with the readiness* of the gospel which is problematic. There are two main options which are not, however, so far apart. In both cases it is about having a solid grasp of the gospel and conviction of its truth which *either* gives a readiness to face Satan's attacks on one's own assurance and obedience *or* gives a readiness to proclaim the gospel to others. If the words of Isaiah 52:7 were indeed in Paul's mind as he wrote, they would point to the latter meaning which would therefore give an offensive rather than a defensive turn to the phrase. Paul is telling his readers that they must be so clear and sure about their message that they are ready and able to pass it on.

d. The shield of faith

The *shield of faith* obviously does have a defensive dimension, offering protection against Satan's *flaming arrows*. Flaming arrows, dipped in pitch and then set alight, could inflict terrible and fatal wounds in first-century warfare, and so the image points to lethal attack and acute danger. Paul is thinking of the whole range of Satan's 'schemes', all his *flaming arrows*, including moral temptation, false teaching and physical persecution. Also in view may be those moments of doubt, fear, discouragement and even despair which Satan exploits to undermine trust in God's goodness, power and wisdom. To defend themselves Roman soldiers were armed with

---

[49] Eph. 4:24.
[50] See e.g., O'Brien, *Ephesians*, pp. 475–479.

large shields, shaped like a door, which covered the whole body,[51] and Paul sees this as a metaphor for faith. As believers face the enemy's most venomous attacks in any one of its varied guises, they need a faith which still holds on to God, and so finds strength in him to persevere and do his will. Such faith was visible in Job as he continued to trust in God despite all his terrible loss and agony; in Paul and Silas singing God's praises in a miserable Philippian gaol (Acts 16:25); in John exiled on Patmos 'because of the word of God and the testimony of Jesus' (Rev. 1:9); and especially in the Lord Jesus Christ as he prayed in Gethsemane.[52] It was visible too in Martin Luther, standing almost alone against the combined power of church and emperor and declaring, 'Unless I am convinced by Scripture and plain reason ... my conscience is captive to the Word of God. I cannot and I will not recant anything, for to go against conscience is neither right nor safe. God help me. Amen.'[53]

Towards the end of Hebrews 11 the writer speaks of those who by faith 'faced jeers and flogging ... were stoned ... sawn in two ... put to death by the sword ... went about in sheepskins and goatskins, destitute, persecuted and ill-treated'.[54] And C. S. Lewis captures something of the character of such faith in words he puts into the mouth of Screwtape: 'Our cause is never more in danger than when a human, no longer desiring, but still intending, to do our enemy's will, looks round upon a universe from which every trace of him seems to have vanished, and asks why he has been forsaken, and still obeys.'[55] It is the shield of faith which enables a person to do that – still to trust God, and so find strength in him and persevere.

e. The helmet of salvation

The armies of Paul's day used helmets, but Paul is certainly thinking of the divine warrior himself who puts on the *helmet of salvation* along with 'righteousness as his breastplate'.[56] He uses a very similar image when he urges the Thessalonians to put on 'the hope of salvation as a helmet'.[57] Here in Ephesians, however, the metaphor speaks of the conviction of the present reality of salvation rather than assurance of its future realization. It is the conviction that God

[51] O'Brien, *Ephesians*, p. 479, n. 168.
[52] Matt. 26:39, 42; Mark 14:35–36; Luke 22:41–42.
[53] R. H. Bainton, *Here I Stand: A Life of Martin Luther* (New York, Nashville: Abingdon-Cokesbury Press, 1950), p. 185.
[54] Heb. 11:36–37.
[55] C. S. Lewis, *The Screwtape Letters* (London: Geoffrey Bles/The Centenary Press, 1942), p. 47.
[56] Isa. 59:17.
[57] 1 Thess. 5:8.

has truly saved: he has justified and raised us, and he is with us to deliver in the midst of the battle. It was a point vitally important for Paul's readers with their fears of sorcery and evil spirits, and earlier in the letter he had already reassured them in just these terms. Jesus has been raised from the dead and is now seated at God's right hand, and as believers they are raised with him and seated with him in the heavenly places (Eph. 1:19–22; 2:6). This is *the helmet of salvation*. By getting a firm hold on those truths and allowing them to transform the way they thought and lived, Paul's readers would be putting the helmet on. Similarly, when Paul was on trial in Rome and facing the authorities without any human support, his conviction of the sure and certain fulfilment of God's saving purpose in his life armed him against the enemy – it was his helmet of salvation: 'The Lord will rescue me from every evil attack, and bring me safely to his heavenly kingdom.'[58]

f. The sword of the Spirit, which is the word of God

The sword is clearly an offensive weapon and one 'worn by every Roman infantryman'.[59] Once again, however, the background to Paul's thinking is surely the mighty word of the Spirit-anointed Messiah prophesied by Isaiah, who would 'strike the earth with the rod of his mouth',[60] rather than the weaponry of first-century Roman soldiers.[61] The Messiah supplies 'his power and weapons to his people for warfare'.[62] Further, the term Paul uses for 'word'[63] 'tends to emphasize the word as spoken or proclaimed'.[64] Along with the Isaianic background this suggests that Paul is primarily speaking of the proclamation of the good news by which the Spirit of God sovereignly brings about the liberation of those held captive by sin and Satan. God's word is the word of truth which still strikes the earth, exposing Satan's lies and bringing freedom to his dupes. In his own relentless preaching Paul demonstrated in practice what he teaches here. Hounded from place to place, never did he re-evaluate his approach to the ministry God had given him. He persisted in the proclamation of the gospel without pause or hesitation, because he was convinced that this was the means uniquely appointed by God

[58] 2 Tim. 4:18.
[59] Arnold, *Ephesians*, p. 461.
[60] Isa. 11:4–5.
[61] O'Brien, *Ephesians*, p. 482.
[62] Arnold, *Ephesians*, p. 462.
[63] It is *rhēma* rather than the more usual *logos* that Paul uses here and which is translated 'word' in English versions.
[64] O'Brien, *Ephesians*, p. 482.

to bring salvation to lost men and women. Moreover, this is doubtless what he had in mind when he wrote to the Corinthians about the divine character of the weapons he used to break down resistance to the knowledge of God. 'The weapons we fight with are not the weapons of the world. On the contrary, they have divine power to demolish strongholds. We demolish arguments and every pretension that sets itself up against the knowledge of God, and we take captive every thought to make it obedient to Christ.'[65]

And the *word of God* is also, of course, the means by which believers arm themselves to face Satan's temptations in their own lives. In his confrontation with the devil Jesus himself repeatedly went back to the Scriptures as he responded to each temptation, 'it is written'.

5. Our prayer (6:18–20)

Finally Paul urges his readers to *pray* (18). Although at this point he drops the military imagery his exhortation to pray does not introduce a new subject but is tightly linked to what precedes. Nor is it a mere appendix to what he has just been saying but fundamental to it all, a fitting conclusion to his words on spiritual warfare and even to the whole book. The spiritual armour is God's and provided by him, and strength for the fight is equally found in him. Ultimately, therefore, if his readers are to stand, the most important thing of all is constant, ongoing communion with God who is their great armourer. Paul is in fact making very much the same point as James in his exhortation already discussed above:[66] 'Submit yourselves, then, to God. Resist the devil, and he will flee from you. Come near to God and he will come near to you.'[67] Believers withstand Satan in the context of submitting themselves to God and coming near to him, and only in that way.

Paul presses the importance of prayer by four times repeating the word *all*. First, his readers must pray *in the Spirit on all occasions*. The warfare they are engaged in is unrelenting and so their praying must also be unrelenting so that they may have uninterrupted access to the resources they need. Moreover, such praying is to be *in the Spirit*, meaning that they are open to the Spirit's prompting and seek his guidance in their petitions, trusting him too to intercede for them in times of perplexity (Rom. 8:26–27). Second, they must pray with *all kinds of prayer*. There will be set times of prayer, spontaneous

---

[65] 2 Cor. 10:4–5.
[66] See above, pp. 215–216.
[67] Jas 4:7–8.

moments of prayer, solitary prayers, prayers with God's people, family prayers, and especially the cultivation of a constant underlying communion with God. Third, they must *be alert and always keep on praying*. The incessant dangers of distraction, complacency and weariness demand a constant and self-conscious alertness. Paul's words remind his readers of Jesus' warning to his disciples that they must 'watch and pray' so as not to fall into temptation (Matt. 26:41). Satan's active pursuit of the believer's destruction (1 Pet. 5:8) and the need to be ready for the Lord's return (Matt. 24:42; Luke 21:36) both call for watchful prayerfulness. And, finally, they must pray *for all the saints*. Spiritual warfare is the affair not just of individual Christians but of the whole church together as people of God. Each member is part of the body, and the spiritual vigour of each is intimately bound up with that of the whole, and vice versa.

Finally, Paul asks them to pray for him (19–20). Remarkably, although he writes from prison, he does not ask for prayer for release from his chains but rather for his communication of the gospel. The chains, which are the cross he bears for Christ, are in fact integral to the warfare he is engaged in. Far from meaning that Satan has got the better of him, they enable him to gain access to men and women themselves captive to the darkness, who might otherwise have no occasion of hearing the good news. In this sense he himself is a model of the warfare he speaks of, which is not against his captors but against the powers that stand behind them.[68] Accordingly there are two focal points to his prayer. First he is concerned for clarity: *that . . . words may be given me* (19). Experienced preacher though he is, he is nevertheless humbly aware of his need for God's grace and wisdom as he shares the most important message of all. Second, he recognizes his need of courage to seize the opportunities that might arise and twice asks for fearlessness: *so that I will fearlessly make known . . . that I may declare it fearlessly*. As he shared the good news in the course of his ministry Paul displayed outstanding courage on numerous occasions: giving his testimony to a crowd that had been trying to kill him just moments before (Acts 21:30 – 22:21); sharing it with a king and a governor (Acts 26); proclaiming the gospel message to his judges as he stood on trial for his life (2 Tim. 4:17); and constantly from town to town facing hostility and violence. To the Corinthians he confessed the weakness, fear and trembling he might feel as he embarked on ministry (1 Cor. 2:3), but he never shrank back from the task entrusted to him. Nevertheless, he felt the need of prayer for continuing fearlessness as in his preaching he struggled *against the rulers, against the authorities . . .*

---

[68] Cf. Lincoln, *Ephesians*, p. 460.

To conclude, spiritual warfare is Christian life. Believers are in a battle and they must respond accordingly or be overcome. Soldiers in physical battle take their position seriously, for the consequence of not doing so is defeat, even death. In Western societies relative ease and affluence easily breed a debilitating complacency which produces spiritual mediocrity and ineffectiveness in mission. But Christ has overcome every enemy: there is no excuse for defeat. Strong in him and clothed in his armour his people may take their stand – confident but not complacent – and 'live as light in a dark world'.[69]

[69] Powlison, 'The Classical Model', p. 98.

Revelation 12:11
21. They overcame him

We have been forewarned that an enemy relentlessly threatens us, an enemy who is the very embodiment of rash boldness, of military prowess, of crafty wiles, of untiring zeal and haste, of every conceivable weapon and of skill in the art of warfare. We must, then, bend our every effort to this goal: that we should not let ourselves be overwhelmed by carelessness or faintheartedness, but on the contrary, with courage rekindled stand our ground in combat.[1]

The purpose of any war is to overcome the enemy, and so it is with spiritual warfare, as Calvin reminds us. Military strategy, tactics, weaponry are all evaluated in terms of their capacity to achieve that one great end. The longbow was a mighty weapon in the fourteenth and fifteenth centuries, and used with great success by the English against French cavalry at Agincourt in 1415. However, longbows were not issued to the troops sent into battle on the beaches of Normandy in June 1944. In a very different conflict they would no longer have been effective. Spiritual warfare is of course entirely different. Nevertheless, the same basic principle applies: the purpose of the conflict is to overcome the enemy, and the weapons used must be such as can achieve that purpose.

In this case the great enemy is Satan, the enemy of God and of his people, whose object is to destroy those people and to frustrate the mission God has given to them. So, in Paul's words, we do not struggle 'against flesh and blood'[2] and, therefore, the 'weapons we fight with are not the weapons of the world'.[3] It is, however, all too easy to misunderstand the battle and to fight wrongly: with angry

---

[1] J. Calvin, *Institutes of the Christian Religion*, ed. J. T. McNeill (Philadelphia: The Westminster Press, 1960), 1.14.13, p. 173.
[2] Eph. 6:12.
[3] 2 Cor. 10:4.

and bitter words, with manipulative and underhand methods, even with blows and violence. Far from enabling believers to overcome their spiritual enemy, the use of such 'weapons of the world' actually puts them in his camp and brings miserable defeat. Christians need to be aware of Satan's subtlety and cunning so that they will not be outwitted by him (2 Cor. 2:11; Eph. 6:11; Gen. 3:1), and perhaps especially so when, like the readers of Revelation, they face severe physical persecution and provocation. At such moments, along with Paul, they must intentionally renounce 'the hidden things of shame'.[4]

How then do they overcome? John passes on to his seven churches the answer he had heard transmitted by a 'loud voice in heaven' in the context of a hymn of victory, briefly summarizing how 'our brothers' had overcome Satan:

> *They overcame him*
> *by the blood of the Lamb*
> *and by the word of their testimony;*
> *they did not love their lives so much*
> *as to shrink from death.*

1. An enemy defeated

The words John hears come in the flow of a narrative already discussed above.[5] Through his death and resurrection the child of the woman has brought about the expulsion from heaven of the dragon and his angels, which was carried out by Michael (Rev. 12:1–9). Following the description of this event the 'loud voice' intones a hymn which both celebrates and explains the meaning of the celestial battle (Rev. 12:10–12). The one who speaks remains anonymous here although a 'loud voice' speaks frequently in Revelation,[6] normally the voice of an angel, once of an eagle, and in other cases probably that of God or Christ, and especially so when speaking from the temple (16:1, 17) or the throne (21:3). Nevertheless, the allusion to 'our brothers' in the words proclaimed by the 'loud voice' suggests that here it is probably Christian believers already in glory who speak, as they do earlier in the book when the souls of martyred saints 'under the altar' also 'called out in a loud voice' (Rev. 6:9–10). At all events, the loudness of the voice and the location from which it sounds indicate the trustworthiness and authority of what it says.

---

[4] 2 Cor. 4:2. New King James literal translation of *ta krypta tēs aischynēs*.
[5] See ch. 9.
[6] 1:10–11; 7:2–3; 8:13; 11:12; 14:7, 9, 18; 16:1, 17; 18:2; 19:17; 21:3.

First, the hymn rejoices in the coming of 'the salvation and the power and the kingdom of our God, and the authority of his Christ'. There is something of a parallel here with the song of Moses and the Israelites which similarly celebrated God's triumph at the Red Sea and his rule (Exod. 15:1–18). There it was the exaltation of the Lord and the hurling down of Pharaoh and his army into the sea (Exod. 15:4–7, 10, 12); in Revelation it is the ascension of Christ (12:5) and the hurling down of Satan (12:7–9): 'For the accuser . . . has been hurled down.' Beyond the celebration, however, the hymn also explains the significance of Satan's expulsion from heaven in the fact that he can no longer accuse the people of God. Satan has been 'hurled down' specifically as 'the accuser of our brothers, who accuses them before our God day and night'.[7] Christ's atoning sacrifice accomplished that, for it is because of the cross that there is no longer any ground for the accusation of God's people, and so no 'place' for the accuser (Rev. 12:8). 'Our brothers' have been set free through the blood of their Saviour.

The celebration of God's kingdom and Satan's defeat was vital to John's readers. The evidence of their eyes – the fierce trials and persecutions they faced – suggested that far from being overcomers they were hopeless losers. The hymn assured them that, on the contrary, in Christ they had already overcome because Satan had been disarmed of his power of accusation. As at the Red Sea, God had overwhelmed the enemy and freed his victims, and the 'satanic evil' which they faced was 'really a defeated power, however contrary it might seem to human experience'.[8] Indeed, the sufferings they were experiencing were actually evidence of their enemy's defeat and frustration, as the words at the end of the hymn suggest: 'He is filled with fury, because he knows that his time is short.'[9] 'It is precisely when Satan has lost the battle for the souls of the saints in heaven that he begins the fruitless persecution of their bodies.'[10]

The hymn then goes on to explain how, on the basis of the accuser's downfall at the hands of Christ, 'our brothers' have themselves also overcome him. It makes three points, closely related to one another and to the rest of the book. They prevail not by escaping the persecution he inflicts but by their identification with

[7] Rev. 12:10.

[8] G. E. Ladd, quoted in G. K. Beale, *The Book of Revelation*, New International Greek Testament Commentary (Grand Rapids: Eerdmans and Carlisle: Paternoster, 1999), p. 663.

[9] Rev. 12:12.

[10] A. Farrer, quoted in A. F. Johnson, 'Revelation', *The Expositor's Bible Commentary*, vol. XII (Grand Rapids: Zondervan, 1981), p. 517. Also mentioned by Beale, *Revelation*, p. 663.

Christ in his victory: cleansed by him, witnessing to him, suffering with him.

2. The blood of the Lamb

First, *they overcame him by the blood of the Lamb*. This is the absolute heart of Christian life, experience and perseverance: Christ shed his blood to make atonement for sins. Consequently 'our brothers' have been freed from their sins (Rev. 1:5), for 'they have washed their robes and made them white in the blood of the Lamb'.[11] It is the first and most fundamental dimension of their victory over Satan, whose power over them was always parasitic on their own sin. Now they are invulnerable to any and every accusation he may seek to bring. 'Through Christ's death they have been declared not guilty of the accusations launched against them.'[12] In Paul's words, written most likely with Satan in mind,[13] 'Who will bring any charge against those whom God has chosen? It is God who justifies. Who is he that condemns?'[14]

It is true of all believers of every age and every people. Their status before God, their righteousness and consequent acceptance by him, is grounded in the work of Christ and in nothing else. In Christ every Christian at the very outset of their life as a believer is cleansed from sin and clothed once for all in his perfect righteousness. They can add nothing to that righteousness, nor can they diminish it. *They start out victorious*, already armed with God's declaration of their acquittal on every charge. It is first of all a matter of objective truth and reality and not about feelings and emotion, although the realization of what God has done should indeed stir a profound sense of wonder, gratitude and love. God has done this and it is the very core and centre of the gospel: as we have already noted, it is this above all that makes the good news truly *good* news.[15] 'Christ died for our sins.'[16]

The knowledge of this truth is central to the believer's perseverance in the face of Satan's hostility. First, it is crucial at those moments of doubt and uncertainty that all Christians experience. There is the constant struggle with sin, and the sense of frustrated impotence in the face of one's own continued stumbling and failing which Paul expressed: 'For I have the desire to do what is good, but I cannot

[11] Rev. 7:14; cf. 22:14.
[12] Beale, *Revelation*, p. 664.
[13] So C. G. Kruse, *Paul's Letter to the Romans*, Pillar NT Commentary (Grand Rapids: Eerdmans and Nottingham: Apollos, 2012), p. 361.
[14] Rom. 8:33–34.
[15] See above, p. 194.
[16] 1 Cor. 15.3.

carry it out. For what I do is not the good I want to do; no, the evil I do not want to do – this I keep on doing.'[17] At such times it is knowledge of what God has already triumphantly accomplished through the *blood of the Lamb* which alone can reassure and sustain, and the consequent certainty that 'there is now no condemnation for those who are in Christ Jesus'.[18] It is a constant reminder that Christian confidence and hope are never rooted in ourselves and our good works but always and only in the cross of Jesus.

Second, it is the vital anchor whenever Satan seeks to slide believers away from faith in the unique and complete efficacy of Christ's work. This is the issue Paul responds to in a number of his epistles. The Colossian church, for example, was apparently adding ascetic regulations and mysticism to the gospel, while the Galatian church was insisting on the necessity of circumcision. The persistent human desire, rooted in sinful pride, to bring some merit to God and so somehow to earn his favour, undermines the very nature of the gospel as pure gift of God; indeed, it perverts it and turns it into 'a different gospel – which is really no gospel at all'.[19] The fundamental truth, *they overcame him by the blood of the Lamb*, is a reminder that however much we may do in the service of God, whatever position we may attain for him, whatever our achievements or our sufferings for him, it is the utter grace and mercy of God's gift in Christ which alone saves. We never move on from the foundation laid by Christ for our salvation. This is the scandal of the gospel, and its glory: 'Not to us, O LORD, not to us but to your name be the glory . . .'[20]

Augustus Toplady's words sum it up:

> Nothing in my hand I bring,
> Simply to thy cross I cling;
> Naked, come to thee for dress,
> Helpless, look to thee for grace;
> Foul, I to the fountain fly;
> Wash me, Saviour, or I die.[21]

3. The word of their testimony

Second, they overcame him *by the word of their testimony*. In John 8:44 Jesus reveals the two fundamental characteristics of Satan: he is

[17] Rom. 7:18–19.
[18] Rom. 8:1.
[19] Gal. 1:6–7.
[20] Ps. 115:1.
[21] A. M. Toplady, 'Rock of Ages', 1763.

a liar and he is a murderer.[22] Further, his lies are the means by which he murders. At the very beginning he deceived Adam and Eve through lies and brought about their expulsion from Eden and the presence of God. Ever since he continues to blind the minds of unbelievers 'so that they cannot see the light of the gospel of the glory of Christ, who is the image of God'.[23]

In absolute contrast to the liar, the Lord Jesus Christ is in his very being the truth (John 14:6). The glory that he bears as 'the One and Only, who came from the Father' is itself a glory 'full of grace and truth';[24] and at his trial before Pilate he defined the whole purpose of his mission as one of testimony to the truth: 'In fact, for this reason I was born, and for this I came into the world, to testify to the truth.'[25] It is through that testimony that he brings freedom to men and women enslaved by sin (John 8:31–38). Witness to the truth is in fact a central theme throughout the Johannine writings, including the book of Revelation, and the great witness is the Lord Jesus Christ himself, the 'faithful and true witness'.[26]

As his disciples – those who have themselves believed his word of truth and been cleansed by his blood – Jesus' followers bear witness as he bore witness. He sent them into the world, as the Father had sent him, to proclaim the message he gave them (John 17:18; 20:21), and it is *the word of their testimony* that overcomes the accuser. Just as Jesus' testimony exposed Satan's lies and thereby overcame him, so too does theirs. Like John the Baptist they testify to 'the Lamb of God, who takes away the sin of the world'.[27] Those who receive their message are freed from their sins by believing in Jesus (Rev. 1:5; cf. John 20:23), and Satan's accusations are thereby nullified and he is overcome.

This means that they fight him indirectly by speaking the word that witnesses to Christ. They do not engage him directly nor do they combat 'territorial spirits' in so-called 'strategic-level' spiritual warfare.[28] It is the word of God, the sword of the Spirit, the message of the cross, that God uses to demolish strongholds and to bring redemption. This is how the gospel advances, how sinners are rescued from the accuser's kingdom of darkness, and how the church is built.

There is, moreover, an implicit warning here. In the letter to the Ephesian church earlier in Revelation (2:1–7) Jesus rebukes the

---

[22] See above, pp. 34–36.
[23] 2 Cor. 4:4.
[24] John 1:14.
[25] John 18:37.
[26] Rev. 3:14; cf. 1:5.
[27] John 1:29.
[28] See the fuller discussion above, pp. 164–166.

church for having forsaken its 'first love' and urgently summons it to repent and 'do the things you did at first'. The identity of that 'first love' has been much debated but it may well have been the church's former faithfulness in declaring 'the word of their testimony'. G. K. Beale argues that this is why at the beginning of that letter Christ identified himself to the Ephesian church as the one who 'walks among the seven golden lampstands':[29] he wanted to remind them that precisely as a lampstand 'their primary role in relation to their Lord should be that of a light of witness to the outside world'.[30] Christ himself is the faithful witness (Rev. 1:5) and as they truly follow him they will also witness. Therefore, if they do not repent of their failure to do so, he will remove their lampstand, for of what use would they be as a lampstand if they cease to bear testimony? This understanding of Christ's rebuke coincides with the theme of Revelation 11 where the two witnesses 'are the two lampstands and the two olive trees', an allusion to the prophecy of Zechariah (Zech. 4:2–6). In short, lampstands bear witness, and churches that lose sight of their great calling to bear witness in a dark world become futile. Not only do they not overcome Satan but they succumb to him, and the Lord of the church finally un-churches them.

4. They did not love their lives so much as to shrink from death

Third, they overcame the accuser in that *they did not love their lives so much as to shrink from death*. The victory that 'our brothers' experience through the blood of the Lamb, and the testimony that they then bear to him, mean that they are exposed to Satan's malice which they encounter especially through the hostility of the world of which he is prince. John himself wrote the book of Revelation from his place of exile on the island of Patmos, where he had been sent 'because of the word of God and the testimony of Jesus';[31] and at the opening of the fifth seal he saw 'under the altar the souls of those who had been slain because of the word of God and the testimony they had maintained'.[32] Not only do the disciples of Christ bear witness as Christ did, but they also share in his sufferings as a result. It was through the shedding of Christ's blood that the skull of the serpent was crushed, and it is by that same principle of the cross that Christ's people continue to overcome him. Indeed, at every point in the hymn Christ is at the heart of their overcoming, for the instruments of their victory over Satan are their purification *by*

---

[29] Rev. 2:1.
[30] Beale, *Revelation*, p. 230.
[31] Rev. 1:9.
[32] Rev. 6:9.

the blood of the Lamb, the word of their testimony to the Lamb, and their participation in the sufferings of the Lamb.

In John's Gospel towards the end of Jesus' earthly ministry some Greeks approached Philip and asked to see Jésus (John 12:20–21). When he heard of the approach of these Gentiles he understood it as a sign of the imminence of his death and resurrection, through which indeed 'all men' including such Greeks would be drawn to him (John 12:23, 32). At that moment he spoke of the necessity of his death: 'The hour has come for the Son of Man to be glorified. I tell you the truth, unless a kernel of wheat falls to the ground and dies, it remains only a single seed. But if it dies, it produces many seeds.'[33] What he says is pre-eminently true of himself, but the words that follow indicate that it is also true in the lives and ministry of his disciples. If they want eternal life they must also hate their lives in this world and accept the trials that will come from following Jesus: 'Whoever serves me must follow me . . .'[34] The same point is emphasized in the synoptic Gospels. When the disciples confessed that Jesus was the Messiah he immediately began to speak of the sufferings he would undergo as Messiah, and then told them that they too must take up their cross if they wished to be his disciples. 'If anyone would come after me, he must deny himself and take up his cross and follow me. For whoever wants to save his life will lose it, but whoever loses his life for me will find it.'[35]

There are two principal applications. First, for those who would overcome there must be a deliberate and conscious dying to self and to personal interests, clearly indicated by Jesus' words summoning his followers intentionally to take up their cross and deny themselves. It is about sacrifice voluntarily embraced rather than persecution brutally imposed, a serious willingness to lay aside personal ambition, desires and needs for the sake of Christ and the gospel. It is above all evident in the sacrifice of the Lord Jesus Christ who intentionally and voluntarily laid down his life: 'I lay down my life – only to take it up again. No one takes it from me, but I lay it down of my own accord. I have authority to lay it down and to take it up again.'[36] Paul too speaks of Jesus' active acceptance of the cross as he 'made himself nothing', took 'the very nature of a servant' and 'became obedient to death, even death on a cross'.[37] In his first letter to the Corinthians Paul explores the implications of taking up the

[33] John 12:23–24.
[34] John 12:26.
[35] Matt. 16:24–25.
[36] John 10:17–18.
[37] Phil. 2:6–8.

cross in the context of his own ministry when he speaks of laying aside his rights for the sake of the gospel: his right to be accompanied in his travels by a wife; his right to draw an income in return for his labour; his right to follow his own cultural preferences (1 Cor. 9:5–14, 19–23). He does not use 'any of these rights'[38] but, on the contrary, 'though I am free and belong to no man, I make myself a slave to everyone to win as many as possible'.[39] In contrast, when believers prioritize their own interests and ambitions, and treat Christian commitment as a spare time hobby, then Satan prevails. In the context of the book of Revelation, the church of Laodicea with its lukewarmness and complacency exemplifies the danger. 'You say, "I am rich; I have acquired wealth and do not need a thing." But you do not realise that you are wretched, pitiful, poor, blind and naked.'[40] It is the danger which threatens innumerable churches in the West, compliantly shaped by a culture whose principal values are those of 'personal peace and affluence'.[41] Satan is overcome when the disciples of Christ consider nothing more precious than to follow him and do his will, whatever the cost may be to their own well-being and prosperity.

Second, not loving one's life *so much as to shrink from death* speaks also of a readiness to accept trials and persecutions that come un-invited because of the gospel. Such a readiness comes from a love of Christ which is greater than the fear of suffering and death. The seven churches of Revelation were clearly facing this issue as they endured painful persecution carried out by the Roman state under the emperor Domitian. Satan's aim, however, was not primarily to afflict them physically but, as with Job, to undermine their faith in God. The purpose of Revelation, therefore, was to encourage its readers to persevere. And so there is praise for the church of Thyatira which did not renounce its faith in Christ 'even in the days of Antipas, my faithful witness, who was put to death in your city',[42] and encouragement for the church of Smyrna where the devil was about to put some of them in prison: 'Be faithful, even to the point of death, and I will give you the crown of life.'[43] The language used here, 'unto death' (*achri thanatou*), anticipates the words of the hymn in Revelation 12:11: they overcome the accuser who do not love their lives 'unto death'. Beyond death he has no weapon that he can use

[38] 1 Cor. 9:15.
[39] 1 Cor. 9:19.
[40] Rev. 3:17.
[41] F. A. Schaeffer, *How Should We Then Live?: The Rise and Decline of Western Thought and Culture* (Grand Rapids: Revell, 1976), p. 246.
[42] Rev. 2:13.
[43] Rev. 2:10.

against them, and death itself is a broken weapon, for it simply ushers them into the immediate presence of Christ. Indeed, they can rejoice in the death they suffer, because it takes them to be 'with Christ, which is better by far'.[44]

At the heart of faithful, fruitful, overcoming Christian discipleship there is a cross; it is that 'strangest victory' which is brought about by dying rather than by killing. And it is fitting that a book on spiritual warfare should end on such a note, especially as it is one that the Western church has so much lost sight of. Ajith Fernando suggests that the problem lies at least in part with Western theological education: 'I have come to feel that Western theological education is not adequately preparing Christians for suffering, and this deficit is causing negative repercussions in the church in the non-Western world.'[45] If so, theological educators should take stock, for the brothers who overcame the accuser *did not love their lives so much as to shrink from death*, just as their Lord did not.

Dietrich Bonhoeffer wrote, 'When God calls a man he bids him come and die',[46] and he himself went on to suffer death for his testimony. So too the apostle Paul time and again throughout his ministry walked knowingly into situations of danger, suffering and possible death: 'I only know that in every city the Holy Spirit warns me that prison and hardships are facing me.'[47] The cross is the mark that distinguishes the faithful church of Jesus Christ in every age and among every people as it witnesses to its crucified Lord through its life as well as its words: 'hacked to pieces, marked with scratches, despised, crucified, mocked – like Christ, but to the sight of God, a pure, holy, spotless dove'.[48]

---

[44] Phil. 1:23.
[45] A. Fernando, 'Is Western Christian Training Neglecting the Cross?', *Trinity World Forum* (Fall, 1998), p. 1.
[46] D. Bonhoeffer, *The Cost of Discipleship* (London: SCM Press, 2001), p. 44.
[47] Acts 20:23.
[48] M. Luther, 'Table Talk', in T. G. Tappert (tr. and ed.), *Luther's Works*, vol. 54 (Philadelphia: Fortress Press, 1967), p. 262.

Study Guide

HOW TO USE THIS STUDY GUIDE

The aim of this study guide is to help you to get to the heart of what Keith has written and challenge you to apply what you learn to your own life. The questions have been designed for use by individuals or by small groups of Christians meeting, perhaps for an hour or two each week, to study, discuss and pray together. When this guide is used by a group with limited time, the leader should decide beforehand which questions are most appropriate for the group to discuss during the meeting and which should perhaps be left for group members to work through by themselves or in smaller groups during the week.

PREVIEW. Use the guide and the contents pages as a map to become familiar with what you are about to read, your 'journey' through the book.

READ. Look up the Bible passages as well as the text.

ANSWER. As you read, look for answers to the questions in the guide.

DISCUSS. Even if you are studying on your own, try to find another person to share your thoughts with.

REVIEW. Use the guide as a tool to remind you what you have learned. The best way of retaining what you learn is to write it down in a notebook or journal.

APPLY. Translate what you have learned into your attitudes and actions, considering your relationship with God, your personal life, your family life, your working life, your church life, your role as a citizen and your world view.

Introduction (pp. 1–11)

1 In what sense is 'spiritual warfare' a biblical concept (pp. 1–2)?
2 In what three ways has spiritual warfare been misunderstood (pp. 3–4)?
3 Describe and evaluate the approaches to spiritual warfare classified in *Understanding Spiritual Warfare: Four Views* (pp. 4–6).

4 Why is the Bible reticent about Satan and demons and which central truths of biblical theology should define our thinking abut Satan, spirits and spiritual warfare (pp. 6–8)?

'It is important to respect what the Bible does not say as well as what it does' (p. 7).

---

5 What is 'the big question'? What false turnings should be avoided and can the question be answered (pp. 8–10)?
6 What topics are tackled in the four sections of the book (pp. 10–11)?

PART 1. THE SOVEREIGN CREATOR AND A FALLEN WORLD

Colossians 1:15–17
1. The sovereign Creator of all (pp. 15–25)

1 What can we know about the church at Colossae and its problem (pp. 15–17)?
2 What do the phrases 'image of the invisible God' and 'firstborn over all creation' tell us about Christ (pp. 17–19)?
3 What are the four stages through which Paul's argument develops in verse 16 and how does it help our understanding of the spirit world (pp. 19–22)?
4 Why does Paul emphasize that Christ is sustainer as well as Lord and creator (p. 22)?
5 What major misunderstanding do these verses address and what practical implications do they have for us today (pp. 22–25)?

Genesis 3:1–5; John 8:44
2. A liar and a murderer (pp. 26–36)

1 What scriptures are used to account for Satan's fall and how appropriate are they (pp. 26–27)?
2 How should we understand the serpent in Genesis 3 (pp. 27–28)?
3 Where can we trace Satan's character as a murderer through Old and New Testament Scripture (pp. 28–30)?
4 In what ways does the serpent's temptation of Adam and Eve serve as a paradigm of temptation in succeeding generations (pp. 30–32)?

'In truth, of course, anything like total independence from God is mere illusion, for the universe he created continues at every moment to be sustained by him. Adam was dependent on God for the air he breathed, the food he ate, the functioning of his own body and the regular operation of the world around him – night and day, seedtime and harvest and so on. In that sense truly to rebel against God would be to opt for non-being' (p. 28).

---

5 What four implications can we draw from the serpent's approach to Adam and Eve and how are they reflected in contemporary society (pp. 32–34)?

6 What does the testimony of Jesus in John 8:44 reveal about Satan himself, about temptation, about those who are tempted and about the answer to lies (pp. 34–36)?

Genesis 3:6–24
3. Sinners, not victims (pp. 37–48)

1 'She was no victim.' What factors in the narrative of Genesis 3 support this interpretation of Eve's action (pp. 37–39)?

2 'Adam's responsibility and the consequent significance of his disobedience were immeasurably greater than Eve's . . .' What is the evidence for this conclusion (pp. 39–40)?

3 In what sense was the aftermath of their choice an apparent anti-climax and what was the reality (pp. 40–41)?

4 How does God's judgment of the serpent differ from that of Adam and Eve (pp. 41–42)?

5 In what ways do the judgments on Adam and Eve differ from each other (pp. 42–43)?

6 What is the deeper meaning of the two verbs describing Adam's work in the garden in Gen. 2:15 (pp. 43–44)?

7 How is the character of God's grace revealed following the disobedience of Adam and Eve (pp. 44–48)?

Job 1 – 2
4. Satan and suffering (pp. 49–59)

1 In what sense are Western rationalists out of step with animistic cultures and religious traditions (pp. 49–50)?

2 How is the word 'satan' used in the Old Testament and what distinguishes its occurrence in Job (pp. 50–51)?

3 What do the first two chapters of Job tell us about Satan's power and motivation (pp. 51–52)?

'A fundamental assumption of the book of Job is, therefore, that God is sovereign and that Satan, although undoubtedly antagonistic and malevolent, is emphatically subject to the divine will' (p. 52).

4 What other passages of Scripture underline the sovereignty of God and the subservience of Satan to God's purposes (pp. 52–54)?
5 What is the 'extraordinary feature of the story of Job'? How does it contrast with the Ancient Near Eastern world and what conclusion should we draw from it (pp. 54–55)?
6 What does Job's response to his suffering tell us about his conception of God and how is it reflected in the experience of Paul (pp. 55–56)?
7 What was God's answer to Job's questions (pp. 57–58)?
8 Does Satan cause all suffering (pp. 58–59)?

Numbers 22 – 25
5. A curse transformed (pp. 60–70)

1 What evidence is there for the prevalence of malevolent sorcery in human history and biblical times (pp. 60–61)?
2 How have commentators assessed Balaam and how do their views square with the narrative of Numbers (pp. 61–62)?
3 What four considerations help to explain Balaam's significance and how do later books of the Bible reinforce this assessment (pp. 62–63)?
4 What biblical evidence is there for the prevalence and significance of occult practices and what implications does this have for the relationship between witchcraft and suffering (pp. 64–67)?
5 How should we understand the relationship between Balaam and God and how does it demonstrate God's sovereignty (pp. 67–69)?

'The people of God need not fear the sorcerer or the witch, supposed manipulators of evil powers. . . . They must, however, beware of their own faithlessness and rebellion, and of their consequences. "Above all else, guard your heart, for it is the wellspring of life" (Prov. 4:23)' (p. 70).

6 What was Balaam's part in Moab's seduction of Israel and their apostasy with the Baal of Peor (pp. 69–70)?

PART 2. THE WARFARE OF THE SON OF GOD

Matthew 4:1–11
6. The testing of the Son of God (pp. 73–83)

1 'The LORD IS a warrior.' What is distinctive about the Lord's warfare in the Old Testament and how is it developed in the New Testament (pp. 73–74)?
2 What factors indicate that Jesus' entry into the desert involved more than fasting and praying in preparation for his ministry (pp. 74–75)?
3 What gives the first temptation its force, as opposed to a merely reasonable, even innocent suggestion (pp. 75–77)?
4 What is the essence of the second temptation and why is the sequel recorded by Luke so appropriate (pp. 77–78)?
5 What issues are involved in the third temptation? In what ways was it absurd, and where in Matthew's Gospel do we find a significant sequel (pp. 78–80)?
6 How has church history illustrated the issues represented in this third temptation (pp. 80–81)?
7 Which Old Testament narratives were being played out again in the temptations of Jesus and with what results (pp. 81–83)?

'God's purposes can only be achieved by God's means, which invariably include servanthood, suffering, persecution, and "not by triumphant self-assertion, not by the exercise of power and authority"' (p. 80).

Mark 5:1–20
7. Releasing the oppressed (pp. 84–96)

1 Who was John Nevius and what conclusions did he draw from his work in nineteenth-century China (p. 84)?
2 What expressions do the New Testament evangelists use to describe demonic 'possession' (pp. 84–85)?
3 What five symptoms of 'demonization' are illustrated in the account of the Gerasene man (pp. 85–87)?
4 Is it legitimate to speak about demon 'possession' and which relevant features emerge from Mark 7:24–30 and other New Testament passages (pp. 87–88)?

5 In what ways do the synoptic Gospels characterize Jesus' deliverance ministry and how did it contrast with that of contemporary exorcists (pp. 88–90)?

6 Why does synoptic terminology indicate the theological significance of Jesus' deliverance ministry (pp. 90–91)?

7 What aspects of Jesus' understanding are seen in (a) plundering the strong man and (b) Satan's fall from heaven (pp. 91–94)?

8 What principles from Jesus' approach can we apply to contemporary issues surrounding deliverance (pp. 94–96)?

Colossians 2:13–15
8. Disarming the powers (pp. 97–108)

1 How does John's Gospel differ from the synoptics in its presentation of Jesus' battle with spiritual powers (pp. 97–98)?

2 In what two new directions does Paul push his argument in Colossians 2:13–15 and how does he stress the hopelessness of the Colossians' condition without Christ (pp. 98–100)?

3 What three details of Paul's language in verse 13 are vital to our understanding (pp. 100–101)?

4 What is the meaning of the term *cheirographon* and how does Paul develop it (pp. 101–102)?

5 What are the implications of the atonement for the *powers and authorities* (pp. 102–104)?

'By the unimaginable, unbelievable sacrifice of his own beloved Son God has completely outwitted and outmanoeuvred the enemy and laid waste to all his purposes. And the day will come when humanity as a whole will know it too' (p. 104).

---

6 What four implications relating to the *powers and authorities* can be drawn from Paul's argument about the cross (pp. 104–108)?

Revelation 12:1–17
9. The dragon hurled down (pp. 109–121)

1 What is apocalyptic and why is the genre difficult for modern readers (pp. 109–110)?

2 What are the two signs in Revelation 12:1–6 and how should they be understood (pp. 110–113)?

3 Who are the protagonists in the *war in heaven* and what is its outcome (pp. 113–114)?

4 What four features of the loud voice in heaven clarify our understanding of the dragon's downfall (pp. 114–117)?

5 What is the significance of the woman's trial, verses 13–17, and what four points emerge from it (pp. 117–119)?

6 What parallels can be drawn between John, Paul, Peter and the author of Hebrews (pp. 119–121)?

'The point is not that the people of God do not face severe trials that may indeed seem to threaten their very existence, but that God preserves them through those trials for the glory to come. For he has already seated them "in the heavenly realms in Christ Jesus", a place of total security' (p. 119).

Revelation 20:7–10
10. The last battle (pp. 122–132)

1 How should the symbolic language of Satan's defeat be interpreted in the light of John 12:31 and Revelation 12:8–9 (pp. 122–124)?

2 What are the two dimensions of Satan's activity when the thousand years are over (pp. 124–126)?

3 What is unusual about the description of the final battle (pp. 126–127)?

4 Is it possible to penetrate the apocalyptic language and discern what will actually happen (pp. 127–128)?

5 Should we view the narratives of Revelation chapters 19 and 20 as linear or cyclical (pp. 128–130)?

6 What are the distinctive emphases of these chapters (pp. 130–131)?

7 What is the final fate of the devil and the two beasts (pp. 131–132)?

'And in all of this God is glorified. Finally, through the work of the Son the whole cosmos is reconciled in that all is brought, willingly or unwillingly, into submission to the Creator' (p. 131).

PART 3. LIBERATED AND LIBERATING

Colossians 1:13–14
11. Delivered from the darkness (pp. 135–145)

1 What are the four particular ways in which believers can live God-pleasing lives (pp. 135–136)?

2 How important was thanksgiving in Paul's thinking and theology, and why (pp. 136–137)?
3 What is the nature of the *dominion of darkness* (a) in heavenly places and (b) on earth (pp. 137–139)?
4 What is the nature of God's deliverance? What four implications can be drawn from it and how does Colossians 1:13–14 relate to 2:13–15 (pp. 140–141)?
5 How are Paul's themes echoed in Galatians and Ephesians (p. 142)?
6 What are the positive consequences of redemption in terms of identity, freedom and obligation (pp. 143–145)?

Ephesians 1:19b – 2:7
12. Seated with Christ (pp. 146–157)

1 Why is human fear so prevalent and why might God's people be considered even more susceptible (pp. 146–147)?
2 What is the background to Paul's letter to the Ephesians (pp. 147–149)?
3 What lessons can the international church today learn from Acts 19:19 (pp. 149–150)?
4 In what two ways does Paul unpack the total sufficiency of God's power in his prayer? Which psalms does he refer to and how do they contribute to his argument (pp. 150–152)?
5 What are the implications of the prepositions 'in' and 'with' in this section of Ephesians (pp. 153–154)?
6 Why does Paul not explicitly address the issue of magic (pp. 154–155)?
7 How is the experience of persecution compatible with believers' union with Christ (pp. 155–157)?

Matthew 28:18–20
13. Moving out (pp. 158–168)

1 What constituted the 'new and revolutionary movement in the history of salvation' (pp. 158–160)?

'Proclaiming the gospel of grace and truth is itself, therefore, an act of spiritual warfare, both provocative and dangerous, and messengers must be alert to that fact' (p. 160).

---

2 What assertion marks the beginning of Jesus' commission and where is it paralleled in Old and New Testament passages (pp. 160–161)?

3 In what respect does the Father's gift exceed Satan's offer at the temptation and what implications does it have for Christ's disciples (pp. 161–162)?

4 Why is the disciples' task of making disciples *of all nations* profoundly subversive and what are the consequences (pp. 162–163)?

5 What two elements in conversion are emphasized in the great commission (pp. 163–164)?

6 What is fundamental to the ministry of Jesus' disciples and what does it not involve (pp. 164–166)?

7 What two declarations frame the great commission (p. 166)?

8 What five assurances are reinforced in the final part of the commission (pp. 166–168)?

Acts 13:4–12
14. Facing the foe (pp. 169–179)

1 What do we know of Paul's early missionary activities and why is the account from Acts 13 onwards significant (pp. 169–171)?

2 What do we know about Sergius Paulus and Bar-Jesus (pp. 170–172)?

3 In what ways was Elymas' opposition more than a merely personal matter (pp. 172–174)?

4 Why is the phrase *filled with the Holy Spirit* important and what was the effect of the Spirit's renewed anointing of Paul (pp. 174–176)?

5 What was the outcome of the spiritual confrontation and which two factors influenced Sergius Paulus (pp. 176–177)?

6 What is meant by 'power encounter' and in what ways does the notion need to be qualified (pp. 177–179)?

2 Corinthians 12:1–10
15. Strong in weakness (pp. 180–190)

'It is a central theme of the whole New Testament and one constantly apparent in church history through the centuries. Christian life and ministry are cross-shaped' (p. 180).

1 What was the nature of Paul's boasting and what factors made it necessary (pp. 181–182)?

2 What features of vocabulary and grammar are significant in Paul's description of his experiences (pp. 182–183)?

3 How should we interpret Paul's *thorn in the flesh* and in what sense was it a *messenger from Satan* (pp. 183–186)?

4 In what two ways does Paul bring out the positive value of Satan's activity in his life (pp. 186–188)?

5 On what grounds does Paul reach this understanding of his sufferings (pp. 188–189)?

6 In what two ways did Paul respond to the discipline he experienced (p. 190)?

PART 4. FIGHTING IN HOPE

Romans 12:1–2
16. Battle for the mind (pp. 193–204)

1 What evidence is there for an intimate relationship between sin and folly (pp. 193–194)?

2 In what four ways does the sacrifice described in these verses move radically beyond the Jewish sacrificial system (pp. 194–195)?

3 Why are Christians living as 'strangers and exiles'? How does this experience differ from that of Israel in the Old Testament (pp. 196–197)?

4 What are the practical implications of Christian non-conformity (pp. 197–198)?

5 What four factors are involved in the process of being transformed (pp. 198–202)?

6 Why is discerning the will of God so 'immensely significant' – both negatively and positively, and how is this significance underlined elsewhere in Scripture (pp. 202–204)?

James 3:13 – 4:10
17. Fighting and quarrelling (pp. 205–218)

1 What is your response to the opening paragraphs of this chapter (pp. 205–206)?

2 How is the history of human violence recorded and depicted in Scripture (pp. 206–208)?

'*After their repudiation of God himself, the sin that lies closest to the heart of human fallenness is the manifold violence that human beings remorselessly inflict on one another. Sin shatters human community, and human beings show only too clearly that they have truly become children of their father, the devil, who "was a murderer from the beginning"' (p. 208).*

3 What is the basis of peace with God and reconciliation and why is a demonstration of peace fundamental to Christian testimony (pp. 208–209)?
4 What characterizes the wisdom from above and in what ways does it differ from false wisdom (pp. 210–211)?
5 In what five ways does James explain the true wisdom from above and what is the outcome of such wisdom (pp. 211–213)?
6 What was the source of the conflict in the community James was writing to (pp. 213–214)?
7 Why is repentance so crucial and what four elements of that repentance does James envisage (pp. 214–217)?

1 John 2:12–17
18. The world and its lusts (pp. 219–230)

1 What do biblical writers mean by 'the world' (p. 219)?
2 What identities have been suggested for the *children, young men* and *fathers* in verses 12–14 and which do you find most convincing (p. 220)?
3 In what ways might John's references to love in verse 15 be misunderstood and what reasons does he give for not loving the world (pp. 220–222)?
4 What should we understand by (a) *the desire of the flesh*, (b) *the desire of the eyes* and (c) *the boastfulness of possessions* (pp. 223–228)?
5 What are the 'two complementary dimensions' in verse 17 and how should we understand the contrast with verse 15 (pp. 228–230)?

1 Corinthians 9:24 – 10:22
19. The snare of complacency (pp. 231–244)

1 Why was 'food sacrificed to idols' such an issue for Christians in Corinth (pp. 231–233)?

2 How does Paul develop and apply his illustration from the games (pp. 233–234)?

3 In what two ways does Paul compare the experience of the Israelites with that of the Corinthian believers (pp. 235–236)?

4 What evidence is there that Paul intended to shock his readers out of their complacency and what four specific incidents does he use to define the nature of their sin (pp. 236–237)?

5 How does Paul conclude the first part of his argument in verses 11–13 (pp. 237–238)?

6 With what tone does Paul make his arguments in verses 14–22 and how does he develop them (pp. 238–244)?

7 Do Paul's arguments have a contemporary application for us (pp. 241–244)?

Ephesians 6:10–20
20. The weapons of our warfare (pp. 245–260)

1 How does Ephesians 6 verses 10–20 relate to the letter as a whole (pp. 245–246)?

2 What resources do Christians possess as they face the devil's malignity (pp. 246–249)?

'*It is the whole* panoplia *and, indeed, nothing other than the* panoplia, *that is needed for the fight if God's people are to prevail. And believers must actively put it on, just as they must consciously and deliberately* be strong in the Lord. *The divine provision of strength and armour does not exclude their personal responsibility to make use of it*' (p. 248).

---

3 'It is important to know the enemy.' What does this passage teach about the enemy, his strategy and our struggle (pp. 249–253)?

4 How should we understand *the belt of truth*, *the breastplate of righteousness* and *feet fitted with the readiness that comes from the gospel of peace* (pp. 253–255)?

5 How should we understand *the shield of faith*, *the helmet of salvation* and *the sword of the Spirit, which is the word of God* (pp. 255–258)?

6 How does Paul underline the importance of prayer and in what terms does he ask for prayers for himself (pp. 258–260)?

Revelation 12:11
21. They overcame him (pp. 261–270)

1 What parallels exist between spiritual warfare and historical conflicts and in what ways is spiritual warfare different (pp. 261–262)?

'It is, however, all too easy to misunderstand the battle and to fight wrongly: with angry and bitter words, with manipulative and underhand methods, even with blows and violence. Far from enabling believers to overcome their spiritual enemy, the use of such "weapons of the world" actually puts them in his camp and brings miserable defeat' (pp. 261–262).

---

2 Who is speaking in this verse, where is it paralleled in the Old Testament and in what sense is it a celebration (pp. 262–263)?
3 What is 'the absolute heart of Christian life, experience and perseverance' and why (pp. 264–265)?
4 How does the issue of truth differentiate Jesus from Satan and why is it so vital to the warfare of the church (pp. 265–267)?
5 Where is the evidence that suffering is an integral part of spiritual warfare (pp. 267–268)?
6 What are the two principal applications of the value of suffering as a Christian (pp. 268–270)?

The Bible Speaks Today: Old Testament series

The Message of Genesis 1 – 11
The dawn of creation
David Atkinson

The Message of Genesis 12 – 50
From Abraham to Joseph
Joyce G. Baldwin

The Message of Exodus
The days of our pilgrimage
Alec Motyer

The Message of Leviticus
Free to be holy
Derek Tidball

The Message of Numbers
Journey to the promised land
Raymond Brown

The Message of Deuteronomy
Not by bread alone
Raymond Brown

The Message of Joshua
Promise and people
David G. Firth

The Message of Judges
Grace abounding
Michael Wilcock

The Message of Ruth
The wings of refuge
David Atkinson

The Message of Samuel
Personalities, potential, politics and power
Mary J. Evans

The Message of Kings
God is present
John W. Olley

The Message of Chronicles
One church, one faith, one Lord
Michael Wilcock

The Message of Ezra and Haggai
Building for God
Robert Fyall

The Message of Nehemiah
God's servant in a time of change
Raymond Brown

The Message of Esther
God present but unseen
David G. Firth

The Message of Job
Suffering and grace
David Atkinson

The Message of Psalms 1 – 72
Songs for the people of God
Michael Wilcock

The Message of Psalms 73 – 150
Songs for the people of God
Michael Wilcock

The Message of Proverbs
Wisdom for life
David Atkinson

The Message of Ecclesiastes
A time to mourn, and a time to dance
Derek Kidner

The Message of the Song of Songs
The lyrics of love
Tom Gledhill

The Message of Isaiah
On eagles' wings
Barry Webb

The Message of Jeremiah
Grace in the end
Christopher J. H. Wright

The Message of Lamentations
Honest to God
Christopher J. H. Wright

The Message of Ezekiel
A new heart and a new spirit
Christopher J. H. Wright

The Message of Daniel
His kingdom cannot fail
Dale Ralph Davis

The Message of Hosea
Love to the loveless
Derek Kidner

The Message of Joel, Micah and Habakkuk
Listening to the voice of God
David Prior

The Message of Amos
The day of the lion
Alec Motyer

The Message of Obadiah, Nahum and Zephaniah
The kindness and severity of God
Gordon Bridger

The Message of Jonah
Presence in the storm
Rosemary Nixon

The Message of Zechariah
Your kingdom come
Barry Webb

The Message of Malachi
'I have loved you,' says the Lord
Peter Adam

The Bible Speaks Today: New Testament series

The Message of the Sermon on the Mount (Matthew 5 – 7)
Christian counter-culture
John Stott

The Message of Matthew
The kingdom of heaven
Michael Green

The Message of Mark
The mystery of faith
Donald English

The Message of Luke
The Saviour of the world
Michael Wilcock

The Message of John
Here is your King!
Bruce Milne

The Message of Acts
To the ends of the earth
John Stott

The Message of Romans
God's good news for the world
John Stott

The Message of 1 Corinthians
Life in the local church
David Prior

The Message of 2 Corinthians
Power in weakness
Paul Barnett

The Message of Galatians
Only one way
John Stott

The Message of Ephesians
God's new society
John Stott

The Message of Philippians
Jesus our Joy
Alec Motyer

The Message of Colossians and Philemon
Fullness and freedom
Dick Lucas

The Message of Thessalonians
Preparing for the coming King
John Stott

The Message of 1 Timothy and Titus
The life of the local church
John Stott

The Message of 2 Timothy
Guard the gospel
John Stott

The Message of Hebrews
Christ above all
Raymond Brown

The Message of James
The tests of faith
Alec Motyer

The Message of 1 Peter
The way of the cross
Edmund Clowney

The Message of 2 Peter and Jude
The promise of his coming
Dick Lucas and Christopher Green

The Message of John's Letters
Living in the love of God
David Jackman

The Message of Revelation
I saw heaven opened
Michael Wilcock